RENMINBI
INTERNATIONALIZATION

Renminbi Internationalization

Achievements, Prospects, and Challenges

BARRY EICHENGREEN

MASAHIRO KAWAI

editors

ASIAN DEVELOPMENT BANK INSTITUTE
Tokyo

BROOKINGS INSTITUTION PRESS
Washington, D.C.

Library of Congress Cataloging-in-Publication data is available

ISBN 978-0-8157-2611-1

9 8 7 6 5 4 3 2 1

Printed on acid-free paper

Typeset in Adobe Garamond

Composition by R. Lynn Rivenbark
Macon, Georgia

Contents

Part III. The Process

Part IV. The View from the People's Republic of China

Foreword

NAOYUKI YOSHINO

In view of the significant increase in the importance of the People's Republic of China (PRC) in the global economy since the turn of the twenty-first century, it is not surprising that its domestic currency, the renminbi, is expected to play a major role in international trade and finance in the coming years. Indeed, the PRC has begun to promote the international use of the renminbi, as evidenced by the progress that has been made on renminbi trade settlements and on renminbi-denominated bond issuance in Hong Kong, China.

The PRC is successfully sustaining a gradual approach to making the exchange rate regime more flexible and is also adopting a unique approach in striking out on its own path to a more open capital account. The PRC is moving gradually and systematically in the direction of greater capital account liberalization, testing out early reforms before proceeding with others. This involves the PRC and other entities freely buying and selling the currency for trade-related purposes and for a limited range of capital account and financial transactions, while the government attempts to continue to exercise control on presumably short-term investments through administrative and other measures. Over the medium term, however, the prospects of the renminbi's taking on a greater international role are likely to be impeded by the weaknesses of the PRC's financial system. Although the PRC's financial markets have improved in some respects since 2000, there are still significant gaps, especially in terms of achieving a sufficiently large and liquid domestic bond market.

Against this backdrop, Barry Eichengreen, George C. Pardee and Helen N. Pardee Professor of Economics and Political Science at the University of California, Berkeley, and Masahiro Kawai, a former dean of the Asian Development Bank Institute (ADBI) and now project professor at the University of Tokyo, spearheaded this comprehensive study that brings together in one volume the range of important issues that are relevant to the renminbi's growing international role: proactive policies to encourage this growth, and the functioning of markets in which this growth is occurring. In particular, the volume authors highlight the implications of the PRC's liberalization strategy: in the next few years, the PRC will have a more open capital account than it does today, but with a number of administrative controls and regulations still in place. Absent the requisite reform of the PRC's domestic financial market, the likelihood of the renminbi's being used widely in international transactions—and thus its potential to be elevated to reserve-currency status, let alone to challenge the U.S. dollar's status as the leading reserve currency—is severely limited.

The book's authors also argue that the international community—especially the Asian region—has an interest in a smooth and successful internationalization of the renminbi. Renminbi internationalization can contribute to a rebalancing of the PRC economy, which benefits the world economy. It is also widely desirable that the PRC's financial markets not be exposed to the risk of a crisis as the PRC moves ahead with its economic policy reforms.

Taken together, the book's authors convey their conviction that the international community should welcome the emergence of the PRC as a source of global liquidity. The recent global financial crisis led to a critical realization that the over-reliance by the international monetary system on a single, dominant reserve currency poses an ever-present danger to the system's stability. Eventually, the internationalization of the renminbi will enable the PRC to be an alternative supplier of safe assets to the rest of the world in which firms, households, and central banks can park their savings, where they will later be available in case of a need for more liquid funding. It is the editors hope that this volume will contribute to a better and more informed discussion of the complex issues surrounding one of the major international and regional financial developments of our time.

NAOYUKI YOSHINO
Dean, Asian Development Bank Institute
Tokyo, October 2014

Preface

The People's Republic of China (PRC) plays an increasingly prominent role in the world economy, and it would seem entirely logical that its currency should also play a prominent role in international financial markets. As if on cue, PRC officials are moving deliberately, but also with surprising speed, to internationalize their country's currency, the renminbi. Not a few observers look forward expectantly, even confidently, to a time in the not-very-distant future when the renminbi will play a global role comparable to that of the U.S. dollar.

But currency internationalization entails challenges. It will require the PRC to build deep, liquid, and stable financial markets and to open them to the rest of the world. Thus, the progress of currency internationalization is an illuminating window onto the larger process of economic reform. Officials in Beijing, acknowledging their country's middle-income status, are seeking to restructure the PRC economy away from the production of manufactures toward services, including financial services. They are seeking to develop the country's financial markets, so that households can hold diversified portfolios of financial assets that better protect them against economic volatility, enabling them to reduce their precautionary saving and increase their consumption. They are moving to commercialize the country's banks and extend supervision and regulation to the shadow banking system of trust companies and investment vehicles, subjecting companies and local governments to the discipline of competitive financial markets and encouraging them to focus on high-quality investments. Renminbi internationalization is a mechanism for encouraging this process of rebalancing from goods to services and from investment to consumption, since effectively encouraging international use of the currency presupposes progress in strengthening and developing the PRC's financial markets. Progress in encouraging wider international use of the currency is also a revealing indicator of how much progress the PRC is making on the broader process of economic restructuring and reform.

Renminbi internationalization also provides a perspective on likely directions for the international monetary and financial system in the twenty-first century. For much of the twentieth century, the system was dominated by the U.S. dollar, reflecting the extent to which the global economy was dominated, commercially and financially, by the United States. Now, with the rise of emerging markets and the transition to a more multipolar world economy, a more multipolar international monetary system seems to be in the cards—yet, a decade and a half into the new century, such a system has failed to emerge. Indeed, some observers blame the instability experienced by the world economy in recent years on the tension between an increasingly multipolar world economy and a still-dollar-dominated global monetary and financial system. If this situation is to change, it will change as a result of the renminbi's gaining a consequential international role in line with its status as the currency of a country poised to overtake the United States as the world's single largest economy.

Thus, the prospects and challenges of renminbi internationalization matter not just for specialists in foreign exchange but for anyone concerned with the prospects for the both the PRC and the world economy more broadly. This may seem like a narrow issue, but it is one with profound and broad implications.

1

Introduction and Overview

BARRY EICHENGREEN AND MASAHIRO KAWAI

Internationalization of the renminbi (RMB, also known as the yuan) is one of the most contentious and widely debated aspects of economic reform in the People's Republic of China (PRC).[1] Renminbi "internationalization"—that is, wider use of the RMB in international transactions, both commercial and financial transactions and those undertaken by central banks and other official institutions—can be understood as a natural response to the growing weight of PRC trade and investment flows in the world economy. Top PRC officials have repeatedly declared currency internationalization to be a stated goal of policy, and the People's Bank of China and other government agencies have pursued a variety of initiatives designed to encourage the currency's wider use. Thus, whether wider international use of the RMB is a spontaneous market reaction or a manifestation of the PRC's growing ability and willingness to influence the shape and structure of the global economy is a matter of interpretation.

So, too, is the role of RMB internationalization in the process of the PRC's economic growth and development. Some will say that the cause of RMB internationalization is being advanced mainly in the interest of financial institutions, which see scope for doing international business in the currency as a lucrative source of potential income. Others argue that currency internationalization is supported by PRC firms that see the ability to do cross-border business in their own

---

1. "RMB" and "yuan" are often used interchangeably, except that the currency unit of China is expressed in yuan, not in RMB.

currency as a useful way of saving costs and maintaining competitive advantage. Those firms do not see why they should have to continue to incur the additional costs of conducting such business in U.S. dollars and having to hedge the resulting exposures.

Similarly, it is argued in some circles that RMB internationalization is a natural corollary of the process of financial development and deepening currently under way in the PRC. As financial markets gain depth, width, and liquidity and are progressively opened to foreign investors, greater international use of the currency will come naturally. The counterpoint is that currency internationalization and the capital account liberalization required to advance it can be or are being used to ratchet up the pressure on PRC regulators to accelerate domestic financial reforms and hasten the process of financial development and opening.

Equally contentious is how quickly international use of the RMB is likely to expand. The PRC is already the world's largest exporter and will soon be the world's largest economy as measured by gross domestic product (GDP). Previous studies such as Chinn and Frankel (2007) suggesting that economic size is an important determinant of the extent of international use of a national currency create a presumption that there should be momentum for more widespread use of the RMB on this ground alone. Other scholars who instead emphasize the issuing country's market liquidity, financial stability, and political structure as determinants of international currency status suggest that the requisite adjustments may take considerably longer. The optimists point to the fact that as much as 28 percent of the PRC's international trade is now settled in RMB and to the rapid growth of RMB bank balances and RMB bond issuance in Hong Kong, China. The pessimists respond that much of the trade is between the PRC and Hong Kong, China—a special case—and that the growth of RMB deposits in Hong Kong, China reflects and is driven by expectations of currency appreciation, an expectation that may not last indefinitely. The optimists note that the last currency to ascend to international status, the U.S. dollar, after World War I, was able to do so quickly once the United States created an independent central bank to enhance market liquidity and once it undertook related institutional reforms. The pessimists object that the dollar lost many of its international gains in the financial crisis of the 1930s. They caution against prioritizing currency internationalization and capital account liberalization over domestic financial development and reform. They worry that allowing capital account liberalization to get too far out ahead of domestic financial reform might raise the risk of just such a crisis.

These are among the issues we seek to address in this chapter. This overview is principally concerned with establishing the facts. Most fundamentally, what is happening in terms of RMB internationalization? How, where, and why is the currency being adopted as an international unit of account, means of payment, and store of value? We are also interested in the economics and political economy of RMB internationalization. How does currency internationalization fit into the

larger process of the PRC's economic reform? How does it fit into the PRC's political economy? Who, for example, is lobbying for and against it? What does this
mean for the international monetary system?

The PRC is not like other countries. This makes it important to ask, critically,
how much can be learned about the prospects and pitfalls of RMB internationalization from the experience of other countries. In particular, the PRC has a much
more extensively controlled capital account of the balance of payments, and a
more heavily controlled financial system and economy generally, than any other
country that has previously aspired to elevate its national unit to international currency status. Thus, previous experience with capital account liberalization and
associated financial risks—not simply in earlier reserve-currency countries but in
emerging markets whose circumstances the PRC's current circumstances more
closely resemble—is directly relevant to the concerns of this paper.

We also inquire into the implications of RMB internationalization not just for
the PRC but for other countries and, more broadly, for the international monetary and financial system. The effects of economic policies and conditions in the
PRC will be stronger on countries that come to rely extensively on the RMB in
their international transactions. Their commercial banks will come to rely more
heavily on RMB funding. Their central banks are likely to place a heavier weight
on the RMB when managing the exchange rate and foreign exchange reserves. It
is therefore useful to attempt to determine which countries, or what kind of countries, we are talking about. Are we talking mainly about Asian countries? In that
case the RMB is more likely to develop into a regional than a global currency.

This brings us to the implications of RMB internationalization for the structure of the international monetary system. Does the emergence of the RMB imply
a world of competing international currencies or a system of overlapping regional
currency blocs? Is a system in which both the U.S. dollar and the RMB play major
global roles likely to display better or worse stability properties than our current
dollar-based system? Will it make for the smoother and more stable provision of
global liquidity over time? Will it make for more disciplined policies on the part
of the reserve-currency countries, since none of them will possess a monopoly of
safe-haven status? Will it make for more volatile exchange rates between the major
currencies, as investors making use of liquid markets in both currencies shift errat-
ically between the dollar and the RMB?

Finally, what are the implications of RMB internationalization for the geography of international financial business and financial centers? Will this business be
conducted offshore in a financial center such as Hong Kong, China or London?
Or will it migrate back onshore, whether to Shanghai or Beijing? What are the
implications of the PRC's approach to RMB internationalization, which relies on
these offshore centers as laboratories for testing out reforms, for these longer-term
developments?

Clearly, there is much to debate and discuss.

The State of Play

In line with its traditional approach to economic and financial reform, the PRC has pursued a strategy of gradualism in seeking to internationalize the RMB. In the first stage, it has encouraged cross-border use of the currency for trade settlement. As firms exporting to the PRC have acquired RMB receipts, they were allowed to maintain those receipts in the form of RMB bank deposits in Hong Kong, China and, subsequently, other offshore financial centers. The banks and firms acquiring those balances were then permitted to use them for a gradually widening range of investments in the PRC. Meanwhile, the People's Bank of China negotiated bilateral currency swap lines with foreign central banks to provide them with RMB liquidity in order to further encourage foreign authorities to permit their banks and firms to do business in RMB. Most recently, PRC authorities have announced the intention of experimenting with more comprehensive capital account liberalization over a limited geographical domain by creating a Shanghai Free Trade Zone that will be largely open to financial transactions with the rest of the world.

Renminbi Trade Settlement

In the first step in the process of RMB internationalization, the PRC focused on promoting use of the currency for trade-related purposes. In July 2009, the PRC launched a pilot scheme that allowed use of the RMB in settlement of trade with Association of Southeast Asian Nations (ASEAN) member states as well as Hong Kong, China and Macao, China in five mainland PRC cities: Shanghai, Guangzhou, Shenzhen, Dongguan, and Zhuhai. In mid-2010, coverage of the scheme was expanded to twenty provinces, permitting firms in those provinces to settle their trade in RMB. Since then, authorization to settle trade in RMB has been extended nationwide, so that essentially all trade by the PRC can now be settled in RMB.

Take-up has been rapid. From a mere 1 percent of the PRC's total foreign trade in the second quarter of 2010, by the second quarter of 2014 RMB trade settlement had ballooned almost twenty-eight-fold, reaching 27.8 percent of the PRC's total trade (see figure 1-1). Since the inception of the scheme, however, more than 80 percent of these trade settlements have been with Hong Kong, China, raising some questions about the generality of use of the RMB in trade settlement with the PRC.

Initially, RMB trade settlement was skewed toward import settlement, as opposed to settlement of PRC exports. For instance, at the end of 2010 the ratio of RMB receipts and payments was 1:5.5 (People's Bank of China 2012). One interpretation of this bias is that it likely reflected the lack of availability of RMB abroad and the incentive to hold RMB offshore in anticipation of the currency's

Figure 1-1. *Renminbi Trade Settlement*

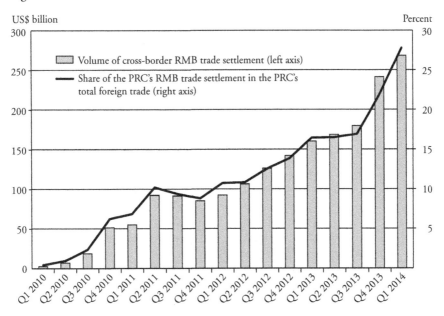

Source: CEIC, China Premium Database (www.ceicdata.com/countries/china); International Monetary Fund, *Direction of Trade Statistics.*

appreciation. In other words, it reflected speculative motives rather than the convenience of invoicing and settling trade in the PRC's currency.

More recently, however, the ratio has narrowed. From 1:1.7 in 2011, it fell to 1:1.3 in the first half of 2013 (People's Bank of China 2013). This trend is in line with the turnaround in expectations of a RMB appreciation since the latter part of 2011. Such consistent expansion in the use of RMB in trade settlement, despite diminished expectations of RMB appreciation in recent years, suggests that RMB internationalization is now being driven by fundamental changes rather than just by speculative motives.

Together with the expansion in RMB trade settlement, RMB deposits in Hong Kong, China have risen dramatically. Although Hong Kong, China banks were allowed to open RMB accounts as early as 2004, it was only in mid-2010, when the RMB settlement scheme was introduced, that RMB deposits in Hong Kong, China took off. Since then, the RMB has been allowed to flow back and forth between Hong Kong, China and the PRC for purposes related to trade settlement, as noted earlier. From about $9.2 billion at the end of 2009 (representing 1.1 percent of total deposits in Hong Kong, China), RMB deposits surged to $47.3 billion by the end of 2010 (5.4 percent of total deposits), $93 billion (9.5 percent) by the end of 2011, and then to $96 billion (about 9 percent) by the end of 2012

Figure 1-2. *Outstanding Renminbi (RMB) Deposits in Hong Kong, China*[a]

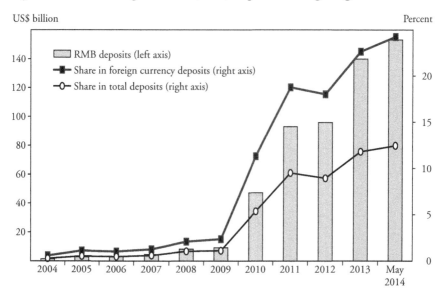

Source: Hong Kong Monetary Authority, *Monetary Statistics* (various years; www.hkma.gov.hk/eng/market-data-and-statistics/monetary-statistics/monetary-base/2014/).

a. The data refer to December of that year, unless otherwise specified.

(see figure 1-2). The rate of increase slowed in 2012, but this may be less a reflection of any diminished attractiveness of the currency than investors in Hong Kong, China shifting away from RMB deposits into other RMB-denominated financial assets. Consistent with this interpretation, the value of RMB deposits in Hong Kong, China subsequently resumed its rise, reaching $140 billion (12 percent of total deposits) at the end of 2013 and then $153 billion (12.5 percent) at the end of May 2014.

Renminbi-Denominated Investment

Although the PRC authorities have continued to control inward and outward foreign direct investment (FDI), the controls in question have been relaxed in recent years. In addition, both the approval process in the use of the RMB for outward FDI by PRC enterprises and the actual use of the RMB for inward FDI in the PRC have been streamlined with the announcement of the Renminbi Outward Direct Investment scheme in January 2011 and the creation of the Renminbi FDI scheme in October of the same year. Since data were made available in early 2012, RMB-denominated and -settled FDI has risen rapidly as a trend, accounting for about a third of the PRC's total FDI flows in mid-2013, close to 60 percent at the end of 2013 and over 80 percent at the end of June 2014 (figure 1-3).

Figure 1-3. *Renminbi-Denominated and -Settled Foreign Direct Investment*

US$ billion   Percent

Legend:
- Inbound direct investment (left axis)
- Outbound direct investment (left axis)
- Share of RMB FDI settlement in the PRC's total FDI (right axis)

Categories: Q1 2012, Q2 2012, Q3 2012, Q4 2012, Q1 2013, Q2 2013, Q3 2013, Q4 2013, Q1 2014, Q2 2014

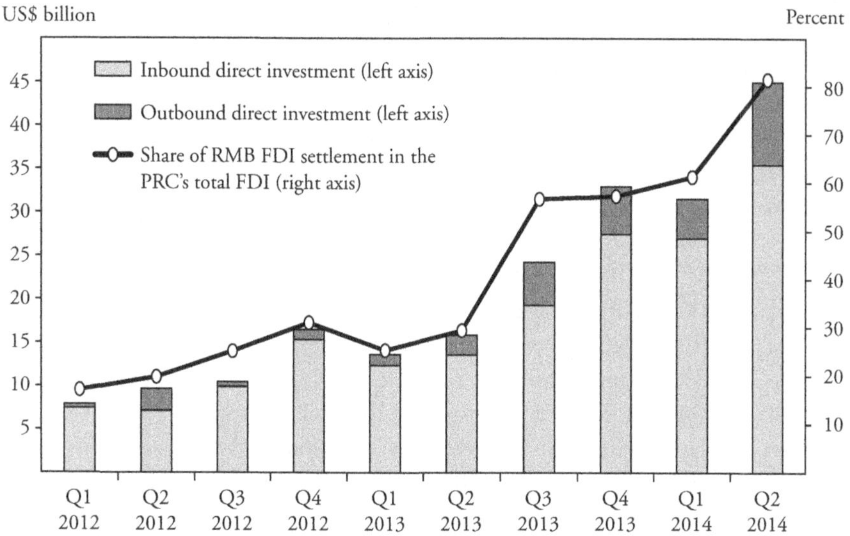

Sources: People's Bank of China (2013); CEIC, "China Premium Database" (www.ceicdata.com/countries/china); Bloomberg (electronic database, various years).

FDI = foreign direct investment.

The strictest controls are on portfolio investment flows, yet these controls have also been relaxed in recent years to expand the range of investors and the type of financial assets that are permitted to engage in cross-border transactions using the RMB. Since April 2006, preapproved institutional investors from the PRC have been allowed to invest in RMB-denominated financial instruments offshore, such as in Hong Kong, China. In August 2010, foreign central banks and certain types of foreign financial institutions were allowed to invest in the PRC's onshore interbank bond market. Then, in December 2011, the Renminbi Qualified Foreign Institutional Investor (RQFII) scheme was introduced to allow prequalified offshore institutions—including foreign central banks—to invest, subject to quota, in the PRC's onshore interbank bond market and equity market. Finally, the quota for RQFII was raised in April 2012, and onshore nonfinancial institutions were allowed to issue RMB bonds in Hong Kong, China in May 2012.

Renminbi Bond Issuance

In addition to relaxing restrictions on inward and outward capital flows, official support by the PRC authorities has fostered the growth of an offshore RMB-denominated (dubbed "dim sum" by bond traders) bond market in Hong Kong, China. Although the first dim sum bond was issued as early as 2007, it was not until

August 2010, when the U.S. corporation McDonald's became the first foreign private company to issue an RMB bond, that the offshore RMB-denominated bond market attracted significant international attention. Issuance then rose from $0.9 billion in 2010 to $4.6 billion in 2011, to $7.1 billion in 2012, and $9.7 billion in 2013. Issuance in the first seven months of 2014 stood at $10.5 billion (figure 1-4), continuing the earlier upward trend. Major issuers of RMB bonds are financial institutions (figure 1-4a), and a large portion of these issuances are made by firms from the PRC; Hong Kong, China; and the rest of the world (figure 1-4b).

Renminbi Currency Swaps and Direct Trading

Since late 2008, the PRC has concluded a series of bilateral RMB-denominated currency swap arrangements with the goal of providing foreign monetary authorities access to RMB liquidity and in return encouraging them to authorize use of the currency by domestic banks and firms. The Republic of Korea was the first counterparty to such an agreement. Its December 2008 bilateral swap arrangement with the People's Bank of China was for 180 billion Chinese yuan (CNY), with a maturity of three years. Prior to its expiration in 2011, the PRC and the Republic of Korea renewed the arrangement, doubling the amount of the swap to CNY360 billion. Where the Republic of Korea led, a variety of other PRC trading partners have followed. As of the end of October 2013, the PRC had signed twenty-five bilateral RMB-denominated swap arrangements with twenty central banks (table 1-1).[2]

Since 2010 the PRC has also promoted direct trading of the RMB with non–U.S. dollar currencies, to eliminate the need for foreign counterparties to first buy and sell dollars in order to move between third currencies and the RMB. It agreed on such direct currency trading with Malaysia (August 2010), the Russian Federation (November 2010), Japan (December 2011, effective in June 2012), and Australia (April 2013). When the PRC signed an agreement with Japan on direct currency trading, it also agreed to allow the Bank of Japan to hold RMB sovereign debt as foreign exchange reserves and to promote the issuance of RMB-denominated bonds by Japanese companies.

Capital Account Liberalization and Currency Internationalization

That successful internationalization of the RMB will require further liberalization of the PRC's capital account is either a boon or a danger, depending on one's point of view. In the eyes of some, opening the capital account is a logical step in the ongoing development of PRC financial markets. Foreign investors are carriers of

---

2. This number does not include the bilateral currency swap arrangements that the PRC signed with six of the ASEAN+3 countries (Indonesia, Japan, the Republic of Korea, Malaysia, the Philippines, and Thailand) between 2001 and 2006 under the Chiang Mai Initiative bilateral currency swap agreements. Three of the six (with Japan, Malaysia, and the Philippines) were denominated in RMB and the other three in U.S. dollars.

Figure 1-4. *Renminbi Bond Issuance in Hong Kong, China*

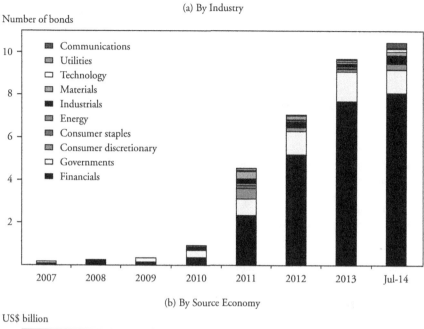

(a) By Industry

Number of bonds

- Communications
- Utilities
- Technology
- Materials
- Industrials
- Energy
- Consumer staples
- Consumer discretionary
- Governments
- Financials

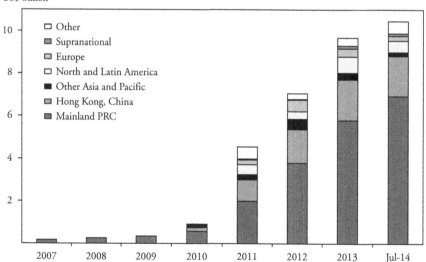

(b) By Source Economy

US$ billion

- Other
- Supranational
- Europe
- North and Latin America
- Other Asia and Pacific
- Hong Kong, China
- Mainland PRC

Source: Bloomberg (electronic database, various years).

advanced financial technology and international best practice. Empirical studies have consistently found that foreign bank penetration and competition, in particular, have positive effects on financial development (see, for example, Levine 1996). Through other eyes, capital account liberalization heightens financial

Table 1-1. *Central Bank Swap Arrangements with the People's Bank of China, December 2008–June 2013*[a]

Bank	Date	Amount (billion yuan)	U.S. dollar equivalent (billion)
Bank of Korea	*12 Dec 2008*	*180*	*26.3*
	26 Oct 2011	360	56.5
Hong Kong Monetary Authority	*20 Jan 2009*	*200*	*29.2*
	22 Nov 2011	400	62.9
Bank Negara Malaysia	*8 Feb 2009*	*80*	*11.7*
	8 Feb 2012	180	28.6
National Bank of the Republic of Belarus	11 Mar 2009	20	2.9
Bank Indonesia	23 Mar 2009	100	14.6
Central Bank of Argentina	2 Apr 2009	70	10.2
Central Bank of Iceland	9 Jun 2010	3.5	0.5
Monetary Authority of Singapore	*23 Jul 2010*	*150*	*22.1*
	7 Mar 2013	300	48.2
Reserve Bank of New Zealand	18 Apr 2011	25	3.8
Central Bank of the Republic of Uzbekistan	19 Apr 2011	0.7	0.11
Bank of Mongolia	*19 Apr 2011*	*5*	*0.8*
	20 Mar 2012	10	1.6
National Bank of Kazakhstan	13 Jun 2011	7	1.1
Bank of Thailand	22 Dec 2011	70	11.1
State Bank of Pakistan	23 Dec 2011	10	1.6
Central Bank of the United Arab Emirates	17 Jan 2012	35	5.5
Central Bank of the Republic of Turkey	21 Feb 2012	10	1.6
Reserve Bank of Australia	22 Mar 2012	200	31.7
National Bank of Ukraine	26 Jun 2012	15	2.4
Banco Central do Brasil	26 Mar 2013	190	30.6
Bank of England	22 Jun 2013	200	32.6

Source: People's Bank of China.

a. The local currency bilateral agreements cover the years after 2008. The agreements shown in italics have been superseded by subsequent agreements between the People's Bank of China and the relevant countries. The dollar equivalents are calculated using the exchange rate on the date of each agreement. The total amount under the twenty open agreements as of June 2013 is about CNY2.2 trillion, or roughly US$360 billion based on the June 2013 exchange rate of CNY6.13 per dollar. A number of bilateral agreements signed before 2008, mostly under the Chiang Mai Initiative, are not included in this table. Many of those agreements are not in the local currencies of the relevant countries.

volatility and the risk of crises, especially in countries with weak regulatory institutions and less-developed financial markets. In this view, history is littered with cases of countries that have experienced serious financial disruptions in the wake of capital account liberalization.

The obvious way to reconcile the two views is to note that the question is not whether or not to liberalize but how to liberalize, in terms of pace and sequencing. Domestic financial market liberalization—introducing market-determined interest rates, deregulating scope of financial businesses and market entry, and promoting competition—should be the first prerequisite. Supervision and regulation of domestic financial firms and markets should then be strengthened considerably in advance of capital account liberalization. Countries that have failed to meet this prerequisite have seen foreign capital inflows fuel risk taking by banks and other investors, a process that has often led to significant disruptions and crises.[3]

The regulatory prerequisites are considerable: Spain, for example, was widely touted as possessing an admirably regulated banking system just before its financial system was laid low by massive capital inflows leading to first a bubble and then a crash. This has led some observers to ask whether capital account liberalization is in fact a feasible objective of policy or whether, given recent experience, countries should in fact resist pressure to move in that direction. Capital account restrictions can be thought of as a second-best form of prudential regulation, where first-best measures—capital requirements, liquidity requirements, and domestic supervision generally—do not suffice (Eichengreen and Mussa 1998). The takeaway from recent experience may be that first best measures cannot be relied on in general. Brazil's use of capital inflow taxes, the Republic of Korea's limits on the foreign currency exposures of its banks, and even Iceland's and Cyprus's exchange controls can be thought of in this light. These observations point in turn to the question of whether the goal, for the foreseeable future, should be full capital account liberalization or limited liberalization, where taxes and restrictions on some types of international financial flows remain in place.

Capital Account Liberalization: Basic versus Full

PRC policymakers are by no means preparing to throw open the capital account. Instead, they are moving gradually and systematically in the direction of greater capital account liberalization, testing out early reforms before proceeding with others. Their stated goal is to achieve only "basic" capital account convertibility by 2015, which means that by then it will be possible to freely buy and sell the currency for trade-related purposes as well as for a limited range of capital account and financial transactions. This presumably means that short-term investments indicating speculative motivations will still be restricted, reflecting the now-conventional wisdom that short-term capital movements create greater risks than long-term foreign investments.

However, this strategy raises as many questions as it answers. Will it be possible to limit short-term flows as policymakers liberalize current account transactions and long-term capital flows, or will market participants be able to use "leads and lags" in trade invoicing and settlement and relabel short-term capital flows as long-term flows to evade remaining restrictions? Will basic capital account convertibility be enough to facilitate significant RMB internationalization, or will foreign

3. See Prasad and Rajan (2008) for issues of capital account liberalization.

institutional investors, including central banks, require free access to the PRC's onshore markets before they are willing to hold significant balances in that form? Can PRC policymakers achieve their goal of transforming Shanghai into a first-tier international financial center without moving all the way to "full" capital account liberalization?

Logically, "full" capital account liberalization would seem more important for some functions of an international currency than others. Full liberalization is not obviously necessary to encourage widespread pricing, invoicing, and settlement of international merchandise transactions in RMB. More importers and exporters are likely to prefer RMB settlement if they can use the resulting balances for a wider range of financial transactions, but some limited financial liberalization might still be enough to encourage them to accept payment in this form. Companies contemplating long-term investments in the PRC would be more willing to accept payment in this form even if PRC policymakers stopped at the stage of basic capital account convertibility. Central banks with foreign exchange reserves far in excess of what they require for purposes of currency market intervention would presumably feel similarly. In contrast, central banks with actual intervention needs and other international investors who value market liquidity would be more inclined to think twice.

The PRC liberalization strategy thus implies that we should see the RMB make progress more rapidly as a currency for trade invoicing and settlement, as a vehicle for outward and inward FDI, and perhaps also as a currency of denomination for international bonds than as a funding currency for international banks or a form of foreign exchange reserves. Limited liberalization is unlikely to be enough, however, for international banks to use the RMB for liquidity management, for global institutional investors to include RMB assets in active portfolios, for multinational corporations to incorporate RMB for cash management programs, and for central banks to hold RMB as one of the most important reserve assets.

The risks of evasion and arbitrage—the likelihood that once the PRC moves to basic capital account convertibility, remaining limits on international capital movements will become increasingly porous and difficult to enforce—should not be underestimated. The PRC, however, has a relatively extensive and long-established administrative bureaucracy experienced in the application of controls. Klein (2012) has found that controls tend to be more effective when they have been in place for an extended period rather than when they are newly imposed in response to excessive inflows or to a crisis. This suggests that PRC policymakers should avoid prematurely removing the control apparatus. It also suggests that as the country moves to basic capital account convertibility, it should contemplate giving its financial regulators greater independence from politics. An independent agency is more likely to apply remaining restrictions in an evenhanded and predictable way—and evenhandedness and predictability are qualities especially valued by international investors.

Interest Rate Liberalization and Exchange Rate Flexibility

Another important point in the sequencing of capital account liberalization is that PRC policymakers need to proceed with interest rate liberalization, exchange rate flexibility, and capital account opening in an integrated way. The freer financial capital is to flow in and out of an economy, the more problematic interest rate floors and ceilings become. For example, the PRC has a long-standing policy of controlling bank deposit interest rates, although bank loan rates have been liberalized. The more opportunities PRC savers have for transferring funds abroad, the more domestic disintermediation will result. This implies that the banks will have to be put on a true commercial footing—it will no longer be possible to rely on them for policy lending—insofar as they are no longer the recipients of subsidized funding.

This shift also implies that the country will have to move toward a more market-determined exchange rate. The People's Bank of China has kept the exchange rate low by intervening in the foreign exchange market and then sterilizing the impact on the money supply by requiring the banks to deposit an increasing share of customer funds at the central bank. Decontrolling deposit interest rates could squeeze bank profitability and make this process more difficult.

These reforms are desirable on multiple grounds. Fully commercializing the state-owned commercial banks, particularly the four large ones, will intensify competition and create pressure to increase efficiency. Distancing these banks from the government will harden their budget constraints. But interest rate liberalization and bank commercialization are not substitutes for rigorous supervision and regulation. Decontrol of deposit interest rates will help to reduce the flow of funds to "shadow banking" systems such as through wealth management assets and local governments' financial platforms, which potentially contribute to the buildup of financial vulnerabilities. Lending rates, which better reflect market demand and supply, will encourage enterprises to concentrate on a smaller number of efficient investment projects and allow private firms and households to have greater access to bank financing.

Finally, a more flexible exchange rate is an important macroeconomic adjustment facilitator as well as shock absorber for countries with relatively open capital accounts. History has shown that open capital accounts and pegged exchange rates are a toxic mix. Country authorities experiencing substantial capital inflows and outflows need to be able to adjust domestic policy in response by allowing the exchange rate to float.

PRC officials are aware of the connection and of the need to make the RMB much more flexible. Exchange rate appreciation in response to balance-of-payments surpluses would raise the prices of locally produced goods and services relative to those of internationally traded goods—locally produced goods and services being where demand will grow most strongly as the PRC rebalances its economy toward consumption.[4] In this respect, then, RMB internationalization should be thought of as integral to the larger ongoing process of rebalancing the PRC economy.[5] The question here is whether reform of the country's exchange rate system is proceeding fast enough, given the pace of capital account opening and currency internationalization.

One reason for a positive answer is that the PRC is a large economy. It is less subject to being inundated by a tidal wave of capital inflows than Cyprus or Ireland or even Spain, for that matter. Hence, the need for sharp adjustments in domestic policy in response to capital movements will be less. At the same time, even a country as large as the United States saw its domestic economic and financial imbalances at least significantly aggravated by capital inflows in the period from 2003 to 2007 (Obstfeld and Rogoff 2009). Hindsight suggests that the country would have been better off had policy been adjusted earlier and more extensively in response to those flows (Borio and Disyatat 2011).

Renminbi Internationalization in Historical Perspective

One way of gauging the scope for RMB internationalization is by comparing the PRC with other countries that have consciously sought to internationalize their currencies. There are only a few such precedents——a fact that may tell us something about the prospects. In this section we focus on two such cases: the United States and Japan.

Lessons from the United States

The U.S. case is striking for the speed with which the dollar was successfully internationalized.[6] The dollar, it is important to recall, played essentially no international role prior to 1914. U.S. banks were prohibited by the National Bank Act from branching abroad in order to originate foreign business. The country lacked a central bank to act as lender and liquidity provider of last resort to domestic financial markets. Its record of financial stability was checkered. The result was that the dollar was not held as foreign exchange reserves by central banks and governments in the rest of the world. It was not used as a currency of denomination for international trade or international bond issuance (bonds issued in foreign financial centers to be marketed to international investors). Importers and exporters—even those in the United States—when seeking trade credit for their international transactions, sourced it not in New York but in London, where it was denominated in pound sterling instead of dollars.

---

4. This shift in relative prices could also come about through relatively high inflation in the PRC, but high inflation has well-known economic and social costs.

5. See Lardy and Borst (2013) for issues of the PRC's rebalancing.

6. Here we draw on Eichengreen (2011).

This situation was transformed in barely a decade, suggesting that the PRC's timetable for RMB internationalization is not entirely without precedent. The key policy initiative was the adoption of the Federal Reserve Act in 1913, which established a central bank to backstop financial markets and permitted commercial banks to branch abroad. U.S. banks moved quickly to expand internationally, a process accelerated by World War I, which interrupted the provision of global financial services by London.

The Federal Reserve System moved equally aggressively to create a market in trade credits ("trade acceptances" in the contemporary parlance), discounting and purchasing such credits as needed to ensure a liquid market and stable prices. For much of the 1920s, the Federal Reserve Bank of New York was the single largest counterparty in this market. The bank also campaigned actively to encourage foreign central banks and governments to hold the U.S. dollar as their foreign exchange reserves. The result was that by 1924, just ten years after the Federal Reserve Bank launched its "dollar internationalization" policy, more foreign exchange reserves were held in dollars than in sterling. More trade credit was sourced in New York and denominated in dollars than was sourced in London and denominated in sterling. Leaving aside the special case of the British Commonwealth and Empire, more international bonds were denominated in dollars than in sterling.

Is it realistic to expect the PRC to emulate this example? The PRC is still a developing country, whereas the United States in 1924 was the richest country in the world, as measured by per capita GDP. On the other hand, per capita GDP measured in 1990 international Geary-Khamis dollars is currently 20 percent higher in the PRC than it was in the United States in 1924, given that the whole world has a much higher per capita income today than ninety years ago.[7] The implicit question is whether ability to attain international currency status depends on a country's absolute or its relative level of economic development. The answer is not self-evident.

As for financial development, the ratio of bank deposits to GDP was 33 percent in the United States in 1913; stock market capitalization as a share of GDP was 100 percent. In the PRC, stock market capitalization is on the order of 50 percent of GDP, while bank deposits are well in excess of 100 percent of GDP, owing to the unusually large role of state-owned commercial banks in the PRC financial system, reflecting the country's history as a planned economy. Overall, the PRC does not have a smaller financial system relative to its GDP than did the United States in 1913 (and it has a considerably larger economy). The implicit question in this case is whether the structure of that financial system—specifically, whether it is bank- or market-based—matters for a country's currency internationalization aspirations.

7. This is according to the Maddison database; see http://www.ggdc.net/maddison/maddison-project/data.htm.

Another noteworthy facet of the U.S. experience is that what was created in 1913 was an independent central bank with the independence and autonomy needed to make credible commitments and gain the confidence of international investors. It is worth recalling that the decision to create an independent central bank was controversial. Delegating monetary and regulatory authority to an independent central bank did not work perfectly; to the contrary, the Federal Reserve was deeply implicated in the Great Depression of 1929–1933.

Yet the decision taken in response to that depression was to strengthen the independence and authority of the Federal Reserve System: the secretary of the U.S. Treasury was stripped of his seat on the Federal Reserve Board, and authority to set discount rates was transferred from reserve banks to the Federal Reserve Board in Washington, D.C. The PRC still lacks an independent central bank with full autonomy to take monetary policy and regulatory decisions. The People's Bank of China is still viewed as an arm of the economic planning mechanism. This is something that will have to change if the PRC is to succeed fully in gaining the confidence of foreign investors that is needed for currency internationalization.

Lessons from Japan's Efforts to Internationalize the Yen

Japan sought but failed to transform the yen into a leading international currency starting in the 1980s. Although the relative weight of the Japanese economy in the world rose substantially in the 1980s and the first half of the 1990s, international use of the yen did not rise as much. It is true that the yen became an international currency, achieving an 8.5 percent share in global foreign exchange reserves in the early 1990s, but its role has been limited in comparison to both the U.S. dollar and the euro.

Several explanations can be given for the low international use of the yen. First, Japanese policy was not supportive of yen internationalization in the 1970s and most of the 1980s. Although Japan in principle liberalized foreign exchange transactions for all purposes in 1980, barriers to free international capital flows remained. It was only in the mid-1980s that Japan adopted a policy of facilitating international use of the yen by removing impediments to its use as an international currency. Until then, the Japanese authorities had taken the view that large capital inflows and outflows might be destabilizing and that such movements would undermine the effectiveness of monetary policy by weakening the central bank's control of the money supply. Although Japan in the second half of the 1990s attempted to encourage yen internationalization by transforming Tokyo into an international financial center comparable to London and New York, this move came too late, as the country was soon mired in a systemic banking crisis.

Second, the prolonged stagnation of the Japanese economy in the 1990s and 2000s—the so-called "two lost decades"—hampered the process of currency internationalization. The bursting of asset price bubbles in the early 1990s, subsequent low economic growth, and a systemic banking crisis in 1997–1998 forced Japanese banks and multinational corporations to retreat from the global markets, including the Asian ones. These entities' declining global and Asian presence had a negative impact on yen internationalization as cross-border bank loans, international bond issuance, and international trade denominated in yen progressively declined over time.

Third, use of the Japanese yen in invoicing Japan's trade was limited for structural reasons, as explained by Kawai (1996). Japan depended on the United States as its major export market, and the U.S. dollar was the dominant invoicing currency there. Japan's neighbors also used the dollar, making it the norm in East Asia and the Pacific and handicapping the efforts of other currencies, like the yen, to gain traction in the region. In addition, a large part of Japan's imports consisted of minerals, fuels, other raw materials, and basic commodities, pricing and invoicing of which are dollar-denominated because of the global nature of their markets. Finally, the bulk of Japan's trade was handled by large trading companies (known as *sogoshosha*) and multinational corporations, which were able to manage exchange risks efficiently by pooling risks, marrying claims and liabilities, and borrowing and lending in foreign currencies, thereby creating no particular incentive to invoice trade in yen.

Fourth, money and capital markets, particularly for Treasury bills and other short-term instruments, were not as well developed or deep in Tokyo as in New York or London due to functional and tax limitations in Tokyo. The lack of such short-term liquid assets in yen discouraged foreign central banks from holding yen as foreign exchange reserves. As a result, the yen was also a relatively unattractive currency in which to carry out international trade and capital transactions for private agents.

The PRC is clearly different from Japan in ways both favorable and unfavorable to RMB internationalization. On the favorable side, whereas Japan was reluctant to internationalize the yen in the 1980s and the first half of the 1990s, the PRC has aggressively promoted currency internationalization, particularly through use of the RMB for trade settlement, offshore bank deposits and bond issuance in RMB, and bilateral currency swaps with foreign central banks, as noted earlier. Similarly, although the PRC's growth rate is sure to decline over the next decades, due if nothing else to a shrinking labor force and aging population, the country can still realistically be expected to sustain a growth rate of 5 to 6 percent into the 2020s, in contrast to the case of Japan, which suffered from stagnation in the 1990s and 2000s. Such strong economic growth will support the continued progress of RMB internationalization.

On the unfavorable side, it is at least conceivable that the PRC could be caught in a middle-income trap, with per capita GDP stuck at low levels. Worse, financial market liberalization and capital account openness could lead to a financial crisis—

a type of crisis Japan or Southeast Asian nations faced in the late 1990s. Thus, one of the biggest challenges for PRC policymakers would be to pursue economic reforms to avoid the middle-income trap as well as to establish effective regulatory and supervisory frameworks and credible crisis-resolution mechanisms to avoid a crisis, or at least to head off a long period of post-crisis stagnation.

Although Japan had fully opened its financial system to the rest of the world by the late 1980s, it was not able to create a deep, broad, and liquid financial market that would have been needed for successful yen internationalization. In other words, capital account openness is necessary but not sufficient for successful currency internationalization. In addition, international investors will demand transparent, rules-based institutions in the PRC if they are to invest substantial amounts of their wealth in RMB. Such institutions are most likely associated with a mature democracy, which the PRC clearly lacks.

Political Prerequisites for Renminbi Internationalization

The small sample of previous cases of currency internationalization makes any generalizations hazardous, but it is nonetheless relevant to observe that in no previous case—not Britain in the nineteenth century, not the United States in the twentieth century, and not even Japan in the 1980s—was currency intervention undertaken in the presence of such a strong state role in the economy as in the PRC. The question is, How fundamentally this will have to change to permit successful currency internationalization? Can the PRC leadership grant independence to its central bank and financial regulators, commercialize or even privatize the state-owned commercial banks, deregulate interest rates, and leave it at that? Or do these limited measures lead to a slippery slope in which (1) state-owned enterprises no longer enjoy privileged access to finance, eventually face hard budget constraints, and ultimately are privatized; (2) prices must be decontrolled more generally; and (3) the state's presence in the economy is systematically reduced?

Then there are the political implications. Can a country with a one-party system liberalize the capital account without undermining its political foundations? If households are able to vote with their feet by deciding what country and currency to invest in, will other forms of voting and political competition inevitably follow?

And, to turn the question around, is political reform a prerequisite for successful currency internationalization? Sterling and the dollar were the currencies of political democracies. Going back in time, earlier international currencies—the Dutch guilder, the Genoese denaro, and the Venetian ducat—were the currencies of republics or self-governing communes. Investors, if they are to hold a significant portion of their wealth in the form of a country's currency, will want reassurance that there are limits on arbitrary action by the issuer. Rule of law is clearly important, and checks on the executive created by political competition are one source of such assurance. This is not to imply that the PRC will have to move to a multiparty democratic system with contested elections in order to successfully internationalize the RMB. It will, however, have to significantly strengthen checks and balances on the Standing Committee of the Communist Party (the Politburo), and the judiciary system—which affects the outcomes of economic and financial disputes—must become independent from the political system, not to mention the Standing Committee. The country will also have to move toward a well-defined federal system in which provincial governments counterbalance the role of the central government. It will have to allow the development of an independent media. It will have to allow the voice of nongovernment organizations to become stronger.

Thus, currency internationalization may have implications not only for the PRC's economic model but also for its political model. Such political prerequisites would be greater if the RMB were to become a global reserve currency.

Implications for the International Monetary System

Finally, we consider the implications of RMB internationalization for the international monetary system. In popular discussion, this issue is commonly framed as whether and when the RMB will displace the U.S. dollar as the leading international reserve currency. However, recent scholarship suggests that this emphasis is misplaced. The conventional view is that there can be only one international reserve currency at a time. Yet recent historical scholarship shows that several international currencies have regularly coexisted and the single-currency model is in fact anomalous. The anomalous period, from this point of view, is the second half of the twentieth century, a unique era when only the United States possessed deep and liquid financial markets open to the rest of the world, and consequently the dollar reigned supreme.

There is no reason why, in the circumstances of the twenty-first century, the dollar and the RMB could not both play major global roles. There is no reason why the United States should continue to possess a monopoly in international finance or why only its financial markets should be deep, liquid, and open. Increasing returns to scale and network externalities create a tendency for importers, exporters, and international investors to gravitate toward one currency as a common unit of account and means of payment. Yet these returns are less pronounced and less attractive in a high-tech world where everyone has access to information on exchange rates in real time and currency conversion costs are low.

Of course, the same arguments suggesting that two currencies can share the international stage at a point in time also admit the possibility of more than two international reserve currencies. Hence, PRC policymakers, when seeking to promote use of the RMB in trade settlements and international investment, should be cognizant of the possibility of competition not just from the U.S. dollar but from other sources, be they additional advanced countries or other emerging markets.

Implications for the International Monetary Fund and Special Drawing Rights

There are also the implications for the International Monetary Fund (IMF). Will the RMB be added to the basket of currencies that makes up special drawing rights (SDR)?[8] Will the IMF when making loans provide RMB credit to its members? Will the PRC acquire a louder voice in decisionmaking in the IMF? Will the IMF headquarters be moved to Beijing or Shanghai when the PRC economy becomes the world's largest?

The answer to all these questions is likely to be "Perhaps, but not all at once." As the RMB comes to be used more widely in trade settlements and as a vehicle for cross-border financial flows, it will become logical for the IMF to provide emergency credit to at least some of its members in this form. And as the PRC's weight in the world economy continues to grow, it will become logical for it to acquire more voice in the deliberations of the IMF. The constraint is the reluctance of the incumbent members with a seat at the table of the IMF's Executive Board and a voice in deliberations to cede authority and accept reduced voting shares. The more PRC policymakers, including the country's IMF executive director, advance policies designed to enhance global monetary and financial stability as opposed to simply defending the country's own interests, the easier it will be to overcome this resistance.

In 2011 the IMF Executive Board laid down the criteria that a country should meet in order for its currency to be included in the SDR basket (International Monetary Fund 2011). First, the currency in question should be actively traded on foreign exchange markets. Second, there should be active markets in exchange-based and over-the-counter foreign exchange derivatives. Third, the country should have market-based interest rate instruments. And, fourth, the currency should be widely held as foreign exchange reserves.

The RMB already meets the first two conditions, although the size of RMB in the global foreign exchange markets is still limited (2.2 percent in 2013). The policy reforms needed for currency internationalization will require it to meet the third. The fourth condition, that foreign central banks and governments hold a significant share of their foreign exchange reserves in the currency, is likely to be the sticking point. The world's central banks, when making reserve-allocation decisions, attach importance to market liquidity, and it will take time for the PRC to develop deep and liquid markets. There is also something of a chicken-and-egg problem. Central banks are more likely to hold a significant fraction of their reserves in RMB if the currency is added to the SDR basket, but in order to add

---

8. The SDR is the unit of account used by the IMF for its transactions with members. It is made up of a basket of internationally used convertible national currencies, that is, the U.S. dollar, the euro, the yen, and sterling.

it to the SDR basket, the IMF will first want to see a significant fraction of reserves held in this form.

Potential Instability of a Multiple Reserve Currency System

There are also worries that a system of competing international currencies could be unstable. Investors, including central banks, could be prone to shifting the composition of their reserve portfolios in response to events, rendering the exchange rates between the major currencies more volatile.

Historically, we have examples of both stable and unstable multiple reserve currency systems: a relatively stable configuration before 1913 when sterling, the French franc, and the German mark all played consequential international roles, and an interwar system, in which sterling and the dollar competed, that suffered from severe instability. The stability of such a system, this history suggests, hinges on the stability of the policy in the issuing countries.

Even if foreign exchange speculators have a tendency to follow trends, central bank reserve managers behave differently. They tend to act as contrarians, buying currencies when they depreciate and their share in the portfolio declines, thus acting like stabilizing speculators (Truman and Wong 2006). The euro crisis might seem to constitute a counterexample. As the crisis deepened and the euro depreciated in 2012, the world's central banks actively reduced the share of their foreign exchange reserves held in euros.[9] Even so, there was no collapse of the euro exchange rate, only the slow and steady depreciation appropriate for a relatively weak European economy.

Role of the Renminbi in Asia's Monetary System

Observers ask further whether the emergence of the RMB will hasten the regionalization of the international monetary system. This would happen if the RMB comes to be widely used for international transactions in Asia, while the role of the U.S. dollar diminishes in the region, leading to the two currencies' sharing the international currency role. There may ultimately be some movement in this direction insofar as the PRC's trade is disproportionately concentrated in Asia. Regionalization may be further encouraged by the negotiation of bilateral currency swap lines between the PRC and neighboring Asian countries. Good political relationships between the PRC and the Asian countries are also important if the RMB is to play a key role. The PRC's territorial conflicts with Japan (in the East China Sea) and with the neighboring ASEAN member states, such as the Philippines and Viet Nam (in the South China Sea), need to be resolved. Even though some ASEAN member states may see a rising role of the RMB in their exchange rate

---

9. This is according to the IMF's Currency Composition of Official Foreign Exchange Reserves (COFER) database (release of March 29, 2013; see www.imf.org/external/np/sta/cofer/eng/cofer.pdf).

policy and reserve holdings and may even stabilize their currencies to the RMB, Japan will not likely move significantly in that direction until these other disputes are resolved and the PRC establishes world-class institutions.

Peering further into the future, it is possible to imagine the currencies of other large Asian economies also someday playing consequential roles in the region. For example, one can imagine the Indian rupee as one day becoming the dominant international currency in South Asia. One can imagine renewed competition from the yen if Japan's economy is successfully revived. In this scenario, Asia will be the home to multiple reserve currencies, including (still) the U.S. dollar, the RMB, the yen, and the Indian rupee. It is not entirely unrealistic to see in the future the PRC, India, Japan, the Republic of Korea, and ASEAN countries cooperate on currency issues to create a common regional currency unit.

Conclusion

The world has an interest in successful RMB internationalization. It wants to see the PRC rebalance its economy, a process to which currency internationalization can contribute. It does not want the PRC to fall prey to instability as it opens its financial markets and reforms its economy.

Beyond that, the world welcomes the PRC's emergence as a source of global liquidity. Globalization in the twenty-first century requires international liquidity to grease its wheels. It needs internationally accepted safe assets in which firms, households, and central banks can park their savings and which they can borrow when there is an increase in the need for liquid funding. For more than half a century, the U.S. dollar has been the source of that liquidity, with U.S. Treasury obligations constituting the single largest and most liquid financial market in the world. However, as other countries, in the catch-up phase of growth, continue to expand more rapidly than the United States, the demand for liquidity globally will outstrip the capacity of the United States to provide it. The fiscal capacity of the U.S. government to stand behind an adequate stock of safe and liquid treasury securities will come under strain.[10] Other sources of international liquidity will have to be developed to supplement the United States and its dollar. The PRC and its RMB are obvious candidates. Thus, the future of globalization may well turn on the success of the PRC's efforts to internationalize the RMB.

References

Borio, Claudio, and Piti Disyatat. 2011. "Global Imbalances and the Financial Crisis: Link or No Link?" BIS Working Paper No. 346 (Basel: Bank for International Settlements, May).

10. For a more extended discussion of these points, see Gourinchas and Jeanne (2012).

Chinn, Menzie, and Jeffrey Frankel. 2007. "Will the Euro Eventually Surpass the Dollar as Leading International Reserve Currency?" In *G7 Current Account Imbalances: Sustainability and Adjustment*, edited by Richard Clarida. University of Chicago Press.

Eichengreen, Barry. 2011. *Exorbitant Privilege: The Rise and Fall of the Dollar and the Future of the International Monetary System*. Oxford University Press.

Eichengreen, Barry, and Michael Mussa. 1998. "Theoretical and Practical Aspects of Capital Account Liberalization." IMF Occasional Paper No. 182. Washington: International Monetary Fund, October.

Gourinchas, Pierre-Olivier, and Olivier Jeanne. 2012. "Global Safe Assets." Paper presented to the BIS Annual Conference, Lucerne, Switzerland (June 22).

International Monetary Fund. 2011. "IMF Executive Board Discusses Criteria for Broadening the SDR Currency Basket." Public Information Notice No.11/137. Washington: IMF.

Kawai, Masahiro. 1996. "The Japanese Yen as an International Currency: Performance and Prospects." In *Organization, Performance and Equity: Perspectives on the Japanese Economy*, edited by Ryuzo Sato, Rama V. Ramachandran, and Hajime Hori, pp. 305–55. Boston, London, Dordrecht: Kluwer Academic Publishers.

Klein, Michael. 2012. "Capital Controls: Gates versus Walls." *Brookings Papers on Economic Activity,* Fall 2012: 317–67.

Lardy, Nicholas, and Nicholas Borst. 2013. "A Blueprint for Rebalancing the Chinese Economy." Policy Brief No.13-02. Washington: Institute for International Economics, February.

Levine, Ross. 1996. "Foreign Banks, Financial Development and Economic Growth." In *International Financial Markets: Harmonization versus Competition*, edited by Claude Barfield, pp. 224–54. Washington: American Enterprise Institute.

Obstfeld, Maurice, and Kenneth Rogoff. 2009. "Global Imbalances and the Financial Crisis: Products of Common Causes." In *Asia and the Global Financial Crisis*, edited by Reuven Glick and Mark Spiegel, pp. 131–72. San Francisco: Federal Reserve Bank of San Francisco.

People's Bank of China. 2012. *China Monetary Policy Quarter 4–2011*. Prepared by the Monetary Policy Analysis Group of the People's Bank of China. Beijing: February 15 (www.pbc.gov.cn/image_public/UserFiles/english/upload/File/2011Q4.pdf).

———. 2013. *China Monetary Policy Report, Quarter 2–2013*. Prepared by the Monetary Policy Analysis Group of the People's Bank of China. Beijing: August 2 (www.pbc.gov.cn/image_public/UserFiles/english/upload/File/Final%20English%20version_2013Q2_%281%29.pdf).

Prasad, Eswar S., and Raghuram G. Rajan. 2008. "A Pragmatic Approach to Capital Account Liberalization." *Journal of Economic Perspectives* 22, no. 3: 149–72.

Truman, Edwin, and Anna Wong. 2006. "The Case for an International Reserve Diversification Standard." Working Paper 06-2. Washington: Peterson Institute for International Economics, May.

PART I

The Context

2

Will History Repeat Itself? Lessons for the Yuan

BENJAMIN J. COHEN

There is a lot of talk about the potential role of the currency of the People's Republic of China (PRC), the yuan, as an international currency. For many observers, internationalization is the yuan's manifest destiny and a by-product of the PRC's remarkable economic success. Widespread use of the yuan is confidently said to be "inevitable" (see, for example, Lee 2010; Subramanian 2011). The yuan has embarked on a Long March toward world status, reminiscent of the historic trek in the 1930s that was so pivotal in bringing the Chinese Communist Party to power in 1949. The only question, it seems, is how many years the Long March will take.

Is such confidence warranted? Recent history has seen the emergence of other currencies that for a time were also expected to soar to the top ranks of the "currency pyramid" (see Cohen 1998, 2004). In the end, their trajectories leveled off well short of what was anticipated. Limits slowed down and ultimately stalled the process of internationalization. Will history repeat itself? Or will the yuan prove to be the exceptional currency that finally manages to keep ascending where others faltered?

In this chapter I discuss lessons that may be drawn from these earlier experiences for the future internationalization of the yuan. Analysis will be limited to the period since World War II. During that period three historical antecedents stand out. These are the German mark (deutsche mark, or DM), the Japanese yen, and the euro. Each seemed destined for greatness, only to fall short of expectations. Much can be learned from their stories—first, about what may drive the internationalization of a currency, and second, about what, ultimately, may set a limit to the process.

The three currencies are examined in turn. In each case, economic and political factors that influenced the eventual outcomes are analyzed. The aim is to identify the key determinants that might be thought to have either promoted or hindered internationalization over time. What factors contributed to the international appeal of each currency, and what factors, in the end, limited their competitiveness? In a separate section I describe the main lessons suggested by these cases for the future prospects of the yuan, followed by a concluding section.

Historical Antecedents

It is axiomatic that a flourishing world economy requires some kind of internationally accepted currency. Without this, nations would be reduced to crude barter, severely curtailing gains from cross-border trade or investment. In the absence of a true world currency backed up by a global central bank, however, participants have little choice but to rely instead on a limited selection of national currencies to play vital international roles. At any given time, only a few currencies actually gain some degree of acceptance for use across borders. The conditions for successful internationalization are daunting, limiting the sample of historical antecedents that may be considered relevant to the aspirations of the yuan today.

Internationalization

Internationalization of a currency involves a multiplicity of roles, as specialists have long recognized. There is, in fact, a standard taxonomy for characterizing the roles of an international currency, which separates out the three familiar functions of money—medium of exchange, unit of account, and store of value—on two levels of analysis: the private market and official policy. This adds up to six roles in all. Sources generally speak of the separate roles of an international currency at the private level in foreign exchange trading (medium of exchange), trade invoicing and settlement (unit of account and medium of exchange), and financial markets (store of value). At the official level, we speak of a currency's role as an exchange-rate anchor (unit of account), intervention currency (medium of exchange), or reserve asset (store of value). Although the six roles are interdependent to some extent, each is distinct in practical as well as analytical terms.

The scope of an international currency is defined by the number of roles it plays. Its domain is defined by its geographic range. At any given time, only a few national currencies tend to play any international role at all. Even fewer play all six roles, and even fewer still are used on a truly global scale. Since World War II, the U.S. dollar has clearly dominated in terms of both scope and domain. Its only close rival these days is the euro, presently the second most important currency in the world, with Japan's yen a bit further behind. Other currencies—such as the pound sterling, Swiss franc, and Canadian and Australian dollars—are also used across borders but on a much more modest scale. These minor currencies can be found mainly in international banking or bond markets, or to a limited extent in central bank reserves. The yuan, by contrast, has gained little traction outside the PRC. Despite current talk of internationalization, the yuan's role on the global stage has yet to be realized.

Essential Qualities of International Currencies

Why are there so few international currencies? At the national level, the role of a currency can be promoted by the coercive powers of the state. Sovereign governments can deploy legal-tender laws and related regulatory measures to compel residents to adopt the national currency for all legitimate monetary purposes. States enjoy a monopoly within their own borders, but at the international level the capacity for coercion is more limited. Monopoly is replaced by competition, and agents must be persuaded rather than compelled to make use of a currency. Competition for market share is the essence of the process of internationalization. A new entrant must have qualities that enhance its appeal relative to that of incumbents or other possible contenders. In short, the currency must be competitive.

What makes a currency competitive? Both economic and political factors are involved. On the economic side, analysts agree that three broad attributes are essential. First, at least during the initial stages of internationalization, is widespread confidence in a currency's future value backed by financial stability in the country of origin. This means that a proven track record of relatively low and stable inflation is required. Second are the qualities of "exchange convenience" and "capital certainty"—a high degree of transactional liquidity and reasonable predictability of asset value. The key to both is a set of deep and well-developed financial markets, sufficiently open to ensure some degree of access by nonresidents. A minimum level of convertibility for foreign transactions is obviously necessary if a currency is to be used internationally. And third, a currency must promise a broad transactional network, since nothing enhances a currency's appeal more than the prospect of acceptability by others. Historically, this factor has usually meant a growing economy that is large in absolute size and well integrated into world markets. Without at least some of these essential attributes, no currency is likely to hold much appeal for international use.

On the political side, both domestic and international considerations play a role. Domestically, political stability and effective governance in the country of origin are critical. Potential users are unlikely to be attracted to a currency that is not backed by adequate protection of property rights and genuine respect for the rule of law. Nor will they be drawn to a regime that lacks a demonstrated capacity for successful policy management.

Internationally, the experience of the dollar suggests that geopolitics and security considerations may also be of considerable importance. At the private level, a militarily powerful nation can provide a "safe haven" for nervous investors (James 2009; Norloff 2010). A strong defense ensures a more secure investment climate. At the official level, currency preferences of governments may be influenced by broader foreign-policy ties—traditional patron-client linkages, informal security guarantees, or formal military alliances. Can it be an accident that with the conspicuous exception of the PRC, most of the big dollar holders around the world are all formal or informal allies of the United States? The greater the ability of an issuing state to project power beyond its borders, the more likely it is that others will feel comfortable using its money.

Candidates for Internationalization

Realistically, few currencies are able to meet all these demanding economic and political qualifications. Given the substantial stakes involved, the competition that is at the heart of the process of internationalization is bound to be unforgiving.

In some cases, currencies are effectively disqualified because they fail to perform all three of the standard functions of money. They are not full-bodied currencies. That is especially true of so-called "artificial currency units" such as the special drawing right (SDR) of the International Monetary Fund (IMF) or Europe's old European Currency Unit (ECU), which have existed primarily as notional units of account.[1] Neither the SDR nor the ECU was ever available for use as a medium of exchange. The same was also true of the "transfer ruble" created by the former Soviet Union for denominating trade within the Soviet-led bloc of socialist nations before the end of the cold war. Trade among bloc members was based on strict bilateral balancing. Monetary values were expressed in transfer rubles, but these existed solely for accounting purposes. Trade with non-bloc members was done entirely in dollars or other Western currencies. The ruble that was used inside the Soviet Union was tightly regulated and rarely adopted for transactions abroad. Despite the Soviet Union's geopolitical importance at the time, its national currency never had any real international standing.

In other cases, currencies are disbarred in practical terms by inconvertibility. Technically, Article VIII of the charter of the IMF imposes a convertibility obligation on all IMF members. To this day, however, a majority of the IMF's membership—mostly the least-developed economies—still take advantage of a legal loophole afforded by the charter's Article XIV to prolong rigid exchange and capital controls. No one would ever consider any of their currencies credible candidates for internationalization.

---

1. This was a basket of the currencies of the European Community member states, used as the unit of account of the European Community before being replaced by the euro on January 1, 1999, at parity.

Interestingly, the PRC, too, still limits the convertibility of its currency. Even among observers who see internationalization as the yuan's destiny, a natural assumption is that a minimum level of convertibility for current and capital-account transactions must come first. It is not clear, however, whether convertibility must be absolute. A critical question posed by the yuan is how much convertibility is necessary to encourage international use. The answer, as we shall see, is not self-evident.

Among convertible currencies, many fail to appeal internationally because they lack one or more essential attributes. Some issuing countries may have a poor record on inflation or lack sufficient depth and liquidity in their financial markets. Others may simply not be big enough to offer a broad transactional network or project power effectively. Others may lack the requisite political stability or rule of law.

Incumbency also matters. Currency choice is notoriously subject to inertia, owing to the often high cost of switching from one currency to another. Why go to the trouble of adapting financial practice to a different currency unless you can be sure that others will make use of it, too? A challenger must not only match at least some of the qualities of existing international currencies, it must also somehow offer advantages sufficient to persuade agents to risk making a potentially costly change. In practical terms, it is not easy to compete with a currency that is already as well established as the U.S. dollar has been since World War II. The U.S. dollar enjoys undoubted incumbency advantages. Not least is the fact that the language of its issuing country, English, happens as well to be the universal language of international business. The idea of converting from one currency to another is less appealing if it also means switching from one language to another.

In recent experience, the currencies that have managed to achieve even marginal acceptance for cross-border purposes are few. Since World War II, the dollar has dominated. Among all other currencies, only the DM, yen, and euro have for a time been competitive enough to also gain a significant share of the market for international money. Much can be learned from the stories of these three currencies.

The Deutsche Mark

At the end of World War II the picture was clear. There was just one international currency of any consequence, the U.S. dollar. Within the so-called sterling area, the United Kingdom's pound sterling was still in use for some cross-border purposes but had already begun a long decline to fringe status (Cohen 1971; Schenck 2010). Ironically, when the first new challenger emerged in the 1960s and 1970s, it was a currency that had not even existed in 1945—the German mark. The DM was created in 1948 as part of a major economic reform in the western zones of occupied Germany, presaging the inauguration a year later of the new Federal Republic of Germany (otherwise known as West Germany). By the 1980s the DM was firmly established as the second most important currency in the world, before being absorbed into the newborn euro in 1999. Both economic and political considerations played pivotal roles in the story.

History

The Federal Republic's beginnings were not auspicious. Following the devastation of war, the former Third Reich lay in ruins, its cities and industries largely destroyed. But then began West Germany's *Wirtschaftswunder*—literally, "economic miracle"—which generated rapid growth and persistent export surpluses. By the end of the 1950s the Federal Republic (created in May 1949 from the three Allied-occupied zones) could already be described as the leading economy on the European continent and the region's preeminent monetary power. By the 1960s the DM's internationalization was well under way. By the 1970s, evidence of the currency's growing prominence was manifest. Though never more than a distant second to the dollar, it was leagues ahead of all other currencies, apart from Japan's yen.

At the private level, the DM quickly emerged as one of the world's most widely used currencies for both foreign exchange trading and trade invoicing and settlement. In the foreign exchange market, a currency's share in total transactions indicates its importance as a "vehicle" for trades among third currencies. Comprehensive data on the currency composition of such transactions in the global market were hard to come by prior to a series of triennial surveys conducted by the Bank for International Settlements (BIS) beginning in 1989. Earlier estimates for turnover in the interbank market in New York, released by the Federal Reserve Bank of New York, put the DM share of trades against the dollar in the range of 31 to 34 percent over the decade of the 1980s (Tavlas and Ozeki 1992). The BIS surveys suggest that globally, in 1989, the DM was involved on one side or the other of 27 percent of all currency trades—far below the dollar's share of 90 percent, but well above that of any other currency except for the yen, whose share as a vehicle currency was comparable. (Since each foreign exchange transaction has two sides, the total of shares adds up to 200 percent.) In 1998, just prior to the birth of the euro, the DM's share of global currency transactions was up slightly, to 30 percent (Bank for International Settlements 1999).

Similarly, by as early as 1980 the DM's share in the denomination of global trade was estimated at 13.6 percent, rising to 15.3 percent by 1992, some 40 percent greater than the Federal Republic's share of total world exports (Thygesen 1995; McCauley 1997). Only the dollar, with a share of global trade close to 50 percent, accounted for a larger proportion of invoicing.

The DM also gained some popularity in financial markets. Most indicative is a composite index of the currency composition of international assets constructed at the BIS for the years 1980 to 1995 (Frenkel and Goldstein 1999). This "international asset" aggregate combined holdings of bonds, notes, and cross-border banking claims for purposes of ready comparison. Over the period covered by the index, the DM attained a market share in the range of 14 to 15 percent. Again, this was second only to the dollar, though well below the dollar's share of half or more.

At the official level, the Federal Republic's currency was quickly adopted by a number of European neighbors as an anchor for the exchange rates of their own currencies. These currencies' stability in relation to the DM became a high priority, for reasons to be explained later in this chapter. Correspondingly, the Federal Republic's currency also became the preferred intervention medium for neighboring central banks, mostly replacing the dollar. According to one informed source (Tavlas 1991), the DM share of exchange-market interventions within Europe rose from around 25 to 30 percent in 1979 to as much as 75 percent by the end of the 1980s. That development in turn encouraged accumulations of DM in reserves, also in preference to the dollar. Estimates culled from various IMF annual reports suggest that the DM came to account for 12 to 16 percent of global reserves during the 1980s and 1990s.

Explaining the DM's Rise

What explains the successful rise of the DM? The roots of its internationalization lay in economics but were reinforced by politics. Two economic factors in particular stood out. One was the Federal Republic's growing importance in world trade, which mainly affected the DM's role as a medium of exchange and unit of account for private market actors. The other derived from West Germany's disproportionate influence on general macroeconomic conditions, particularly within Europe, which mostly affected the currency's use at the official level. Both factors were amplified at the political level by the process of regional integration that began with the Coal and Steel Community in 1950 and the Rome Treaty of 1955—what has since become known as the "European project."

Together, these economic and political considerations promoted a broad, albeit uneven, scope to the DM's internationalization. The DM played all six roles of an international currency to a greater or lesser extent. In terms of domain, however, the DM was quite localized, prevailing mainly around Europe. Elsewhere, the currency was less competitive. The DM's geographic range was regional, not global like the dollar's.

TRADE. As indicated, a broad transactional network, reflecting a large and open economy, is generally considered essential to the internationalization of a currency. That proposition certainly seems to be confirmed by the German case. There is little doubt that the increased use of the DM for trade invoicing and settlement was directly linked to the Federal Republic's growing importance in international commerce, both as exporter and importer. By the 1990s, Germany had become the world's second-largest trading nation, with a share of global trade (exports plus imports) of around 10 percent—well behind the United States but ahead of Japan. On the selling side, the Federal Republic ranked as the second-largest exporter, with a pronounced comparative advantage in differentiated manufactured goods such as machinery and transport equipment. These are the sorts of products that in advanced economies typically are priced in the seller's own currency. (The major exception to this norm was Japan, as we shall see.) Conversely, on the buying side the large size of the Federal Republic's domestic market gave German importers leverage to insist on denominating trade in DM, to avoid exchange risk. Thus, use of the DM was stimulated on both sides.

But the effect was distinctly regional in scale, limited primarily to the Federal Republic's immediate neighbors. In the broader global economy, West Germany was by no means a giant among nations—only about one-fifth the size of the U.S. market and equal to just 60 percent of Japanese GDP. Its place in the world was substantial but hardly overwhelming. Within Europe, however, the Federal Republic was dominant—about 30 percent larger than France and 40 percent larger than the United Kingdom. In its own vicinity, the Federal Republic's large market was bound to exercise a strong gravitational pull.

The regional bias was in turn reinforced by the European project of integration. By the 1980s nearly the entire continent west of the Iron Curtain was drawn together by a network of trade agreements that reduced or eliminated barriers to commerce in the region. Some countries were full members of the Common Market, known today as the European Union (EU). Others were effectively included under other accords. Europe's increasingly close commercial ties naturally added to the weight of the regional leader's currency. With barriers falling, intra-European trade could logically be expected to grow faster than trade with countries elsewhere, and no economy was more important within the region than that of the Federal Republic. As nearby countries grew increasingly dependent on West Germany, both as a market and a source of supply, it was only natural that they would be prepared to do more business using the DM.

MACROECONOMICS. A record of low inflation is also considered essential to internationalization. This proposition seems to be confirmed by the German case. The German public has a well-known aversion to inflation, dating back to the hyperinflation that swept the country after World War I. A pronounced "stability culture" has long prevailed, fully reflected in the hard-line policies of the Federal Republic's central bank, the Bundesbank. Throughout the post–World War II period, West Germany consistently ranked among the least inflationary of all economies. That preference was bound to have a disproportionate influence on general macroeconomic conditions across Western Europe, given the Federal Republic's central position in regional import and export markets. Neighboring states were driven to keep their own prices in line in order to avoid a loss of competitiveness relative to the Federal Republic. The imperative was to stop real exchange rates (nominal exchange rates adjusted for inflation differentials) from rising.

This meant that many European governments felt under pressure to match the Federal Republic's high interest rates as best they could. It may have been a bit of a caricature to suggest, as some observers did, that the Deutsche Bundesbank was making monetary policy for all of Europe—a simplification that came to be known as the "German dominance hypothesis." Econometric evidence suggests a more nuanced picture, where interest rates often moved in tandem but were less than perfectly correlated (Von Hagen and Fratianni 1990; Laopodis 2001). There is little question that a distinct asymmetry prevailed that closely resembled the sequential Stackelberg leadership model of game theory, with the Bundesbank as the acknowledged leader. Other central banks then decided whether (or by how much) to follow German policy in response.

The same imperative also explains why stability of other currencies in relation to the DM became a high priority. Neighbors felt compelled to anchor their nominal exchange rates to the DM as a kind of check to their own inflationary propensities. As one informed commentary put it (Frenkel and Goldstein 1999): "The gradual hardening of exchange rate commitments . . . became the mechanism by which previously high-inflation members chose to discipline their own monetary policies, and it was to the Bundesbank and its anti-inflationary credibility that these countries turned for monetary policy leadership" (720). By the end of the 1980s the Deutsche Bundesbank (1988, 14) was boasting that the DM "performs the function of a key currency, acting as a 'stability anchor' for the other pertinent currencies."

It was only natural, therefore, that most interventions in Europe would be carried out in the German currency and that a larger share of reserves would now be maintained in DM. Here, too, the impact was reinforced by the European project, which from the late 1960s onward featured repeated attempts to promote some form of regional monetary integration. First, in 1972, came the so-called "snake," a mutual intervention system aiming to link the currencies of West Germany and its Common Market partners together in a joint float. When that experiment proved unsustainable, agreement was reached in 1978 to launch a new European Monetary System (EMS), designed in effect to create an improved "supersnake" for Europe. At the heart of the EMS was the Exchange Rate Mechanism (ERM), where in principle all interventions to sustain the joint float would be symmetrical within a matrix of bilateral cross-rates. In practice, however, the ERM soon evolved into something more like a spoke-and-wheel construct with West Germany's currency at the center, forming a de facto DM zone. Studies show that by the 1980s almost all of Europe's currencies were shadowing the DM to an extent (Bénassy-Quéré and Deusy-Fournier 1994; Frankel and Wei 1995).

Limits to the DM's Internationalization

Yet for all its achievements, German's currency never came close to true global status. Even before its absorption into the euro, the DM had clearly reached its limit and remained a distant second to the dollar. Four factors, both economic and political, explain why.

First was sheer inertia, reflecting the dollar's undoubted incumbency advantages in most parts of the world. Outside Europe, the DM offered no significant gains relative to the dollar. Only within the European neighborhood was Germany's gravitational pull sufficient to make the DM truly competitive. Elsewhere, the dollar retained its traditional edge.

Second was the inaccessibility and relative backwardness of West Germany's financial markets, as compared with the global market for the dollar. Although convertibility of the DM (along with most other European currencies) for current account transactions was introduced as early as 1958, a panoply of capital controls persisted until as late as the mid-1980s, restricting foreign participation; the financial system could hardly be described as open. Moreover, institutional development was hindered by a variety of complex regulations and taxes. West German bond and equity markets were notably thinner than corresponding markets in New York or London, offering a limited range of financial instruments. Accordingly, trading in DM-denominated claims was narrow and expenses were high, hampering transactional liquidity. It was hardly surprising, therefore, that use of the Federal Republic's currency as an investment medium, though not insignificant, would lag considerably behind its other international roles.

Third was a notable reluctance on the part of the West German government to do much to promote internationalization of the DM. Until the early 1980s the Bundesbank actively sought to restrict cross-border use—for example, by exercising firm command over the issue of DM obligations in the external bond market (Neumann 1986, 110). At issue was control of monetary policy, which was very critical to West Germany's anti-inflationary stability culture. Public authorities feared that in time an undue constraint might be imposed on policy at home by an excessive accumulation of liabilities abroad—an apprehension that was widely shared by financial interests and other key constituencies across German society (Henning 1994). Over the longer term, it was thought, shifting currency preferences could generate much exchange rate volatility and uncertainty, threatening both price stability and export revenues. At no point did the government take a proactive stance on internationalization. If the DM were going to emerge as a rival to the dollar, it would have to do it on its own.

Finally, there was the security dimension. The Federal Republic may have been a stable democracy with full respect for property rights and an earned reputation for effective policy management. However, it was also on the front line of the cold war, hardly what might be considered a safe haven for investors. For understandable historical reasons, the West German government was reluctant to challenge legal restrictions on its ability to rebuild a strong military machine capable of projecting power abroad, relying instead on the protection of the United States. Foreign governments, therefore, had no reason to look to West Germany for leadership on security issues. If they were going to be attracted to using the DM, it would have to be for economic, not political reasons. As we know, the DM's economic appeal was limited largely to the European region, setting a natural limit to the currency's scope and domain.

The Yen

In many ways the story of the Japanese yen is similar to the German mark's. At the end of World War II, Japan lay in ruins, with its economy shattered and its currency virtually worthless. Then, Japan, too, enjoyed an economic miracle, with growth rates from the late 1950s onward that were the envy of the world. By the late 1960s, Japan's GDP had come to be the second-largest in the world—larger even than Germany's. By the late 1970s the international standing of the yen was well established. Yet Japan's currency ultimately reached its limit; indeed, more recently, it has in most respects gone into seemingly irreversible decline. Here, too, both economic and political considerations played pivotal roles.

History

The rise of the yen was impressive but uneven in both scope and domain. At both the private and official levels, the currency came to be used much more as a store of value than as a medium of exchange or unit of account. Geographically, its reach, like that of the DM, remained primarily regional, for the most part limited to the nations of East Asia. Overall, the yen never managed to climb above third place among international currencies, behind both the dollar and the DM.

The yen's internationalization was most notable in financial markets, where persistent appreciation made the currency an especially attractive store of value. According to the composite index constructed at the BIS, the yen's share of claims in international asset markets accelerated swiftly from little more than 3 percent in 1980 to 12.4 percent in 1995 (Frenkel and Goldstein 1999). Growth was especially rapid in the offshore bond market, where the proportion of new issues denominated in yen more than tripled between 1980 and 1995, from under 5 percent to above 17 percent (Iwami 2000). By the 1990s the yen's share of the bond market matched that of the DM, though both remained well short of the dollar's share. The Japanese currency was especially popular in the East Asian region—most notably, in larger neighbors like Indonesia, the Republic of Korea, Malaysia, the Philippines, and Thailand—where the yen supplanted the dollar as the predominant vehicle for foreign borrowing. Within Japan, nonresident holdings of both bank deposits and securities expanded steadily through the 1980s and into the 1990s.

Likewise, for central banks the yen became an attractive complement to the dollar or DM for purposes of portfolio diversification. IMF estimates suggest that during the 1980s and early 1990s the yen's share of global reserves more than doubled, from just over 3 percent to close to 8 percent. That was only half the portion accounted for by the DM but well ahead of any other currency. Once again the yen was favored most in East Asian nations, where the currency's share of reserves topped 17 percent by 1990 (Tavlas and Ozeki 1992; Kawai 1996).

For other uses, the yen's performance was respectable but by no means over-powering. In foreign exchange markets, the yen share of currency trades acceler-ated over the course of the 1980s to a peak of 27 percent in 1989 but never did surpass the proportion accounted for by the DM (Bank for International Settle-ments 1999). Here, too, the appeal was mainly regional. Japan's currency was most favored as a vehicle in East Asia, in financial centers such as Singapore and Hong Kong, China, where the proportion of business done in yen was considerably higher than anywhere else. Likewise, in the invoicing of global trade, available evi-dence suggests that there was some expansion of use, but from a very low base and again concentrated mainly in East Asia. The yen's share in the denomination of trade more than doubled during the 1980s but in 1992 still accounted for less than 5 percent of the world total. That represented little more than half of Japan's share of global exports (Thygesen 1995).

Finally, there was the yen's potential as a possible anchor for the exchange rates of other currencies. Over the course of the 1980s and into the 1990s there was much debate about whether, or to what extent, Japan and its neighbors might be coalescing into some kind of yen bloc, comparable to the emerging DM zone in Europe. In fact, most governments in the East Asian region preferred to maintain a managed float. Usually the float was in line with a currency basket of some kind, though the components of their baskets were rarely disclosed. Econometric analy-sis suggests that increasingly some of Japan's neighbors—including, in particular, the Republic of Korea, Singapore, and Thailand—did begin to shadow the yen more closely, putting greater weight on the yen relative to the dollar (Frankel 1993; Frankel and Wei 1995). However, in no economy other than the Republic of Korea did the yen actually surpass the dollar as an anchor; no country ever for-mally pegged its currency to the yen. If there was a yen bloc, it was a feeble one. In the words of one contemporary analyst (Maehara 1993): "From a policy per-spective, it appears that the yen has not yet been perceived as a key regional cur-rency to the extent that the deutsche mark is incorporated as an anchor currency in the European Monetary System" (164). As another source declared more bluntly, "The yen zone is reduced to Japan" (Bénassy-Quéré and Deusy-Fournier 1994, 138). Correspondingly, there was also very little increase in the use of Japan's currency for intervention purposes.

Explaining the Rise of the Yen

As with the DM, the roots of the yen's internationalization lay mainly in eco-nomics, although in the yen's case—in contrast to the DM—there was little rein-forcement from politics. Unlike Europe, post–World War II Asia never sought any sort of formal integration; there was no local equivalent of the European project. Nor did the Japanese government at the time actively promote foreign use of its currency. Widespread adoption of the yen occurred in the absence of—not because of—affirmative political support. Economic motivations dominated.

To begin with, there was Japan's enviable record of low inflation, confirming again the importance of monetary stability in the process of internationalization. Over the course of the 1980s Japan recorded the lowest price increases of any advanced economy. Annual inflation averaged about 2.6 percent, lower even than Germany's 2.9 percent (Tavlas and Ozeki 1992). At the same time, decades of trade surpluses had made Japan the world's greatest creditor nation, even as the United States was becoming a net debtor. Together with the sustained strength of the yen's exchange rate and a seemingly stable political system, these considerations were bound to make the currency an attractive store of value for investors and central banks alike. A strong demand for yen-denominated claims was assured.

A series of regulatory reforms also supported increased access to a growing yen supply. During the first decades after World War II, Japan's financial system was the most tightly managed of any industrial nation, which inhibited wider use of the yen. Domestic markets for equities and securities were relatively underdeveloped, and financial institutions were rigidly segmented. Beginning in the mid-1970s, however, a gradual process of deregulation began, prompted in particular by a slowing of Japan's economic growth. Interest rates were soon freed, encouraging investor appetite for a rapidly rising volume of public debt, and new markets were created or expanded for government liabilities, certificates of deposits, and other financial instruments. The traditional segmentation of institutions was relaxed and supervisory practices were strengthened, gradually increasing both exchange convenience and capital certainty.

Most important, capital controls were largely eliminated, which opened the domestic system to greater foreign participation. Earlier, strict limitations on the movement of funds restricted both inward and outward investments, even though convertibility of the yen for current account transactions was restored as early as 1964. But that, too, began to change by the 1980s. In 1980, nonresident access was eased by a new Foreign Exchange and Trade Control Law, which established the principle that cross-border capital flows should now be free unless specifically restricted. In 1984, Tokyo committed to a panoply of further liberalization measures outlined in an agreement negotiated with the United States. The so-called Yen/Dollar Agreement grew out of discussions of the Working Group on Yen/Dollar Exchange Rate Issues—the Yen/Dollar Committee—which had been created jointly by the U.S. Treasury and the Japanese Ministry of Finance in 1983. Subsequent years saw a flurry of measures to widen the scope of allowable foreign activity in domestic banking and capital markets (Shigehara 1991; Kawai 1996). Overall, the process of liberalization was by no means complete, as contemporary accounts emphasized (Garber 1996). Cumulatively, the government's initiatives did suffice to increase Japan's integration into world financial markets and to promote use of the yen for investment and reserve purposes.

Finally, there was the massive size of Japan's economy and foreign trade, exerting a strong gravitational pull on markets elsewhere. Without the promise of a broad transactional network, the yen would never have become the third most popular vehicle in foreign exchange trading, nor would East Asian governments have given it so much weight in the management of their exchange rates. In the 1980s Japan was seen as a new giant on the world stage, destined perhaps to surpass even the United States as an economic power. The appeal of the yen for international use naturally followed. For many, it was only a matter of time before the currency would take its rightful place alongside the dollar and the DM at the peak of the global monetary system (Kwan 1994; Hale 1995).

Limits to the Internationalization of the Yen

The anticipated rise of the yen failed to happen. As in the case of the DM, a limit was eventually reached: internationalization of the yen peaked somewhere around the mid-1990s. Ever since then the currency's standing has gradually declined. In banking markets, the yen share of cross-border claims has declined from 14 percent in the early 1990s to under 4 percent by 2010. Similarly, in bond markets the share has fallen from above 17 percent to under 3 percent. In currency markets the drop has been from 27 percent to 19 percent, and in central bank reserves, from near 8 percent to less than 4 percent. No one today speaks of Japan's currency as a future number one (or even number two). What happened? In this instance, five factors may be cited.

First, once again, was the force of inertia. By the time the yen became prominent in the 1980s, there were already two well-established rivals, the dollar globally and the DM in Europe. The incumbency advantages of these two currencies were hard to overcome. Outside East Asia, the yen offered no significant advantages relative to either one.

Second was the crash of the Japanese market after the bursting of its so-called "bubble economy" in 1989. In ensuing years, the country was plagued by stagnation, frequent recessions, and persistent price deflation, even as the neighboring PRC charged ahead with double-digit growth rates. Over time the gravitational pull of the Japanese economy simply became weaker and weaker.

Third was the unique pattern of invoicing in Japanese trade that discouraged foreign adoption of the yen as a medium of exchange. Unlike most other advanced economies, Japan did relatively little of its overseas business in its own currency— that is, the invoices were not denominated in yen. Whereas in the United States virtually all exports were denominated in dollars and in Germany 80 percent was in its own currency, in Japan the corresponding figure at the time was only some 30 to 35 percent. Most exports were denominated in dollars, reflecting the central importance of the U.S. market as a destination for Japanese goods. The practice represented a rational "pricing to market" strategy to maintain market share in the United States. Only sales to developing countries tended to be denominated in yen. Over time there was some increase in yen invoicing, mainly due to the growing salience of East Asia as an export market (Sato 1999). But as noted, even at its peak the currency's share in global trade remained remarkably small.

Fourth was the role of public policy in Japan, which for years was notably unhelpful. Like the Germans, the authorities in Tokyo were for a long time resistant to internationalization of their currency, which they, too, feared might in time impose an undue constraint on domestic monetary management. Some in the government did take a more positive tone. Most notable was the Council on Foreign Exchange and Other Transactions, an advisory body to the Ministry of Finance, which in 1985 called for further financial liberalization to enhance the yen's international appeal. For the most part, however, the regulatory reforms of the 1980s were adopted reluctantly, partly to stimulate domestic growth, as indicated, but also as a grudging concession to the United States. Through the Yen/Dollar Committee, Washington pressured Tokyo to liberalize its financial structure in hopes of raising demand for the yen. The idea was to engineer an appreciation of the yen that would improve the competitiveness of U.S. goods vis-à-vis Japan. Yen internationalization was seen by most Japanese not as a goal to be sought, but rather as a price to be paid to retain the goodwill of the Americans.

In fact, appreciation did occur, particularly after the well-publicized Plaza Accord of 1985, but with consequences that were not anticipated at the time. In order to soften the adverse effects of the appreciation, Japan's central bank pushed interest rates to historically low levels. The result was a marked increase in speculation in the equities and real estate markets, which fed the bubble that finally burst in 1989. Many in Japan have blamed the United States, at least in part, for the prolonged deflation that followed, harking back to the pressures Washington exerted through the Yen/Dollar Agreement and Plaza Accord (see, for example, Okina, Shirakawa, and Shiratsuka 2001; Hamada and Okada 2009).

Interestingly, as Tokyo struggled to come to grips with the country's post-bubble downturn, opinion on internationalization shifted. Over the course of the 1990s, strengthening the international role of the yen became a declared policy objective in the hope that it would help promote economic recovery at home (Grimes 2003). Most dramatic was a multiyear financial liberalization program announced by the government in 1996, dubbed the "Big Bang" in imitation of the swift deregulation of the United Kingdom's capital markets a decade earlier. Under the Big Bang, all remaining capital controls were to be eliminated and the Finance Ministry scheduled a variety of other ambitious measures, including tax reductions and increases in the range of available financial products. Especially after the Asian financial crisis of 1997–98, the government made a concerted effort to promote broader use of the yen for a variety of purposes, guided by the recommendations of a Study Group on the Promotion of Yen Internationalization established by the Ministry of Finance. But by that time it was too late. As economic stagnation dragged on, Tokyo's campaign failed to reverse the declining interest in the yen. The government admitted defeat in 2003 when it officially abandoned the strategy. In the words of one Japanese observer, "It was clear that any further attempt to internationalize the yen . . . would be futile" (Takagi 2012, 83).

Finally, there was also a security dimension. Like Germany, post–World War II Japan was considered to be a stable democracy with full respect for property rights and effective policy management. Investors were probably attracted for those reasons. But as powerful as it was in economic terms, Japan lacked the political means to influence the currency preferences of foreign governments. It was in no position to offer leadership on security issues. Limited by its occupation constitution to a modest self-defense force, Tokyo was incapable of projecting military power beyond the country's home islands. Indeed, Japan was obliged to seek protection under the security umbrella of the United States. Also, there were no nations in the region prepared to follow Japan's lead. Memories were still fresh of Tokyo's wartime atrocities and prewar attempts to build an imperial Greater East-Asia Co-Prosperity Sphere. Here, too, as in the case of the DM, it appeared that if others were to be attracted to use the yen, it would have to be for economic, not political reasons.

The Euro

The last antecedent to be considered is the euro, Europe's joint currency. In 1999 the European Union (EU) began its grand experiment: the new Economic and Monetary Union (EMU), with the euro as its centerpiece. Although the EU story is still in progress, its contours are by now clear, and they bear a strong resemblance to the experience of the yen (albeit on a more compressed time scale). After a fast start following the currency's birth, progress of the euro toward internationalization appears to have quickly reached a limit. Since the beginning of the global financial crisis in 2008, it may even have gone into reverse.

History

A fast early start was not unexpected, given the euro's credentials. From the moment of its birth, Europe's new currency clearly enjoyed many of the qualities necessary for competitive success on the world stage. One such quality was a large economic base in the membership of the eurozone, which initially numbered eleven countries, including some of the world's richest economies, and has now expanded to eighteen. Others were deep and resilient financial markets, unquestioned political stability, and an enviably low rate of inflation, all backed by a joint monetary authority, the European Central Bank (ECB), which was fully committed to preserving confidence in the currency's future value. For many observers, the global future of the euro seemed secure; for some, it seemed that Europe's currency might even overtake the dollar as the world's preeminent currency (Chinn and Frankel 2008; Papaioannou and Portes 2008). Hence it was no surprise that in the euro's early days, international use seemed to expand exponentially.

Soon, however, momentum slowed. The currency's fast start appears to have peaked sometime around 2003–2004; thereafter, use for cross-border purposes leveled off at rates well below those enjoyed by the dollar. In effect, the euro did little more than hold its own compared to the past aggregate market shares of the EMU's "legacy" currencies. Given the fact that Germany's DM had already attained a number two ranking in global monetary relations, second to the dollar, anything less for the euro would have been a real shock. Some observers expected a straight-line extrapolation of the euro's early acceleration far into the future. Now, this does not seem to have been warranted. The euro appears to have bumped up against a ceiling.

Limits were evident in terms of both scope and domain. In terms of scope, growth of euro usage was broad but, like that of the DM before it, sharply uneven across functional categories. The early expansion of international use was especially dramatic in the issuance of debt securities, reflecting the promised integration of Europe's financial markets. There was also some modest increase in the euro's share of trade invoicing and central bank reserves. But in other categories, such as foreign exchange trading or banking, there was little penetration. The ECB's (European Central Bank 2008, 7) polite way of putting this was that use of the euro turned out to be "heterogeneous across market segments."

Furthermore, the euro's domain turned out to be starkly bifurcated, just as it had been for the DM. For the most part, internationalization of the euro has been confined to economies with close geographical or institutional links to the EU and the euro zone. These include the EU's newest members, all destined eventually to join the monetary union, as well other candidate states (for example, Croatia or Montenegro) and nonmember neighbors such as Norway and Switzerland. They also include several nations around the Mediterranean littoral as well as a number in sub-Saharan Africa. Where trade and financial ties are deep, the euro obviously enjoys a special advantage. Elsewhere, however, in stark contrast, scale of use drops off abruptly. The evidence, concludes the ECB (European Central Bank 2010, 7), clearly confirms "the strong regional character of the euro's international role."

Worse, since 2008 some of the euro's achievements have even been reversed as the global crisis has lingered and Europe's debt and banking problems have multiplied. Given the adverse circumstances, says the ECB (European Central Bank 2012, 7, 9), the currency has remained notably "resilient." But that is at best a backhanded compliment, referring mainly to the relative stability of the euro's exchange rate. In terms of actual use, key indicators have started to trend downward. For example, the global share of debt securities issued in euros, which peaked at one third in 2004, began to slide in 2009, and by the end of 2011 was down to less than one quarter (European Central Bank 2012, 58). Similarly, the euro's share of international reserves, which exceeded 27 percent as recently as 2009, fell to below 24 percent by the end of 2012. According to the IMF, most of the decline was accounted for by developing countries, where central banks sold off €45 billion in 2012, cutting their holdings by 8 percent. Clearly, "resilience" is in the eye of the beholder. The best we really can say is that it could have been worse.

Limits to Internationalization of the Euro

The reasons for the euro's early rise are clear. Despite the skepticism of some, including me (Cohen 2003), the currency's credentials appeared obvious. Yet it failed to live up to its potential. Why? Here four factors seem paramount.

First is the familiar force of inertia, which in this instance acted as a double-edged sword. Within the European region itself, where the DM already predominated, adoption of the euro was only to be expected. In the eyes of many, the euro was simply the DM writ large. As the DM's successor the new currency would inevitably inherit the natural hinterland of the old. In fact, however, beyond the immediate neighborhood, the force of inertia worked the other way, favoring the U.S. dollar, with all its incumbency advantages. In this respect, the euro was able to make no more headway than the DM or the yen before it.

Second has been the absence of any proactive policy by European authorities to promote a major role for the euro. Like the German and Japanese governments before it, officials of the EMU have been at best ambivalent about internationalization. From the beginning, policy has remained studiously neutral, in principle neither discouraging nor encouraging wider use by foreigners. According to an authoritative early statement by the ECB (European Central Bank 1999, 31), development of the euro as an international currency might simply be one of many possible by-products of monetary union. If it occurred at all, it would be a market-driven process; policymakers would take no action to directly enhance the currency's appeal. That message has been repeated many times since.

Third, once again, is the security dimension. How could the EMU—a gaggle of states with limited military capabilities and divergent foreign-policy interests—possibly substitute for the global influence of the United States? How could others look to Europe for protection? As the economist Adam Posen (2008, 80) comments: "The European Union, let alone the euro area itself, is unable or unwilling to offer these systemic or security benefits beyond a very limited area" (80). Bessma Momani (2008), a political scientist, echoes Posen: "While there are viable currency alternatives to the U.S. dollar, there are no alternatives to the US military security umbrella" (309). Few governments had any political interest in switching their currency allegiance to a weaker patron.

Finally, and perhaps most important of all, is the issue of the euro's internal governance. For all their other limitations, this was never a question for the DM or yen. No one doubted that Germany and Japan were capable of effective policy management. The euro, as the joint currency of a club of sovereign states, is obviously different—in effect, a currency without a country. A fundamental mismatch exists between the domain of the EMU and the jurisdictions of its member governments, which makes decisionmaking problematic at best. The euro is the product of an interstate treaty rather than the expression of a single sovereign power. Therefore, outsiders can consider the currency only as good as the political agreement underlying it—and as recent experience in Europe has vividly demonstrated, the requisite agreement is often tenuous at best. Foreigners cannot be blamed for not wishing to put too many eggs into that fragile basket.

A Decalogue of Commandments

What lessons do these three cases suggest for the future prospects of the yuan? Although the sample is admittedly small, much can be learned from the history of the DM, the yen, and the euro. Since the PRC appears to be determined to promote internationalization of the yuan, the lessons may be framed as a series of "dos and don'ts" for Beijing—ten commandments for the Long March toward world status.

1. Don't Underestimate the Power of Inertia

International currency use is obviously path-dependent. It is not a level playing field; institutionally and linguistically, market actors and governments are already locked into certain patterns of behavior. Thus, newcomers start at a distinct competitive disadvantage that may be difficult to overcome. Inducing agents to switch is not impossible—the yuan's three antecedents all showed that barriers to entry can be overcome to some extent—but the challenge, clearly, is daunting. The yuan needs to be not just as good as the dollar or other international currencies. It must, somehow, promise to be better than existing incumbents to surmount the powerful force of inertia.

Much depends on what happens to the existing incumbents. The preeminence of the dollar has long been threatened by the United States' persistent payments deficits and accumulating foreign debt, which many believe must sooner or later erode its global competitive advantage. Barry Eichengreen (2011) has stated, "As a result of the financial mismanagement . . . the dollar's singular status is in doubt" (5–6). Switching away from the dollar could become increasingly attractive, paving the way for greater use of the yuan. Yet even then the yuan would face formidable obstacles because of the lingering presence of other potential rivals. The yuan would not be the default choice. In the European neighborhood, the euro still enjoys a special advantage. Likewise, the dollar is apt to retain its appeal in the Western Hemisphere and perhaps also in the Middle East. Even the yen, for all its troubles, remains a popular option in financial markets. The most likely outcome would not be a new monetary order dominated by the yuan, but rather something closer to a multicurrency universe—what I have elsewhere called a "leaderless currency system" (Cohen 2011), with several "peer" competitors in contention and no single currency at the top.

2. Don't Be Passive

Lesson 1 implies that it is vital to actively support the internationalization process through public policy. The fact that none of the yuan's three antecedents managed to achieve its full promise cannot be blamed entirely on the ambivalence or resistance of its issuing authority; many others factors were also involved. But the lack of official backing surely did not help. Affirmative government action may not be *sufficient* to bring the yuan to the top of the currency pyramid, but arguably, it may be *necessary*. Judging from the many actions that have already been taken by Beijing to promote international use of the yuan (Cohen 2013), the PRC's leaders would appear to need no convincing on that point.

3. Don't Be Too Ambitious

A global domain for the yuan, rivaling the worldwide reach of the dollar, may be a worthy goal, but it is unlikely to be immediately attainable. Both logic and experience suggest that internationalization tends to start close to home, building on close geographical and institutional linkages, and only then may go on to true world status. It stands to reason that, initially at least, a currency will be most appealing to neighbors with extensive trade or financial ties. That is the way the process worked with all three antecedents discussed in this chapter, each of which started in a specific region. Going further back in history, one could argue that the same was true for the early rise of both the pound sterling and the dollar. A realistic proactive strategy for the yuan would be to consolidate a firm base in East Asia before reaching out to other parts of the globe.

4. Do Sustain Price Stability

To be competitive, a currency must inspire confidence. In this regard, the three antecedents confirm the importance of a record of relatively low inflation, especially for a currency's use as a store of value. The yuan is unlikely to hold much appeal to investors or central banks if its future value is not reasonably assured. To date, the PRC's central bank, the People's Bank of China (PBOC), has been notably successful in keeping a lid on the rate of price increases despite decades of rapid economic expansion. However, few would deny that the task has been made easier by a wide panoply of government controls over interest rates, the quantity and allocation of credit, cross-border capital flows, and the yuan exchange rate. Many of these controls are slated for relaxation or removal as the country moves to make market forces play a "decisive" role in the economy, as the ruling party's central committee put it after its most recent meeting in November 2013. The question is whether the PBOC will be able to sustain its record of success in a more liberalized financial environment. Doubts are to be expected as long as the PBOC falls short of the degree of political independence enjoyed by the Federal Reserve and all other major central banks.

5. Do Maintain a Reputation for Effective Policy Management

All three antecedents confirm the importance of stable and effective economic governance as a source of confidence. The early rise of each of the three currencies was associated with rapid economic growth, a trade surplus, and high employment. In the cases of the DM and the yen, it helped that Germany and Japan became major creditor nations. Nonresidents had no reason to fear for the solvency of either currency. Conversely, the subsequent setbacks for the yen and euro were clearly attributable, at least in part, to stunning policy reversals—in one case, the bursting of Japan's bubble economy; in the other, a wave of sovereign debt and banking problems.

Many are tempted to blame those policy reversals on others. For example, many Japanese have held the United States at least partly responsible for the bubble economy of the 1980s that subsequently brought them so much pain. Likewise, many Europeans attribute their tribulations today to the global crisis that started with the excesses of the U.S. housing market before 2007. The issue is not how troubles start but how well a government deals with them once the storm breaks. For three decades, the PRC's record of overall economic success was unmatched. More recently, however, blemishes have begun to appear, including slower growth, rising labor costs, increasing levels of debt, glaring income inequalities, and severe environmental problems. Could the PRC face a similar type of policy reversal? To maintain trust in the yuan, Beijing must keep the ship of state on an even keel.

6. Do Cultivate Extensive Trade Relations

A broad transactional network was critical to all three antecedents' early internationalization. Where a high proportion of the issuer's exports were denominated in the home currency, as was the case for both the DM and the euro, extensive trade relations encouraged broader use for purposes of invoicing and settlement. In all three instances, the gravitational pull of strong trade ties led to closer exchange rate relationships and greater use for intervention and reserve purposes as well. As the world export leader, the PRC would seem to be in an excellent position to boost use of the yuan as a medium of exchange.

Trade volume alone will not be enough; the structure of trade relations will also make a difference. Despite its great weight as a trading nation, the PRC today is similar to Japan in that only a small percentage of its exports is denominated in its own currency. To a large extent this is due to the distinctive character of the PRC's foreign trade structure, which to date has been highly networked. With its low labor costs, the PRC has made itself into the "world's workshop" by encouraging imports of high-valued-added inputs and components (for example, computer chips) that could then be processed or assembled into lower-value-added final products for export. In such a network structure it makes sense to "price to market," denominating all the links of the production chain in one widely accepted international currency such as the dollar. This situation is not likely to change substantially unless the PRC can succeed with plans to move up the technological scale to more home-grown, high-value-added industrial goods, as it has already done with solar panels and wind turbines. As mentioned earlier, across the industrial world exports of differentiated manufactured goods tend to be invoiced and settled in the seller's own currency. The more the PRC is able to move its production structure in that direction, the easier it will be to expand the yuan's role in international trade.

7. Do Broaden Convertibility

Convertibility for current account transactions would seem to be a minimum requirement to get the process of internationalization going. But what about the capital account? The stories of the DM and the yen both demonstrate that widespread adoption of a currency for cross-border use is possible even in the presence of a substantial array of capital controls. Serious financial liberalization did not begin in either Germany or Japan until well after their currencies had already gained broad acceptance. This would seem to suggest that full convertibility of the yuan is by no means necessary to encourage wide adoption. But it is also clear that the achievements of the DM and yen might have been even greater had full convertibility been introduced earlier. A degree of currency internationalization was sacrificed for the sake of maintaining a grip on domestic financial conditions.

Today, the PRC faces the same trade-off. Some broadening of capital account convertibility seems necessary to promote interest in the yuan as an investment medium or reserve asset, but how much convertibility is a matter of choice. At a minimum, market actors and central banks would need to be given full freedom to establish yuan bank accounts and to buy and sell selected classes of PRC bonds and stocks. Few foreigners are likely to see yuan-denominated claims as attractive if they cannot be acquired or sold at will. Equally important would be the right to issue new yuan debt or equities in the PRC in order to facilitate portfolio balancing. Internationalization on the asset side must be complemented by internationalization on the liability side. At the same time, however, trading in certain classes of liquid claims—especially in more speculative sectors such as options, futures, or other exotic derivatives—might well remain prohibited or tightly regulated to reduce the risk of destabilizing capital flows. The idea would be to encourage greater use of the yuan as a store of value while minimizing resulting vulnerabilities.

Complicating the trade-off is the fact that today many more currencies are convertible than was the case in the 1970s and 1980s, offering market actors and central banks a wider range of opportunities. In principle, this would seem to increase the pressure on Beijing to liberalize fully. Given the PRC's great economic importance, even a partial opening of the capital account could be expected to attract wider use of the yuan. Although the availability of more accessible alternatives might slow down the yuan's Long March to an elevated status, it would be unlikely to stop the currency's ascent. In practice, some range of restrictions on more speculative market sectors could be preserved to sustain financial control at home.

8. Do Promote Financial-Market Development

Convertibility alone is not enough; access is just part of the story. The cases of the DM and yen also demonstrate how important it is to promote the development of deep and resilient financial markets capable of meeting the needs of international investors and central banks. Opening the capital account is just the beginning. Equally important is assurance of an adequate degree of exchange convenience and capital certainty. Sectors that are to be opened to foreign investors must offer both low transaction costs and a level of turnover high enough to ensure that large new orders will not generate major price shifts. Achieving these goals takes time, and it is no secret that the PRC still has a long way to go on these matters.

9. Don't Ignore Domestic Political Institutions

Among the qualities that made the DM and yen attractive were domestic political stability and unquestioned respect for the rule of law. Both West Germany and Japan were reborn after World War II as functioning pluralistic democracies, where agents could reasonably assume that contractual obligations would be fairly and effectively enforced. Gone was the arbitrariness and unpredictability of authoritarian government. Had circumstances been otherwise, it is hard to imagine either country's currency gaining much traction in international markets. Recall that non-nationals cannot be compelled to make use of a currency; they must be persuaded. They are unlikely deliberately and unnecessarily to expose themselves to serious political risk.

In the PRC's case this would seem to suggest that some degree of domestic political reform will be essential to assure adequate respect for property rights and thus increase the appeal of the yuan. Trust in the country's institutions must be laboriously cultivated. In this regard, too, the PRC still has a long way to go. As one astute observer (Lo 2013) has said, "China faces a credibility problem. . . . Without political reform supporting deeper structural reforms, the internationalization process would either stall or go astray" (162).

10. Don't Ignore Geopolitics

Foremost among factors that limited adoption of the yuan's three antecedents was the security dimension—the inability of any of their issuers to match the military prowess of the United States. Neither the DM, the yen, nor the euro could offer the same kind of security guarantees that Washington routinely extends to foreign governments that use its currency. Unlike the antecedents, however, the PRC is rapidly developing an ability to project power beyond its borders, which could in time encourage some states to switch their monetary allegiance. Much depends on how others perceive Beijing's foreign policy intentions. Will the PRC use its power defensively, to help promote peace in East Asia or elsewhere, or aggressively, to pursue controversial national goals (such as territorial claims in the East China Sea and South China Sea)? The outcome is yet to be seen.

Concluding Remarks

I began this chapter with the question: Will history repeat itself? Will the yuan falter on the road to internationalization like the DM, the yen, and the euro? Or will the yuan prove to be an exception, as the currency that finally managed to keep ascending where others faltered? A look at the past cannot provide an infallible guide to the future, but a review of three recent antecedents does help to identify the factors, both economic and political, that seem most likely to determine the yuan's prospects. I have summarized the principal lessons to be drawn from these earlier experiences in ten commandments.

The main message of my analysis is that the challenge of yuan internationalization is formidable. Some very demanding conditions must be satisfied. The principal conditions may be summarized in six questions:

1. Can Beijing sustain its record of price stability and effective policy management (commandments 4 and 5)?

2. Can the country succeed in shifting its industrial and trade structure toward exports of more advanced differentiated products (commandment 6)?

3. Can the yuan's convertibility be broadened (commandment 7)?

4. Can domestic financial markets be adequately developed (commandment 8)?

5. Can the country's political institutions be trusted (commandment 9)?

6. Can geopolitical tensions be avoided (commandment 10)?

Contrary to predictions of the yuan's rise, positive answers to all these questions are by no means guaranteed. If these conditions cannot be met, the Long March to the internationalization of the yuan may never reach its destination.

References

Bank for International Settlements. 1999. *Central Bank Survey of Foreign Exchange and Derivatives Market Activity, 1998.* Basel: Bank for International Settlements.

Bénassy-Quéré, Agnes, and Pierre Deusy-Fournier. 1994. "La Concurrence pour le statut de monnaie internationale depuis 1973" [The competition for international currency status since 1973]. *Économie Internationale* 59, no. 3: 107–44.

Chinn, Menzie, and Jeffrey A. Frankel. 2008. "Why the Euro Will Rival the Dollar." *International Finance* 11, no. 1: 49–73.

Cohen, Benjamin J. 1971. *The Future of Sterling as an International Currency.* London: Macmillan.

———. 1998. *The Geography of Money.* Cornell University Press.

————. 2003. "Global Currency Rivalry: Can the Euro Ever Challenge the Dollar?" *Journal of Common Market Studies* 41, no. 4: 575–95.

————. 2004. *The Future of Money.* Princeton University Press.

————. 2011. *The Future of Global Currency: The Euro Versus the Dollar.* London: Routledge.

————. 2013. "The Yuan's Long March." In *Power in a Changing World Economy: Lessons from East Asia*, edited by Benjamin J. Cohen and Eric M. P. Chiu, pp. 144–59. London: Routledge.

Deutsche Bundesbank. 1988. "Forty Years of the Deutsche Mark." *Monthly Report* 40 (May): 13–23.

Eichengreen, Barry. 2011. *Exorbitant Privilege: The Rise and Fall of the Dollar and the Future of the International Monetary System.* Oxford University Press.

European Central Bank. 1999. "International Role of the Euro." *Monthly Bulletin*, August, 31–53.

————. 2008. *Review of the International Role of the Euro.* Frankfurt: European Central Bank.

————. 2010. *Review of the International Role of the Euro.* Frankfurt: European Central Bank.

————. 2012. *Review of the International Role of the Euro.* Frankfurt: European Central Bank.

Frankel, Jeffrey A. 1993. "Is Japan Creating a Yen Bloc in East Asia and the Pacific?" In *Regionalism and Rivalry: Japan and the United States in Pacific Asia*, edited by Jeffrey A. Frankel and Miles Kahler, pp. 53–85. University of Chicago Press.

Frankel, Jeffrey A., and Shang-Jin Wei. 1995. "Emerging Currency Blocs." In *The International Monetary System: Its Institutions and Future*, edited by Hans Genberg, pp. 111–43. New York: Springer.

Frenkel, Jacob A., and M. Goldstein. 1999. "The International Role of the Deutsche Mark." In *Fifty Years of the Deutsche Mark: Central Bank and the Currency in Germany since 1948*, edited by Deutsche Bundesbank, pp. 685–729. Oxford University Press.

Garber, Peter M. 1996. "The Use of the Yen as a Reserve Currency." *Bank of Japan Monetary and Economic Studies* 14 (December): 1–21.

Grimes, William W. 2003. "Internationalization of the Yen and the New Politics of Monetary Insulation." In *Monetary Orders: Ambiguous Economics, Ubiquitous Politics*, edited by Jonathan Kirshner, pp. 172–94. Cornell University Press.

Hale, David D. 1995. "Is It a Yen or a Dollar Crisis in the Currency Market?" *Washington Quarterly* 18, no. 4: 145–71.

Hamada, Koichi, and Yasushi Okada. 2009. "Monetary and International Factors behind Japan's Lost Decade." *Journal of the Japanese and International Economies* 23, no. 2: 200–219.

Henning, C. Randall. 1994. *Currency and Politics in the United States, Germany, and Japan.* Washington: Institute for International Economics.

Iwami, Toru. 2000. "A Vulnerable Power in the World Economy: Japan's Economic Diplomacy and the Yen." CIRJE Discussion Papers. University of Tokyo, Economics Department (www.cirje.e.u-tokyo.ac.jp/research/dp/2000/2000cf73.pdf).

James, Harold. 2009. *The Creation and Destruction of Value: The Globalization Cycle.* Harvard University Press.

Kawai, Masahiro. 1996. "The Japanese Yen as an International Currency: Performance and Prospects." In *Organization, Performance, and Equity: Perspectives on the Japanese Economy*, edited by Ryuzo Sato, Rama V. Ramachandran, and Hajime Hori, pp. 305–55. Boston: Kluwer Academic Publishers.

Kwan, Chi Hung. 1994. *Economic Interdependence in the Asia-Pacific Region: Towards a Yen Bloc.* London: Routledge.

Laopodis, Nikiforos T. 2001." International Interest-Rate Transmission and the 'German Dominance Hypothesis' within EMS." *Open Economies Review* 12, no. 4: 347–77.

Lee, Jong-Wha. 2010. *Will the Renminbi Emerge as an International Reserve Currency?* Manila: Asian Development Bank.

Lo, Chi. 2013. *The Renminbi Rises.* London: Palgrave Macmillan.

Maehara, Yasuhiro. 1993. "The Internationalization of the Yen and Its Role as a Key Currency." *Journal of Asian Economics* 4, no. 1: 153–70.

McCauley, Robert N. 1997. "The Euro and the Dollar." Essays in International Finance No. 205. Princeton University Press, Department of Economics, International Finance Section.

Momani, Bessma. 2008. "Gulf Co-Operation Council Oil Exporters and the Future of the Dollar." *New Political Economy* 13, no. 3: 293–14.

Neumann, Manfred J. 1986. "Internationalization of German Banking and Finance." In *Internationalization of Banking: Analysis and Prospects*, edited by Korea Federation of Banks, pp. 67–144. Seoul: Korea Federation of Banks.

Norloff, Carla. 2010. *America's Global Advantage: US Hegemony and International Cooperation.* Cambridge University Press.

Okina, Kunio, Masaaki Shirakawa, and Shigenori Shiratsuka. 2001. "The Asset Price Bubble and Monetary Policy: Japan's Experience in the Late 1980s and the Lessons." *Monetary and Economic Studies* 19 (S-1): 395–450.

Papaioannou, Elias, and Richard Portes. 2008. "The International Role of the Euro: A Status Report." Economic Paper 317. Brussels: European Commission.

Posen, Adam. 2008. "Why the Euro Will Not Rival the Dollar." *International Finance* 11, no. 1: 75–100.

Sato, Kiyotaka. 1999. "The International Use of the Japanese Yen: The Case of Japan's Trade with East Asia." *World Economy* 22, no. 4: 547–84.

Schenck, Catherine. 2010. *The Decline of Sterling: Managing the Retreat of an International Currency.* Cambridge University Press.

Subramanian, Arvind. 2011. *Eclipse: Living in the Shadow of China's Economic Dominance.* Washington: Peterson Institute for International Economics.

Takagi, Shinji. 2012. "Internationalizing the Yen, 1984–2003: Unfinished Agenda or Mission Impossible?" BIS Papers 61. Basel: Bank for International Settlements.

Tavlas, George S. 1991. "On the International Use of Currencies: The Case of the Deutsche Mark." Essays in International Finance, no. 181. Princeton University, Department of Economics, International Finance Section, March.

Tavlas, George S., and Yuzuru Ozeki. 1992. "The Internationalization of Currencies: An Appraisal of the Japanese Yen." IMF Occasional Paper 90. Washington: International Monetary Fund.

Thygesen, Niels, ed. 1995. "International Currency Competition and the Future Role of the Single European Currency." Final Report of a Working Group on European Monetary Union-International Monetary System. London: Kluwer Law International.

Von Hagen, Jurgen, and Michele Fratianni. 1990. "German Dominance in the EMS: Evidence from Interest Rates." *Journal of International Money and Finance* 9, no. 4: 358–75.

3

How Far Can Renminbi Internationalization Go?

YU YONGDING

Over the five years since the launch of the renminbi trade settlement scheme in 2009, renminbi internationalization has made impressive inroads. In Hong Kong, China, a renminbi offshore market has been established from which international investors have benefited greatly. Coveting the gains, many economies are trying to follow suit. Renminbi offshore markets in Singapore, Taipei,China, and some European countries have begun to take shape. However, all is not well with renminbi internationalization. Although the progress in renminbi trade settlement has more or less met market expectations, the use of the renminbi as a store of value has been lackluster in recent years, after the initial dramatic increase in the renminbi deposits held by nonresidents in Hong Kong, China. The question of how far renminbi internationalization can go has become a common concern in the international financial community.

In this chapter I attempt to identify the factors behind the evolution of renminbi internationalization and explain why a certain pattern in renminbi internationalization has emerged during this evolution. I argue that despite impressive progress, changes in the domestic conditions in the People's Republic of China (PRC) and the international environment will likely cause internationalization to slow in the future. There is still a long way to go for the renminbi to become a true international currency.

An important point I make here is that the PRC should maintain its gradualist approach toward capital account liberalization, despite the fact that accelerating capital account liberalization could significantly boost renminbi internationalization. In this chapter I discuss the following topics:

—The evolution of the motivations of the PRC monetary authority for promoting renminbi internationalization

—The problems of and progress in renminbi internationalization made with the government's road map, according to which the government first allows the renminbi to flow out of borders through renminbi import settlement and then allows nonresidents who hold the renminbi to invest in renminbi assets on the mainland

—The relationship between internationalization and capital account liberalization

—Different prospects for renminbi internationalization according to different road maps

—Concluding remarks

Why and How Renminbi Internationalization Was Brought into the Policy Agenda

The issue of renminbi internationalization had barely been mentioned in China before 2009. Since then, however, it has quite suddenly become one of hottest topics among Chinese economists, and one of the most important, if not the single most important, international economic policy of the Chinese government. What happened to bring this about?

The Global Financial Crisis and the Decision to Internationalize the Renminbi

No other country except the PRC has ever made the internationalization of its own currency a national policy. The government of Japan initially launched the internationalization of the yen only reluctantly, yielding to the pressure from the United States (Takagi 2009), but the PRC is the only country that has tried to internationalize its own currency on its own initiative. Why did the PRC decide to push renminbi internationalization rather suddenly, in the beginning of the second quarter of 2009.

In the 1990s, the government of the PRC made the integration of the country's economy with the global economy a national policy. There were two important reasons for this. The first was to participate fully in the international division of labor. Entry into the World Trade Organization (WTO) is a landmark event. The second was to participate fully in the global financial system. In 1994, the renminbi was devalued and a managed floating system was introduced. The PRC liberalized its current account by accepting Article VIII of the International Monetary Fund (IMF) in 1996 and set a road map for capital account liberalization at roughly the same time. It was expected that, in a few years' time, the capital account would be fully liberalized and the renminbi fully convertible. However, the Asian financial crisis brought the process of capital account liberalization to an abrupt halt. During the crisis, the renminbi was repegged to the U.S. dollar and capital control was tightened. These two measures helped the PRC weather the storm of the Asian financial crisis. In 2001, the PRC came out of the crisis unscathed.

In the 2000s, the maintenance of an annual growth rate higher than 8 percent was regarded as indispensable for the creation of the 8 million to 10 million jobs each year needed to absorb the growing working-age population and became the single most important policy objective for the PRC government. Maintaining a competitive exchange rate for promoting exports was a key monetary policy objective. Faced with strong appreciation pressure on the renminbi, which in turn was created by large current and capital account surpluses, the PRC monetary authority adopted a policy of tight controls over capital inflows but loose controls over capital outflows. However, because of the strong renminbi appreciation expectations, hot money flowed in unabatedly and increased pressure on the renminbi to appreciate in value. In response, the People's Bank of China (PBOC) intervened in the foreign exchange market extensively, which in turn led to rapid accumulation of foreign exchange reserves. They skyrocketed from about US$500 billion in 2003 to more than US$2 trillion before the onset of the global financial crisis.

The global financial crisis hit the global economy badly and the PRC was not an exception. Despite PRC financial institutions' exposure to the financial derivatives originating in the United States and direct losses caused by the fall in the prices of assets such as mortgage-backed securities (MBSs) and collateralized debt obligations (CDOs) being limited, the PRC was on the brink of massive capital losses on its foreign exchange reserves, especially on its U.S. government–sponsored enterprise (GSE) bonds.

The fact that the PRC had fallen into a dollar trap meant that the PRC had to be satisfied with low returns on its foreign exchange reserves and bear large capital losses. In 2008–09, the PRC's bigger worry was capital losses because of default, dollar devaluation, and inflation. When the Federal National Mortgage Association (Fannie Mae) and the Federal Home Loan Mortgage Corporation (Freddie Mac) were on the brink of bankruptcy, some officials within the PRC government were extremely concerned. At the time, the PRC held more than $400 billion in GSE bonds. Only when the two GSEs were placed into conservatorship, on September 6, 2008, were those officials able to a breathe a sigh of relief.

The Federal Reserve's quantitative easing accompanied by the U.S. Treasury's intervention succeeded in stabilizing the U.S. financial market. The PRC became less concerned about a default on the U.S. GSE bonds. With rapid expansion of the Federal Reserve's balance sheet, however, the PRC had to worry about the devaluation of the U.S. dollar and inflation in the future, all of which inevitably would lead to significant capital losses of the PRC's foreign exchange reserves.

On March 13, 2009, at a news conference for the annual meeting of the National People's Congress, Premier Wen Jiabao for the first time expressed publicly his worries about the safety of PRC assets in the United States, stating: "We lent such [a] huge fund to the United States and of course we're concerned. . . . To speak truthfully, I am a little bit worried."[1] It was unusual for the premier to speak openly like this.

What was the PRC supposed to do? The most obvious answer was to diversify away from U.S. government securities, and the PRC certainly has done something on this front. However, as the American economist Paul Krugman pointed out, "[The People's Republic of] China now owns so many dollars that it can't sell them off without driving the dollar down and triggering the very capital loss its leaders fear." In fact, the PRC has continued to add new foreign exchange to its reserves at a dazzling speed.[2]

On March 23, 2009, ten days after Premier Wen's comments, PBOC Governor Zhou Xiaochuan published an essay in which he posed the question "What kind of international reserve currency do we need to secure global financial stability and facilitate world economic growth?" (Zhou 2009). He pointed out that the goal of the reform of the international monetary system was "to create an international reserve currency that is disconnected from individual nations and is able to remain stable in the long run, thus removing the inherent deficiencies caused by using credit-based national currencies." Zhou expressed the wish to create such a supranational currency on the basis of special drawing rights (SDRs). According to Zhou, "The role of the SDR has not been put into full play due to limitations on its allocation and the scope of its uses." He suggested that the IMF and countries concerned should "actively promote the use of the SDR in international trade, commodities pricing, investment and corporate book-keeping" and "create financial assets denominated in the SDR to increase its appeal." Zhou's proposal is an attempt to deprive the U.S. dollar of its "exorbitant privilege" (a term coined in the 1960s by France's minister of finance, Valéry Giscard d'Estaing), which is a desire shared by many countries in the world. As a first step, Zhou hoped that a wider use of the SDR as a unit of account, means of exchange, and store of value will help the PRC reduce the risks its U.S. dollar–denominated foreign exchange reserves are facing.

However, the call for the reform of the international monetary system went nowhere. On March 24, 2009, President Barack Obama dismissed Governor Zhou's proposal by saying that there was no need for a world currency and that the U.S. dollar was very strong at the current time. Surprisingly, even the PRC government failed to treat the idea of the reform of the international monetary system seriously. A few days after Governor Zhou's essay was published, a spokesman of the Ministry of Foreign Affairs distanced the government from his

1. "Premier Worries about Safety of Chinese Assets in US," Xinhua (Chinese news agency), March 13, 2009.
2. Paul Krugman, "China's Dollar Trap," *New York Times,* April 4, 2009.

proposal by saying that the proposal for a supranational reserve currency was no more than a personal idea.

What about the strengthening of the regional financial cooperation? May 2000 saw the start of the Chiang Mai Initiative (CMI)—a network of bilateral currency swap arrangements among the ASEAN (Association of Southeast Asian Nations) ten countries plus China, Japan, and Korea. Its purpose was to enable countries in East Asia to reduce the amount of foreign exchange reserves they had to hold individually for the defense of their own currencies and their reliance on IMF bailout loans. Although the CMIM has given the PRC an outlet to diversify its huge foreign exchange reserves, it could not do much to help the PRC with this. Despite all the efforts, the CMI rescue mechanism was never triggered during the subprime crisis. The Chiang Mai Initiative Multilateralization (CMIM) Agreement was launched in March 2010, after the crisis. Its aim was to provide more, and more effective, financial support to ASEAN+3 countries when they needed greater liquidity. (The ASEAN+3 countries are the ten ASEAN member states—Brunei Darussalam, Cambodia, Indonesia, Lao PDR, Malaysia, Myanmar, Philippines, Singapore, Thailand, and Viet Nam—plus the PRC, Japan, and the Republic of Korea.) Each CMIM participant was entitled to swap its local currency with U.S. dollars for an amount up to its contribution multiplied by its purchasing multiplier. The total size of the CMIM was US$120 billion.

CMIM was a step forward in regional financial cooperation when compared with the CMI, which was a network of bilateral currency-swap agreements. Ideally, on the basis of the CMI, East Asian countries could move toward the creation of a regional monetary union and a regional currency, but the variety of interests among those countries make this idea look unrealistic. After the euro crisis, the idea of a regional currency has been all but forgotten. There has not been much talk about regional financial cooperation in the PRC during and since the global financial crisis.

Before 2009 there were only sporadic discussions on renminbi internationalization. On March 9, 2008, the senior deputy governor of the PBOC, Wu Xiaoling, said that conditions for renminbi internationalization were not mature and it was not on the agenda yet.[3] On September 17, 2008, Wu pointed out that two conditions must be met to make the renminbi international: the renminbi must be made fully convertible and the width and depth of the renminbi financial market must be made comparable with the width and depth of the U.S. dollar financial market.[4]

3. "Wu Xiaoling: The Result of the PBOC's Macro-Regulation Is Significant and RMB Internationalization Is Not on Agenda" (in Chinese), *Financial Daily*, March 10, 2008 (http://news.xinhuanet.com/).

4. "Wu Xiaoling: The Internationalization of the Renminbi Must Meet Two Prerequisites" (in Chinese), *Shanghai Securities Daily*, September 17, 2008 (http://bank.hexun.com/2008-09-17/108 952514.html).

In December 2008, some economists discussed the possibility of issuing "Panda bonds" (bonds denominated in renminbi) by nonresidents (Yu 2008). The liquidity shortage caused by the failure of Lehman Brothers gave the renminbi an opportunity to play a role in alleviating the global liquidity shortage. In fact, after the collapse of Lehman Brothers, the Republic of Korea suffered an acute liquidity shortage. It sought help from the PRC, which was sitting on a huge pile of foreign exchange reserves so it certainly could help. However, there were worries in the PRC about possible dollar devaluation, which would cause losses to the PRC on its dollar-denominated loans. Nevertheless, the PRC could lend renminbi to the Republic of Korea by purchasing Panda bonds issued by Koreans, who in turn could use the borrowed renminbi to buy dollars from the PRC. Thus, the Republic of Korea could obtain the dollars it needed and the PRC could promote renminbi internationalization as well as reduce its holdings of dollar-denominated government securities. However, neither government showed interest in exploring such a possibility. With the Federal Reserve's swap arrangements with the Republic of Korea, the liquidity problems were solved rather quickly. The PRC lost an opportunity to promote renminbi internationalization by lending renminbi to a foreign country.

Interest in renminbi internationalization surged rather suddenly in 2009. The causes of this rising interest can be summarized as follows. First, the reform of the international monetary system was very difficult without the support of the U.S. government. Few industrialized countries were really serious about replacing the U.S. dollar with the SDR. At the same time, the PRC leadership had no stomach to challenge the supremacy of the U.S. dollar. This perhaps is the reason why Governor Zhou's proposal for a "supranational currency" was dismissed as "personal" by other Chinese officials. At the time, the mantra of the PRC leadership was "Don't rock the boat." Another issue was technical: the reform of the international monetary system is not only an important political and economic issue but also a technically complicated one. PRC technocrats were not yet sophisticated enough to handle all the complications of this issue. Hence, after having caused a stir, the PRC disengaged quickly and left countries such as the Russian Federation and France to talk about the reform of the international monetary system. In the PRC, people started asking, "If the regional financial cooperation is going nowhere and the international community has not yet made up its mind on the use of the SDR as a unit of account, means of exchange, and store of value in place of the U.S. dollar, why can't the PRC use its own currency to fulfill these functions?" Compared with the reform of the international monetary system and the promotion of the use of the SDR, renminbi internationalization would allow the PRC to pursue its policy objectives on its own initiative without waiting for outsiders' consent.

Second, as a result of the liquidity shortage and credit crunch caused by the collapse of the MBS and CDO markets, the renminbi's international acceptability increased significantly. On December 12, 2008, the PBOC and the Bank of Korea signed a currency-swap agreement of 200 billion yuan. In the following three months, the PBOC signed similar agreements with the Hong Kong Monetary Authority (HKMA), the Central Bank of Malaysia, the Bank of Russia, Bank Indonesia, and the Central Bank of Argentina. The strong position of the renminbi in the wake of the subprime crisis led the PRC to believe that the renminbi could be made an international currency.

Third, national pride could also have been a contributing factor. This is similar to when the Japanese government claimed that the use of the yen in international transactions was not "commensurate with the share of the Japanese economy in the world and Japan's status as the world's largest net creditor nation" (Takagi 2009, 75). This argument means nothing to economists, but it may mean a lot to politicians in decisionmaking positions.

The consensus view is that the internationalization of a national currency brings important benefits to the issuing country because the internationalization of a national currency would (1) reduce exchange rate risks for the country's enterprises, (2) reduce the need for holding more foreign exchange reserves, (3) promote trade by reducing transaction costs, and (4) improve the competitiveness of the currency-issuing country's finance sectors. These benefits should be obvious enough to encourage the PRC to pursue renminbi internationalization.

However, something puzzling still remains. First, renminbi internationalization is a long-term project and will take years, if not decades, to realize. Hence, it is difficult to imagine how renminbi internationalization can help the PRC reduce exchange risks and preserve the value of its foreign exchange reserves, as well as meet other objectives, in the wake of the subprime crisis.

Second, by the second half of 2009, the U.S. financial market had stabilized, and there was no longer an immediate threat to the safety of the PRC's foreign exchange reserves by default, dollar devaluation, and a fall in the prices of U.S. government securities.

Third, currency internationalization requires capital account liberalization. Each step in renminbi internationalization is more or less conditional on certain steps in capital account liberalization. However, because the PRC's financial system is still fragile and many domestic financial reforms are still incomplete, the liberalization of the capital account may cause serious financial instability to the country's economy. The PRC monetary authority knows well the costs and benefits of renminbi internationalization as well as the risks that capital account liberalization will create.

Then why did the PRC suddenly become so interested in promoting renminbi internationalization? According to Wu (2011), "The ideal sequencing for renminbi internationalization is to reform the exchange rate regime ('formation mechanisms') first, and then to promote the convertibility of the renminbi under capital account and make the renminbi a settlement currency."[5] However, as Wu pointed out,

> It is too difficult to reach consensus among all parties concerned on how to reform the exchanger rate (regime). Hence, the PBOC looks one way and rows another. The promotion of the use of the renminbi for international trade settlement . . . will force us to speed up capital account liberalization with a "fight or die" attitude. Because so many renminbis have flown out of [the People's Republic of] China via renminbi import settlement, you have to create channels to allow these renminbis to flow back. Without channels for recycling, no one will be interested in using renminbis for trade settlement. Thus, pressures will be built up to force open [the People's Republic of] China's capital account.

In Wu's view, "Within five years, [the People's Republic of] China should be able to realize the convertibility of renminbis under capital account." Here, capital account liberalization was treated as the objective per se rather than a condition for renminbi internationalization. A June 2011 *Wall Street Journal* report made a wild guess that Governor Zhou "used the language of economic nationalism to push an agenda that ultimately would loosen state control of the economy by making the yuan, also known as the renminbi, or RMB, more dependent on market forces than government orders. . . . Make the policy arguments so attractive that decision makers will approve the ideas without realizing the implications."[6] In fact, the passage of time has made the PBOC's intention to use renminbi internationalization to promote capital account liberalization increasingly clear.

It is fair to say that the PBOC indeed wishes, via renminbi internationalization, to reduce exchange rate risks and to increase the foreign exchange reserves it holds, promote trade, and improve the competitiveness of the PRC's finance sectors. However, besides and beyond these commonly understood objectives, promoting capital account liberalization is perhaps a more immediate and important objective for the PBOC.

How Renminbi Internationalization Has Been Pursued

Having decided to promote renminbi internationalization, the Chinese government decided to design a road map for the process. So far the government has followed the road map, but some of the most important actual effects of internationalization are turning out to be the opposite of its proclaimed purposes.

5. "Wu Xiaoling: Top Layer Design and the Reform of Financial System" (in Chinese), *Shanghai Securities Daily*, August 27, 2011.

6. Bob Davis, "Were China's Leaders Conned?" *Wall Street Journal*, June 2, 2011.

The Road Map for Renminbi Internationalization

Different routes can be taken to promote renminbi internationalization. The PBOC has adopted what I call a "functional approach," that is, to promote the use of the renminbi as a settlement currency and investment currency, and finally somehow to make the renminbi the currency of foreign central banks' foreign exchange reserves. It is worth noting that this approach is exactly the same as that proposed by Zhou regarding the use of the SDR as a supranational currency in place of the U.S. dollar.

In line with the "functional approach," there are still different routes that can be pursued to internationalize the renminbi. It can begin with either running a trade deficit or a capital account deficit. The United States is running a current account deficit and so it can provide dollars to the rest of the world via its current account. Normally, if a country is running a current account surplus, it will be able to provide liquidity to the rest of the world by running a capital account deficit. Japan is a case in point. The PRC's international balance-of-payments structure is abnormal in that it runs both a current account surplus and a capital account surplus at the same time. How to provide renminbi liquidity to the rest of the world is a big challenge for the PRC's monetary authority.

As a country with "twin surpluses," to make the renminbi available overseas as a first step for the internationalization of the renminbi the PRC had to choose to promote the use of the renminbi either as an import settlement currency or as an investment currency for outbound foreign direct investment (FDI) and foreign lending. The PRC's monetary authority chose the former route. Then, in order to encourage nonresidents to accept renminbi payments and create a renminbi fund pool by holding renminbi, channels have to be created for nonresidents to invest their renminbi proceeds in renminbi assets—so-called "renminbi recycling mechanisms." Residents in Hong Kong, China are encouraged to hold renminbi deposits, renminbi corporate bonds, and renminbi government bonds. They are also allowed to invest in the PRC's A-share markets (renminbi share markets), within some limits. It is assumed that following the increase in the holding of renminbi-denominated assets, nonresidents will use more and more renminbi in trade and financial transactions. According to officials with the PBOC, as a result of the extensive use of renminbi in trade and financial transactions and investment, the renminbi will in some way be used increasingly as foreign exchange reserves by foreign central banks and will eventually become a key international currency. To supplement this basic approach that begins with using the renminbi as an import settlement currency, the PRC government and the PBOC also promote renminbi internationalization via channels such as signing currency-swap agreements with foreign central banks, ministries of finance holding each other's government bonds, and reducing the use of the dollar as a vehicle currency in bilateral trade via official agreements with relevant foreign governments.

The fundamental problem with the PRC's road map for renminbi internationalization is that because it is running a current account surplus, it cannot provide the renminbi liquidity to the rest of the world without correspondingly increasing assets denominated in foreign currency, especially the U.S. dollar. On the one hand, if the gap between renminbi import and export settlements fails to increase, the renminbi available in offshore markets as store of value (as investment currency) and liquid assets will fail to increase. On the other hand, the increase in the gap between renminbi import and export settlements means that China has to hold increasingly more dollar-denominated assets corresponding to the increase in the PRC's renminbi liabilities, which is just what the PBOC has been trying to avoid by promoting renminbi internationalization. Hence, for a country with a current account surplus, relying on renminbi trade settlement to provide offshore markets with renminbi liquidity defeats the very objective of renminbi internationalization (Yu 2012).

Progress in Renminbi Internationalization

Since the launch of renminbi internationalization in 2009, impressive progress has been made in using the renminbi as settlement currency and investment currency. Progress has also been made in promoting the renminbi as reserve currency. But all this progress has had material costs, and the question of the sustainability of renminbi internationalization is as yet unanswered.

RENMINBI AS UNIT OF ACCOUNT. Use of the renminbi as a unit of account in trade and financial transactions should be the foundation of renminbi internationalization in the PRC's chosen road map. However, how to promote the use of the renminbi as an invoice currency for trade transactions and as a denomination currency for financial transactions has not been discussed in the road map. For most foreign observers, the use of the renminbi as a trade settlement currency means that the renminbi is also used as an invoice currency. However, to use the renminbi as a settlement currency does not necessarily mean that the renminbi has been used as an invoice currency. Use of the renminbi as an invoice currency is beneficial for foreign exporters because its value is appreciating. For importers in the PRC, however, this fact means that they will forfeit the possible gains from the appreciation. Similarly, PRC exporters should be happy to use the renminbi as an invoice currency, but their foreign counterparts should be reluctant to do so. After five years of promoting renminbi internationalization, still no official or nonofficial statistics are available on the use of the renminbi as an invoice or denomination currency. However, anecdotal evidence shows that most PRC enterprises that use the renminbi for trade settlement do not use the renminbi to invoice trade.

THE RENMINBI AS A SETTLEMENT CURRENCY. Impressive progress has been made in the use of the renminbi as a settlement currency. Since the third quarter of 2010, the amount of renminbi trade settlement increased dramatically. According to the HKMA, the volume of renminbi used in cross-border trade settlement between the mainland of the PRC and Hong Kong, China reached 2.6 trillion yuan by the end of 2012. The share of renminbi trade settlement in the PRC's total trade has increased from 3 percent in 2010 to 8.4 percent in 2011 to 11 percent in May 2013.[7]

According to the HKMA (Hong Kong Monetary Authority 2013), total renminbi trade settlement handled by banks in Hong Kong, China in 2012 surpassed 2.6 trillion yuan (US$413 billion), a year-on-year increase of 37 percent, and represented over 90 percent of the cross-border trade in the mainland of the PRC settled in renminbi.[8]

THE RENMINBI AS A STORE OF VALUE.   Based on the renminbi pool created via renminbi import settlement, a renminbi offshore market has been growing rapidly in Hong Kong, China. Renminbi offshore markets in London, Singapore, and Taipei,China are also beginning to take shape.

Renminbi deposits. One of the most important measurements for the progress in renminbi internationalization is the increase in renminbi deposits held by residents of Hong Kong, China, which serve as the basis for the use of the renminbi as a store of value. From the middle of 2010 to the third quarter of 2011, renminbi deposits held by Hong Kong, China residents skyrocketed. It was widely expected that the total amount of renminbi deposits will surpass 1 trillion yuan by the end of 2012.[9]

However, the momentum of demand for renminbi deposits in Hong Kong, China suddenly lost ground in the fourth quarter of 2011. According to the HKMA, total renminbi deposits and outstanding renminbi certificates of deposit stood at 720 billion yuan at the end of 2012 (China Daily 2013).[10] This slowdown could be attributed to the weakening of renminbi appreciation expectations, which in turn was attributable to the weakening of the PRC's international balance of payments.

Renminbi bonds. The most popular category of renminbi bonds is called "dim sum" bonds, which are denominated in renminbi and issued in Hong Kong, China.

The PRC's Ministry of Finance issued 20 billion yuan in government bonds in Hong Kong, China on August 23, 2011. This particular issue was regarded as a major boost to renminbi internationalization and a "big gift" to the people in Hong Kong, China.

---

7. Li Jingxia, "White Paper on Cross-Border RMB Business Issued by the Bank of China," *China Business News,* July 15, 2013.

8. According to a more recent report, renminbi trade settlement in 2010 accounted for only 2.5 percent of the PRC's total trade. In 2011, the corresponding figure rose dramatically, to 9 percent of total trade (see "HK Banks' RMB Trade Settlement Up 37% in 2013," *China Daily,* February 27, 2013).

9. As of the end of September 2011, renminbi deposits in Hong Kong, China reached 622.2 billion yuan.

10. "HK Banks' RMB Trade Settlement Up 37% in 2013," *China Daily,* February 27, 2013.

According to the HKMA, total issuance of dim sum bonds in 2012 amounted to 112.2 billion yuan and the outstanding amount of dim sum bonds reached 237.2 billion yuan, representing a 62 percent increase over the amount at the end of 2011 (Hong Kong Monetary Authority 2013). However, in 2013 dim sum bond issues failed to make important headway.

Renminbi loans. In 2010, the total amount of renminbi customer deposits in banks in Hong Kong, China was 315 billion yuan, yet renminbi loans extended by them totaled only 2 billion yuan. The loan-to-deposit ratio was less than 1 percent. The striking asymmetry between renminbi deposits and renminbi loans was attributable to the fact that the interest rate on renminbi loans was relatively high and renminbi appreciation expectations were still strong. The asymmetry has been reduced since the fourth quarter of 2011. The improvement in the asymmetry between deposits and loans can be attributed to the increase in cross-border trade finance and syndicated loans. However, compared with Hong Kong, China's overall loan-to-deposit ratio, the asymmetry is still very serious. Early in 2013, the Qianhai cross-border lending pilot scheme was launched in Qianhai—a small locality in Shenzhen bordering Hong Kong, China—enabling companies incorporated in Qianhai to borrow renminbi loans from banks in Hong Kong, China for the development of Qianhai.

Renminbi trade credit. According to a note released by SWIFT in May 2012, the share of renminbi in trade finance has been increasing rapidly, despite the fact that the share of renminbi trade payment by value in global payments is still negligible, accounting for just 0.34 percent of total trade payment.[11] Up to the time of the release of the note, the renminbi's market share of the global issuance of letters of credit by value was 4 percent. This makes the renminbi the third largest currency in the global issuance of letters of credit by value, after the U.S. dollar and the euro.

Renminbi direct investment. Since January 2011, PRC enterprises have been allowed to invest offshore in renminbi. Enterprises can raise renminbi funds onshore and remit the funds offshore via onshore banks. Onshore banks' offshore branches can raise renminbi funds onshore and extend loans to enterprises for offshore investment.

Renminbi qualified foreign institutional investors. The most important development in renminbi internationalization is the introduction of Renminbi Qualified Foreign Institutional Investors (RQFII). The China Banking Regulatory Committee, the PBOC, and the State Administration of Foreign Exchange jointly initiated the RQFII scheme on December 16, 2011. According to this scheme, qualified foreign institutional investors are allowed to invest in the PRC's A-share market in renminbi. At the beginning, the RQFII quota was 20 billion yuan. In

---

11. "A Bronze Medal for RMB in Trade Finance," *SWIFT RMB Tracker* (online journal), May 23, 2012 (www.swift.com/resources/documents/SWIFT_RMB_Tracker_May_2012.pdf).

April 2012, the quota was raised to 50 billion yuan. In November 2012, it was increased to 200 billion yuan.

The renminbi as a reserve currency. Initially, the PBOC's swap agreements with other central banks were mainly aimed at providing liquidity support to its counterparts. Renminbi funds obtained by foreign central banks are deposited in the accounts held with the PBOC as PBOC liabilities. At a later stage, the swap agreements are mainly aimed at encouraging foreign central banks to hold renminbi as foreign exchange reserves. Correspondingly, foreign central banks conduct swaps with the PBOC for the purpose of diversification and other benefits.

Besides currency swaps, foreign central banks also buy renminbi bonds as foreign currency reserves. Since September 2010, when Malaysia became the first country to do this, many countries have jumped on the renminbi reserves bandwagon.

Renminbi Internationalization and Capital Account Liberalization

Capital account liberalization is a prerequisite of renminbi internationalization, so the road map of renminbi internationalization implies a road map for China's capital account liberalization. A fundamental question facing the Chinese government is, which is the horse, and which the cart? Should China's capital account liberalization be shaped to accommodate the needs of renminbi internationalization, or the other way around: Should the pursuit of renminbi internationalization be constrained by a well-thought-out sequence of capital account liberalization?

The Impact of Renminbi Internationalization on Capital Controls

The bulk of the PRC's capital account had been liberalized before renminbi internationalization was launched in 2009, but in some key areas capital flows are still subject to tight controls and the renminbi is not convertible in some transactions or convertibility is limited in others. First, in principle households are not allowed to invest abroad. They can do so only via so-called qualified domestic institutional investors (QDII). By the end of 2012, 106 financial institutions had obtained QDII status and the total quota for QDII investment was US$86.6 billion. More important, each resident's annual purchase of foreign exchange is capped at U.S.$50,000. Second, overseas borrowing by domestic financial and nonfinancial corporations is subject to strict restrictions. Third, foreign investment in the PRC's equity market is also subject to strict restrictions. Foreign investors can invest in the PRC's B-share market (shares denominated in foreign currencies). They are not allowed to invest in the A-share market (shares denominated in renminbi) unless they invest via the Renminbi Qualified Foreign Institutional Investor (RQFII) scheme. Currently the quota for RQFII is US$160 billion. Fourth, nonresidents'

Figure 3-1. *The Renminbi (RMB) Offshore Market and Cross-Border Capital Flows*

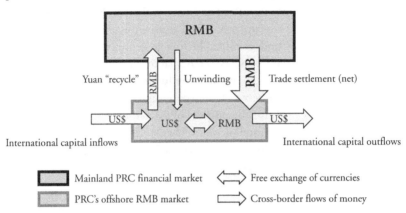

Source: Author.

investment in the PRC's real estate market is also subject to various restrictions (Chao 2013). It can be seen that the PRC's remaining capital control is mainly aimed at short-term cross-border capital flows. The current debate in China is whether the PRC should speed up the dismantling of the remaining controls according to a timetable or whether the PRC should eventually open its capital account—although this, too, is a debatable issue.

Before the launch of renminbi internationalization, there were two main channels of short-term cross-border capital flows: first, *over-invoicing imports* and *under-invoicing exports* or *under-invoicing imports* and *over-invoicing exports,* depending on the changes in renminbi appreciation expectations; second, carrying physical notes across borders or exchanging money through underground money dealers. The situation has changed significantly since the launch of renminbi internationalization. Large amounts of renminbi now can legally and easily move across the borders via the renminbi offshore market in Hong Kong, China (figure 3-1).

From the figure it can be seen that, via import settlement, renminbi flow into Hong Kong, China. This can be done via the transactions between mainland firms and their subsidiaries in Hong Kong, China in the name of renminbi import settlement. It can also be seen that the "recycling mechanisms" allow the renminbi in Hong Kong, China to be invested in renminbi-denominated assets in the mainland PRC. In this way, international investors are able to bypass the PRC's capital controls to invest in renminbi assets that are still forbidden or restricted under the current capital control regime. It is worth emphasizing that although the renminbi trade settlement scheme and recycling mechanisms have partially dismantled the control over short-term cross-border capital flows, restrictions remain. Renminbi that move between the mainland PRC and Hong Kong, China have to do so through a settlement system operated by the Bank of China, and the quarterly net flows are capped. Furthermore, investment of the "recycled" renminbi in the mainland PRC is subject to restrictions both in quantity and market destinations (see figure 3-1).

A New Stage of Capital Account Liberalization

In February 2012 the PBOC released a policy research report, "China Stands in the Period of Strategic Opportunity for Capital Account Liberalization," in which four arguments were made that deserve notice:

1. The PRC is in a period of "strategic opportunity" for capital account liberalization; hence its capital account liberalization should be accelerated.[12]

2. There will be no large risks if the PRC opens its capital account.

3. The traditional view of the sequencing of capital account liberalization does not apply to the PRC. The liberalization of the interest rate, the exchange rate, and the capital account can be implemented at the same time "in a coordinated way."

4. There should be a timetable for the liberalization of the capital account.

In 2013 some officials from the PBOC went so far as to say that without the liberalization of the capital account, there would be no liberalization of the interest rate and exchange rate. In other words, the liberalization of the capital account is now regarded as a prerequisite for interest rate and exchange rate liberalization, not the other way around. For example, in those officials' view, if the capital account, including short-term cross-border capital flows, is not fully liberalized, the exchange rate decided by the current account balance and long-term capital flows is not a truly market-determined exchange rate.[13]

As of 2012, five years into the global financial crisis, for the majority of PRC economists "The more important and more immediate benefit from renminbi internationalization is that . . . [it] will add momentum to reforms," which "include the opening of the capital account, increasing exchange rate flexibility, liberalizing the interest rates, opening the capital markets and reducing entry barriers to the financial industry" (Ma 2012, 9).

It is worth noting that in the PBOC research mentioned earlier, renminbi internationalization and the relationship between renminbi internationalization and capital account liberalization were barely mentioned. It can be seen that capital account liberalization is no longer viewed as just a condition for renminbi internationalization. Instead, it is regarded as a powerful external force that can be used

12. Soncheng Sheng, "China Stands in the Period of Strategic Opportunity for Capital Account Liberalization," *China Daily,* February 24, 2012.

13. Personal communications from participants in internal conference on renminbi internationalization held in Beijing on June 30, 2013. The conference was sponsored by the Boyuan Foundation.

to push through domestic reforms and restructuring. Even though renminbi internationalization is still a policy goal and is being pursued, scrapping the remaining capital controls has come to dominate the PRC's policy agenda.[14]

A Digression: Literature on Capital Account Liberalization

In the literature, the main arguments for free movement of capital include the following:

—Free flows of capital lead to optimal allocation of resources.

—Capital controls do not work and lead to more market distortions.

Theoretically, in a perfect world the free flow of capital across the globe improves welfare—but the world is not perfect. In an imperfect world, there is no consensus on whether the free movement of cross-border capital flows is optimal. It is not difficult to show that with imperfect information and market distortion, a free flow of capital can lead to misallocation of resources (Ocampo, Spiegel, and Stiglitz 2008).

Before the Asian financial crisis, capital controls were universally regarded as "bad," but the mood of economists as well as government officials changed after the crisis. The IMF gradually shifted its stance on the liberalization of capital accounts, admitting that it is necessary to carefully manage and sequence the liberalization process in order to minimize concomitant risks (Ostry and others 2010; Ostry and others 2011; Ostry and others 2012).

After the 2008–09 global financial crisis, more countries resorted to capital controls in one way or another to deal with capital-flow volatility. The IMF has recently done a lot to destigmatize the use of capital controls alongside macro-economic and prudential policies (Ostry and others 2011).

Perhaps the only exception in this new trend in capital controls is the PRC, whose central bank declared that the country is in "a strategic period of window of opportunities to accelerate capital account liberalization" (Sheng 2012).

Few PRC economists oppose the eventual total liberalization of the capital account and full convertibility of the renminbi. The key difference among PRC economists lies in the issue of sequencing. There are different views on the importance of sequencing in the literature. The conventional view emphasizes the importance of achieving macroeconomic stability and developing domestic financial institutions, markets, and instruments before liberalizing the capital account (Johnston 1998). This approach can be called the "gradualist approach." An alternative view stresses constraints on reforms and the limited capacity of countries to reform themselves in the absence of external pressures for reform. This view can be called the "big bang approach" in capital account liberalization.[15] A middle view

14. It seems that the government has adjusted its policy on capital account liberalization again. Recently the tone has become more cautious.

15. Galbis (1994) is a survey of the early literature on the sequencing of capital account liberalization.

is that capital account liberalization should be part of a concurrent, integrated, and comprehensive approach to macroeconomic and structural reform (Galbis 1994). The middle way is called the "integrated approach" (Kawai and Takagi 2010).

The PBOC seems to have become more sympathetic toward the big-bang approach as a result of the frustrations of trying the gradualist approach that it has taken since the 1970s.

The PRC's capital account liberalization has kept roughly to the following sequence: liberalizing current account before liberalizing capital account, liberalizing FDI before liberalizing indirect investment, liberalizing long-term capital before liberalizing short-term capital, liberalizing portfolio before liberalizing borrowing, liberalizing capital inflows before liberalizing capital outflows, and so on. However, the issue of sequencing capital account liberalization is not just about the sequencing of items in the capital account for liberalization. More important is the question of how to build up institutional capacity to manage the risks and minimize the distortions that develop in the course of capital account liberalization.

According to a report by the World Bank and the IMF (2005, 317):

Sequencing is the setting of priorities among financial sector measures, and the appropriate sequencing and coordination of reforms is important for the following reasons:
—Inappropriate sequencing of reforms could cause excessive risk taking and financial instability.
—Limited institutional capacity necessarily requires some prioritization of reform elements.
—Given the numerous policy and operational reforms in each area of financial policy, setting priorities could facilitate and encourage the adoption of reforms; hence, this aspect of financial sector assessments is important.

In a report they wrote for the IMF Ishii and Habermeier (2002) state that since financial liberalization will trigger financial and macroeconomic risks, risk management capacity and its infrastructure should be built up in individual financial markets. They divide markets into categories in order of complexity and riskiness: money and exchange markets, government bond markets, banking and financial services to target groups, corporate debt and equity markets, and derivatives and asset-backed securities. Ishii and Habermeier's categories of measures for building up risk management capacity are as follows:
—Market and product development
—Risk mitigation
—Financial system infrastructure
—Financial institutions' restructuring and recapitalization
Obviously, building up risk management capacity in each financial market in a concerted way should precede the full liberalization of the capital account. For

example, the development of government bond markets and the establishment of a risk-free yield curve provide the benchmark for pricing corporate bonds and other more risky securities and derivative products. Hence, the formation of the risk-free yield curve in the government bond market should precede the liberalization of capital's access to and exit from the government bond market and other more sophisticated financial markets. Otherwise the risks created by free movements of capital into and out of these markets will be impossible to manage. In contrast, it is difficult to see how free access to and exit from the government bond market by foreign investors can automatically lead to the buildup of risk management capacity in the market, and why it is a better strategy than the one in which the buildup of risk management capacity takes precedence over opening up the market to foreign investors.

Prerequisites for Full Capital Account Liberalization

The PRC has now entered the stage of liberalizing short-term cross-border capital flows or, more or less equivalently, the full convertibility of the renminbi. If it is accepted to fully liberalize the country's capital account, some prerequisites must be met, and a key question is whether it is realistic and affordable for the PRC to set a timetable to complete capital account liberalization "basically" before 2015 and fully before 2020.

Before liberalizing the capital account fully and making the renminbi fully convertible, the government needs to deal with many more problems. Without having solved these problems, a hasty liberalization of short-term cross-border capital flows is dangerous.

First, macroeconomic stability must be achieved. If the economy suffers from high inflation and serious asset bubbles, the liberalization of short-term capital flows will create large volatility in capital flows, which in turn will further destabilize the economy. Currently the PRC's inflation is moderate, but despite the government crackdown, house prices have been increasing continuously. At least in some first-tier cities there are serious real estate bubbles. Furthermore, because of prevalent overcapacity, profitability is low and falling across industries. The PRC's growth is under serious downward pressure, and investors' confidence in the economy has reached a record low since the global financial crisis.

Second, financial institutions should be strengthened. High leverage and a high ratio of nonperforming loans could make the financial system very vulnerable to changes in capital flows, which in turn would make capital flows more volatile. As of summer 2014 the PRC's local government debt and corporate debt are very high. The nonperforming loan rate is not high at the moment but may soon rise rapidly. The country's financial vulnerability has risen significantly since the global financial crisis and the PRC's 4 trillion yuan stimulus package, with enterprise debt estimated to exceed 120 percent of gross domestic product (GDP) and broad money supply (M2) amounting to more than 180 percent of GDP.

Third, the PRC's financial markets should be further liberalized and a rational interest structure must be created. The benchmark PRC interest rate is commercial banks' interest rate on one-year deposits, which is set by the PBOC. There is no short-term interest rate in the interbank money market that can be used as a benchmark interest rate. At the same time, there is no well-functioning risk-free yield curve in the government bond market. So there is no well-functioning interest rate system. As a result, it is difficult to price financial assets in different financial markets rationally. This, on top of a high corporate leverage ratio, means that the PRC's risk management capacity is weak, which makes the financial system in the mainland PRC vulnerable to cross-border speculative attacks.

Fourth, the PRC's exchange rate is still subject to frequent intervention by the PBOC. The PRC is bound to lose its monetary independence with an inflexible exchange rate and open capital account. Although the sterilization policy by the PBOC was successful in retaining the independence of monetary policy in the past at a considerable cost, with an entirely open capital account, it is doubtful that the PBOC can maintain monetary independence. Furthermore, the lack of flexibility in interest and exchange rates has already created conditions for persistent interest rate and exchange rate arbitrage at the expense of the country's national welfare.

Fifth, emerging economies are under the shadow of the Federal Reserve's quantitative easing tapering. Historical experience has shown that whenever U.S. interest rates rise, there will be massive capital outflows from developing countries. If the tapering coincides with the PRC's dismantling of its control over short-term cross-border capital flows, the consequences could be disastrous.

Last but not least, the PRC's economic reforms remain incomplete, with property rights not yet clearly defined. Amid ambiguity over ownership and pervasive corruption, the free flow of capital across borders could be used to facilitate money laundering and asset stripping, which in turn would incite social tensions. Thus, the completion of "economic system reform" is of utmost importance as a precondition for full capital account liberalization.

In short, because of the PRC's current economic and financial instability and the volatility of global financial uncertainty, an unforeseen shock could trigger large-scale capital flight, leading to significant currency devaluation, skyrocketing interest rates, bursting asset bubbles, bankruptcy and default for financial and nonfinancial enterprises, and, ultimately, the collapse of the country's financial system. Although the likelihood that this worst-case scenario will happen is very low, its consequences would be devastating, and the PRC cannot take this risk. In my view, the full liberalization of the capital account should be the last step of economic reforms. The PRC should stick to its gradualist approach. The liberalization of the interest rate and exchange rate should be completed, adequate risk management capacity should be built up, and the major points of vulnerability in the economy should be eliminated before full liberalization.

So what are the implications of this discussion of capital account liberalization for renminbi internationalization? Renminbi internationalization is closely related to capital account liberalization, and many important steps of renminbi internationalization are conditional on the corresponding development in capital account liberalization. If the PRC does not accelerate capital account liberalization to give nonresidents free access to its financial markets, the incentive for nonresidents to hold the renminbi will be limited, and after the initial euphoria, the pace of renminbi internationalization is likely to slow down, at least in the area of using the renminbi as investment currency.

Despite the enthusiasm shown by the PBOC for speeding up the liberalization of capital control in the recent past, pragmatism prevailed eventually. In fact, in the first quarter of 2013, when PRC enterprises again were using letters of credit enabled by the renminbi trade settlement scheme to engage in interest rate arbitrage and caused very large capital inflows, the PBOC did not liberalize short-term cross-border capital movement to facilitate the arbitrage but instead, jointly with the customs authority, clamped down on the activities in a prompt manner. As a result, short-term capital inflows have fallen significantly since April 2013.

The Prospects for Renminbi Internationalization

Despite the fact that renminbi internationalization has made impressive progress so far, there are reasons to believe that this process may suffer serious setbacks some time in the future, and the road map of renminbi internationalization may need to be adjusted.

Different Routes to Renminbi Internationalization

According to an upbeat forecast by the Bank of China, in 2015, the total amount of renminbi trade settlement will reach 6.4 trillion yuan, and renminbi deposits in Hong Kong, China will surpass 5 trillion yuan. In the same year, the issuance of renminbi bonds will reach 1 percent of the PRC's GDP, surpassing 640 billion yuan, and renminbi FDI will account for 35 percent of total FDI, surpassing 500 billion yuan (Chen 2013). But only time will tell whether this upbeat prediction of renminbi internationalization will come true.

There are three possible options to further promote renminbi internationalization:

1. To continue to implement the original road map: renminbi import settlement–recycling mechanisms–renminbi pool in Hong Kong, China–export settlement, and so on.

2. To make a major adjustment to the original road map by providing renminbi liquidity to the rest of the world via the capital account instead of the current account.

3. To liberalize the capital account fully and let market forces have full play in realizing renminbi internationalization.

The Renminbi's Prospects for Use as a Trade Settlement Currency

Experience so far shows that exchange rate and interest rate arbitrages are two key drivers for progress in renminbi internationalization. Since late 2011, due to the shrinkage of the PRC's current account surplus and the precariousness of capital flows, expectations that the renminbi would appreciate weakened significantly. In 2013, however, following changes in domestic and international conditions, expectations of renminbi appreciation strengthened once more. Efforts in rebalancing the country's current account in the foreseeable future are likely to be intensified and the renminbi exchange rate made more flexible. As a result, exchange rate arbitrage is likely to exert less influence on the use of renminbi in trade settlement.[16]

Nevertheless the interest rate spread between the PRC and its major trade partners will persist, because the PRC's trade partners are likely to continue to maintain loose monetary policy but the PRC is likely to maintain a relatively tight monetary policy in the foreseeable future. In 2013, due to the return of renminbi appreciation expectations and large interest rate spreads between China and developed countries, via the channels opened up by renminbi internationalization, the flow of hot money into China surged, resulting in an increase of China's foreign exchange reserves by US$500 billion in just one year.

Although renminbi appreciation expectations have weakened and the exchange rate variation has grown, as long as the PRC continues to run twin surpluses and the PBOC continues to intervene in the foreign exchange market to contain the appreciation of the renminbi, the interest rate arbitrage will be not only profitable but also basically risk-free. Risk-free interest rate arbitrage by PRC enterprises seems to have been the most important contributing factor to the increase in renminbi trade settlement.

In the long run the increase in renminbi trade settlement will be decided mainly by two factors. The first is the PRC's growth. If the economy can maintain its growth momentum and stability in the future, naturally the PRC's trade partners will be increasingly interested in using the renminbi as a settlement currency. The greatest attraction for the PRC and its trade partners to use the renminbi for trade settlement should be the reduction in transaction costs. The second factor is the dollar's future position. The weakening of the dollar certainly will increase the renminbi's appeal, which in turn will increase the chance for the renminbi to be used not only as a trade settlement currency but also as a vehicle currency.

In recent years, especially after the fourth quarter of 2011, the use of the renminbi as a trade settlement currency has shown two trends. First, the use of the renminbi for trade settlement has maintained a strong growth momentum, due to arbitrage activities as well as the PRC's steady growth.

---

16. For a more detailed description of exchange rate arbitrage activities since the introduction of the renminbi trade settlement scheme, see Yu (2012).

The second factor is that the ratio of renminbi import settlement to renminbi export settlement has become more balanced. Experience studies show that this ratio is highly correlated with the offshore–onshore renminbi market spread (Zhang and Xu 2011). When the trade settlement scheme had just been introduced, the volume of renminbi import settlement was considerably larger than that of renminbi export settlement.[17] This situation changed rather dramatically in the fourth quarter of 2011. Capital flight from Hong Kong, China to the developed world because of the eurozone financial crisis made the offshore renminbi cheaper than the onshore renminbi. As a result, instead of selling the renminbi for the dollar in Hong Kong, China via renminbi import settlement, PRC enterprises sold the dollar for the renminbi in Hong Kong, China via renminbi export settlement.

A more balanced renminbi settlement ratio is also related negatively with the use of the renminbi as a store of value, especially as an investment currency. The narrowing exchange rate spread and the remaining restriction on using the renminbi to invest in renminbi-denominated financial assets have made renminbi assets less attractive for nonresidents. As a result, the renminbi that had been injected into offshore markets via renminbi import settlement in the offshore market found their way back to the mainland via renminbi export settlement. This partially explains why a more balanced ratio of renminbi import settlement to renminbi export settlement coincides with the stagnation of renminbi deposits in Hong Kong, China.

It can be expected that, in the longer run, in order to rebalance the economy, the PBOC will reduce its intervention in the foreign exchange market. The chance for the renminbi exchange rate to fluctuate in two directions will increase significantly. As a result, the arbitrage will no longer be risk-free, which in turn will reduce the demand for the renminbi by nonresidents, who obtain the renminbi via renminbi import settlement and use the renminbi for arbitrage purposes. It would not be at all surprising if at some point in the future, the share of renminbi settlement in the PRC's total trade settlement stops increasing or even falls.

With macroeconomic factors playing a less important role, the use of the renminbi for trade settlement will be decided by factors at the enterprise and industrial levels, a topic to which I will return.

The Prospects for Using the Renminbi as a Store of Value

The scale of the renminbi used as a store of value, for investing in renminbi-denominated assets both within and outside the PRC, depends on China's supply of renminbi in offshore markets, which in turn is decided mainly by the net injection of renminbi into renminbi offshore markets via renminbi trade settlement according to the PBOC's current road map for renminbi internationalization.

17. The author has discussed this issue extensively in other writings. See, for example, Yu (2012).

Because the PRC is a trade surplus country, if both its imports and exports are all settled in renminbi, the net injection of renminbi into offshore markets has to be negative. Under this circumstance, it is impossible to promote the use of renminbi as a store of value (investment currency and foreign exchange reserves) and international liquidity via the trade settlement channel. To inject renminbi liquidity into the rest of the world, the amount of renminbi import settlement must be larger than that of renminbi export settlement, and the difference between these two amounts equals the new liquidity, which in turn translates into an increase in renminbi assets held by nonresidents, if demand exists. From the PRC's point of view, the increase in its renminbi liabilities must be matched by an equal increase in the PRC's foreign assets, the bulk of which would most likely be U.S. government securities. The PRC's foreign liabilities are denominated mostly in renminbi and its foreign assets are almost exclusively denominated in foreign currencies, in particular, the U.S. dollar. The further increase in the PRC's renminbi liabilities and dollar assets means that the currency structure of these foreign liabilities and assets has worsened further. This is a fundamental problem with the PBOC's road map for renminbi internationalization.

Furthermore, if renminbi appreciation expectations fade as a result of the PRC's rebalancing, nonresidents' desire to hold renminbi assets will fade correspondingly. In early 2011, many leading investment banks predicted that by the end of 2012, renminbi deposits in Hong Kong, China would surpass 1 trillion to 2 trillion yuan. Now, well into 2013, the customer renminbi deposits in Hong Kong, China are still holding at 600 billion to 700 billion yuan.[18]

Renminbi lending and borrowing activities in offshore markets can lead to an increase in the renminbi pool via renminbi monetary multipliers in Hong Kong, China or other renminbi offshore markets. The amount of liquidity, however, is constrained ultimately by the net injection of renminbi. If the net injection to an offshore market fails to increase—if the "renminbi monetary base" in the offshore market fails to increase—the scope for the renminbi pool to increase will be very limited.

Here the route of injecting renminbi via the capital account seems more promising. That is, if the PRC cannot provide renminbi liquidity by running a current account deficit, it can do so by running a capital account deficit. In fact, before 1981, the United States provided dollar liquidity to the rest of the world mainly via an "official account deficit"—a capital account deficit rather than a current account deficit.

If a country runs a current account surplus, normally it runs a capital account deficit. When it injects its own currency into the rest of the world by running a

18. Other factors may also contribute to the stagnation of renminbi deposits in Hong Kong, China. Among them is the development of other offshore centers such as in London, Singapore, and Taipei,China. More financial instruments for renminbi investment may also be a contributing factor.

capital account deficit, normally, borrowers will use the currency to buy products exported by the country. As a result, not only the country's foreign assets but also part of its exports will be denominated in its own currency.

The PRC is a twin surplus (current account and capital account) country. To inject liquidity into the rest of the world can lead to more complicated changes in the currency structure of the PRC's foreign assets and liabilities. However, a very important advantage of using the capital account to inject renminbi liquidity into the rest of the world is that it will increase renminbi-denominated assets and lead to the improvement in the PRC's currency structure of assets and liabilities. At the same time, it will promote the use of the renminbi as an export settlement currency. Certainly the renminbi import settlement channel can be maintained while the capital account is used to inject renminbi liquidity, but its impact on the currency structure of the PRC's foreign assets and liabilities should not be ignored.

The PRC can promote renminbi internationalization by lending renminbi to foreign borrowers. Panda bonds and Renminbi Outward Direct Investment (RODI) are good vehicles for such an endeavor. Officials from the PBOC recently emphasized that the thrust of the PRC's capital account liberalization at the current stage is to facilitate PRC enterprises' outward direct investment (ODI). The Ministry of Commerce is taking action to change the rules and regulations to support ODI. The PRC can also buy more Panda bonds and make more contributions to the IMF and other keystone international organizations.

The reform of the international monetary system has been shelved for a while, but the idea is still alive and can become fashionable again. The PRC should continue the effort to promote the reform of the international monetary system by injecting renminbi-denominated funds to keystone international organizations and create conditions for making the renminbi a component of the SDR.

Certainly, this route of injecting renminbi liquidity into the rest of the world via the capital account has its own problems. First, after four years of using import settlement to inject renminbi liquidity to offshore markets, the decisionmakers may be reluctant to change course, because of the cost of the change ("path dependence"). Second, as mentioned, the PRC may not be able to continue to run a current account surplus, which is equivalent to saying that it may not be able to continue to provide net renminbi liquidity to the rest of the world via its capital account, because its ability to run a capital account deficit will be limited. Third, the bulk of the PRC's ODI is destined for the Middle East and North Africa, where civil war and political conflict may erupt at any time. In short, the path of injecting renminbi into the rest of the world and encouraging foreign investors to hold more renminbi assets via the route of exporting capital is also bound to be bumpy. Last but not least, because China is still a poor country with a per capita income of just US$6,700, it is debatable whether China should be a capital exporting country.

The PRC's financial market is already very open to FDI and other forms of long-term credit. Long-term capital does not need to use offshore markets to evade capital controls. International capital that seeks to enter the PRC via offshore markets very likely is short-term speculative capital, where the aim is to profit from interest rate and exchange rate arbitrage. Ironically, as a result of the PBOC's further opening up of the PRC's financial market to international investors, the role of offshore markets will diminish correspondingly.

The PRC can surely provide renminbi liquidity via currency swaps with other central banks. Currency swaps are useful measures for reducing the dependence on the U.S. dollar for liquidity. These swaps are short- or medium-term bilateral liquidity arrangements, however, which will become unwound sooner or later. Currency swaps will not pose a challenge to the domination of the U.S. dollar. Despite all the virtues of the currency swaps, it is difficult to imagine how the PRC can continuously supply liquidity and promote renminbi internationalization in a significant way via this route.

An unexpected development in renminbi internationalization in recent years is the significant increase in the use of the renminbi as a reserve currency by foreign central banks. This is not only a reflection of the PRC's economic strength but also a result of the weakening status of traditional reserve currencies such as the U.S. dollar and the euro. This implies that the renminbi's expansion efforts will also be influenced by the change in the international standing of the U.S. dollar. The more current wrangles in Washington erode the confidence, the more scope there will be for the renminbi to make inroads into becoming an international reserve currency.

Microeconomic Foundation for Renminbi Internationalization

According to a February 2012 survey of 782 importers and exporters in the mainland PRC, the motivations of the enterprises for the use of the renminbi as a settlement currency in order of importance are reduction in foreign exchange risk, renminbi appreciation expectations, financial benefits, operational convenience, counterparty requests, and others (Brewer 2012).

One important question: If renminbi appreciation expectations cease or interest rate spreads between renminbi assets and foreign assets are reduced to zero, will PRC importers continue to use renminbi to purchase dollars in Hong Kong, China and hence supply enough liquidity for renminbi offshore markets and enable the renminbi to play a role as a store of value?

A similar question can be asked about the demand for renminbi in offshore markets: If renminbi appreciation expectations cease and the interest rate spread between the PRC's benchmark interests and international benchmark interests is reduced to zero, will foreign investors still be interested in holding the renminbi in renminbi offshore markets?

Despite all the fanfare about the acceleration of capital account liberalization, it is likely that the PRC government eventually will again adopt the gradualist approach to capital account liberalization. At the same time, as a result of the slowdown of the country's economy and the correction of imbalances, the use of the renminbi as an invoice and settlement currency will increasingly be decided by the specific nature of PRC firms, industrial organizations, business models, types of products traded, bargaining power of PRC firms and their counterparts, and so on. Following the gradual opening of the capital account, renminbi internationalization will continue to make progress, but perhaps at a much slower pace than people have expected.

Renminbi internationalization will no longer be driven by arbitrage, but rather by the behavior of enterprises. In other words, only when people are still interested in using renminbi for trade settlement, even absent channels for recycling, can the use of renminbi as a settlement currency be sustainable.

Many theoretical and empirical studies explore the selection of an invoice currency (Grassman 1973; Goldberg and Tille 2008; Friberg and Wilander 2008; Kawai 1996; Ito and others 2010). According to these studies, industrial- and enterprise-level factors—such as a country's industrial structure, corporation organizations, enterprise business models and marketing strategies, types of products available, and development of relevant financial markets—may fundamentally influence an enterprise's choice of invoice currency and hence settlement currency.[19] It should be recognized that over the past few years few studies have been conducted on the microeconomic foundation of the use of the renminbi as an invoice and settlement currency (although many papers on renminbi internationalization have appeared). Hopefully, more studies on this issue will be published.

As for the use of the renminbi as an investment and reserve currency, under an open capital account, demand for renminbi-denominated assets will depend on conditions that are more fundamental than arbitrage opportunities and offshore markets. Eichengreen (2013) has pointed out: "An international currency that is widely used in private commercial and financial transactions and held by central banks and governments as reserves has three essential attributes: scale, stability, and liquidity" (149).

There is no doubt that meeting these conditions is time-consuming. At the moment, the PRC's most urgent tasks are readjustment of its economic structure, rebalancing of its economy, further financial reform, and liberalization of interest rates and the exchange rate. Renminbi internationalization should be prioritized appropriately. Haste does not bring success.

---

19. Ito and others (2010) found that most Japanese firms use the same currency for both invoicing and settlement.

Conclusion

Since the launch of renminbi trade settlement schemes in 2009, renminbi appreciation and interest rate spread have been the two key drivers for the progress in renminbi internationalization. Renminbi import settlement enabled renminbi to flow into Hong Kong, China and establish a renminbi pool there because of the coexistence of two exchange rates for the renminbi. Whenever the renminbi is under appreciation pressure, liquidity flows into Hong Kong, China. As a result of appreciation expectations and the opportunities for investment in renminbi-denominated assets in the mainland PRC, which have higher returns, renminbi deposits in Hong Kong, China and renminbi bond issuance increased very rapidly.

Since late 2011, however, the shrinkage of the PRC's current account surplus and the precariousness of capital flows dramatically weakened renminbi appreciation expectations. As a result of a narrowing or reversing of the offshore–onshore renminbi market spread, residents in Hong Kong, China were no longer eager to hold renminbi deposits while PRC importers became less interested in purchasing U.S. dollars in Hong Kong, China.

Yet renminbi trade settlement has continued to increase, despite the disappointment in the increase in the renminbi pool and the less-than-satisfactory increase in renminbi bond issuance in Hong Kong, China. The sheer size of the PRC's trade and improvements in transactional convenience by using the renminbi for settlement must be a key contributing factor, but interest rate arbitrage also plays an important role. The decline in the offshore–onshore renminbi market spread contributes to the emergence of a more balanced ratio of renminbi import settlement to renminbi export settlement.

An unexpected development in renminbi internationalization in recent years is the significant increase in the use of the renminbi as a reserve currency by foreign central banks, reflecting not only the PRC's economic strength but also the weakening status of traditional reserve currencies such as the U.S. dollar and the euro. This implies that renminbi expansion efforts will also be influenced by the change in the preference for the U.S. dollar.

A fundamental constraint for renminbi internationalization is the PRC's capital controls. The question facing the PRC government at the moment is whether it should abandon the remaining controls over short-run cross-border capital flows. It seems that the PBOC has lost patience with the slow progress in domestic reforms, and is pushing for the big-bang approach in capital account liberalization to force though much-needed internal changes. Certainly, other things being equal, capital account liberalization will give an extra boost to renminbi internationalization.

However, in my view, the PRC should put its own house in order before fully opening its capital account and making the renminbi freely convertible. For example, macroeconomic stability has to be achieved, the high leverage ratio should be reduced, a rational and flexible interest rate structure must be created, risk management capacity across industries should be established, and intervention in the foreign exchange market should be minimized. All of this takes time. Hasty capital account liberalization could lead to dire consequences if these tasks have not been completed.

I suspect that the high risks involved will lead the PRC government eventually to return to a gradualist approach to capital account liberalization. Hence, renminbi internationalization will continue to enjoy steady progress, but there will be no sensational developments. After the capital account has been fully liberalized and renminbi dynamics are no longer driven by arbitrage, the progress of renminbi internationalization will depend increasingly on the specific nature of PRC firms, industrial organizations, business models, types of products traded, and bargaining power of PRC firms and their counterparts, in addition to the continuous expansion of the economy. There is no doubt whatsoever that the renminbi will become a major international currency, but the internationalization journey is a long one. The PRC is only at the beginning.

References

Brewer, David. 2012. "Sir David Brewer on RMB Trade between the UK and China." Video. Presentation at the China-Britain Business Council–HSBC conference The Rising Role of the Renminbi: A Corporate Perspective. Hong Kong, China, May 24 (www.hsbcnet.com/gbm/riseofthermb# for video of presentation and link to other PowerPoint presentations).

Chen, Manjiang. 2013. "Renminbi Internationalization and China's Capital Account Liberalization." Internal report. Beijing: Bank of China, August 23.

Eichengreen, Barry. 2013. "ADB Distinguished Lecture. Renminbi Internationalization: Tempest in a Teapot?" *Asian Development Review* 30, no. 1: 148–64.

Friberg, Richard, and Fredrik Wilander. 2007. "Price Setting Transactions and the Role of Denominating Currency in FX Markets." Working Paper Series 201. Stockholm: Central Bank of Sweden.

Galbis, Vicente. 1994. "Sequencing of Financial Sector Reforms: A Review." IMF Working Paper. Washington: International Monetary Fund, September.

Goldberg, Linda S., and Cédric Tille. 2008. "Vehicle Currency Use in International Trade." *Journal of International Economics* 76, no. 2: 177–92.

Grassman, Sven. 1973. "A Fundamental Symmetry in International Payment Patterns." *Journal of International Economics* 3, no. 2: 105–16.

Hong Kong Monetary Authority. 2013. "Development of Offshore Renminbi Business in Hong Kong: Review and Outlook." *InSight* (online magazine), February 21 (www.hkma.gov.hk/eng/key-information/insight/20130221.shtml).

HSBC Bank. 2013. "RMB Cross-Border Service" (www.hsbc.com.cn/1/2/commercial-banking/business-banking/rmblibrary).

Ishii, Shogo, and Karl Habermeier. 2002. "Capital Account Liberalization and Financial Sector Stability." IMF Occasional Paper 211. Washington: International Monetary Fund.

Ito, Takatoshi, Satoshi Koibuchi, Kiyotaka Sato, and Junko Shimizu. 2010. "Why Has the Yen Failed to Become a Dominant Invoicing Currency in Asia?" NBER Working Paper 16231. Cambridge, Mass.: National Bureau of Economic Research.

Johnston, R. Barry. 1998. "Sequencing Capital Account Liberalization." *Finance and Development* 25, no. 4: 20–23.

Kawai, Masahiro. 1996. "The Japanese Yen as an International Currency: Performance and Prospects." In *Organization, Performance and Equity: Perspectives on the Japanese Economy*, edited by Ryuzo Sato, Rama V. Ramachandran, and Hajime Hori, pp. 305–55. Boston, London, Dordrecht: Kluwer Academic Publishers.

Kawai, Masahiro, and Shinji Takagi. 2010. "A Survey of the Literature on Managing Capital Flows." In *Managing Capital Flows*, edited by Masahiro Kawai and Mario B. Lamberte, pp. 46–72. Cheltenham, U.K., and Northampton, Mass.: Edward Elgar.

Ma, Jun. 2012. "Roadmap for RMB Internationalization." Report. *Asia Economics Special.* Hong Kong, China: Deutsche Bank AG, June 25.

Ocampo, Jose Antonio, Shari Spiegel, and Joseph E. Stiglitz. 2008. "Capital Market Liberalization and Development." In *Capital Market Liberalization and Development*, edited by Jose A. Ocampo and Joseph E. Stiglitz, pp. 1–47. Oxford University Press.

Ostry, Jonathan D., Atish R. Ghosh, Marcos Chamon, and Mahvash S. Qureshi. 2012. "Tools for Managing Financial-Stability Risks from Capital Inflows." *Journal of International Economics* 88, no. 2: 407–21.

Ostry, Jonathan D., Atish R. Ghosh, Karl Habermeier, Marcos Chamon, Mahvash S. Qureshi, and Dennis B.S. Reinhardt. 2010. "Capital Inflows: The Role of Controls." IMF Staff Position Note SPN/10/04. Washington: International Monetary Fund, February 19.

Ostry, Jonathan D., Atish R. Ghosh, Karl Habermeier, Luc Laeven, Marcos Chamon, Mahvash S. Qureshi, and Annamaria Kokenyne. 2011. "Managing Capital Inflows: What Tools to Use." IMF Staff Discussion Note SDN/11/06. Washington: International Monetary Fund.

Sheng, Soncheng. 2012. "Conditions for China's Capital Account Liberalization Have Matured." Report. Beijing: People's Bank of China, February 23.

Takagi, Shinji. 2009. "Internationalising the Yen, 1984–2003: Unfinished Agenda or Mission Impossible?" Paper presented at the BIS-BoK seminar Currency Internationalization: Lessons from the Global Financial Crisis and Prospects for the Future in Asia and the Pacific. Seoul, March 19–20 (www.bis.org/repofficepubl/arpresearch200903.04.pdf).

Yu, Yongding. 2008. "American Government Bonds and Panda Bonds." *Journal of Finance and Economics* [Cai Jing Za Zhi] 25 (December 8).

———. 2012. "Revisiting the Internationalization of the Yuan." ADBI Working Paper Series 366. Tokyo: Asian Development Bank Institute, July.

World Bank and International Monetary Fund. 2005. "Sequencing Financial Sector Reforms." In *Financial Sector Assessment: A Handbook*, pp. 317–24. Washington: World Bank.

Zhang, Bin, and Qiyuan Xu. 2011. "RMB Internationalization in the Context of Exchange Rate and Capital Account Control" (in Chinese). Unpublished paper. Chinese Academy of Social Sciences (Beijing), Institute of World Economics and Politics.

Zhao, Qingming. 2013. "The Progress of Capital Account Liberalization Depends on the Progress of Institutional Capacity Building." Unpublished manuscript. Beijing: Construction Bank of China, Research Department.

Zhou, Xiaochuan. 2009. "Reform the International Monetary System." Unpublished paper (www.bis.org/review/r090402c.pdf), March 23.

PART II

The Implications

4

Global Ramifications of the Renminbi's Ascendance

ESWAR PRASAD

In terms of size and dynamism, the economy of the People's Republic of China (PRC) stands out among the emerging markets. It has already become the world's second-largest economy and is now one of the largest contributors to global growth. If the PRC continues on its present growth track, it may soon take over from the United States as the world's largest economy. These developments have led to intense speculation that the PRC's currency, the renminbi, will soon become one of the major international currencies.

The potential for the renminbi to develop quickly into an international currency is not without historical precedent.[1] One important question, however, is whether the PRC economy is ready for this shift in terms of other aspects that matter, besides size. Discussion of the renminbi's ascendance might seem premature, since the PRC has neither a flexible exchange rate nor an open capital account, both of these once considered essential prerequisites for a country's currency to have a major role in global financial markets. Still, the government of the PRC has recently taken a number of steps to increase the international use of the renminbi. Given the PRC's sheer size and its rising share of global gross domestic product (GDP) and trade, these steps are gaining traction and portend a growing role for the renminbi in global trade and finance.

---

1. The speed of the dollar's ascent as it vaulted past the pound sterling is documented by Eichengreen and Flandreau (2009).

In this chapter I briefly summarize some of the steps taken by the PRC government to promote the international use of the renminbi, which in turn is linked to moves to open up the PRC's capital account. I then review the potential implications of these changes for capital flows into and out of the PRC. I also discuss the prospects for the renminbi to become a reserve currency and the implications that could have for international liquidity, the Asian monetary system, and the global configuration of reserve currencies.

Steps toward Reserve Currency Status

A great deal of hyperbole surrounds the renminbi, and some commentators go so far as to argue that its displacement of the dollar as the dominant reserve currency is imminent.[2] Before evaluating these claims, it is important first to clarify some concepts. Popular discussions of the renminbi's emergence on the international stage tend to conflate three related but distinct aspects of a currency's role in international finance.

1. Internationalization—its use in denominating and settling cross-border trade and financial transactions, that is, its use as an international medium of exchange.

2. Capital account convertibility—the country's level of restrictions on inflows and outflows of financial capital. A fully open capital account has no restrictions on cross-border capital flows.

3. Reserve currency—whether the currency is held by foreign central banks as protection against balance-of-payments crises.

A currency's international usage and its convertibility are different concepts, and neither one is a necessary or sufficient condition for the other. The renminbi is a prime example of a currency that is increasingly being used in international transactions even though the PRC keeps capital flows restricted. And of course there are many economies that have fully open capital accounts but whose currencies do not have broad acceptance in global markets. An additional wrinkle is that a fully open capital account does not necessarily imply a floating exchange rate. For instance, Hong Kong, China has an open capital account, but its currency is in effect pegged to the U.S. dollar, through a currency board arrangement.

---

2. Prasad and Ye (2012) provide a systematic evaluation of the PRC's progress in each of the dimensions of the renminbi's progress as an international currency. Chen, Peng, and Shu (2009) and Subramanian (2011) argue that the renminbi is well on its way to becoming a major, if not dominant, reserve currency. Dobson and Masson (2009), Eichengreen (2011), and Kroeber (2011) offer more nuanced and skeptical views. Angeloni and others (2011) discuss probabilities of alternative scenarios, noting that the renminbi may gain more prominence if the euro does not mount a serious challenge to the dominance of the U.S. dollar. See also Prasad (2014).

It turns out that all three conditions—capital account convertibility, floating exchange rate, and internationalization—are necessary for a currency to become a reserve currency. I begin by considering how much progress the PRC has made on each of these dimensions and how they are interconnected.

Renminbi Internationalization

The PRC has begun to promote the international use of the renminbi, but with its customary cautious and gradual approach. With its sophisticated financial markets and strong supervisory and other institutions, Hong Kong, China provides a perfect testing ground for these policy reforms. Meanwhile, its status as an international financial center means that Hong Kong, China could actively help build up the renminbi's role, at least in Asia.

As early as 2004, personal renminbi business had been initiated in Hong Kong, China when residents were allowed to open deposit accounts denominated in renminbi. In 2007, the PRC began to take a number of additional steps in promoting the international use of its currency, in most cases using Hong Kong, China as the platform:

—Permitting the settlement of trade transactions with the renminbi

—Easing restrictions on cross-border remittances of the renminbi for settlement

—Allowing the issuance of renminbi-denominated bonds in Hong Kong, China and the mainland PRC

—Permitting selected banks to offer offshore renminbi deposit accounts

Given the PRC's rapidly expanding trade volumes, promoting a greater use of the renminbi in trade settlement is a logical first step in the currency's internationalization process. In a relatively short period, cross-border trade settlement in the currency has expanded rapidly. In 2012, trade settlements in renminbi amounted to roughly 12 percent of the PRC's total trade in goods and services.

As with most other data for the PRC, there is a hidden story behind the numbers. For the first couple of years, data for these settlement transactions broken down separately for imports and exports showed that most of the renminbi trade settlement was for transactions that represented imports by the PRC. Payments by PRC importers in renminbi allowed foreign traders to acquire renminbi that were difficult to acquire offshore through other channels. By contrast, there was little settlement in renminbi of the PRC's exports, suggesting that recipients of exports from the PRC either have limited amounts of the currency or are disinclined to reduce their holdings.

One interpretation of this one-sided pattern of trade settlements is that it reflects the desire of foreign traders to bet on the renminbi's appreciation by acquiring as much of the currency as possible. This is another indication of how the PRC's rising trade and financial integration with global markets will make it increasingly difficult to tightly manage the currency's external value.

Settling trade transactions in renminbi requires access to that currency. During 2012, remittances of renminbi used for cross-border settlement in Hong Kong, China averaged roughly US$35 billion per month, compared to US$9 billion per month in the second half of 2010. Cross-border renminbi settlement is not confined exclusively to Hong Kong, China, but Hong Kong, China's banks play a dominant role. To support renminbi settlement, Hong Kong, China's interbank market initiated a renminbi settlement system in March 2006, in order to provide a variety of services such as check clearing, remittance processing, and bankcard payment services. Renminbi clearing transactions were virtually zero until mid-2010, when financial institutions in Hong Kong, China were allowed to open renminbi-denominated accounts. Since then, both the volume and value of transactions have increased dramatically. Another major development is the rising issuance of renminbi-denominated bonds, better known as dim sum bonds, in Hong Kong, China. The issuance of dim sum bonds rose sharply during 2007–2011 before leveling off at about CNY110 billion (US$18 billion) in 2012.

All of these steps are gaining traction, although they are still modest in scale. Still, the initiation and rapid expansion of different elements of the offshore renminbi market signal that the currency is gaining a significant foothold in the Asian region's trade and financial transactions. However, some caveats are in order. First, dim sum bond issuance remains somewhat narrow in scope, in that such issuance is still strongly confined to banking and financial institutions. Second, a large portion of the issuance currently comes from the mainland PRC. Third, various reports suggest that a significant portion of cross-border renminbi settlement is used mainly for cross-border arbitrage between companies in the mainland PRC and their Hong Kong, China subsidiaries. These factors imply that the influence of offshore renminbi use still has some way to go to reach its full potential.

Capital Account Liberalization and Exchange Rate Flexibility

On paper, the PRC still has a large number of restrictions on the free flow of capital across its borders. Many of the restrictions on both inflows and outflows have been loosened over time, consistent with the active promotion of the renminbi as an international currency. In most cases, constraints on outflows and inflows have been made less stringent rather than being eliminated entirely.[3]

In recent years, the government has encouraged outflows by corporations and institutional investors (such as pension funds and insurance companies) in order to offset some of the pressures for currency appreciation arising from trade sur-

---

3. For more details on measures taken by the PRC in recent years to open up its capital account, see Prasad and Ye (2012) and the IMF's Annual Reports on Exchange Arrangements and Exchange Restrictions.

pluses and capital inflows. For instance, in 2009 the government dropped review and approval requirements for outward remittances of funds for direct investment abroad by Chinese corporations and financial institutions. In 2007, the limit on foreign exchange purchases by residents for remittance abroad for personal reasons was increased to US$50,000 a year, a high limit for an economy where the annual per capita income is now about US$8,000.

Controls on inflows are also being gradually eased, although many restrictions remain in place. The government has always welcomed foreign direct investment, not just for the money that foreign investors provide but, more important, for the technological and managerial skills they bring with them. Now the government has started allowing approved foreign investors—dubbed Qualified Foreign Institutional Investors (QFIIs)—to buy Chinese stocks as well, although they are limited to a certain amount of investments per year. The upper limit on portfolio investments by individual QFIIs has been raised but still remains at a modest US$1 billion, and the period for which these investments are "locked up" has been reduced.[4]

Although capital account restrictions are a useful way to evaluate an economy's openness, an alternative approach to do this is to examine the total amount of foreign assets and liabilities relative to GDP. The level of the PRC's gross external position has grown rapidly, roughly tripling in size over the last five years to more than US$7.5 trillion in 2011. The ratio of gross external assets plus liabilities to GDP is now greater than 100 percent.

In terms of openness levels the PRC's gross external position exceeds those of all the other key emerging markets and also that of Switzerland. Its openness as a share of GDP lags behind the proportions of the reserve currency economies. Among emerging markets, however, the PRC's de facto measure of openness is relatively high, exceeding the levels of countries such as Brazil and India. To the extent that de facto openness is somewhat higher and grows more than the rise in de jure openness, recent steps taken to selectively loosen capital account restrictions do seem to have stoked greater financial flows.

In short, although the PRC still has an extensive capital control regime in place, it is selectively and cautiously dismantling these controls. Partly as a result of this dismantling, the country's capital account is becoming increasingly open in de facto terms, but the government is far from allowing the extent of free flow of capital that is typical of reserve currencies.

---

4. The total quota for QFIIs was raised to US$80 billion in 2012. The upper limit on portfolio investments by individual QFIIs was raised to US$1 billion. The period for which these investments are "locked up" and cannot remit their principal abroad ranges from three to twelve months, depending on the type of institution. By February 2013, the China Securities Regulatory Commission had granted QFII licenses to 215 foreign institutions, and the State Administration of Foreign Exchange had approved aggregate quotas amounting to US$41 billion.

The Exchange Rate Regime

The renminbi was pegged to the dollar from 1997 to 2005. Although it was allowed to appreciate gradually against the dollar starting in July 2005, the currency continues to be managed tightly relative to the dollar. With the onset of the global financial crisis, the hard peg to the dollar was reinstituted in July 2008 before being relaxed again in June 2010. By limiting the flow of money, the capital account restrictions help in controlling the value of the renminbi, which now trades both onshore (CNY) and offshore (CNH; H is a reference to Hong Kong, China). Onshore trade takes place through the PRC Foreign Exchange Trade System, which is in effect managed by the People's Bank of China (PBOC). The offshore trades mostly take place on Hong Kong, China's interbank market. Mainland government regulations mandate these separate markets for the trading of renminbi. The onshore market is subject to the mainland capital account restrictions and the renminbi's value on that market is therefore more under the PBOC's control. In contrast, the offshore market is not subject to direct official control or intervention.

The two rates have moved in lockstep for much of the period since the end of 2010, reflecting the rising integration of the PRC's onshore and offshore financial markets. Before this period, renminbi-related activities in the offshore market were quite limited, which contributed to a marked deviation of the offshore exchange rate from that of the onshore rate—the renminbi was typically more valuable offshore. The two exchange rates became more closely linked after a series of developments in the last quarter of 2010 boosted renminbi-denominated financial transactions. This includes the approval granted to financial institutions and banks in Hong Kong, China to open renminbi accounts and for Hong Kong, China banks to access the onshore interbank market; activation of a swap line between the PBOC and the Hong Kong Monetary Authority; and a flurry of renminbi-denominated bond issuance activities. These measures have lowered transaction costs for eligible financial market participants to access both markets.

As things stand, however, offshore renminbi trading is still restricted by a variety of regulations that limit market participation to a select group—mostly financial institutions. This sometimes leads to quirky outcomes. For instance, a deviation of the two exchange rates resurfaced temporarily in mid-2011, but this time in the opposite direction—the offshore exchange rate rose markedly above the onshore exchange rate, and this gap persisted for a while. That is, the renminbi was worth more onshore rather than on offshore markets. Such episodes suggest that the integration of the two markets is far from complete.

Despite various moves to make the renminbi's exchange rate more flexible, including a widening of the daily fluctuation band around the previous day's midpoint to plus or minus 1 percent, the renminbi continues to be tightly managed against the U.S. dollar.

Characteristic Capital Account Liberalization

Is the PRC putting the cart before the horse by pushing forward with capital account opening before freeing up its exchange rate?[5] There is considerable evidence that opening up the capital account without a flexible exchange rate is risky. A fixed or tightly managed nominal exchange rate makes it harder to cope with capital flow volatility because the exchange rate cannot act as a shock absorber. Another source of risk is that an open capital account often encourages an accumulation of external debt. The PRC's external debt is about 8 percent of GDP, much lower than that of any other major emerging market. The PRC's overall external balance sheet shows that its economy is quite well insulated from external shocks, as net foreign assets amounted to nearly US$1.8 trillion at the end of 2011. In other words, the PRC has enough foreign assets not only to meet all its external debt obligations but also to more than cover all of its foreign liabilities.

The bigger risks may be domestic ones. The combination of a tightly managed exchange rate and an increasingly open capital account impedes the ability of the central bank to use monetary policy instruments such as interest rates to maintain domestic price stability. Despite its relatively closed capital account, this constraint applies to the PRC as well, because the capital account is in fact rather porous and becomes even more so when interest differentials with the rest of the world increase and the incentives to evade controls become larger. If the United States has low rates while the PRC ought to have higher interest rates to manage inflation, the central bank of the PRC is constrained in raising rates as that may suck in more inflows. Indeed, the expectations of renminbi appreciation that resulted from the tight management of the renminbi's value may have fueled more speculative inflows in previous years.

Moreover, lifting restrictions on capital flows could also be risky for the financial system. Freeing up outflows further while maintaining a cap on deposit interest rates could cause households and corporations to shift deposits out of the banking system. Banking sector earnings are heavily dependent on net interest margins that are mandated by the government through the deposit rate ceiling and, until recently, the lending rate floor (the floor was removed in July 2013). Hence, massive deposit withdrawals can damage banks and strain the entire domestic financial system.

How worried should the PRC be about these risks? The government has enough control of its financial markets and enough resources to back up its banks

---

5. For a discussion of the issue of sequencing capital account liberalization in the context of the PRC, see Prasad, Rumbaugh, and Wang (2005) and references therein. A burgeoning literature looking at specific aspects of the PRC's exchange rate management and capital account liberalization includes Frankel (2005, 2011), Eichengreen (2011), Lardy and Douglass (2011), Yam (2011), and Yu (2012). Goodfriend and Prasad (2007) discuss the implications of the PRC's exchange rate regime for monetary policy formulation and implementation. For a description of the challenges facing the PRC's financial system, see Lardy (2011) and Prasad and Ye (2012). For a broader discussion of the PRC's economic challenges and the need for reforms, see Prasad (2009, 2011).

that these risks are probably not likely to morph into a full-blown banking or broader financial crisis. Nevertheless, it could take a lot of government money to keep the system stable in difficult times. It is not easy to lay out a crisis scenario where the wheels come off the PRC financial system, but there are many fragilities in the banking system and in the unregulated part of the financial system that are cause for serious concern. A capital account that is becoming increasingly open could bring some of these tensions to a simmer and perhaps even cause them to boil over. So how is the PRC managing the difficult act of getting the sequence of its reforms right?

Gradual Reforms

Some commentators have argued that a piecemeal approach to reforms may not be tenable for the PRC when it comes to issues such as exchange rate flexibility and capital account liberalization. The logic seems simple: making the currency more flexible gradually could lead to a wave of capital flooding into the economy, notwithstanding capital controls, as there would be a tempting opportunity for a one-way bet on the currency's appreciation. Some researchers have also argued that there are good reasons for the PRC to move ahead with exchange rate flexibility before opening up the capital account.[6]

In practice, the government has managed to sustain a gradual approach to making the exchange rate regime more flexible. It has also undertaken capital account opening in small steps but more aggressively than it has moved forward on letting the exchange rate float more freely. The PRC government likes to stay in control and not take any major risks, and it was clear that it wanted to take a similar approach even with respect to large-scale macroeconomic reforms. So how could it implement a gradual opening without losing control of the capital account in a more drastic manner?

By 2007, the renminbi was under enormous pressure to appreciate: the PRC was piling up ever-larger trade surpluses and capital flows were pouring in as a result of the strong desire of foreign investors to participate in and benefit from the PRC growth story. The government was eager to encourage some private capital outflows to offset the capital inflows.

In August 2007, the government unveiled the "through train," a channel that made it easier for mainland retail investors to directly buy equities in Hong Kong, China. Anticipation of large sums of money gushing into Hong Kong, China pushed the Hang Seng stock-market index to a record high in October. The mere prospect that the program might end up being not just a success but a wild success that could result in their losing control of the channel prompted PRC regulators to have second thoughts. They were particularly concerned about the surge

6. See Prasad, Rumbaugh, and Wang (2005), and Prasad and Rajan (2005, 2006, 2008).

in the Hang Seng index and fears that PRC households could lose money if they took the opportunity to invest in Hong Kong, China just when that market was perhaps becoming overvalued. Later that year, the "through train" ran out of track and came to a halt as the government scrapped the plan even before it actually came into full-fledged operation.

The government's next step to liberalize outflows was a safer approach through an expansion of the Qualified Domestic Institutional Investor (QDII) scheme in 2010. QDIIs include securities firms and asset management companies as well as some large institutional investors such as insurance companies. QDIIs could gather funds from retail investors, pool those funds, and then invest abroad. There was of course some risk involved, but the fact that the QDIIs would presumably have better information and invest more wisely than the average retail investor improved the risk–benefit trade-off. More important, the QDII approach gave the government much more control as to when and how much money could be taken offshore because the QDIIs were given specific investment quotas each year.

This approach to allowing for private capital outflows in a controlled manner is better in many ways than the inefficient approach of having the government recycle foreign currency inflows through official channels in the form of reserve accumulation. The QDII approach reduces the need for foreign exchange market intervention, gives private investors a chance to diversify their portfolios by increasing foreign investments, and also prods PRC banks to shape up by increasing competition in the financial system.

Capital Outflows

Even as the country's economy continued to post relatively good growth rates in the aftermath of the financial crisis and became the main driver of world growth, political uncertainty related to the leadership transition during the summer and fall of 2012 led to concerns about capital flight from the PRC.

What was true even in 2012 was that weaker inflows and stronger outflows (including an increase in foreign currency deposits as exporters held more of their earnings abroad in foreign currencies) led to a more balanced position of capital outflows and inflows. These swings seemed to be quite similar to those experienced by many other emerging markets.

In the first half of 2012, with the eurozone debt crisis worsening, investors worldwide seemed to be more concerned about safety than high returns. Consequently, there was a flow of capital out of emerging markets around the world to safe havens, especially the United States but also Japan and Switzerland. In August 2012, the European Central Bank announced its Outright Monetary Transactions backstop for sovereign debt of the eurozone periphery economies. That eased immediate concerns about global spillovers from eurozone problems and capital started flowing back to emerging markets, including the PRC.

These changes in the patterns and timing of flows illustrate one important point—that the PRC is looking like a lot of other emerging markets in terms of what factors lead to capital flowing in or out. There is little basis for panic about the PRC not continuing to receive waves of inflows almost irrespective of global financial conditions. In fact, the period before 2012 might have been more of an aberration as the attractiveness of the PRC growth story seemed to override other considerations related to world interest rates and other financial market conditions.

While gross capital outflows from the PRC have increased significantly over the past two years, these are consistent with the government's steps to liberalize out-flows. Non-government outflows are likely to increase further as Chinese corpo-rations look for investment opportunities abroad and as financial market devel-opment allows households to take advantage of avenues to diversify their savings into foreign investments.[7] In short, there is little reason (so far) to panic about the PRC's rising capital outflows—they may be a sign of a maturing economy rather than a troubled one.

Global Configuration of Reserve Currencies

With the capital account becoming more open and the currency gaining greater if still modest acceptance in international financial markets, does the renminbi have a future as a reserve currency?

Some economists have argued that the PRC's sheer size and dynamism will lead to its currency becoming a global reserve currency. While the PRC's growth over the last three decades is indeed awe-inspiring, it is essential to keep in mind that the PRC has become big and influential before it has become rich and, more importantly, before it has well-developed financial markets or broadly trusted pub-lic institutions. After all, if size were the main criterion, it is unlikely that a small country like Switzerland, which has a GDP less than one-tenth that of the PRC, would have one of the main reserve currencies in the world.

There is no clear template for what it takes for a currency to become a reserve currency but, based on historical evidence, there are a few criteria that matter. It is worth considering each of these criteria to see how the PRC measures up.

—Economic size: A country's size and its shares of global trade and finance are important—but not crucial—determinants of the status of its reserve currency. The PRC now accounts for 10 percent of world GDP (15 percent if measured by purchasing power parity rather than market exchange rates) and 9 percent of world trade. In 2011–12, it is estimated to have accounted for about one quarter of world GDP growth.

---

7. For a discussion of the PRC's outward investment strategy, see Rosen and Hanemann (2009) and Scissors (2011). For more on PRC households' saving behavior, see Chamon and Prasad (2010) and Chamon, Liu, and Prasad (2010).

—Open capital account: Reserves must be acceptable as payments to a country's trade and financial partners, which requires that the currency be easily tradable in global financial markets. This is difficult if a country imposes restrictions on capital flows and if its foreign exchange markets are thin and subject to direct control by the government. The PRC is gradually and selectively easing restrictions on both inflows and outflows. The capital account has become increasingly open in de facto terms, but extensive capital controls are still in place.

—Flexible exchange rate: Typically reserve currencies are traded freely and their external value is market-determined, although this does not preclude occasional bouts of intervention by the country's central bank in foreign exchange markets. The PRC still has a tightly managed exchange rate, but it will become increasingly hard to manage as the capital account becomes more open.

—Macroeconomic policies: Investors in a country's sovereign assets must have faith in its commitment to low inflation and sustainable levels of public debt, so the value of the currency is not in danger of being eroded. The PRC has a lower ratio of explicit public debt to GDP than most major reserve currency economies and has maintained moderate inflation in recent years.

—Financial market development: A country must have broad, deep, and liquid financial markets so that international investors will have access to a wide array of financial assets denominated in its currency. The PRC's financial markets remain limited and underdeveloped, with a number of constraints such as a rigid interest rate structure.

Although the PRC measures up favorably in the first four areas, the last one—financial market development—is likely ultimately to determine winners and losers in the global reserve currency sweepstakes. This is where the PRC falls short and is unlikely to catch up to the United States and other reserve currencies anytime soon.[8]

Getting Financial Markets Ready

Financial market development in the home country is one of the key determinants of a currency's international status.[9] Historically, each reserve currency has risen on the international stage under unique circumstances and has been spurred by different motivations, but one constant is that this rise has always required financial markets that can cope with the varied and voluminous demands of private and official foreign investors. There are three relevant aspects of financial market development:

---

8. Angeloni and others (2011) note that in addition to strong financial markets, a reserve currency should be backed up by (1) the reliability of rules and institutions, (2) the quality and predictability of fiscal and monetary policies, (3) the ability of policymakers to respond to unexpected shocks, and (4) political cohesion. Some authors also argue that network externalities are important, as they generate economies of scale and scope. See, for instance, Chinn and Frankel (2008).

9. On the importance of home-country financial market development for a currency to become a reserve currency, see Tavlas (1990), Chinn and Frankel (2007), Forbes (2009), and Obstfeld (2011).

1. Breadth—The availability of a broad range of financial instruments, including markets for hedging risk

2. Depth—A large volume of financial instruments in specific markets

3. Liquidity—A high level of turnover (trading volume)

Without a sufficiently large and liquid debt market, the renminbi cannot be used widely in international transactions. For foreign central banks and large institutional investors to find the currency attractive they will need access to renminbi-denominated government and corporate debt as "safe" assets for their portfolios. At the same time, both importers and exporters may be concerned about greater exchange rate volatility resulting from an open capital account if they do not have access to derivatives markets to hedge foreign exchange risk. Thus, depth, breadth, and liquidity are all relevant considerations in assessing the readiness of a country's finance sector to cope with an open capital account and elevate its currency to reserve currency status.

The PRC's financial system remains dominated by banks, with the state directly controlling most of the banking system. Policies that favor the banking sector relative to the rest of the financial system—including the interest rate structure that sets a ceiling for deposit rates—are detrimental to broader financial market development.

One dimension in which the PRC has made progress is the development of its equity markets. In 2005, reforms were introduced to allow non-tradable shares in Chinese companies to float freely. These reforms had a dramatic effect. Market capitalization and turnover surged immediately thereafter and have grown sixfold since then, while trading volume has increased more than tenfold. Capitalization and turnover in Chinese equity markets now exceed those of most other economies, with the notable exception of the United States, which remains dominant in terms of its share of global equity market capitalization and turnover. In principle equity markets provide renminbi-denominated instruments that can be held by both domestic and foreign investors, but there are still significant restrictions on foreign investors' participation in these markets. Moreover, PRC stock markets are volatile and prone to concerns about weak corporate governance and shoddy accounting practices, so the country's deep equity markets may be of limited help in making the renminbi an international currency in the near future.

By most measures, the size and liquidity of the PRC's debt market lag far behind those of existing reserve currency economies. The stock of domestic debt securities has risen sharply during the last few years but from a very low base. Non-financial corporate debt was practically nonexistent until 2005. The size of the PRC's government bond market, measured by the market value of the stock of outstanding bonds, was about US$1.5 trillion as of March 2012, compared with US$13.3 trillion for the United States. The turnover ratio on government bonds—the ratio of transactions in a given year relative to the outstanding stock of bonds—is about one for PRC, compared with a ratio of around fourteen for the United States. In addition to the limited turnover, the PRC restricts foreign investors' participation in its government bond markets, which could affect its currency's scope to become a reserve currency. However, the PRC has a relatively high turnover ratio in its corporate bond market, which is consistent with the rapid growth of the corporate debt market, though even that market is still small in absolute terms, at about one-sixth the size of the U.S. corporate bond market.

The PRC's overall domestic debt market is valued at US$3.4 trillion (as of March 2012, significantly lower than that of the top three reserve currency areas—the United States, the eurozone, and Japan. The U.S. domestic debt securities market has a capital value nearly ten times this size. Interestingly, the quantity of the PRC's outstanding domestic securities is greater than that of the United Kingdom and Switzerland, two reserve currency economies. This suggests that the size of the domestic debt market per se does not necessarily prevent the renminbi from going global.

The PRC's aspirations to make the renminbi a global reserve currency rest in large part on the pace of development of the government debt market. Reserve currencies are expected to issue high-quality and creditworthy government debt or government-backed debt instruments that can serve as a hedge against domestic currency depreciation during a global downturn. The current level of government debt in the PRC is relatively low compared with the debt levels of reserve currency areas and with other major emerging markets. The low level of debt provides more credibility about the government's fiscal and inflation policies, but the limited supply of safe and liquid renminbi-denominated assets works against the renminbi's ascendance to reserve currency status.

Although the absolute size of the debt securities market in the PRC is small from a cross-country perspective, it should not mask the country's rapid growth in these markets. Domestic debt securities, especially corporate sector debt, were at negligible levels only a decade ago. The share of nonfinancial corporate debt in total domestic debt outstanding is also rising, accounting for a share of 20 percent and a value of US$700 billion in March 2012.

The growth of the PRC's debt markets suggests that the pace of the country's financial market development is consistent with its intention to make its currency accepted as an international currency. Nevertheless, achieving reserve currency status for the renminbi is probably a long way off.

Limited Use in International Financial Transactions

The pace of the internationalization of the PRC's currency depends on its use in international financial transactions as well. The choice of currency for denomination and settlement of trade flows is contingent on the extent to which that currency can also be used in international financial transactions.[10]

---

10. Data on foreign exchange market turnover, derivatives markets, and currency denomination of international debt securities are taken from the Bank for International Settlements website. See Prasad and Ye (2012) for further discussion of the concepts and data.

Foreign exchange market turnover is a good indicator of a currency's potential for developing into a vehicle currency. The renminbi accounts for less than 1 percent (out of 200 percent, as each transaction involves two currencies) of all turnover in foreign exchange markets. This is true of other emerging markets' currencies as well. The U.S. dollar is dominant in this dimension, accounting for 85 percent of turnover. The five major reserve currencies combined account for 162 percent of total turnover. In terms of the geographic distribution of foreign exchange turnover, however, the PRC has the advantage of having Hong Kong, China as an important financial center for settling foreign exchange transactions. Hong Kong, China accounts for 5 percent of global foreign exchange market turnover (compared to 27 percent for the United Kingdom and 18 percent for the United States). This puts the renminbi on a competitive footing relative to other emerging market currencies in terms of attaining the role of an international currency.

Overall, the spot and derivatives markets for trading in the renminbi remain underdeveloped. The PRC's currency has the lowest spot transactions turnover among all major economies. The renminbi's foreign exchange derivatives trading volume across the board is far smaller than that of the major reserve currencies. The PRC does have a major presence in markets for commodity futures. Based on the number of futures/options traded, three of the PRC's commodity futures exchanges are among the top twenty derivatives exchanges in the world. This is encouraging in terms of broader financial development, but a large commodity derivatives market may be of limited use from the perspective of promoting international use of a currency.

Another indicator of the currency's potential use in international financial transactions is the relative size of international debt securities (that is, debt issued outside the home country) in different currencies of issuance. The existing reserve currencies clearly dominate, with the U.S. dollar and the euro accounting for about 83 percent of outstanding international bonds and notes. The top five reserve currencies combined account for 96 percent of these instruments. Only a paltry 0.1 percent of international debt is denominated in renminbi. The same is true for other major emerging-market currencies.

Financial Markets: The Weak Link in the Global Renminbi Project

The main conclusion to be drawn from the discussion so far is that the PRC falls short on many key dimensions of financial market development, and its steps to aggressively promote its currency's international role are likely to be impeded over the medium term by the weaknesses of its financial system.

The PRC's financial markets have improved in some respects during the last decade, but there are still significant gaps, especially in terms of achieving sufficiently large and liquid debt markets. More important, the structure and quality of debt markets will also need to be changed to fully prepare for a currency used widely in international financial transactions and reserve holdings. With relatively low external and government debt positions, the PRC's debt markets can in principle expand rapidly without serious threat to inflation credibility or vulnerability to external risks. Effective regulation of corporate debt markets is an important priority so that these markets can expand without generating financial instability. Moreover, to satisfy their demand for relatively safe renminbi-denominated assets, foreign investors—both official and private—will eventually need to be given greater access to the PRC's debt markets if the renminbi is to become a true international currency.

Thus far, the use of commercial policies to increase the offshore use of the renminbi has been the centerpiece of the PRC's currency internationalization process. The latest move on this front is a revival of the "through train" concept, but now in the form of an extended QDII scheme (QDII2), which would allow high-net-worth mainland residents to invest directly in Hong Kong, China's equity market using renminbi funds. Although this broad approach has been effective in promoting the renminbi's global role without risking the potential deleterious effects of capital account liberalization, the full potential of the renminbi's international use cannot be realized without more active onshore development. This development would encourage private initiatives to use the renminbi for trade and financial transactions. Ultimately, it will be difficult to fully develop the PRC's foreign exchange and derivatives markets in the absence of substantial capital account liberalization.

The Renminbi and the Special Drawing Right

In March 2009, PBOC Governor Zhou Xiaochuan issued a paper titled "Reform the International Monetary System" on the PBOC's website (Zhou 2009). It laid out the case for special drawing rights (SDRs) to play a more prominent role in global finance and suggested that the composition of the SDR needed to keep up with changing times by incorporating the currencies of the major emerging market economies.

SDRs constitute an international reserve asset created by the International Monetary Fund (IMF). The SDR exists only on the books of the IMF and its value is based on a basket of four reserve currencies: the U.S. dollar, the euro, the yen, and the pound sterling. SDRs are distributed among IMF members on the basis of their quotas at the institution. In effect, these allocations get added to a country's international reserves, since they can be exchanged for "real" hard currencies at the IMF with no questions asked or conditions attached.

The proposal to give SDRs more prominence was seen as a direct shot across the bow of the U.S. dollar. It was also widely interpreted as staking a claim for the renminbi's global importance to be recognized by its inclusion in the exclusive group of currencies in the SDR basket, which does not even include some smaller reserve currencies such as the Swiss franc.

There was considerable discussion in 2011 about a proposal to include the renminbi in the SDR basket. The government of France, during its presidency of the Group of Twenty (G-20) in 2011, promoted this proposal at different venues, viewing it as an important component of the reform of the international monetary system. At a G-20 conference in Nanjing in March 2011, President Nicolas Sarkozy of France put the issue squarely on the table, arguing that the SDR basket should be enlarged to include emerging market economies' currencies, starting with the renminbi. The communiqué issued at the conclusion of the November 2011 G-20 Summit in Cannes noted, "We agreed that the SDR basket composition should continue to reflect the role of currencies in the global trading and financial system and be adjusted over time to reflect currencies' changing role and characteristics."

The PRC itself has been more circumspect about the prospects of expanding the SDR basket. Yi Gang, the deputy governor of the PBOC and head of the State Administration of Foreign Exchange, urged the IMF to conduct more research into a shadow SDR and argued that "the IMF should consider including currencies of the BRICS [Brazil, Russian Federation, India, the PRC, and South Africa] countries and other emerging economies when it next reviews its Special Drawing Right (SDR) system by 2015." The BRICS are the world's largest fast-growing emerging economies. But Yi was also quoted as saying that the PRC was in no hurry for the renminbi's inclusion in the basket, because so far the SDR had been only a symbolic currency basket.[11]

As of 2014, SDRs accounted for about 5 percent of world official reserve asset holdings, so the direct effect of including the renminbi in the SDR basket would not be substantial. The symbolic effect, however, would be substantial, because even the prospect of the renminbi's becoming a part of the SDR basket would encourage central banks around the world to begin adding renminbi assets to their reserve portfolios. Technically, the renminbi cannot become a part of the SDR basket because it is not a convertible currency. However, the notion that a freely usable currency ought to qualify for the SDR basket has been thrust into the debate, based on the argument that the renminbi already meets the criteria for a freely usable currency—it is being increasingly used in trade settlement transactions and in the denomination of deposit accounts offshore.

The IMF's position in 2010 was clear and was summarized as follows in a report on its Executive Board's discussion of the matter: "Directors noted that although [the People's Republic of] China has become the third-largest exporter of goods and services on a five-year average basis and has taken steps to facilitate international use of its currency, the Chinese renminbi does not currently meet the criteria to be a freely usable currency and it would therefore not be included in the SDR basket at this time. Directors urged that this issue be kept under review in light of develop-

11. Yi Gang quoted in Lu Jianxin and Kazunori Takada, "China FX Head Proposes Adding BRICS Currencies to SDR," Reuters, May 4, 2011.

ments." Thus, it appeared that the IMF intended to apply the convertibility criterion strictly, which would be logical because any currency that is part of the SDR basket would presumably automatically be counted as an official reserve currency.

Technically, the SDR basket consists of the four currencies that are issued by IMF members (or monetary unions that include IMF members) that are the largest exporters, and that have been determined by the IMF to be "freely usable." The latter condition was added as a formal criterion only in 2000 and is clearly open to interpretation. The IMF's operational definition of a freely usable currency requires that it be widely used to make payments for international transactions and widely traded in the principal exchange markets. Thus, the criterion of convertibility is not strictly essential for a currency's inclusion in the SDR basket. By contrast, the IMF's own balance-of-payments definition of a freely usable currency is one that is liquid, convertible, and used for the settlement of international transactions. The composition of the SDR basket is governed by operational rather than technical criteria, so the lack of convertibility is not a hindrance to including the renminbi (or other emerging market currencies) in the basket.

In November 2011, the IMF proposed the following four indicators for evaluating a currency's potential for inclusion in the SDR basket:

1. Volume of transactions in foreign exchange spot markets
2. Volume of transactions in foreign exchange derivatives markets and over-the-counter derivatives
3. Existence of an appropriate market-based interest rate instrument
4. Currency composition of official reserve holdings

There are no clear benchmarks for any of these criteria, suggesting that the decision as to whether to include a currency in the SDR basket is ultimately a political decision, as long as some minimal thresholds are met on each criterion. The PRC most likely already meets the first criterion and is making progress on the second. Interest rate liberalization would be necessary to meet the third one. The IMF has also suggested that an ancillary indicator could be the number of countries holding a currency in their international reserve portfolios. This would certainly suit the PRC well—a number of countries have begun to publicly discuss the possibility and desirability of holding renminbi assets in their reserve portfolios, even if the actual (or proposed) amounts are small as of now. Regardless of the outcome of this debate on whether the renminbi should be part of the SDR basket, the debate's mere existence is a powerful signal of the PRC's ascendance in the world economy.

The People's Bank of China as a Provider of Liquidity

Despite its underdeveloped financial markets, the PRC is trying to create a new playbook for its currency. Indeed, the renminbi is already making its presence felt on the international stage, in part as the result of policy actions by the government and in part because of the sheer size and growing role of the PRC in international trade and finance.

Since 2009 the PBOC has moved aggressively to establish bilateral swap lines with other central banks in order to facilitate and expand the use of the renminbi in international trade and financial transactions. The PRC had in fact established swap lines with many Asian central banks even before it started to actively promote the international use of its currency. Most of these were dollar-renminbi swaps under which the PRC would provide U.S. dollars in exchange for the local currency of the counterparty economy. In other words, the foreign exchange reserves of economies such as the PRC would often serve as an additional credit line facility if the counterparty economy were to face a liquidity crunch due to a balance-of-payments or financial crisis.

There is one crucial difference between the earlier swap arrangements and those the PBOC has signed since 2009. Every single one of the swaps in place now is in terms of local currencies—that is, the PBOC commits to exchange other central banks' currencies for renminbi. By early 2013, twenty central banks had signed such local currency swap agreements with the PBOC (see table 4-1). Eager to expand its renminbi business and with the goal of making London a major center for renminbi-denominated activity, by early 2013 even the Bank of England had signed such a swap line, making it the first G-7 central bank to sign one with the PBOC.

The PRC's bilateral swap lines with foreign central banks directly support the renminbi's greater international use. The amounts of these bilateral agreements have been relatively small so far. The modest amounts notwithstanding, the PBOC is clearly making an active effort to make the central banks of a broad group of economies comfortable and familiar with renminbi-denominated instruments and financial facilities.

Another interesting development is that, despite its lack of convertibility, the renminbi is already beginning to play a modest role in a few central banks' reserve portfolios.[12] Chile, Malaysia, and Nigeria are widely believed to have pioneered this trend, starting in the second half of 2011. Official statements and other accounts suggest that other central banks are also considering adding renminbi assets to their reserve portfolios. An interesting point is that these holdings cannot in principle be counted as reserves by the IMF, given the present status of the renminbi's lack of convertibility, but this does not seem to matter for these central banks, because they view renminbi-denominated assets—just as they do other major reserve-currency-denominated assets—as providing insurance against balance-of-payments pressures.

12. Foreign central banks that want to buy PRC bonds for their reserve portfolios have to get permission from the PRC government through the QFII scheme. Sovereign wealth funds have to do the same. In December 2012, in response to strong demand for higher access limits, the State Administration of Foreign Exchange removed the ceiling on inward investments by sovereign wealth funds, central banks, and monetary authorities.

Table 4-1. *Central Bank Swap Arrangements with the People's Bank of China, December 2008–June 2013*[a]

Bank	Date	Amount (billion yuan)	U.S. dollar equivalent (billion)
Bank of Korea	*12 Dec 2008*	*180*	*26.3*
	26 Oct 2011	360	56.5
Hong Kong Monetary Authority	*20 Jan 2009*	*200*	*29.2*
	22 Nov 2011	400	62.9
Bank Negara Malaysia	*8 Feb 2009*	*80*	*11.7*
	8 Feb 2012	180	28.6
National Bank of the Republic of Belarus	11 Mar 2009	20	2.9
Bank Indonesia	23 Mar 2009	100	14.6
Central Bank of Argentina	2 Apr 2009	70	10.2
Central Bank of Iceland	9 Jun 2010	3.5	0.5
Monetary Authority of Singapore	*23 Jul 2010*	*150*	*22.1*
	7 Mar 2013	300	48.2
Reserve Bank of New Zealand	18 Apr 2011	25	3.8
Central Bank of the Republic of Uzbekistan	19 Apr 2011	0.7	0.11
Bank of Mongolia	*19 Apr 2011*	*5*	*0.8*
	20 Mar 2012	10	1.6
National Bank of Kazakhstan	13 Jun 2011	7	1.1
Bank of Thailand	22 Dec 2011	70	11.1
State Bank of Pakistan	23 Dec 2011	10	1.6
Central Bank of the United Arab Emirates	17 Jan 2012	35	5.5
Central Bank of the Republic of Turkey	21 Feb 2012	10	1.6
Reserve Bank of Australia	22 Mar 2012	200	31.7
National Bank of Ukraine	26 Jun 2012	15	2.4
Banco Central do Brasil	26 Mar 2013	190	30.6
Bank of England	22 Jun 2013	200	32.6

Source: People's Bank of China.

a. The local currency bilateral agreements cover the years after 2008. The agreements shown in italics have been superseded by subsequent agreements between the People's Bank of China and the relevant countries. The dollar equivalents are calculated using the exchange rate on the date of each agreement. The total amount under the twenty open agreements as of June 2013 is about CNY2.2 trillion, or roughly US$360 billion based on the June 2013 exchange rate of CNY6.13 per dollar. A number of bilateral agreements signed before 2008, mostly under the Chiang Mai Initiative, are not included in this table. Many of those agreements are not in the local currencies of the relevant countries.

All these moves are modest in size but are symbolically important in signaling the shift in perception about the renminbi's stability and its future role in the international monetary system. The clamor on the part of so many countries—small and large, within and outside Asia—to develop bilateral financial arrangements with the PRC is striking.

One recent bilateral arrangement that is likely to shape finance in Asia is the pact that the PRC and Japan signed in December 2011 to promote the use of their currencies for bilateral trade and investment flows.[13] Trade between the two economies amounted to about US$300 billion in 2010, while bilateral investment flows are estimated to be less than US$100 billion. Assuming that all these transactions are currently settled in dollars but will eventually be settled in the two countries' currencies, the effect of switching from dollar-intermediated transactions would still be relatively modest at the global level.

Over time, the effects could be larger, especially because the decline in currency transaction costs and exchange rate uncertainty could boost trade and financial flows between the two countries. The PRC has also given permission for the Japan Bank for International Cooperation to issue a renminbi-denominated bond, while Japan has indicated that it will buy some PRC government bonds, presumably to add to its reserve portfolio. Again, these moves are more important symbolically than quantitatively, but they may be setting the stage for more significant developments as the PRC's capital account becomes more open.

Building Bridges to a Rising Power

Why are so many economies eager to sign currency swap lines with the PRC and even hold its currency as part of their reserve portfolios? This may be less a sign of the renminbi's inevitable march to global dominance than a low-cost bet on a likely outcome of a convertible and more widely accepted global currency. Equally important is the desire on the part of many economies to maintain a good economic relationship with the PRC in anticipation of its growing economic power.

Holding renminbi reserves may in effect be a simple way of trying to buy protection from the PRC, which in turn may be better motivated to provide help to a central bank that has helped the renminbi in its early stages of ascendance. The amounts may be small but the symbolism is hard to miss. Central banks around the world are preparing for a future in which the renminbi will start playing an increasingly prominent role in international finance and may ultimately become a reserve currency.

The Renminbi's Impact on the Asian and International Monetary Systems

Promoting the currency's international role is tied up with many complex domestic and geopolitical considerations. As with all of its policies, in this case as well the PRC is working simultaneously toward multiple objectives. For now the PRC will continue promoting the international use of the renminbi using Hong Kong, China as a platform. When the government on the mainland of the PRC determines that its financial markets are finally strong enough to allow for a more open

---

13. For details on the PRC-Japan agreement, see People's Bank of China, "Enhanced Cooperation for Financial Markets Development between PRC and Japan," press release, December 25, 2011.

capital account, promotion of Shanghai as an international financial center could take precedence, especially as that would fit better with the objective of domestic financial market development.

While using Hong Kong, China as the main staging ground for the internationalization of the renminbi, the PRC government is also working to promote competition among financial centers eager to engage in renminbi business. Regional and international financial centers such as Bangkok, London, Singapore, and Tokyo are all being given opportunities to engage in renminbi transactions. This competition is useful for Beijing to be able to continue its program of internationalizing the renminbi without the usual prerequisite of opening the capital account and providing more renminbi liquidity.

Over the next five years, the PRC is likely to have a more open capital account than it does today but with numerous administrative controls and regulations still in place. This will allow the renminbi to play an increasingly significant role in Asian as well as global trade and finance, but in a manner that allows the government to retain some control over capital flows.

Even with only gradual financial market development, the renminbi is likely to be included in the basket of currencies that constitute the IMF's SDR basket within the next four to five years. The prospect of the renminbi's inclusion in the SDR basket could be seen as a way for the IMF—and the international community that it represents—to exercise leverage over the PRC in internalizing the global repercussions of its domestic policies.

Although the renminbi is likely to become a significant reserve currency over the next decade, it is unlikely to challenge the dollar's dominance. There is still a huge gulf between the PRC and the United States in the availability of safe and liquid assets such as government bonds. The depth, breadth, and liquidity of U.S. financial markets will serve as a potent buffer against threats to the dollar's preeminent status. Rather than catching up to the United States by building up debt, the challenge for the PRC is to develop its other financial markets and increase the availability of high-quality renminbi-denominated assets.

Although the PRC's rapidly growing size and dynamism are enormous advantages that will help promote the international use of its currency, especially within the Asian region, its low level of financial market development is a major constraint on the pace at which the renminbi attains reserve currency status. Moreover, in the absence of an open capital account and free convertibility of the currency, it is unlikely that the renminbi will become a prominent reserve currency, let alone challenge the dollar's status as the leading one.

Will the Renminbi's Rise Add Stability to Regional and Global Finance?

Economic theory offers no clear guidance as to how many currencies would be best for a world economy that is becoming increasingly closely integrated. The existence of multiple currencies but with just one principal reserve currency has fueled a number of complications, such as persistent global current account imbalances, suggesting that this constellation may not be the optimal one for promoting the stability of the global financial system.[14]

If multiple reserve currencies are indeed desirable, how should one assess the prospects of other currencies being able to compete with the dollar? The history of the rise and fall of reserve currencies has some useful lessons, as discussed earlier. The key is for a country to have public institutions that are trusted by domestic and foreign investors, good economic policies, and well-developed financial markets. These are the relevant criteria that put a country's currency in a position to develop into a reserve currency.

The argument for a world with multiple reserve currencies in a stable competitive equilibrium might be obvious if the world economy were starting as a tabula rasa. However, the argument is far from clear-cut given the present state of financial markets and the level of international financial integration. Events during the financial crisis present a counterargument to the notion that having more reserve currencies is better.

The dollar's dominance allowed the Federal Reserve to act as a credible global lender of last resort, a role that few other central banks are capable of playing. However, there is a risk of confusing cause and effect here. One of the reasons the world was in search of dollar liquidity during the crisis is that many global banks had sought large amounts of cheap dollar funding to finance their worldwide operations. U.S. monetary conditions, which led to an aggressive search for yield through financial innovations, and the fertile ground provided by U.S. financial markets for such sophistry were important elements in making many global banks so dependent on dollar liquidity.

This discussion suggests that the renminbi's rising prominence as an alternative to the dollar could add to the stability of the regional and international financial systems. This in turn requires that the PRC's macroeconomic policies and financial market development and regulation be conducive to the PRC's own macroeconomic and financial stability. This favorable outcome will also depend on whether the domestic financial markets and institutional development allow the renminbi to become a credible safe-haven currency. Moreover, as long as the PRC continues to itself demand safe assets through its foreign exchange market interventions, it will not be in a position to become a net supplier of safe assets to the rest of the world.

Summary and Conclusion

The renminbi's prospects as a global currency will ultimately be shaped by broader domestic policies, especially those related to financial market development,

---

14. The discussion in this section draws on Prasad (2014).

exchange rate flexibility, and capital account liberalization. As the country's financial markets become more developed and private investors increase the international diversification of their portfolios, these shifts in the PRC's outward investment patterns are likely to become more pronounced. Thus, the various policy reforms that are needed to support the international role of the renminbi could also create significant changes in the PRC's economy and the patterns of its capital inflows and outflows.[15]

Given its size and economic clout, the PRC is adopting a unique approach to the renminbi's role in the global monetary system. As with virtually all other major reforms, the PRC is striking out on its own path to a more open capital account. This is likely to involve removing explicit controls even while attempting to exercise "soft" control over inflows and outflows through administrative and other measures. Over the next five years, the PRC will have a more open capital account than it does today, but with numerous administrative controls and regulations still in place. This will allow the renminbi to play an increasingly significant role in global trade and finance, but in a manner that allows the government to retain some control over capital flows.

Indeed, as illustrated earlier, the renminbi is beginning to play a role in international trade transactions and also starting to appear in the reserve portfolios of certain emerging-market central banks. These shifts, at present more symbolic than substantive, will develop critical mass over time; they have the potential to start transforming the global monetary system.

Liberalization of outflows would not only reduce reserve accumulation but also generate more collateral benefits. It would provide Chinese households with opportunities to diversify their savings portfolios internationally and stimulate domestic financial reforms by creating competition for domestic banks that currently have a captive domestic source of funds. Initiatives to encourage corporate outflows have focused on large state-owned firms and a concentrated set of sectors such as natural resources. For the renminbi to take on a more international role, outflows of foreign direct investment should involve more participation from the private sector.

In this context the issue of sequencing becomes complicated. Absent financial market development, the benefits of capital account opening may be limited even if the risks are low, as in the case of the PRC. As noted earlier, in principle residents can take the equivalent of US$50,000 out of the country each year, but the absence of well-developed securities markets makes it difficult for most households to take advantage of these opportunities to pursue the international diversification of their savings portfolios.

---

15. Prasad (2009) argues that capital account opening, especially if accompanied by greater exchange rate flexibility, could also strengthen the PRC's domestic economic structure. It would facilitate financial sector reforms, allowing for a rebalancing of growth away from reliance on exports and investment-driven growth to a more balanced model of growth, with higher private consumption. Also see Kose and others (2009) on the indirect benefits of capital account liberalization.

In this context, the liberalization of inflows is an important part of the overall picture. This liberalization would allow foreign investors to play a role in developing and deepening the PRC's financial markets. Liberalizing portfolio equity inflows typically helps improve liquidity in the domestic equity markets of emerging economies. This, along with the entry of foreign banks, would increase competition in the banking sector, which in turn would be beneficial for private savers and borrowers. Other segments of the PRC's finance sector, including the insurance sector, have been dependent on capital controls and other entry restrictions to stay competitive. These segments will face greater competition with more open inflows. With effective regulation, this could lead to significant efficiency gains.

Capital account liberalization could also have broader benefits. For instance, an open capital account would catalyze progress toward the PRC's objective of making Shanghai an international financial center.

An interesting issue is whether there is a policy goal short of full capital account convertibility that provides a better risk-benefit trade-off. Yam (2011) has argued that the long-term objective for the PRC ought to be full capital account convertibility, which he defines as relaxation of capital controls but maintenance of "soft" controls in the form of registration and reporting requirements for regulatory purposes. He draws a careful distinction between this and an entirely unfettered capital-flow regime, referred to as free capital account convertibility. This is a subtle but important distinction that has resonated well with the PRC leadership, given that by this definition full convertibility provides a path to an open capital account without entirely ceding control to market forces.

To summarize, the renminbi is already well on its way to becoming a widely used currency in international trade and finance. It is likely that the renminbi will become a competitive reserve currency within the next decade, eroding but not displacing the dollar's dominance.

References

Angeloni, Ignazio, Agnès Bénassy-Quéré, Benjamin Carton, Zsolt Darvas, Christophe Destais, Jean Pisani-Ferry, André Sapir, and Shahin Vallée. 2011. "Global Currencies for Tomorrow: A European Perspective." CEPII Research Report. Paris: CEPII.

Chamon, Marcos, and Eswar S. Prasad. 2010. "Why Are Saving Rates of Urban Households in China Rising?" *American Economic Journal: Macroeconomics* 2, no. 1: 93–130.

Chamon, Marcos, Kai Liu, and Eswar S. Prasad. 2010. "Income Uncertainty and Household Savings in China." NBER Working Paper 16565. Cambridge, Mass.: National Bureau of Economic Research.

Chen, Hongyi, Wensheng Peng, and Chang Shu. 2009. "The Potential of the Renminbi as an International Currency." BIS Asian Research Program Research Papers. Basel: Bank for International Settlements.

Chinn, Menzie, and Jeffrey A. Frankel. 2007. "Will the Euro Eventually Surpass the Dollar as Leading International Reserve Currency?" In *G7 Current Account Imbalances: Sustainability and Adjustment,* edited by Richard Clarida, pp. 283–338. University of Chicago Press.

———. 2008. "Why the Euro Will Rival the Dollar." *International Finance* 11, no. 1: 49–73.

Dobson, Wendy, and Paul R. Masson. 2009. "Will the Renminbi Become a World Currency?" *China Economic Review* 20, no. 1: 124–35.

Eichengreen, Barry. 2011. "The Renminbi as an International Currency." Unpublished paper. University of California, Berkeley.

Eichengreen, Barry, and Marc Flandreau. 2009. "The Rise and Fall of the Dollar, or When Did the Dollar Overtake Sterling as the Leading Reserve Currency?" *European Review of Economic History* 13: 377–411.

European Central Bank. 2013. "The International Role of the Euro." Report. Frankfurt: European Central Bank, July.

Forbes, Kristin. 2009. "Financial Deepening and Global Currency Usage." In *The Euro at Ten: The Next Global Currency?*, edited by Jean Pisani-Ferry and Adam Posen, pp. 41–52. Washington: Peterson Institute of International Economics.

Frankel, Jeffrey. 2005. "On the Renminbi: The Choice between Adjustment under a Fixed Exchange Rate and Adjustment under a Flexible Rate." NBER Working Paper 11274. Cambridge, Mass.: National Bureau of Economic Research.

———. 2011. "Historical Precedents for the Internationalization of the RMB." CGS/IIGG Working Paper. New York: Council on Foreign Relations Press (link to download paper at www.cfr.org/china/historical-precedents-internationalization-rmb/p26293).

Goodfriend, Marvin, and Eswar S. Prasad. 2007. "A Framework for Independent Monetary Policy in China." *CESifo Economic Studies* 53, no. 1: 2–41.

International Monetary Fund. 2010. "IMF Executive Board Completes the 2010 Review of SDR Valuation." IMF Public Information Notice 10/149. Washington: International Monetary Fund, November 17.

———. 2011a. "Criteria for Broadening the SDR Currency Basket." IMF Policy Paper. Washington: International Monetary Fund, September 23.

———. 2011b. "IMF Executive Board Discusses Criteria for Broadening the SDR Currency Basket." IMF Public Information Notice 11/137. Washington: International Monetary Fund, November 11.

Kose, M. Ayhan, Eswar S. Prasad, Kenneth Rogoff, and Shang-Jin Wei. 2009. "Financial Globalization: A Reappraisal." *IMF Staff Papers* 56, no. 1: 8–62.

Kroeber, Arthur. 2011. "The Chinese Yuan Grows Up Slowly: Fact and Fiction about China's Currency Internationalization." Policy paper. Washington: New America Foundation.

Lardy, Nicholas R. 2011. *Sustaining China's Growth after the Global Financial Crisis*. Washington: Peterson Institute for International Economics.

Lardy, Nicholas R., and Patrick Douglass. 2011. "Capital Account Liberalization and the Role of the Renminbi." Working Paper 11-6. Washington: Peterson Institute for International Economics.

Obstfeld, Maurice. 2011. "The SDR as an International Reserve Asset: What Future?" Unpublished paper. University of California, Berkeley, Department of Economics, March 27 (http://eml.berkeley.edu/~obstfeld/SDR_Obstfeld.pdf).

Prasad, Eswar S. 2009. "Is China's Growth Miracle Built to Last?" *China Economic Review* 20, no. 1: 103–23.

———. 2011. "Rebalancing Growth in Asia." *International Finance* 14, no. 1: 27–66.

———. 2014. *The Dollar Trap: How the U.S. Dollar Tightened Its Grip on Global Finance*. Princeton University Press.

Prasad, Eswar S., and Raghuram G. Rajan. 2005. "Controlled Capital Account Liberalization: A Proposal." IMF Policy Discussion Paper 05/7. Washington: International Monetary Fund.

———. 2006. "Modernizing China's Growth Paradigm." *American Economic Review* 96, no. 2: 331–36.

———. 2008. "A Pragmatic Approach to Capital Account Liberalization." *Journal of Economic Perspectives* 22, no. 3: 149–72.

Prasad, Eswar S., and Lei Ye. 2012. *The Renminbi's Role in the Global Monetary System.* Brookings Report. Wahsington, D.C.: Brookings Institution.

Prasad, Eswar S., Thomas Rumbaugh, and Qing Wang. 2005. "Putting the Cart before the Horse? Capital Account Liberalization and Exchange Rate Flexibility in China." IMF Policy Discussion Paper 05/1. Washington: International Monetary Fund.

Rosen, Daniel H., and Thilo Hanemann. 2009. "China's Changing Outbound Foreign Direct Investment Profile: Drivers and Policy Implications." Policy Brief 09-14. Washington: Peterson Institute for International Economics.

Scissors, David. 2011. "Chinese Outward Investment: More Opportunity than Danger." Heritage Foundation Backgrounder 2579. Washington: Heritage Foundation.

Subramanian, Arvind. 2011. *Eclipse: Living in the Shadow of China's Economic Dominance.* Washington: Institute of International Economics.

Tavlas, George. 1990. "On the International Use of Currencies: The Case of the Deutsche Mark." IMF Working Paper 90/3. Washington: International Monetary Fund, January.

Yam, Joseph. 2011. "A Safe Approach to Convertibility for the Renminbi." Working Paper 5. Hong Kong, China: Chinese University of Hong Kong, Institute for Global Economics and Finance.

Yu, Yongding. 2012. "Revisiting the Internationalization of the Yuan." ADBI Working Paper Series 366. Tokyo: Asian Development Bank Institute.

Zhou, Xiaochuan. 2009. "Reform the International Monetary System." Beijing: People's Bank of China.

5

The Rise of the Redback: Evaluating the Prospects for Renminbi Use in Invoicing

HIRO ITO AND MENZIE CHINN

One of the key puzzles in international finance is why certain currencies become international currencies. "International currency" status confers both substantial privileges and burdens, although conventional wisdom places greater weight on the former. But what, exactly, is an international currency? Table 5-1 summarizes the various functions of an international currency.

The table shows that there are several dimensions to consider in terms of the degree to which a currency fulfills the characterization of being international. Money has many roles, of relevance to different actors. Clearly, an international currency can fill some roles of money while not fulfilling others.

With the rapid economic ascent of the People's Republic of China (PRC)—its sheer economic size and outsized role in trade flows—it is entirely natural that questions should arise regarding the evolution of the PRC's currency, the renminbi (RMB). The RMB's potential for internationalization has been actively debated, but the issue has remained largely speculative, because the RMB remained unconvertible, and capital controls were in place. Recently, however, policy declarations and measures aimed at increasing the use of the RMB in trade invoicing and other transactions have led to a significant increase in its use in international markets, making the prospects for an internationalized RMB look increasingly less aspirational and more concrete.

Still, progress is uneven, with current initiatives focused on the medium-of-exchange dimension. As of the last quarter of 2012, 14 percent of the PRC's trade

Table 5-1. *Roles of an International Currency*

Function of money	Governments	Private actors
Store of value	International reserve holdings	Currency substitution (private dollarization)
Medium of exchange	Vehicle currency for foreign exchange intervention	Invoicing trade and financial transactions
Unit of account	Anchor for pegging local currency	Denominating trade and financial transactions

Source: Adapted from Kenen (1983).

was settled in yuan—a significant increase from zero in 2009. As of the beginning of 2013, $1.9 billion of yuan-denominated bonds, so-called dim sum bonds, were in circulation. In 2012, the PRC accounted for 27 percent of the world's money supply, larger than its GDP (in purchasing price parity) share of 8 percent. The PRC's borders are no longer sealed.

In contrast, in the dimension of use as a store of value, the rise of the RMB, sometimes called the "redback," is a potential challenge to the current international monetary system, which is heavily dependent on the greenback—the U.S. dollar. About 60 percent of global foreign exchange reserves are held in U.S. dollars, although the United States accounts for 20 percent of global output, 11 percent of trade, and 30 percent of financial assets trade.

Many argue that such a dollar-centric international monetary system creates an unstable environment for the world economy by providing the United States with privileged access to funds ("exorbitant privilege"), while constraining developing economies with the opposite effect ("original sin," the inability to issue sovereign debt in their own currency). As Eichengreen (2011) argues, a new international monetary system with multiple reserve currencies—the dollar, the euro, and the RMB—might be more stable than the current unipolar system. That is because the loss of exorbitant privilege by the United States would discipline the nation's public finance.

The conventional wisdom holds that the arrival of such a multipolar international currency system is a long way off, although there are dissenters. Since the RMB is the only viable competitor among emerging market economies (Chinn 2012), the issue of internationalization of the RMB is now a global issue. Nonetheless, because most observers believe that major reserve currency status for the RMB is a long way off, we focus here particularly on the private actor role of an international reserve currency: its use in trade invoicing.[1]

Whether and how fast the RMB will become an international currency depends on some key points. First, it depends on how soon and in what ways the PRC

---

1. Use of the RMB seems to have progressed more rapidly as an anchor, either formally or informally, than it has along other dimensions. See Subramanian and Kessler (2012) and, for a critique, Spencer (2013).

implements two policies, allowing greater market determination of the value of the RMB and liberalizing transactions of capital across its borders. The value of the currency needs to be able to fluctuate freely so that international investors can read signals from the market and consider portfolio strategy accordingly. Investors also need to be able to find it easy to acquire or redeem yuan-denominated bonds at their convenience in terms of both time and location. Fulfillment of both of these conditions appears to be far off.

The PRC has been extremely cautious in implementing both external and internal financial liberalization.[2] The global financial crisis of 2008 and the euro debt crisis that followed have naturally deepened reservations regarding the wisdom of financial liberalization by emphasizing the potential short-term costs of financial liberalization over the long-term gains (Kaminsky and Schmukler 2002). However, observers have also long pointed out the high degree of financial repression and the potential risk of financial losses associated with gross inefficiencies in the current system, all of which may be mitigated by financial liberalization. Further capital account liberalization is an inevitable policy choice for the PRC in the medium run in light of the way the country's financial system, long dominated by state-owned financial institutions and the government, impedes smooth transformation of saving to productive investment. The question is how orderly liberalization can proceed such that the tumultuous fate of other emerging market economies is avoided.

Thus, one important key to the RMB becoming an international currency hinges upon the PRC's commitment to liberalizing capital account transactions, though its pace may not satisfy people both inside and outside the country.[3] In this chapter we are interested in exploring the relationship between the context of the inevitable path of financial globalization and the RMB's potential path in becoming an international currency.

Against this backdrop, we investigate how the PRC's efforts to liberalize its capital account transactions would affect the use of the RMB for invoicing in international trade. An increased use of a currency as an invoicing currency is not a sufficient condition for it to become an international currency. In fact, despite the rapid growth of the RMB's use in trade in the last few years, the share of the RMB in average daily foreign exchange turnover was only around 2 percent as of April 2013.[4] (The share of the RMB among the reserve currencies is essentially zero.)

We focus on the impact of the PRC's financial liberalization on the use of the RMB in invoicing for international trade for two reasons. First, the data for currency

2. See Huang, Wang, and Lin (2013) and Hung (2009), among others.

3. Thus far, the PRC has attempted to foster use of the RMB via development of offshore markets in the yuan (sometimes referred to as the CNH).

4. The Bank for International Settlements Triennial Central Bank Survey for 2013 (Bank for International Settlements 2013) reports as preliminary results as of April 2013 that the share of the RMB in average daily foreign exchange turnover is 2.2 percent, rising from 0.9 percent as of 2010. The volume of RMB turnover soared from $34 billion in 2010 to $120 billion as of April 2013, becoming the ninth most actively traded currency in 2013.

invoicing for trade, although quite limited, are not as limited as the data for currency denomination for securities transactions, and therefore allow us to conduct a reasonable empirical analysis. Second, currency invoicing in trade is an important first step for a currency to become an international currency. Therefore, it is appropriate for us to forecast for the foreseeable future with more reasonable scenario analysis.

In this chapter we first survey the literature regarding capital account liberalization and openness, and its impact on reserve holding, asset denomination, and currency invoicing in international trade. We then empirically investigate the determinants of currency invoicing with special focus on capital account liberalization. Armed with estimates of the important relationships, we investigate the various scenarios for RMB use in currency invoicing based upon differing rates of progress in capital account liberalization.

We attempt to answer the following questions:

1. What factors, including capital account liberalization, affect the use of currencies in terms of invoicing in international trade?

2. How does the RMB's recent experience differ from that of other currencies in terms of their use for invoicing exports?

3. How would foreseeable capital account liberalization implemented by the PRC affect the level of use of the RMB in international trade?

4. What can we expect for the internationalization of the RMB once the PRC furthers financial liberalization efforts? Would the RMB proceed smoothly toward the status of international currency, along other dimensions?

Theory and Evidence on the Link between Capital Account Openness and the Use of a Currency in International Financial Markets

Capital Account Openness and Its Impact on Reserve Holding, Asset Denomination

The literature on developed country reserve currencies suggests that the increasing relative economic mass of key emerging market economies will lead to a greater role for their respective currencies. However, if previous empirical findings are relevant, the key factor will not be GDP alone but rather, financial market development and openness to the rest of the world (Chinn and Frankel 2007, 2008).

Financial development involves the creation of institutions that are able to funnel large amounts of capital from savers to borrowers in an efficient manner. Empirical work suggests that institutional development (rule of law, a low degree of corruption) as well as having open capital markets is important (Chinn and Ito 2006). To the extent that the largest emerging-market countries with currencies that are candidates for reserve status have relatively closed and underdeveloped financial markets, the path forward is unclear.

As long as countries restrict capital flows in a heavy-handed fashion and limit convertibility, use of their respective currencies in international transactions, including financial transactions, is unlikely to increase rapidly. Financial repression—a state where financial markets do not function at their full capacities because of government's active interventions and regulatory controls—in a currency's issuer country would also limit the desirability of the currency in international transactions.

To make these points concrete, suppose that many of the reserves are held in the form of government bonds. If it is difficult to purchase and sell government bonds across borders (and especially if there is no secondary market for the bonds), and agents are worried about the default risk associated with the bonds, then the currency those government bonds are denominated in will not be a good candidate for a reserve currency.

The nature of policy preferences is key to determining the pace of developments. In particular, policymaking officials will determine when and how much they are willing to surrender the policy autonomy associated with capital controls and repressed financial systems in favor a more internationalized currency.[5]

Theory and Evidence of Trade Invoicing

The literature on trade invoicing goes back to the 1970s when the eurodollar markets started appearing and cross-border capital transactions became more active in the advanced economies despite tight capital controls under the Bretton Woods system. Especially in Europe, the absolute dominance of the dollar in international trade and finance ended, and the pound sterling, the French franc, and the deutsche mark started becoming the major currencies used in invoicing or for settling international trade transactions.

Grassman (1973) found that a much larger portion of Swedish exports is invoiced in Swedish kronor than are imports, and argued that exporters tended to invoice in their own currency because exporters usually have more bargaining power (so-called Grassman's law). Krugman (1984) supported this idea but argued that the relative sizes of trading partners matter: when an importer is larger than an exporter, Grassman's law does not apply.

As the Bretton Woods system broke down in 1973, the uncertainty and the risk arising from exchange rate movements became issues to consider in determining which currency to use for invoicing international trade transactions. Which to use

---

5. In the context of the "impossible trinity" or the "trilemma," even if a country removes capital controls, it could still retain monetary autonomy as long as it allows flexible movements in its currency's exchange rates (Aizenman, Chinn, and Ito 2013; Obstfeld, Shambaugh, and Taylor 2005). However, if its currency becomes international, its use outside its borders increases, which means the amount of currency out of the reach of the monetary authority increases and the country loses its grip on monetary policy—as occurred with the U.S. dollar (Goldberg 2010).

for trade invoicing essentially comes down to producer currency pricing, pricing a product in the producer's currency, versus "pricing to the market," pricing a product in the local currency (Krugman 1987; Dornbusch 1987). This is basically a question of whether to avoid demand uncertainty or price uncertainty. Producers who price their products in their home country's currency do not face any price uncertainty, but the demand for the product could be uncertain since the price is subject to exchange rate fluctuations. Conversely, if they price their products in the local currency of the export destination, demand uncertainty can be minimized but the price or the revenue of the product can be uncertain.

Thus, not only bargaining power but also exchange rate volatility matters for trade invoicing. The latter also raises the issue of transaction costs of a currency as another factor that affects the choice of invoicing currency. McKinnon (1979) focused on the impact of product differentiation on the choice of invoicing currency. He argued that exporters from industrialized European countries tended to price their products in their home countries because they tended to export differentiated manufactured goods. Facing the downward demand curve, the producers of differentiated goods can exercise more market power, which allows them to avoid bearing the exchange rate risk. Conversely, exporters of relatively homogeneous primary goods, who are price takers in the market (market participants who have no control over the price) tend not to price in their home currency. In such a market, currencies with low transaction costs tend to be preferred. Given the tradition and the depth of the dollar's market, the dollar is usually a dominant vehicle currency in the commodity markets.

Goldberg and Tille (2008) argued in a seminal paper that when demand elasticity is high or there are competitive substitutes in the export destination market, exporters will opt for pricing in the currency used by competitors so that they can limit the fluctuations of their prices relative to those of the competitors' goods—the so-called "coalescing effect." Bacchetta and Van Wincoop (2005) used a general equilibrium model and showed that exporters who have higher market shares of the export market or who produce more differentiated products tend to invoice in their own currency.

Although microeconomic factors such as those just discussed affect the choice of invoicing currency, researchers have also argued that the choice of invoicing currency can be affected by "inertia." Krugman (1980) argued that once a currency is established as the invoicing currency, it becomes difficult for users to switch to another currency—more so if the currency is widely used and liquid.[6] Rey (2001) examined this issue theoretically, and argued that if more than one currency were used in invoicing, it would yield higher transaction costs, which would be passed

---

6. Chinn and Frankel (2007, 2008) point to the inertia that affects the choice of reserve currencies. However, they also argue that there is a "tipping point," or threshold, above which the share of a currency in central banks' reserves would rise rapidly due to externality.

on to export prices. Hence, if a particular currency is dominantly used, as the market size gets bigger the transaction costs are lowered. Such a "thick market externality" leads the currencies of countries with higher levels of trade volumes and openness to be chosen as invoicing currencies. Similarly, Bacchetta and Van Wincoop (2005) predicted that the currency formed in a monetary union should be used more extensively than the sum of the currencies it replaces because of its enlarged market share.

The "thick market externality" or the inertia in the choice of currency invoicing may not be a sufficient condition for major currencies such as the U.S. dollar to be dominantly used in international trade. The United States, the issuer of the dollar, provides vast, liquid, and deep financial markets, which significantly help reduce the transaction costs of the currency and increase the liquidity and usability of the dollar. In other words, the depth and openness of financial markets affect the transaction costs associated with use of the currency and thus affect the choice of the invoicing currency. As Caballero, Farhi, and Gourinchas (2008), Chinn and Ito (2007), and Chinn, Eichengreen, and Ito (2011) show, the level of financial development and the extent of financial openness affect current account balances, and countries with deeper and more open financial markets tend to run a worsened current account balance or a deficit. Hence, a country's financial development and openness can affect the availability and usability of its own currency abroad, and therefore the transaction costs of the currency. Goldberg and Tille (2008), however, using data on the bid–ask spread for each sample country's currency relative to the U.S. dollar, find only a moderate role for transaction costs in the foreign exchange markets. Kamps (2006) finds that countries with forward exchange markets tend to invoice more in their home currencies.

The empirical literature on the choice of currency for trade invoicing is much thinner than the theoretical literature, owing to limited data availability. Few countries disclose currency invoicing data.[7] Hence, most empirical studies on currency invoicing have focused on individual countries, for example, Donnenfeld and Haug (2003) for Canada, Wilander (2004) for Sweden, Ligthart and Werner (2012) for Norway, Ito and others (2010) for Japan, and Da Silva (2004) for the Netherlands. Goldberg and Tille (2008) and Kamps (2006) are the exceptions, having conducted cross-country analysis on the determinants of trade invoicing, although the scope of country coverage tends to be small and highly unbalanced.[8]

---

7. Exceptions are the European Union and several Asian countries. The ECB has been reporting the share of euro use in trade invoicing for euro and non-euro countries since the early 2000s, and the currency share data are available in Eurostat. Japan, Thailand, and Indonesia have been relatively consistent in reporting currency share data for the country's trade. See table 5A-1 for sources of our trade invoicing data.

8. For further literature reviews, see Goldberg and Tille (2008), Kamps (2006), Auboin (2012), Maziad and others (2011), and European Central Bank (2005).

Empirical Analysis of Major Currencies' Shares of Trade Invoicing

We conduct panel data analysis to examine the determinants of export invoicing while focusing on the impact of financial liberalization. Using our data set, we first discuss the general trend of currencies used for trade invoicing. Then we present the results of our panel data analysis and robustness checks.

Currency Shares in Trade Invoicing: Stylized Facts

Although it is clear that the U.S. dollar has been dominant in trade invoicing, a closer look at individual countries' experiences suggests that the countries' behavior of choosing currencies for trade invoicing is rather heterogeneous. In this section we introduce our data set on the shares of major currencies used for trade invoicing, then discuss the general trends of the use of major currencies in trade invoicing.

THE AUGMENTED CURRENCY INVOICING DATA SET. In this study we update and expand the data set constructed by Goldberg and Tille (2008) and Kamps (2006), relying on data provided on the websites of central banks and other government agencies, as well as other past and more recent studies that looked into the issue of trade invoicing (see table 5A-1 in the appendix to this chapter). Although a large portion of our data set relies on the data compiled by Kamps (2006), the coverage of currency shares in export and import invoicing is considerably expanded, especially with respect to the use of the euro. Hence, our analysis is based on a longer, more complete time series than the two earlier data sets.

Regarding our data sets, please note: Although our focus is on analyzing the determinants of currency use for trade invoicing, data limitations force us to rely on a data set that includes both invoicing and settlement currencies. Our data set on the shares of invoicing currencies for exports and imports—the U.S. dollar, the euro, and the domestic currencies—mixes data on currencies used for both invoicing and settlements for trade transactions. Strictly speaking, the currency for trade invoicing and that for actual settlements may differ. However, reporting government agencies often do not make it clear whether they are reporting the currency of invoicing or settlement. Although, as Page (1977, 1981) finds, the differences in the invoicing or settlement currencies is sometimes negligible, for a newly internationalized currency such as the RMB the difference can be large. In fact, the PRC only publishes the data on RMB settlements, not invoicing. Yu (2012) argues that notwithstanding the growth in the amount of RMB use in settlements for the PRC's imports, a large bulk of the imports settled in RMB is initially invoiced in dollars. This scheme reflects the persistent appreciation expectations for the RMB. Conceptually, in order to become an international currency, a candidate currency should be used for trade invoicing rather than settlements. Here we must bear in mind that the PRC's data on settlements may overstate the actual use of the currency as an invoicing currency. We use the phrases "currency for invoicing" and "currency for trade settlements" interchangeably.

Our data set covers fifty countries, including the PRC, but with a varying extent of coverage depending on the type of invoiced currency and whether the data are for exports or imports. For example, Japan's data go back to 1969 for both exports and imports, but for some countries data are available for only a single year or a single currency (often the U.S. dollar or the euro).[9]

STYLIZED FACTS. Using our augmented and updated data set on trade invoicing, we now discuss how the choice of currency for trade invoicing has changed over time and differs among countries or regions.

Figure 5-1, showing the shares of the use of the U.S. dollar in export invoicing for individual countries compared to the shares of the countries' exports to the United States in the countries' total exports, makes it clear that the dollar retains a dominant role. If the U.S. dollar did not play a dominant role or the role of the vehicle currency, we would expect the dollar invoicing share in export transactions of countries to be proportional to the share of the United States as a destination of countries' exports. In fact, the figure clearly shows that countries invoice their exports in dollars much more than proportionally to the share of their exports to the United States.

Figure 5-2 shows the shares of exports invoiced in individual countries' home currencies against the shares of their exports in the world's total exports. We can see that the PRC, which provides about 10 percent of the world's exports, is an outlier given its low level of export invoicing with its home currency. Excluding the PRC, there is a moderate positive correlation between the shares of exports invoiced in the home currency and the shares of exports in the world exports. Although the other two large exporters, Germany and Japan, also appear to be off the fitted line, the PRC's deviation dwarfs the other deviations, indicating that the level of home currency invoicing is much lower than would be expected from its share in the world's exports.

Figures 5-3 and 5-4 further illustrate the dominant role of the dollar in trade invoicing. These two figures show the sample-average shares of the dollar, the euro, and the home country's currency for the invoicing of exports (figure 5-3) and

9. Goldberg and Tille (2008) cover twenty-five countries, whereas Kamps (2006) expands the former data set and covers forty-two countries. Our data set updates the share of euro invoicing in both exports and imports to 2012, using a series of the European Central Bank's reports (2005, 2007–12) on the role of the euro and Eurostat. We also augment the data set with longer time series for Australia (2000–03, 2006–11), Indonesia (1991–2012), the Republic of Korea (1976–2005), Thailand (1993–2012), and Japan (1969–2012), as well as data from earlier years (1970s) for several advanced economies using earlier papers such as Scharrer (1981), Tavlas (1993), Tavlas and Ozeki (1992), Magee and Rao (1980), and Page (1977). For more details see table 5A-1.

Figure 5-1. *U.S. Dollar as the Vehicle Currency, 2007–11*

Exports to the United States

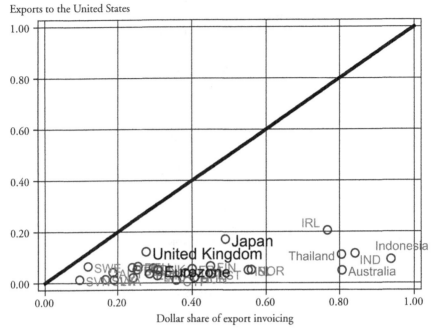

Dollar share of export invoicing

Source: Authors' calculations; see table 5A-1 in the appendix for data sources.

imports (figure 5-4).[10] Note that when calculating the share of the U.S. dollar in trade invoicing, we do not include the use of the U.S. dollar by the United States but include it in the share of the home currency. Similarly, the euro share does not include the use of the euro by the eurozone countries; it is included in the share of the home currency.[11]

In both export and import transactions, the U.S. dollar has the highest share, although it was on a declining trend until the mid-2000s. The recent rise in the dollar share may reflect the effects of the global financial crisis and the euro debt crisis. In both instances, there was "flight to quality," which benefited dollar-denominated assets and led to more dollar invoicing in international trade. Conversely, the share of the euro by non-eurozone countries in both export and import transactions was on a steadily rising trend until the mid-2000s, followed by a decline in the share in the last years of the sample period.[12] The use of the home currency has been increasing for both exports and imports, but it mainly reflects

10. Because the data set is highly unbalanced, annual averages of the currency shares are highly subject to data availability. To mitigate this, we report five-year averages of the currency shares.

11. These rules are applied throughout the chapter, including the estimation exercises.

12. The euro share before the introduction of the euro in 1999 reflects the sum of the uses of the "legacy currencies" before they were replaced by the euro (Kamps 2006).

Figure 5-2. *Home Currencies' Shares of Export Invoicing versus Home Countries'*
Shares of Exports in the World's Total, 2007–11

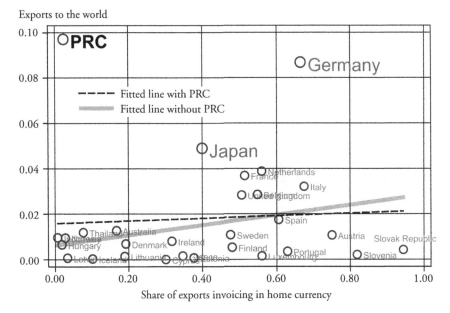

Source: Authors' calculations; see table 5A-1 for data sources.

the use of the euro by the eurozone countries. In general, we see evidence of the operation of Grassman's law (Grassman 1973), mentioned earlier: the share of home currency invoicing is higher for exports than for imports.

The extent of reliance on the dollar as a major invoicing currency seems to differ across regions. Figure 5-5 illustrates the shares of currencies in export invoicing for the EU countries.[13] For this group of countries, the euro is the most commonly invoiced currency. Considering that the home currency in the figure also includes the use of the euro by the euro member countries, the share of the euro invoicing overall is even higher. The share of the U.S. dollar for this group of countries was stable at around 30 to 35 percent in the sample period.

Figure 5-6 shows the shares of invoicing currencies for a selection of Asian and Pacific countries, excluding Japan. It is clear that the countries in this region have relied heavily on the U.S. dollar as the vehicle currency. The main cause for the high reliance on the dollar is the regional supply chain network that primarily uses the U.S. dollar as the currency for transactions. Also, the main export market for products from the Asian supply chain is the United States. As Goldberg and Tille

13. The figure shows the averages of currency shares for the current twenty-seven EU countries as of 2014, regardless of the year of accession to the union. Hence, strictly speaking, the average is calculated for the EU member countries and former candidate countries.

Figure 5-3. *Average Shares of the Dollar, the Euro, and Home Currencies in Export Invoicing*

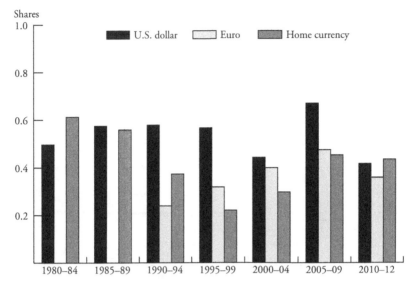

Source: Authors' calculations; see table 5A-1 for data sources.

Figure 5-4. *Average Shares of the Dollar, the Euro, and Home Currencies in Import Invoicing*ᵃ

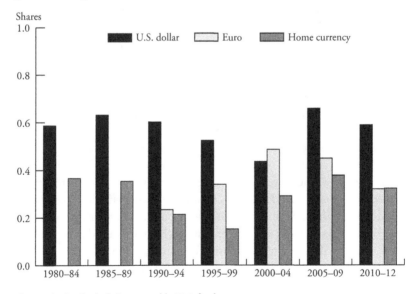

Source: Authors' calculations; see table 5A-1 for data sources.

a. The use of the U.S. dollar in trade invoicing by the United States is not included in the U.S. dollar average share, but it is included in the home currency's share. Similarly, the use of the euro by the eurozone countries is not included in the euro's share, but is included in the home currency's share.

Figure 5-5. *Average Shares of the Dollar, the Euro, and Home Currencies in Export Invoicing, European Union Countries*[a]

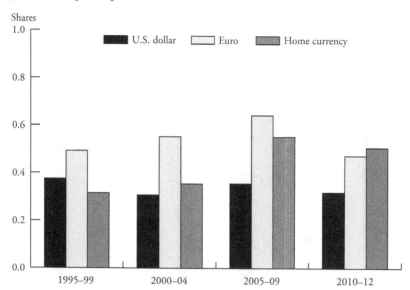

Source: Authors' calculations; see table 5A-1 for data sources.

a. The countries in the European Union subsample are Austria, Belgium, Bulgaria, Cyprus, Czech Republic, Denmark, Estonia, Finland, France, Germany, Greece, Hungary, Iceland, Italy, Latvia, Lithuania, Luxembourg, Malta, Netherlands, Poland, Portugal, Romania, Slovak Republic, Slovenia, Spain, Sweden, and the United Kingdom.

(2008) and Ito and others (2010) argue, firms tend to price to market, that is, invoice their exports in the importer's currency, the U.S. dollar, so as to protect their competitiveness in the destination market.[14] The Asian dollar bloc therefore stands as a big challenge to the PRC's ambitions for the RMB to become the regional international currency.[15]

We have only four years of observations for the PRC, but what we have reflects the country's financial liberalization policy. In the immediate aftermath of the global financial crisis of 2008, the PRC government became active in promoting RMB trade settlements, with the hope that firms would be able to reduce exchange rate risk if they could invoice trade transactions in yuan. The People's Bank of China (PBOC) prepared the environment for RMB settlements by signing currency swap agreements with countries. By the spring of 2013, the PBOC

14. Takagi (2009) argues that established practices of pricing and invoicing trade in the U.S. dollar in Asia hampered the internationalization efforts of the Republic of Korea's won, despite the country's increased presence as a major exporter.

15. We could also argue that given the indispensable role of the PRC in the Asian supply chain network, if the RMB could replace the dollar as the major invoicing currency in the Asian region, the use of the RMB could rise dramatically.

Figure 5-6. *Average Shares of the Dollar, the Euro, and Home Currencies in Export Invoicing, Asia and Pacific Countries (Excluding Japan)*[a]

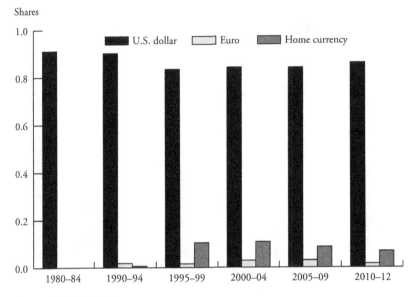

Shares

Source: Authors' calculations.
a. Australia, the PRC, India, Indonesia, the Republic of Korea, Malaysia, Pakistan, and Thailand.

had signed swap agreements with the monetary authorities of twenty countries and areas, for the total value of CNY1,936.2 billion ($317.9 billion).[16] In July 2009 the government started a policy of allowing several pilot firms to settle trades using the RMB through designated domestic banks and banks in offshore markets in Hong Kong, China. By fall 2013 the scope of the policy had been expanded to the national level, and banks in other economies (such as Singapore, the PRC, Japan, Australia, New Zealand, and Taipei,China) were allowed to deal with offshore RMB (that is, CNH) for trade settlements. As of the end of 2012, about 80 percent of RMB trade settlement was conducted through the offshore

16. The economies and areas the PRC signed currency-swap agreements with are as follows: the Republic of Korea (CNY180 billion in 2008, renewed to CNY360 billion in 2011); Hong Kong, China (CNY200 billion in 2008, renewed to CNY400 billion in 2011); Malaysia (CNY80 billion in 2009); Belarus (CNY20 billion in 2009); Indonesia (CNY100 billion in 2009); Argentina (CNY70 billion in 2009); Iceland (CNY3.5 billion in 2010); Singapore (CNY150 billion in 2010); New Zealand (CNY25 billion in 2011); Uzbekistan (CNY0.7 billion in 2011); Mongolia (CNY5 billion, later increased to CNY10 billion, in 2011), Kazakhstan (CNY7 billion in 2011); Thailand (CNY70 billion in 2011); Ukraine (CNY15 billion in 2012); Brazil (CNY190 billion in 2011); Pakistan (CNY10 billion in 2011); United Arab Emirates (CNY35 billion in 2012); Malaysia (CNY100 billion, later increased to CNY180 billion, in 2012); Turkey (CNY10 billion in 2012); and Australia (CNY200 billion in 2012). For more details on the PRC's swap agreements, see Garcia-Herreno and Xia (2013), Huang, Wang, and Fan (2013), and Yu (2013).

Figure 5-7. *Shares of Home Currency Invoicing for the Trade of Japan and the People's Republic of China*

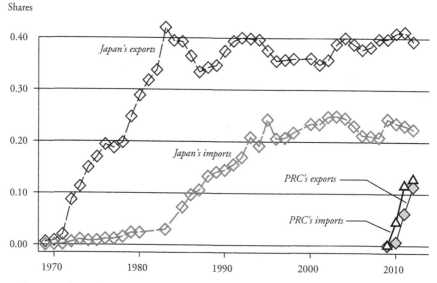

Source: Authors' calculations; see table 5A-1 for data sources.

market in Hong Kong, China, and other economies are eager to become offshore RMB markets.[17]

The data on RMB use for trade settlement reflect this short history of the liberalization of RMB trade settlement. As of the end of 2009, the first year of policy implementation, a mere 0.02 percent of total trade was settled in RMB. According to the People's Bank of China (2011 to 2013) the ratio only grew to 2.2 percent in 2010. In 2011 it started taking off; the share of RMB use in trade settlements rose to about 6.6 percent in 2011 and 8.4 percent in 2012.[18]

Let us look at the development of RMB trade settlement in a global context. In figure 5-7 we first compare the experience of RMB invoicing with that of a previous challenger for the international currency, the Japanese yen. As of the end of the 1960s, a few years after the currency became convertible in 1964, only 0.6 percent of Japan's exports were invoiced in yen, and essentially none of Japan's imports

17. Many authors have produced in-depth reviews and analyses of the PRC's efforts at financial liberalization and internationalization of the RMB, including Chen and Cheung (2011), Prasad and Ye (2012), Ito (2011), Subramanian and Kessler (2012), Huang, Wang, and Lin (2013), Vallée (2012), and Yu (2012, 2013).

18. According to the Society for Worldwide Interbank Financial Telecommunication (SWIFT), the percentage of RMB settlement in the PRC's trade was 10 percent in 2011 and 14 percent in the first quarter of 2012.

Figure 5-8. *Share of the U.S. Dollar, the Euro, and the Japanese Yen in Japan's Export Invoicing*

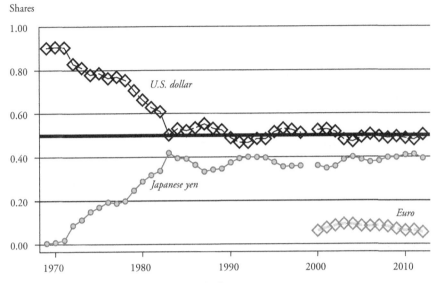

Source: Authors' calculations; see table 5A-1 for data sources.

were invoiced in yen. The share of yen invoicing for exports peaked in 1983, hitting 42 percent, although that of imports only reached 3 percent. Figures 5-8 and 5-9 show that since the mid-1980s the share of yen in export invoicing has hovered around 35 to 40 percent, and that of the U.S. dollar, around 50 percent. In contrast, the share of yen in import invoicing has stabilized at 20 to 25 percent; the U.S. dollar has maintained higher levels of around 70 percent. After all the discussions and initiatives regarding the internationalization of the yen, the currency has failed to become a dominant currency, even for the country's own trade.[19]

Figure 5-7 also illustrates the development of the ratio of RMB invoicing with respect to total exports and imports. The PBC only publishes the RMB settlement figures for total trade, so there is no breakdown for exports and imports. However, it also reports the ratios of RMB receipts to payments in international trade trans-

19. This is in sharp contrast with the German deutsche mark (DM). The share of DM invoicing for exports remained consistently around 80 percent for the entire 1980s and for imports increased from 43 percent in 1980 to 53 percent in 1988 (Tavlas 1993). Frankel (2011) explains that both Japan and West Germany were reluctant to internationalize their currencies when these currencies began to gain shares in the 1980s, because internationalization of the currencies might create appreciation pressure on the currencies and thus could hurt the international competitiveness of the countries' exporting sectors. In the 1990s Japan changed its policy stance and started promoting the internationalization of the yen. Soon after, however, the economy went into a long recession, which led the demand for the currency to fall.

Figure 5-9. *Share of the U.S. Dollar, the Euro, and the Japanese Yen in Japan's Import Invoicing*

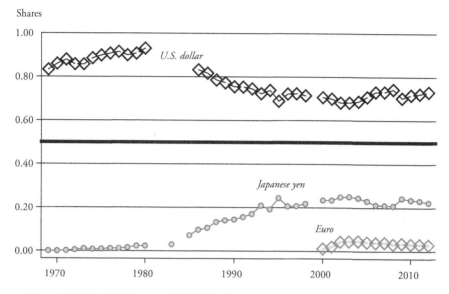

Source: Authors' calculations; see table 5A-1 for data sources.

actions. Using the ratios as well as the published total volumes of RMB trade settlements, we estimate the shares of RMB use for export and import settlements.[20]

Figure 5-7 shows a rapid rise in the share of RMB use for both export and import invoicing in recent years, even though the government only started to allow RMB invoicing in 2009. Whereas the share of the yen for exports has always been higher than that for imports, consistent with Grassman's law, the RMB has had an opposite experience. According to the PBOC (People's Bank of China 2011), the ratio of the RMB receipts to payments was 1:5.5 in 2010, though it improved to 1:1.7 in 2011. This lopsidedness reflects the government's intention to increase the use of the RMB overseas.

Another, more recent challenger as an international currency is the euro. Figure 5-10 shows that the use of the euro for trade invoicing has had a moderately rising trend since its introduction in 1999. As was the case with the yen, the share of euro invoicing is higher for exports than for imports, and the gap between export and import invoicing seems to have been widening in recent years, possibly reflecting the euro debt crisis. The larger-scale use of the euro for trade invoicing makes

20. The PBOC's 2012 *Annual Report* does not report the ratio of RMB receipts to payments in international trade. However, given that the ratio improved from 1:9 in 2009 to 1:1.7 in 2011, it is reasonable to assume the ratio has become close to 1:1. We assume this when we calculate the shares of RMB in export or import invoicing for 2012.

Figure 5-10. *Shares of Home Currency Invoicing for the Trade of the
People's Republic of China's and the Eurozone*

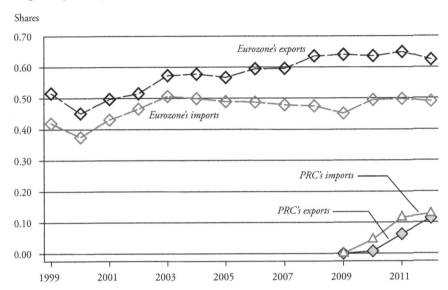

Source: Authors' calculations; see table 5A-1 for data sources.

it clear that the RMB still has a long way to go before it becomes international to
the same extent.

Panel Analysis on the Determinants of Export Invoicing

Now that we have observed different paths of development for the use of currencies in trade invoicing, we conduct a panel data analysis to investigate the determinants of trade invoicing and the role of financial liberalization.

THE MODEL AND CANDIDATE DETERMINANTS OF EXPORTING INVOIC-
ING CURRENCIES.   Here, we investigate the determinants of the use of three currencies, the dollar, the euro, and the home country's currency, by using the data
set for fifty countries, including both advanced and emerging-market economies,
for which the currency share data are available. However, the data limitations for
other variables reduce the number of countries included in our panel data analysis to thirty-three to forty-three countries, depending on the currency of focus, for
the period 1970 to 2011. As we have already described, the data availability of the
currency share data makes the data set highly unbalanced.

We use an empirical specification similar to that used by Goldberg and Tille
(2008) and Kamps (2006), but test other variables that have been suggested as contributors to the share of currency in trade invoicing including financial openness.

The specification relates the share of export invoicing in a specific currency to

$$(5\text{-}2) \qquad \lambda_{EXit}^{C} = \beta_1 + \beta_2 X_{it}^{C}\; \beta_3 D_{it}^{C} + \gamma_1 FL_{it}^{C} + \epsilon_{it}^{C}.$$

λ_{EXit}^{C} indicates the share of exports from country i in year t invoiced in currency C, where C can be the dollar, the euro, or the home country's currency.[21] That is, we repeat this estimation for export invoicing in these three types of currencies. The vector X_{it}^{C} includes the economic factors of country i that affect the share. In X_{it}^{C}, we include EX_{it}^{C}, the share of country i's exports to the United States or the eurozone when C is either the dollar or the euro, respectively, or country i's export share in world exports when we run the estimation for the home currency's share in export invoicing. Vector X_{it}^{C} also includes the share of commodity exports in total exports (*Commd*); relative income level to the United States (*Rel_inc*); exchange rate volatility ($ExVol_{it}^{C}$) and inflation differentials ($InfDif_{it}^{C}$) relative to the United States, the eurozone, and the world, depending on the currency of interest; and a measure for financial development (FD_{it}).[22]

Because it is natural to assume each country is exposed to its own idiosyncratic shocks that are not systematically intrinsic to itself, we estimate a random effects model. We also run the estimations with fixed effects as a robustness check for the possibility of each country's intrinsic characteristics (such as institutional or regulatory environment) affecting the choice of invoicing currencies.

Vector D_{it}^{C} includes the dummies pertaining to currency arrangement (CA_{it}^{C}), such as pegs to the dollar or the euro (or the deutsche mark prior to the introduction of the euro), and also pertaining to whether or not country i participates in the European Union (EU_i).[23] We also include a vector of time effects. One is the dummy for the Bretton Woods period (*BW*); it takes the value of one for all observations before 1973. The other is the dummy for the introduction of the euro (*Euro*); it takes the value of one for all observations after 2002, when the euro was introduced and the national "legacy currencies" ceased circulating in the market.

We focus on the estimate of the variable for capital account openness, FL_{it}^{C}. For the measure of capital account openness, we use the Chinn-Ito index of capital account openness (Chinn and Ito 2006, 2008, and updates). *KAOPEN* is based

21. Again, we do not include the use of the dollar by the United States in the share of the dollar use, but include it in the share of the home currency. Similarly, we do not include the use of the euro in trade invoicing by the eurozone countries in the euro share, but include it in the share of the home currency.

22. "Commodity" includes fuel, food, and metal products, as categorized by the *World Development Indicators*. The exchange rate for the United States, which is included in the "home currency" estimation, is the one against the special drawing right (SDR).

23. The dummy for the EU membership is time-invariant, that is, the dummy is assigned for the entire sample period regardless of the year of entry to the union. This is due to stylized facts that the invoicing behavior would differ for EU member countries even before they actually become members, partly because of the existence of precursor organizations such as the European Community and also because of geographical reasons for other countries that did not participate in the precursor organizations (such as former communist states). We follow Kamps (2006) on this.

on information regarding regulatory restrictions on cross-border capital transactions reported in the International Monetary Fund *Annual Report on Exchange Arrangements and Exchange Restrictions*.[24] Specifically, *KAOPEN* is the first standardized principal component of the variables that indicate the presence of multiple exchange rates, restrictions on current account transactions, on capital account transactions, and the requirement of the surrender of export proceeds (see Chinn and Ito 2006, 2008).[25]

The inclusion of these variables is based on the past literature on trade invoicing. Now we briefly discuss the theoretical rationales for testing the variables and what we should expect for the estimates of the variables.

Share of exports. Larger exporters are expected to have more bargaining power in the market. They can exploit externalities arising from the economies of scale for the use of the currency as well. Hence, we should expect a positive estimate for this variable, especially for the home currency. However, at the same time, for the estimation of the U.S. dollar share, given that the U.S. markets are quite competitive, we can expect the "coalescing effect"; exporters tend to invoice in the currency of the export market to minimize the fluctuations of their prices relative to those of their competitors. This prediction suggests the estimate would be positive.[26] We use data from the IMF's *Direction of Trade*.[27]

Commodity exports as a percentage of total exports. Commodities are almost exclusively denominated in the U.S. dollar, which is consistent with McKinnon's (1979) argument that homogeneous goods tend to be invoiced in a single, low-transaction-cost currency. We should expect a positive effect on the dollar share, but a negative one on the euro and the home currency's shares.

Relative income. We use this variable as a proxy for the extent of differentiation in exported goods. When the extent of competitiveness is high in the destination market or there are other competitive substitutes available in the market, exporters tend to invoice in the local market's currency ("coalescing effects"; see Goldberg and Tille 2008). That is, the more differentiated goods a country exports, the more likely it is to invoice its exports in its home currency. However, we do not have good measures in the cross-country context. Hence, we use the relative per capita income level to the United States as a proxy. The expected sign is negative for both the dollar and euro estimations, but positive for the home currency estimation.[28]

24. These annual reports are available as pdfs at the IMF website, for example, www.imf.org/external/pubs/nft/2013/areaers/ar2013.pdf.

25. The index is normalized to range between 0 and 1. High values indicate a more open capital account. For more details on the index, see "The Chinn-Ito Index" (http://web.pdx.edu/~ito/Chinn-Ito_website.htm).

26. This can be true for the euro share estimation.

27. For more information on this database, see the IMF website at www.imf.org/external/pubs/cat/longres.cfm?sk=19305.0

28. We use the data from Penn World Table 7.1 for real per capita income (see "PWT 7.1," https://pwt.sas.upenn.edu/php_site/pwt71/pwt71_form.php).

Exchange rate volatility and inflation differentials. A more unstable macroeconomic environment would make investors shy away from holding a currency that is subject to such uncertainty. Higher inflation is also associated with an unstable macroeconomic environment. Volatile exchange rates or an unstable macroeconomic environment for a certain currency would make investors flee to hard currency or real assets. Hence, a country with a volatile exchange rate or high inflation tends to rely more on the U.S. dollar and less on its home currency as a medium of trade. For both variables, the estimates should take positive signs for the U.S. dollar, and to a lesser extent the euro, too. For the home currency, both variables should have negative estimates.[29]

Financial development/size. A currency for which large, liquid, and deep markets exist should face lower transaction costs, and therefore should be used more as an invoicing currency. Hence, we examine the impact of financial development on the invoicing currencies while incorporating the level of liquidity, the size, and the depth of the markets with respect to the world market. For that, we use a variable for "financial development/size" (*FD_SIZE*) which we define as the product of private credit creation (as a share of GDP: *PCGDP*) and the relative size of private credit creation of country i to the world total private credit creation (*PRIV_SIZE*).[30] Because a currency associated with a larger and deeper market tends to be used more intensively for trade invoicing in that currency, we expect a negative estimate for the U.S. dollar share coefficient, but a positive one for the home currency share coefficient while that for the euro can be ambiguous.

Financial openness. We consider the effect of financial openness as being similar to that of domestic financial development. Considering that full convertibility of a currency is a necessary, if not sufficient, condition for that currency to become an international currency, the effect of financial openness has to be evaluated separately from that of domestic financial development. A currency of a more open financial market could provide more usability and investment opportunities for international investors. Hence, the more open the capital account is for the issuer country of a currency, the more likely it is that the country will invoice its trade in that currency. Therefore, the impact of financial openness on the shares of the dollar and the euro should be negative and the impact on the home currency share should be positive.

Monetary union and exchange rate arrangements. Bacchetta and van Wincoop (2005) show that the currency for a currency union can make the best use

---

29. Inflation differentials are included as the differentials with the U.S. rate of inflation in the estimations for the U.S. dollar share and the home currency share. For the euro share estimation, inflation differentials with the eurozone rate of inflation are included. For exchange rate volatility, the estimations for the dollar share and the home currency share use the exchange rate against the U.S. dollar, and the estimation for the euro share uses the exchange rate against the euro.

30. *PCGDP* is extracted from the World Bank's Financial Structure Database, first introduced by Beck, Demirgüç-Kunt, and Levine (2001).

of economies of scale and therefore tends to be used more extensively in trade than the sum of the currencies it replaces. If a country pegs its currency to another anchor currency such as the U.S. dollar or the euro, it should surely tend to invoice its trade in the anchor currency.[31]

ESTIMATION RESULTS. Table 5-2 reports the results for both random and fixed effects. Both random and fixed effects models yield similar results; we focus our discussions on the results from the random effect models.

First of all, for all the currencies we find evidence that export market share matters. The larger the share of its exports that goes to the United States or the eurozone, the more likely it is for a country to invoice in dollars or euros, respectively. In the case of the dollar share, the coalescing effect is in effect; given the vast size of the U.S. market and its supposedly high degree of competition, exporters tend to invoice in the U.S. dollar to minimize fluctuations in the prices of their products in the local market's currency (that is, the U.S. dollar) and to retain their market shares. The same observation is applicable to the euro share estimation. Also, if they have a larger export share in the world, exporters tend to invoice their exports in the home currency as well.[32]

If a country exports more commodities, it tends to invoice more in dollars and less in the euro, suggesting that the dollar is a vehicle currency especially for commodity exports. The positive estimate result is obtained for the home currency share estimations—although significantly only in the fixed effects model, which is somewhat counterintuitive. The more differentiated products it exports (which we proxy for by using the relative income level to the U.S. in PPP), the more likely it is to invoice in the home currency (and weakly in the euro) and the less likely to invoice in dollars. These results also provide evidence that the dollar functions as the vehicle currency in international trade. A country with higher inflation tends to invoice its exports in U.S. dollars. The estimate on the inflation differential variable is negative in the euro and home currency share estimations, but only statistically significant in the euro share estimation with fixed effects. The fixed effects estimation for the dollar share suggests that a country with volatile exchange rates also tends to invoice its exports in dollars.

---

31. For the pre-euro period, the dummy is assigned for countries pegging their currencies to the deutsche mark.

32. The findings that the variables for the shares of exports have positive signs for all of the three estimations may appear puzzling. However, while the share variables for the estimations for the U.S. dollar share or the euro share refer to the share of country i's exports to the U.S. or the eurozone, respectively, the export share variable for the home currency estimation represents country i's export share in *world* exports. In other words, as far as the exports share variable is concerned, the estimations for the dollar share or the euro share are not directly comparable with those for the home currency share, which makes all the export share variables having positive signs acceptable. As for the estimations for the dollar or the euro share, our findings suggest that if a country has a greater presence in either the United States or the eurozone area, exports from that country would face a stronger need to invoice in the dollar or the euro to maintain their market presence. As for the estimations for

While financial openness does not affect the share of dollar invoicing, the size of domestic financial markets does matter for it: a country with deeper and larger financial markets is *less* likely to invoice its exports in dollars.[33] Although financial openness does not matter for the U.S. dollar share, it does matter for the share of the euro or the home currency in export invoicing. The more open financial markets a country has, the more it tends to invoice in either the euro or the home currency. Since our measure of financial openness can refer to capital account openness in both directions of capital flow, our findings suggest that financial liberalization may allow countries to diversify investment instruments in international financial markets, which may make euro-denominated assets look more accessible to domestic investors and therefore make euro invoicing more acceptable. At the same time, greater financial openness may lead to more usability and investment opportunities of the home currency for international investors; therefore it may lead to more invoicing in the home currency.

On average, the EU countries have lower shares of dollar invoicing by twenty-six percentage points, while they tend to have higher shares of their home currencies (including the euro for the eurozone countries) by twenty-one percentage points.

After the collapse of the Bretton Woods system in 1973, the share of home currency invoicing rose by nine percentage points, although we do not detect any significant change in the U.S. dollar share. After the euro entered circulation in 2002, the share of dollar invoicing declined by (an insignificant) one percentage point while the share of the euro for non-eurozone countries increased four to seven percentage points.

Countries that peg their currencies to the dollar tend to invoice their exports in dollars. A similar conclusion can be reached for those countries that peg their currencies to the euro; countries that peg their currencies to the euro tend to invoice in euros while tending to reduce their home currency invoicing.

Further Analyses

DE FACTO VERSUS DE JURE MEASURES OF FINANCIAL OPENNESS. Although we used the Chinn-Ito index to reflect the de jure, or regulatory, environment for cross-border capital transactions, one could argue that the reality of cross-border capital transactions is much more complex and so can differ from the picture we depict through the lens of a regulatory framework.[34] In other words,

---

the home currency, if a country has a greater presence in the world, exporters from that country seem able to exercise greater bargaining power so that they can invoice in their home currency.

33. When we include *PCGDP* or *PRIV_SIZE* individually, *PCGDP* does not turn out to be a significant contributor to any of the currency share estimations, but *PRIV_SIZE* is found to be a negative contributor to the U.S. dollar share estimation. These findings suggest that the relative size of financial markets, rather than their depth, matters for the choice of whether or not to invoice exports in the U.S. dollar.

34. Researchers have constructed different de facto and de jure measures of financial openness. For more details on comparisons across different measures of financial openness, see Kose and others (2006) and Quinn, Schindler, and Toyoda (2011).

Table 5-2. Determinants of a Currency's Share of Export Invoicing[a]

	U.S. dollar random 1970 to 2011 (1)	U.S. dollar fixed 1970 to 2011 (2)	Euro random 1990 to 2011 (3)	Euro fixed 1990 to 2011 (4)	Home random 1970 to 2011 (5)	Home fixed 1970 to 2011 (6)
Share of exports	0.491	0.354	0.617	0.678	2.557	2.224
	(0.116)***	(0.164)**	(0.099)***	(0.131)***	(0.697)***	(0.791)***
Commodity exports Percent	0.270	0.198	-0.133	-0.127	0.232	0.331
	(0.086)***	(0.126)	(0.082)*	(0.100)	(0.118)	(0.140)**
Relative income	-0.153	-0.295	0.117	0.882	0.395	0.552
	(0.058)***	(0.120)**	(0.094)	(0.165)***	(0.088)***	(0.140)***
Exchange rate volatility	0.008	0.034	-0.025	-0.021	-0.016	-0.029
	(0.029)	(0.029)	(0.029)	(0.027)	(0.025)	(0.025)
Financial development/size	-0.406	-0.356	-0.080	-0.105	-0.047	-0.092
	(0.082)***	(0.094)***	(0.165)	(0.159)	(0.090)	(0.098)
Inflation differential	0.314	0.356	-0.107	-0.138	-0.213	-0.218
	(0.110)***	(0.114)***	(0.081)	(0.077)*	(0.172)	(0.175)
Financial openness	0.005	0.004	0.082	0.059	0.058	0.069
	(0.031)	(0.032)	(0.027)***	(0.026)**	(0.032)*	(0.034)**

European Union states	-0.259 (0.049)***		0.068 (0.062)		0.207 (0.080)**	
Years after 2002	-0.011 (0.011)	-0.012 (0.012)	0.066 (0.011)***	0.037 (0.011)***	0.010 (0.012)	0.004 (0.012)
Bretton Woods	-0.013 (0.027)	-0.003 (0.027)			-0.089 (0.025)***	-0.091 (0.026)***
Pegged to U.S. dollar	0.055 (0.029)*	0.048 (0.030)	0.017 (0.035)	-0.006 (0.033)	-0.045 (0.041)	-0.060 (0.042)
Pegged to euro	-0.029 (0.023)	-0.030 (0.024)	0.105 (0.022)***	0.082 (0.022)***	-0.094 (0.021)***	-0.092 (0.021)***
Constant	0.571 (0.055)***	0.568 (0.074)***	-0.041 (0.064)	-0.221 (0.091)**	-0.156 (0.082)	-0.145 (0.091)
N	336	336	285	285	326	326
Number of countries	43	43	34	34	37	37
Overall R^2	0.73	0.27	0.67	0.20	0.58	0.38
W/in R^2	0.25	0.26	0.39	0.45	0.26	0.27

Source: Authors' calculations; see table 5A-1 for data sources.

a. Standard errors are in parentheses.

* = $p < 10\%$; ** = $p < 5\%$; *** = $p < 1\%$.

the extent of financial openness depicted by a de jure index such as the Chinn-Ito index can differ from what can be measured by a de facto index that is based upon actual volumes or prices of cross-border capital transactions.

According to the Chinn-Ito index, the PRC and India have not made progress in opening markets for capital account transactions and have been lagging behind the Russian Federation and Brazil and other developing countries (see figure 5-11[a]). But if we measure the extent of capital account openness by the actual size of cross-border capital transactions, we get a different picture. In figure 5-11(b) we show the extent of financial openness by using another often-used quantity-based de facto measure: the ratio of the sum of total stocks of external assets and liabilities to GDP, using the data set compiled by Lane and Milesi-Ferretti (2007). According to this measure, the BRIC countries (Brazil, the Russian Federation, India, and the PRC) are generally progressing toward greater financial openness. The PRC appears to be steadily increasing the extent of financial openness and to be more financially open than Brazil.[35]

We repeat this empirical exercise while including the de facto measure of financial openness instead of the de jure measure (not reported). The results of our regression are that the estimate of the de facto measure of financial openness in the U.S. dollar share estimation is significantly positive; in the euro share estimation is significantly negative; and in the home currency share estimation is insignificant with its magnitude close to zero. Notably, all these results are either inconsistent with or contradictory to theoretical predictions. These results primarily reflect the inclusion of financial-center countries such as the UK, Ireland, and Luxembourg in the sample. When we interact the de facto measure of financial openness with the dummy for high values of the measure (such as de facto measure > 3) to control for the financial-center countries, we can obtain results more consistent with theoretical predictions. However, the results are quite sensitive to what we use as the threshold for the financial-center countries. In sum, we do not think the de facto measure gives us consistent results.

OTHER FACTORS. We should suspect other potential determinants of currency choice for export invoicing so that we can minimize missing variable bias.

We first test the effect of legal development. A currency might be used more intensively in trade if it is associated with an economy where legal systems and institutions are sufficiently well developed to guarantee smooth and predictable

35. This kind of de facto measure has its own drawbacks, however. For one thing, the extent of "openness" can differ depending on how the sizes of the volumes of cross-border capital transactions are normalized. For example, normalizing the sum of total assets and liabilities as a ratio of GDP would make the index appear unnecessarily low for large economies such as the United States, and would make the one for an international financial center such as Ireland, Luxembourg, Singapore, or Hong Kong, China appear extremely high. Second, de facto measures can be susceptible to business cycles as well as the ebb and flow of cross-border capital flows. In figure 5-11(b), the Russian Federation appeared to be becoming more "financially open" in the late 1990s, but part of this is due to a shrinkage of the denominator, the country's GDP.

Figure 5-11. *Different Measures of Financial Openness*

(a) Chinn-Ito De Jure Index

De jure measure of financial openness

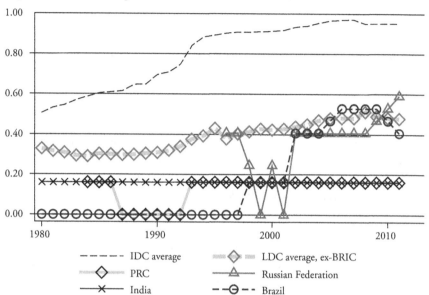

(b) De Facto Measure of Financial Openness in the BRICs (Brazil, Russian Federation, India, and the People's Republic of China)

De facto measure of financial openness

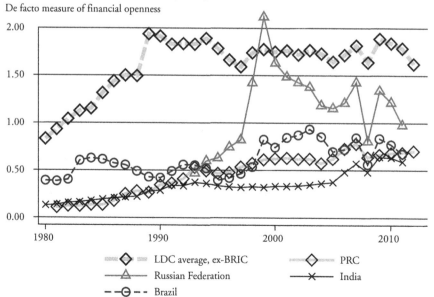

Source: Authors' calculations; see table 5A-1 for data sources.

transactions. Hence, we also expect higher levels of legal or institutional development to lead to more home currency invoicing and less invoicing in the vehicle currency, the U.S. dollar. We use the variable *LEGAL* as a measure of general legal and institutional development, which is the first principal component of law and order (*LAO*), bureaucratic quality (*BQ*), and anticorruption measures (*CORRUPT*).[36] The estimated coefficient on *LEGAL* is found to be insignificantly positive for the U.S. dollar share estimation, significantly negative for the euro share estimation, and insignificantly positive for the home currency share estimation (results not reported). We do not have sufficient evidence to support the hypothesis that legal development matters for the choice of invoicing currency.

Next, we investigate the effect of financial crises. Any financial crisis can throw the credibility of the currency of the crisis country into question, thereby discouraging the use of that currency for trade settlements or invoicing. And a financial crisis that involves expectations for future depreciation or devaluation leads traders to avoid the currency more decisively.

Hence, we include the dummy for currency, banking, or debt crisis individually in each of the three estimations. We use the crisis dummies from Aizenman and Ito (2013) to identify the three types of crisis.[37] The results indicate that countries that experience a banking crisis tend to increase the share of the U.S. dollar for their export invoicing by 4 percentage points and they also tend to *decrease* the share of the euro by 2.4 percentage points.[38] The effect of the banking or other type of crisis on the home currency share turns out to be insignificant.

We also investigate whether the recent global financial crisis had any impact on the choice of invoicing currencies. When we replace the crisis dummy with a dummy variable for the years after 2008, we find that countries on average increase the share of U.S. dollar invoicing by 5.8 percentage points. However, the crisis does not affect other currency shares, suggesting that the global financial crisis may have led investors and traders to flee to the U.S. dollar.

Overall, a crisis, particularly a banking crisis, contributes to more U.S. dollar invoicing, reflecting the role of the dollar as a safe-haven refuge.

Furthermore, we test whether net investment positions matter for the choice of a currency for export invoicing. The currency of a net creditor country may become more available outside the home country, which may make it easier to

36. *LAO, BQ,* and *CORRUPT* are extracted from the International Country Risk Guide database. Higher values of these variables indicate better conditions.

37. To identify currency crisis, Aizenman and Ito use the exchange market pressure index, which uses the exchange rate against the currency of the base country, which is the country a country follows most closely in determining its monetary policy. See Aizenman, Chinn, and Ito (2013) for details. The banking crisis dummy is based on Laeven and Valencia (2008, 2010, 2012). For the debt crisis dummy, they augment the data set by Reinhart and Rogoff (2009) with other sources, including the World Bank's *Global Development Finance* (World Bank 2012). For more details, see Aizenman and Ito (2013, appendix).

38. The estimation results are available from the authors upon request.

invoice in that currency. When we include the variable for net investment positions (as a share of GDP), on the basis of the Lane and Milesi-Ferretti data set, we find that the estimate is significantly positive for the home currency share estimation, suggesting that countries with better net investment positions tend to be able to invoice their exports in their own currency. However, we must take this result with a grain of salt because of potential endogeneity issues. That is, history has told us that countries with international currencies often find it easier to get finance from international financial markets and then to turn into debtor countries, as happened to the United States and the United Kingdom.

Last, we test whether exchange rate changes contribute to the choice of invoicing currencies. One contributing factor to the internationalization of the RMB is the one-sided—that is, only appreciation—expectations of the currency's exchange rate. As long as the PRC continues to experience more rapid productivity growth than advanced economies, which is expected to continue in the foreseeable future, the RMB can continue on the appreciation trend.

If the currency of exporters is on an appreciation trend, nonresidents outside the home country would have more incentive to hold the home country's currency and therefore would agree with invoicing in the home currency. Similarly, the appreciation trend of the home currency may help lower the share of the U.S. dollar use.

Hence, we include in the regressions for the shares of the U.S. dollar and the home currency the centered three-year moving average of the rate of depreciation as a proxy for currency depreciation trend. The rate-of-depreciation variable should have a positive coefficient in the U.S. dollar share regression; a currency appreciation trend (that is, negative rates of depreciation) would lead to a decrease in the U.S. dollar share, whereas it should have a negative estimate in the home currency share regression. A currency appreciation trend would lead to an increase in the home currency share.[39]

It turns out that the estimate on the rate of depreciation in the U.S. dollar share estimation is significantly positive, but that the estimate in the home currency share estimation is insignificantly positive.[40] In other words, appreciation of the home currency does lead to a fall in the share of U.S. dollar invoicing in exports, but it may not necessarily mean that exporters would invoice in their home currencies.

OTHER SPECIFICATIONS. We also test using different specifications to incorporate the unique traits of the currency share data. First, we incorporate the fact that the dependent variable for the share of a currency use ranges between 0 and 1. The truncation of the dependent variable suggests that we conduct a robustness check using the tobit estimation method. The nonlinearity of the estimation method may better fit with the nature of changes in the shares of currencies used for trade invoicing, which entails persistency or inertia, as we have shown.

---

39. We also control for large rates of depreciation (when the three-year moving average rate of depreciation is greater than 30 percent).

40. Results are available from the authors upon request.

Second, as another way of dealing with the possible nonlinearity of the currency share data, we transform the dependent variable into the logistic form, following Chinn and Frankel (2007, 2008). They argue that the share of a currency in central banks' reserves can develop in a nonlinear fashion so that the share of a currency can rise rapidly once it surpasses a "tipping point," or threshold, due to externality. To better capture the nonlinearity, Chinn and Frankel transform the share of a currency in central bank reserves as log (share/(1-share)).Although the nature of the development of invoicing currency shares differs from that of the shares of reserve currencies, we conduct a robustness check by transforming our dependent variables in the same way as Chinn and Frankel.

Third, we suspect that the shares of the dollar, the euro, and the home currency are correlated because the shares must sum to 1. In other words, positive disturbances in one currency should be associated with negative disturbances on average across the other currencies, making the error terms of the three estimation models correlate with each other. Because our data set is far from complete or balanced, such correlation does not have to be the case in a strict sense—in fact, there are some cases where the sign of the estimate remains the same across the three estimations for several variables, which would be inconsistent if we had complete data on the three types of currency shares. Nonetheless, we test the possibility that the error terms across the three estimations are correlated by employing the seemingly unrelated regression (SUR) estimation.

Summarizing the results from these alternative econometric specifications, we find most of the estimates in accord with those obtained using ordinary least squares (OLS), often with greater statistical significance. One exception is exchange rate volatility, which turns out to have estimated coefficients contrary to priors.[41] While the financial development/size variable often had a significantly negative coefficient for the home currency share regression, contradictory to theoretical predictions, the estimate in the U.S. dollar share estimation is significantly negative in all the nonlinear models. This supports the OLS result that a country with deeper and larger financial markets is *less* likely to invoice its exports in the U.S. dollar. The variables whose results are persistently consistent with the OLS estimation results include the variables for the share of exports, commodity exports, and relative income all for the three estimations. Financial openness is also often found to be a significantly positive contributor to the share of home currency invoicing, suggesting that the positive effect of greater financial openness on the share of home currency in export invoicing is robust.

41. Considering that this variable contains outliers, these contradictory results can be due to the outliers.

Implications and Prospects for the People's Republic of China

With the estimation results in hand, we are now interested in examining the implications of our results for the path of RMB internationalization. We first compare predicted and actual shares of some currencies, including the RMB, within the sample period. Then we examine the prospects for the use of RMB for export invoicing for the foreseeable future by making predictions of the RMB share outside our sample period.

Goodness of Fit

Figure 5-12(a) shows both the predicted and actual shares of the RMB in the PRC's export invoicing. The prediction is based on the estimates (with random effects) reported in table 5-2. Overall, the actual use of RMB for settling PRC exports is much smaller than our estimation model suggests, although the recent rapid rise in RMB settlements of exports makes it look as though the actual settlement ratios are getting closer to the predictions. Looking at when the PRC started liberalization of RMB invoicing in 2009, our model suggests that about 20 percent of the PRC's exports *should* be invoiced in RMB, although the actual use of the RMB was essentially nonexistent. As for 2011, where our model predicts the share of RMB use in PRC's exports to be 21 percent, the actual share is still a meager 6.2 percent. Cui, Shu, and Chang (2009) argue that, on the basis of the correlation between the pricing-to-market (PTM) coefficients found in their panel analysis and the actual share of home currency invoicing in exports, the PRC has the potential of invoicing 20 to 30 percent of its exports in its home currency, which is similar to our predictions.

Although there is a possibility that the estimates in our model suffer from omitted variable bias, comparison with other countries' experiences tells us that there is more to it than just omitted variable bias. Figure 5-12(b) illustrates the predicted and actual shares of the yen among the currencies used for export invoicing, and figure 5-12(c) shows the predicted and actual shares of U.S. dollar use in Japan's exports. It appears that the actual level of yen export invoicing finally reached the level predicted by the model in 1983–more than ten years after yen invoicing started taking place. But this was followed by the actual share's again hovering at lower levels than the model predicts. In the dollar invoicing, we can observe the opposite (figure 5-12[c]): the actual use of the dollar is persistently higher than the model predicts. The fact that yen invoicing did not become as prevalent as predicted while dollar invoicing was more prevalent than predicted indicates that "inertia" does affect the choice of currency for trade invoicing.

Figures 5-12(b) and 5-12(c) suggest that the underperformance of RMB invoicing can be attributed to the RMB's recent advent as an invoicing currency and the persistence or the "inertia" of the use of other currencies, particularly that of the U.S. dollar, as the vehicle currency for trade invoicing.[42] Once a currency becomes a dominant invoicing or settlement currency, it tends to continue to be dominant.[43]

Figure 5-12(d) shows the share of the euro—a newly introduced and internationalized currency—used for the eurozone's exports.[44] The model again predicts much higher levels of euro invoicing; in fact the actual use of the euro has been rising, gradually narrowing the gap between the prediction and reality.

Prospects of Renminbi Export Invoicing

So where is the RMB heading in the near future? To answer this question, we implement out-of-sample predictions for 2015 and 2018, using the estimates we obtained in the baseline regression (see table 5-2).

For the out-of-sample predictions, we need to make assumptions about the explanatory variables. We summarize the assumptions we make for the forecasting exercise in table 5A-2 (see appendix). Some of the assumptions are based on the IMF's forecasts reported in the *World Economic Outlook* (as of April 2013). Some other variables are assumed to be the same as the average of the relevant variables in the last five years of the sample period, 2007 to 2011.

We also conduct some scenario analysis to see how the RMB share in export invoicing can be affected by hypothetical paths of financial liberalization. The baseline assumption for the Chinn-Ito index of financial openness (*KAOPEN*) is that for 2015 the PRC will increase the level of financial openness to 0.35, higher than the current level of 0.16 but not as high as that of Brazil, Colombia, and Indonesia, all of which scored 0.41 in 2011. For 2018, we assume the level of the PRC's financial openness continues to rise up to 0.50, more financially open than Turkey (0.45 as of 2011). We also think about both optimistic and pessimistic scenarios and make predictions for these scenarios as points of reference. Under the pessimistic scenario, the level of financial openness for the PRC is the same in 2015 as the 2011 level, 0.16. In 2018, we assume it rises to 0.25, a level still lower than in the baseline scenario for 2015. Under the optimistic scenario, *KAOPEN* rises rapidly to 0.60 in 2015 and to 0.95 in 2018, a level comparable to those of high-income countries.

Figure 5-13 illustrates our predictions for the 2008–2011 period, 2015, and 2018. Based on the baseline prediction, the share of RMB invoicing for the PRC's

42. Cui, Shu, and Chang (2009) also mention the persistency of invoicing practice in other non-RMB currencies.

43. We observe similar patterns when we repeat the same exercise for the Korea won, Indonesia rupee, and Thai baht, the currencies for which we have longer time series of invoicing currency shares. That is, the actual use of the dollar tends to be persistently higher than the model predicts and declines only slowly, or the actual use of the home currency tends to be lower than the model suggests, even when the share of the home currency starts rising, with the gap between the two slowly narrowing.

44. For this prediction, we also include the data for the eurozone in the regression exercise as one entity (in addition to individual eurozone countries); the estimation exercise reported in table 5-2 does not include the euro.

Figure 5-12. *Predicted versus Actual Shares of Currencies in Export Invoicing*

(a) Shares of the Renminbi in the People's Republic of China's Export Invoicing

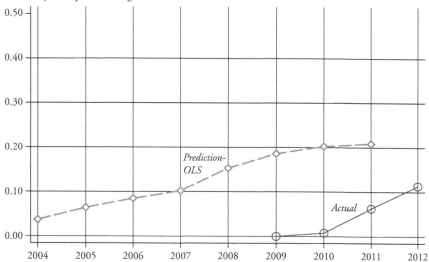

(b) Shares of the Japanese Yen in Japan's Export Invoicing

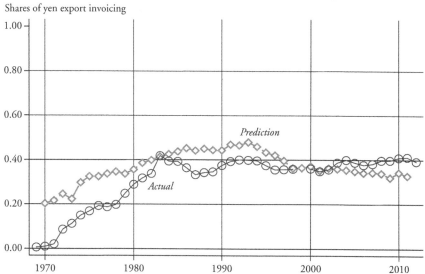

Source: Authors' calculations; see table 5A-1 for data sources.

(continued)

Figure 5-12. *Predicted versus Actual Shares of Currencies in Export Invoicing*
(continued)

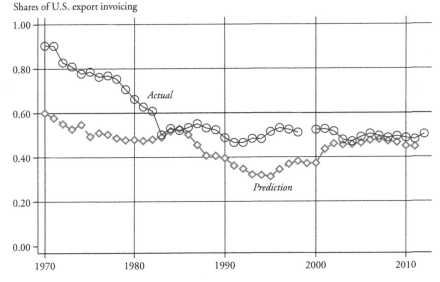

(c) Shares of the U.S. Dollar in Japan's Export Invoicing

Shares of U.S. export invoicing

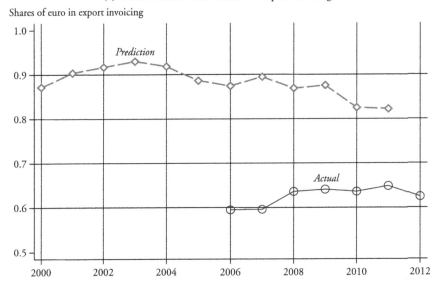

(d) Shares of the Euro in Eurozone's Export Invoicing

Shares of euro in export invoicing

Source: Authors' calculations; see table 5A-1 for data sources.

Figure 5-13. *Forecasting the Renminbi's Share in the People's Republic of China's Export Invoicing*

Share of RMB in export invoicing

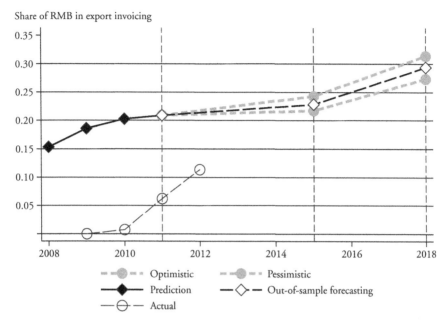

Source: Authors' calculations; see table 5A-1 for data sources.

exports would rise to 22.8 percent in 2015 and 29.4 percent in 2018. Despite the significant coefficient on *KAOPEN*, the different scenarios on financial liberalization do not appear to make much difference. Even in the optimistic scenario, the share of RMB invoicing rises only to 31.4 percent in 2018, which is not much different from the baseline scenario.[45]

Considering that the gap between the predicted and actual paths for the share of RMB export invoicing can be due to the inertia of invoicing currencies, we can expect the gap to narrow over the years to come. Hence, our predictions probably show the upper end of the actual path of RMB internationalization in terms of export invoicing.

As for the foreseeable future, the PRC may allow greater exchange rate flexibility, leading to greater volatility. In addition, it is likely the PRC's financial markets will continue to grow faster than they did from 2007 to 2011; or the country could experience higher than expected inflation. All these factors would tend to decrease RMB use (although the insignificant coefficients suggest little effect). If the PRC

45. However, we have shown that the financial openness variable is one of the robust variables to other (nonlinear) estimation models. Hence, financial openness is still one important contributor to the share of home currency use for export invoicing.

experiences an even greater increase in its relative income level or export market share, or both, then the PRC's share of RMB invoicing might also increase. Nonetheless, the convergence to the predicted values should take place as the use of RMB in export invoicing rises and creates scale benefits.

Conclusions

One of the important keys to the RMB's becoming an international currency is how widely and how soon the RMB becomes a major currency for trade invoicing or settlement. Although RMB use for trade settlement began only in 2009, its use has risen rapidly since then. Many have argued that the future of the RMB as an invoicing currency is closely tied with the issue of the PRC's commitment to liberalizing capital account transactions. In this chapter we investigated the determinants of currency choice for trade invoicing in a cross-country context while focusing on the impact of capital account liberalization.

Our data of trade invoicing reconfirmed that the U.S. dollar still plays an important role as the vehicle currency. Although the use of the euro as an invoicing currency had been steadily increasing before the euro debt crisis, a rise in the risk involving the currency seems to have contributed to the plateauing or even the decline of the currency's use in recent years. In contrast, both the global financial crisis and the euro sovereign debt crisis seem to have helped the U.S. dollar to increase its use for trade invoicing. Furthermore, in the Asian region, countries have relied heavily on the U.S. dollar as the vehicle currency, reflecting the reliance of the regional supply chain network on the U.S. as the ultimate export destination. Such an Asian dollar bloc stands as a large challenge to the PRC's ambitions for the RMB to become the regional international currency

Although the liberalization of the use of the RMB for trade transactions took place only in 2009, the share of RMB use has been rapidly rising in recent years. The RMB has been used more for import invoicing than for export invoicing, whereas in other currencies the share of the use for exports is usually higher than that for imports. This reflects the government's goal to increase the use of RMB overseas and to support the government-run efforts to internationalize the currency. Despite the rapid increase in use for trade invoicing, however, the RMB is still far behind the Japanese yen and the euro—the two previous challengers to the U.S. dollar's dominance—in its use as an invoicing currency.

Our panel data analysis provides results consistent with previous studies. Focusing on variables that have not been tested in the past studies, we find that countries with more developed and larger financial markets tend to invoice *less* in the U.S. dollar. At the same time, countries with more open capital accounts tend to invoice in either the euro or their home currency. Hence, financial development and financial openness are among the keys to challenging the dominance of the dollar in general and to internationalizing the RMB for the PRC.

Our estimates suggest that in the last few years of our sample period—2009 to 2011—the use of the RMB in export invoicing should have been higher, around the low- to mid-twenties as a percentage of total exports, rather than the actual share of less than 10 percent in 2011. The underperformance of RMB export invoicing can be attributed to inertia—once a currency is used for trade invoicing or settlements, it becomes difficult for traders to switch from one currency to another. In fact, both the yen and the euro were not used as much as the model predicts, especially at their inception as international currencies. That inertial tendency is likely to persist.

To provide some outlook on the use of the RMB as a trade invoicing currency, we implemented out-of-sample prediction for 2015 and 2018, using the baseline estimation results. Based on the projections, the share of RMB invoicing for the PRC's exports will rise to 22.8 percent in 2015 and to 29.4 percent in 2018. Despite the statistically significant coefficient on *KAOPEN,* drastically different assumptions regarding financial liberalization do not appear to make much difference.

Other factors could affect the future path of RMB use for export invoicing, including exchange rate volatility, the relative size and depth of the PRC's financial markets, its relative income level, and its export market share. Nonetheless, our predictions probably show the upper end of the actual path of RMB export invoicing. The convergence to the predicted levels could accelerate as the increased use of the RMB in export invoicing creates scale benefits.

Appendix

Appendix tables 5A-1 and 5A-2 are on the following pages.

Table 5A-1. *Availability of Currency Invoicing Data for Fifty Countries for the U.S. Dollar, the Euro, and Home Currencies*

Country	Currency	Years export data available	Years import data available	Sources
Austria	U.S. dollar	1973, 1975, 2006, 2010, 2012	2006, 2010, 2012	Scharrer (1981); Eurostat
	Euro	2006, 2008–12	2006–12	ECBank
	Home	1973, 1975, 2006, 2008–12	1975, 2006–12	
Belgium	U.S. dollar	1971, 1975, 1976, 2002–04, 2010	1972, 1976, 2002–04, 2010	Kamps (2006); ECB; Eurostat, Scharrer (1981)
	Euro	2000–11	2000–11	
	Home	1971, 1975, 1976, 2000–11	1972, 1976, 2000–11	
Bulgaria	U.S. dollar	1998–2006	1998–2006	Kamps (2006); Hristov and Zaimov (2001); ECB
	Euro	1998–2011	1998–2011	Bulgarian National Bank (2006)
	Home			
Croatia	U.S. dollar	1998–2004	1998–2004	Kamps (2006)
	Euro	1998–2009	1998–2009	ECB
	Home			
Cyprus	U.S. dollar	2003, 2004, 2010, 2012	2003, 2004, 2010, 2012	Kamps (2006); ECB; Eurostat
	Euro	2003–12	2003–12	
	Home	2007–12	2007–12	
Czech Republic	U.S. dollar	1999–2004	1999–2004	Kamps (2006); ECB
	Euro	1999–11	1999–2011	
	Home	2001–03	2001–03	
Denmark	U.S. dollar	1971, 1975–76, 1999–2004, 2010, 2012	1972, 1976, 1999–2004, 2010, 2012	Scharrer (1981), Kamps (2006); ECB; Eurostat
	Euro	1999–2004, 2010, 2012	1999–2004, 2010, 2012	
	Home	1971, 1975–77, 1999–2004, 2010, 2012	1972, 1976, 1977, 1999–2004, 2010, 2012	

Country	Currency			Sources
Estonia	U.S. dollar	2003, 2010, 2012	2003, 2004, 2010, 2012	Kamps (2006); ECB; Eurostat
	Euro	2001–12	2001–12	
	Home	2010–12	2010–12	
Finland	U.S. dollar	1971, 1975, 1976, 2010, 2012	2010, 2012	Scharrer (1981); Eurostat
	Euro	2006, 2010, 2012	2006, 2010, 2012	ECB
	Home	1971, 1975, 1976, 2006, 2010, 2012	2006, 2010, 2012	
France	U.S. dollar	1972, 1975–76, 1980, 1992, 1999–2003, 2010, 2012	1980, 1992, 1999–2003, 2010, 2012	Scharrer (1981); Park and Shin (2009); Kamps (2006); ECB; Eurostat; Tavlas and Ozeki (1992)
	Euro	1999–2012	1999–2012	
	Home	1972, 1975–77, 1980, 1988, 1992, 1999–2012	1977, 1980, 1988, 1992, 1999–2012	
Germany	U.S. dollar	1972, 1975, 1976, 1980–88, 1992, 2002–04, 2009, 2010, 2012	1972, 1976, 1980–88, 1992, 2002–04, 2006, 2010	Scharrer (1981); Park and Shin (2009); Kamps (2006); ECB; Eurostat; Tavlas (1993); Tavlas and Ozeki (1992)
	Euro	2002–07, 2009–12	2002–07	
	Home	1972, 1975, 1976, 1977, 1980, 1987, 1992, 2002–07, 2009–12	1972, 1976, 1977, 1980, 1988, 1992, 2002–07	
Greece	U.S. dollar	2001–04, 2012	2001–04, 2010, 2012	Kamps (2006); Eurostat; ECB
	Euro	2001–12	2001–11	
	Home	2001–12	2001–11	
Hungary	U.S. dollar	1992–2004, 2010, 2012	1992–2004, 2010, 2012	Kamps (2006); Eurostat; ECB
	Euro	1992–2004, 2008–09, 2010, 2012	1992–2004, 2008–09, 2010, 2012	
	Home	1999–2004, 2010, 2012	1999–2004, 2010, 2012	

(continued)

Table 5A-1. *Availability of Currency Invoicing Data for Fifty Countries for the U.S. Dollar, the Euro, and Home Currencies (Continued)*

Country	Currency	Years export data available	Years import data available	Sources
Iceland	U.S. dollar	2010	2010	Eurostat
	Euro	2010	2010	
	Home	2010	2010	
Ireland	U.S. dollar	2006, 2010	2006, 2010	Eurostat
	Euro	2006–11	2006–11	ECB
	Home	2006–11	2006–11	
Italy	U.S. dollar	1971, 1975–76, 2010, 2012	1972, 1976, 2010, 2012	Scharrer (1981); Kamps (2006); ECB; Eurostat, Tavlas and Ozeki (1992)
	Euro	2001–10, 2012	2001–10, 2012	
	Home	1971, 1975–77, 1980, 1987, 2001–10, 2012	1972, 1976–1977, 1980, 1987, 2001–10, 2012	
Latvia	U.S. dollar	2000–04, 2010, 2012	2000–04, 2010, 2012	Kamps (2006); ECB; Eurostat
	Euro	2000–12	2000–12	
	Home	2010, 2012	2010, 2012	
Lithuania	U.S. dollar	1999–2005, 2010, 2012	1996–2005, 2010, 2012	Kamps (2006); ECB; Eurostat
	Euro	1999–2012	1996–2012	
	Home	1999–2005, 2010, 2012	1996–2005, 2010, 2012	
Luxembourg	U.S. dollar	2002–04, 2010, 2012	2002–04, 2010, 2012	Kamps (2006); ECB; Eurostat
	Euro	2000–12	2000–12	
	Home	2000–12	2000–12	
Macedonia, FYR	U.S. dollar	1998–2004	1998–2004	Kamps (2006)
	Euro	1998–2009	1998–2009	ECB
	Home			

Country	Currency			Source
Malta	U.S. dollar	2012	2010, 2012	ECB
	Euro	2000–03, 2012	2000–03, 2010, 2012	
	Home	2000–03, 2012	2000–03, 2010, 2012	
Netherlands	U.S. dollar	1971, 1975, 1976, 1998–2002, 2010, 2012	1998–2002, 2010, 2012	Scharrer (1981); Kamps (2006); Eurostat
	Euro	1998–2002, 2006, 2010, 2012	1998–2002, 2006, 2010, 2012	
	Home	1971, 1975–77, 1998–2002, 2006, 2010, 2012	1977, 1998–2002, 2006, 2010, 2012	
Norway	U.S. dollar	2010	2010	Eurostat
	Euro	2010	2010	
	Home	2010	2010	
Poland	U.S. dollar	1994–2004	1994–2004	Kamps (2006); ECB
	Euro	1994–2009	1994–2009	
	Home	1998–2004	1998–2004	
Portugal	U.S. dollar	2002–04, 2010	2002–04, 2010	Kamps (2006); Eurostat, ECB (2012)
	Euro	2000–11	2000–11	
	Home	2000–11	2000–11	
Romania	U.S. dollar	1999–2005	1999–2005	Kamps (2006); ECB (2012)
	Euro	1999–2011	1999–2011	
	Home			
Slovak Republic	U.S. dollar	1999–2003, 2010	2010	Kamps (2006); ECB; Eurostat
	Euro	1999–2011	2002–11	
	Home	2008–11	2008–11	
Slovenia	U.S. dollar	2000, 2001, 2003, 2004, 2010, 2012	2000, 2001, 2003, 2004, 2010, 2012	Kamps (2006); ECB; Eurostat
	Euro	2000–12	2000–12	
	Home	2006–12	2006–12	

(continued)

Table 5A-1. *Availability of Currency Invoicing Data for Fifty Countries for the U.S. Dollar, the Euro, and Home Currencies (Continued)*

Country	Currency	Years export data available	Years import data available	Sources
Spain	U.S. dollar	1998–2004, 2010, 2012	1998–2004, 2010, 2012	Kamps (2006); ECB
	Euro	1998–2012	1998–2012	
	Home	1998–2012	1998–2012	
Sweden	U.S. dollar	1973, 1993, 2010, 2012	1968, 1973, 1993, 2010, 2012	Scharrer (1981); Grassman (1973)
	Euro	2010–12	2010–12	ECB
	Home	1973, 1977, 1993, 2010, 2012	1968, 1973, 1977, 1993, 2010, 2012	
Switzerland	U.S. dollar	1977		Scharrer (1981)
	Euro			
	Home	1977	1973	
Turkey	U.S. dollar	2002–04	2002–04	Kamps (2006); ECB
	Euro	2001–09	2001–09	
	Home	2002–04	2002–04	
United Kingdom	U.S. dollar	1977, 1980, 1992, 1999–2002, 2010–12	1980, 1992, 1999–2002, 2010–12	Scharrer (1981); Park and Shin (2009); Kamps (2006);
	Euro	1999–2002, 2010–12	1999–2002, 2010–12	Eurostat
	Home	1968, 1977, 1980, 1988, 1992, 1999–2002, 2010–12	1980, 1988, 1992, 1999–2002, 2010–12	
Ukraine	U.S. dollar	2001–04	2002–04	Kamps (2006)
	Euro	2001–07	2002–07	
	Home	2003–04	2003–04	
Asia-Pacific				
Australia	U.S. dollar	1997–2011	1997–2011	Australian Bureau of Statistics
	Euro	1997–2011	1997–2011	
	Home	1997–2011	1997–2011	

People's Republic of China	U.S. dollar			People's Bank of China (2010 to 2013)
	Euro			
	Home	2009–12	2009–12	
India	U.S. dollar	2005, 2008	2005, 2008	Kamps (2006)
	Euro	1998, 2005, 2008	1998, 2005, 2008	
	Home			
Indonesia	U.S. dollar	1991, 1994–2012	1991–2012	Kamps (2006); Bank of Indonesia (www.bi.go.id/web/en/Data+Statistik)
	Euro	1991, 1994–2012	1991–2012	
	Home	1991, 1994–95, 1997–2012	1991–2012	
Japan	U.S. dollar	1969–2012	1969–80, 1986–2012	Yarita (1999); Park and Shin (2009); Kamps (2006)
	Euro	2000–12	2000–12	Japan Ministry of Finance
	Home	1969–2012	1969–80, 1983, 1985–2012	
Republic of Korea	U.S. dollar	1976–2005	1980–2005	Bank of Korea
	Euro	1990, 1995, 1996, 2000–05	1990, 1995, 1996, 2000–05	
	Home			
Malaysia	U.S. dollar	1995, 1996, 2000	1995, 1996	Kamps (2006)
	Euro	1995, 1996	1995, 1996	
	Home	1995, 1996		
Pakistan	U.S. dollar	2001–03	2001–03	Kamps (2006)
	Euro	2001–03	2001–03	
	Home			
Thailand	U.S. dollar	1993–2012	1993–2012	Bank of Thailand (www.bot.or.th/English/Statistics/Pages/index1.aspx)
	Euro	1993–2012	1993–2012	
	Home	1993–2012	1993–2012	

(continued)

Table 5A-1. *Availability of Currency Invoicing Data for Fifty Countries for the U.S. Dollar, the Euro, and Home Currencies (Continued)*

Country	Currency	Years export data available	Years import data available	Sources
North America				
Canada	U.S. dollar	2001		Kamps (2006)
	Euro			
	Home	2001		
United States	U.S. dollar	1980, 1988, 1992	1980, 1988, 1992, 2003	Park and Shin (2009); Tavlas and Ozeki (1992)
	Euro		2003	Kamps (2006)
	Home	1980, 1988, 1992	1980, 1988, 1992, 2003	
Middle East and Africa				
Algeria	U.S. dollar	2003, 2004		Kamps (2006)
	Euro	2003, 2004	2003, 2004	
	Home			
Israel	U.S. dollar	2000, 2004		Kamps (2006)
	Euro	2000, 2004		
	Home			
Morocco	U.S. dollar			Kamps (2006)
	Euro		2003	
	Home			
South Africa	U.S. dollar	2003		Kamps (2006)
	Euro	2003		
	Home	2003		
Tunisia	U.S. dollar	1995–2001	1995–2001	Kamps (2006)
	Euro			
	Home			

Source: Authors' compilation.
ECB = European Central Bank.

Table 5A-2. *Assumptions for Out-of-Sample Predictions*

Variable	Assumptions
Share of exports	Based on predictions in WEO
Commodity exports	Same as the average in the 2007–11 period
Relative income	Based on predictions in WEO
Exchange rate	Same as the average in the 2007–11 period
Financial development	PCGDP is assumed to be the same as in the 2007–11 average. The relative size of the market is based on linear extrapolations. We use the product of the two variables.
Inflation difference	Same as the average in the 2007–11 period
Financial openness	KAOPEN
	For People's Republic of China:
	<Middle course> 2015: 0.35; 2018: 0.50
	<Pessimistic course> 2015: 0.16; 2018: 0.25
	<Optimistic course> 2015: 0.70; 2018: 0.80
Pegged to U.S. dollar	Same as the average in the 2007–11 period
Pegged to euro	Same as the average in the 2007–11 period

Source: Authors.

References

Aizenman, Joshua, Menzie D. Chinn, and Hiro Ito. 2013. "The 'Impossible Trinity' Hypothesis in an Era of Global Imbalances: Measurement and Testing." *Review of International Economics* 21, no. 3: 447–58.

Aizenman, Joshua, and Hiro Ito. 2013. "Living with the Trilemma Constraint: Relative Trilemma Policy Divergence, Crises, and Output Losses for Developing Countries." NBER Working Paper No. 19448. Cambridge, Mass.: National Bureau of Economic Research (www.nber.org/papers/w19448).

Auboin, Marc. 2012. "Use of Currencies in International Trade: Any Changes in the Picture?" WTO Staff Working Paper ERSD-2012-10. Geneva: World Trade Organization, Economic Research and Statistics Division.

Bacchetta, Philippe, and Eric van Wincoop. 2005. "A Theory of the Currency Denomination of International Trade." *Journal of International Economics* 67, no. 2: 295–319.

Bank for International Settlements. 2013. *Triennial Central Bank Survey on Foreign Exchange Turnover in April 2013: Preliminary Global Results.* Basel: Bank for International Settlements.

Beck, Thorsten, Asli Demirgüç-Kunt, and Ross Levine. 2001. "A New Database on Financial Development and Structure." Policy Research Paper No. 2147. Washington: World Bank.

Bulgarian National Bank. 2006. *Annual Report.*

Caballero, Ricardo, Emmanuel Farhi, and Pierre-Olivier Gourinchas. 2008. "An Equilibrium Model of 'Global Imbalances' and Low Interest Rates." *American Economic Review* 98, no. 1: 358–93.

Chen, Xiaoli, and Yin-Wong Cheung. 2011. "Renminbi Going Global." HKIMR Working Paper No. 08/2011. Hong Kong: Hong Kong Institute for Monetary Research.

Chinn, Menzie D. 2012. "A Note on Reserve Currencies with Special Reference to the G-20 Countries." Paper prepared for International Growth Centre, India Central Programme, May 13 (www.ssc.wisc.edu/~mchinn/Reserve%20Currencies%20and%20G20_revd.pdf).

Chinn, Menzie D., Barry Eichengreen, and Hiro Ito. 2011. "A Forensic Analysis of Global Imbalances." NBER Working Paper No. 17513. Cambridge, Mass.: National Bureau of Economic Research, October.

Chinn, Menzie D., and Hiro Ito. 2006. "What Matters for Financial Development? Capital Controls, Institutions, and Interactions." *Journal of Development Economics* 81, no. 1: 163–92.

———. 2007. "Current Account Balances, Financial Development and Institutions: Assaying the World 'Savings Glut.' " *Journal of International Money and Finance* 26, no. 4: 546–69.

———. 2008. "A New Measure of Financial Openness." *Journal of Comparative Policy Analysis* 10, no. 3: 309–22.

Chinn, Menzie D., and Jeffrey A. Frankel. 2007. "Will the Euro Eventually Surpass the Dollar as Leading International Reserve Currency?" In *G7 Current Account Imbalances: Sustainability and Adjustment*, edited by R. Clarida. University of Chicago Press.

———. 2008. "Why the Dollar Will Rival the Euro." *International Finance* 11, no. 1: 49–73.

Cui, L., Chang Shu, and Jian Chang. 2009. "Exchange Rate Pass-Through and Currency Invoicing in China's Exports." *China Economic Issues*, Number 2/09 (published by Hong Kong Monetary Authority).

Da Silva, Jorge. 2004. "Determinants of the Choice of Invoicing Currency: From Dutch Guilders to Euros in Dutch Goods Trade." Unpublished paper. Tilburg University (Netherlands).

Donnenfeld, Shabtai, and Alfred Haug. 2003. "Currency Invoicing in International Trade: An Empirical Investigation." *Review of International Economics* 11, no. 2: 332–45.

Dornbusch, Rudiger. 1987. "Exchange Rates and Prices." *American Economic Review* 77, no. 1: 93–106.

Eichengreen, Barry. 2011. *Exorbitant Privilege: The Rise and Fall of the Dollar and the Future of the International Monetary System*. Oxford University Press.

European Central Bank. 2005. "Review of the International Role of the Euro." Frankfurt: European Central Bank.

———. 2007. "Review of the International Role of the Euro." Frankfurt: European Central Bank.

———. 2008 to 2013. "International Role of the Euro." Frankfurt: European Central Bank.

Frankel, Jeffrey. 2011. "Historical Precedents for Internationalization of the RMB." Center for Geoeconomic Studies and International Institutions and Global Governance (CGS/IIGG) Working Paper. Washington: Council on Foreign Relations.

Garcia-Herreno, Alicia, and Le Xia. 2013. "China's RMB Bilateral Swap Agreements: What Explains the Choice of Countries?" BBVA Research Working Paper No. 13/18. Hong Kong, China: BBVA Research.

Goldberg, Linda. 2010. "What Is the Status of the International Roles of the Dollar?" *Vox* (online journal), March 31 (www.voxeu.org/article/dollar-s-international-roles).

Goldberg, Linda, and Cedric Tille. 2008. "Vehicle Currency Use in International Trade." *Journal of International Economics* 76, no. 2: 177–92.

Grassman, Sven. 1973. "A Fundamental Symmetry in International Payments Patterns." *Journal of International Economics* 3, no. 2: 105–16.

Hristov, Kalin, and Martin Zaimov. 2001. "Shadowing the Euro: Bulgaria's Monetary Policy Five Years on," BIS Papers No. 17. Basel: Bank for International Settlements.

Huang, Yiping, Daili Wang, and Gang Fan. 2013. "Path to a Reserve Currency: Internationalization of RMB and Its Implications." Paper presented at the ADBI conference Currency Internationalization: Lessons and Prospects for the RMB. Tokyo, August 8.

Huang, Yiping, Xun Wang, and Nian Lin. 2013. "Financial Reform in China: Progress and Challenges." In *The Ongoing Financial Development of China, Japan, and Korea*, edited by H. Patrick and Y. C. Park. Columbia University Press.

Hung, Juann H. 2009. "China's Approach to Capital Flows since 1978." In *China and Asia: Economic and Financial Interactions*, edited by Y. W. Cheung and K. Wang. New York: Routledge.

International Monetary Fund. 2013. *World Economy Outlook,* April 2013, Washington: International Monetary Fund.

Ito, Takatoshi. 2011. "The Internationalization of the RMB: Opportunities and Pitfalls." A CGS-IIGG Working Paper. New York: Council on Foreign Relations.

Ito, Takatoshi, Satoshi Koibuchi, Kiyotaka Sato, and Junko Shimizu. 2010. "Why Has the Yen Failed to Become a Dominant Invoicing Currency in Asia? A Firm-Level Analysis of Japanese Exporters' Invoicing Behavior." NBER Working Paper 16231. Cambridge, Mass.: National Bureau of Economic Research, July.

Kaminsky, Graciela, and Sergio Schmukler. 2002. "Short-Run Pain, Long-Run Gain: The Effects of Financial Liberalization." World Bank Working Paper No. 2912. Washington: World Bank.

Kamps, Anne. 2006. "The Euro as Invoicing Currency in International Trade." Working Paper Series No. 665. Frankfurt: European Central Bank.

Kenen, Peter. 1983. "The Role of the Dollar as an International Reserve Currency." Occasional Papers No. 13, Group of Thirty. Washington: International Monetary Fund.

Kose, M. Ayhan, Eswar Prasad, Kenneth Rogoff, and Shan-Jin Wei. 2006. "Financial Globalization: A Reappraisal." IMF Working Paper WP/06/189. Washington: International Monetary Fund.

Krugman, Paul. 1980. "Vehicle Currencies and the Structure of International Exchange." *Journal of Money, Credit and Banking* 12, no. 3: 513–26.

———. 1984. "The International Role of the Dollar." In *Exchange Rate Theory and Practice*, edited by J. Bilson and R. Marston. University of Chicago Press.

———. 1987. "Pricing to Market When the Exchange Rate Changes." In *Real Financial Linkages among Open Economies*, edited by S. W. Arndt and J. D. Richardson. MIT Press.

Laeven, Luc, and Fabian Valencia. 2008. "Systematic Banking Crises: A New Database." IMF Working Paper WP/08/224. Washington: International Monetary Fund.

———. 2010. "Resolution of Banking Crises: The Good, the Bad, and the Ugly." IMF Working Paper No. 10/44. Washington: International Monetary Fund.

———. 2012. "Systematic Banking Crises: A New Database." IMF Working Paper WP/12/163. Washington: International Monetary Fund.

Lane, Philip R., and Gian Maria Milesi-Ferretti. 2007. "The External Wealth of Nations Mark II: Revised and Extended Estimates of Foreign Assets and Liabilities, 1970–2004." *Journal of International Economics* 73, no. 2: 223–50.

Ligthart, Jenny E., and Sebastian E. V. Werner. 2012. "Has the Euro Affected the Choice of Invoicing Currency?" Working Paper Series No. 1414. Frankfurt: European Central Bank.

Magee, Stephen P. and Ramesh K. S. Rao. 1980. "Vehicle and Nonvehicle Currencies in International Trade." *American Economic Review* 70, no. 2 (May): 368–73.

Maziad, Samar, Pascal Farahmand, Shengzu Wang, Stephanie Segal, and Faisal Ahmed. 2011. "Internationalization of Emerging Market Currencies: A Balance between Risks and Rewards." IMF Staff Discussion Note SDN/11/17. Washington: International Monetary Fund.

McKinnon, Ronald. 1979. *Money in International Exchange.* Oxford University Press.

Obstfeld, Maurice, Jay C. Shambaugh, and Alan M. Taylor. 2005. "The Trilemma in History: Tradeoffs among Exchange Rates, Monetary Policies, and Capital Mobility." *Review of Economics and Statistics* 87, no. 3: 423–38.

Page, S. A. B. 1977. "The Currency of Invoicing in Merchandise Trade." *National Institute Economic Review* 8, no. 1: 77–81.

————. 1981. "The Choice of Invoicing Currency in Merchandise Trade." *National Institute Economic Review* 98, no. 1: 60–72.

Park, Chul Park, and Kwanho Shin. 2009. "Internationalisation of Currency in East Asia: Implications for Regional Monetary and Financial Cooperation." Basel: Bank for International Settlements (www.bis.org/repofficepubl/arpresearch200903.09.pdf).

People's Bank of China. 2010 to 2013. *Annual Reports.* Beijing: People's Bank of China.

Prasad, Eswar, and Lei Ye. 2012. "The Renminbi's Role in the Global Monetary System." IZA Discussion Papers, No. 6335. Bonn: Institute of Labor Studies.

Quinn, Dennis, Martin Schindler, and A. Maria Toyoda. 2011. "Assessing Measures of Financial Openness and Integration. *IMF Economic Review* 59: 488–522.

Rey, Helen 2001. "International Trade and Currency Exchange Source." *Review of Economic Studies* 68, no. 2: 443–64.

Scharrer, Hans-Eckart. 1981. "Currency Diversification in International Trade and Payments: Empirical Evidence." In *Europe and the Dollar in the World-Wide Disequilibrium*, edited by J. R. Sargent and M. Van den Adel. Alphen aan den Rijn, Netherlands: Sijthoff & Noordhoff International Publishers.

Spencer, Michael. 2013. "A 'Yuan Bloc' in Asia? Not Yet." Global Economic Perspectives. Frankfurt: Deutsche Bank Research, February 7.

Subramanian, Arvind, and Martin Kessler. 2012. "The Renminbi Bloc Is Here: Asia Down, Rest of the World to Go?" Working Paper WP 12-19. Washington: Peterson Institute for International Economics.

Takagi, Shinji. 2009. "Internationalizing the Yen, 1984–2000: Unfinished Agenda or Mission Impossible?" Paper presented at the BoK-BIS seminar on currency internationalization, Lessons from the Global Financial Crisis and Prospects for the Future in Asia and the Pacific. Seoul, March 19 (www.bis.org/repofficepubl/arpresearch200903.04.pdf).

Tavlas, George S. 1991. "On the International Use of Currencies: The Case of the Deutsche Mark." Essays in International Finance 181. Princeton University.

Tavlas, George S., and Yuzuru Ozeki. 1992. "The Internationalization of Currencies: An Appraisal of the Japanese Yen." IMF Occasional Paper 90. Washington: International Monetary Fund.

Vallée, Shahin. 2012. "The Internationalization Path of the Renminbi." Bruegel Working Paper 2012/05. Brussels: Bruegel, March 13.

Wilander, Fredrik. 2006. "An Empirical Analysis of the Currency Denomination in International Trade." Unpublished paper. Stockholm School of Economics.

World Bank. 2012. *Global Development Finance—External Debt of Developing Countries.* Washington, D.C.: World Bank.

Yarita, Takashi. 1999. "Nihon no Boueki Kessai ni Kansuru Toukei Shiryou nit suite" [Concerning Data on Trade Settlement Currencies]. *Waseda Economic Studies* 48 (December).

Yu, Yongding. 2012. "Revisiting the Internationalization of the Yuan." ADBI Working Paper 366. Tokyo: Asian Development Bank Institute.

————. 2013. "How Far Can Internationalization of the RMB Go?" Unpublished paper. Beijing: Chinese Academy of Social Sciences.

6

The Renminbi and Exchange Rate Regimes in East Asia

MASAHIRO KAWAI AND VICTOR PONTINES

The recent rise of the People's Republic of China (PRC) as the world's largest trading nation (measured by trade value) and second-largest economic power (measured by GDP) has been accompanied by the PRC's greater economic influence over emerging economies in East Asia.[1] The dependence of these economies on the PRC through trade and investment has increased over time.

The PRC used to peg its currency, the renminbi (RMB), tightly to the U.S. dollar, but over the ten years since 2005 it has engineered currency appreciation against the dollar by allowing a certain degree of exchange rate flexibility. The PRC shifted its exchange rate arrangement from a conventional U.S. dollar peg to a crawling peg regime in July 2005. Although it temporarily restored a conventional U.S. dollar peg regime from August 2008 to May 2010, it once again shifted to a crawling-peg-like regime in June 2010. In general, the degree of exchange rate flexibility has increased over time.

In addition, the PRC has been pursuing a policy of internationalizing the RMB in the wake of the global financial crisis. The authorities started to allow firms to

---

1. In this paper East Asia includes the People's Republic of China (PRC), the Asian newly industrialized economies outside the Association of Southeast Asian Nations (Republic of Korea, Taipei,China, and Hong Kong, China), Mongolia, and member states of the Association of Southeast Asian Nations (Brunei Darussalam, Cambodia, Indonesia, Lao People's Democratic Republic, Malaysia, Myanmar, Philippines, Singapore, Thailand, and Viet Nam). To broaden our study we have included India.

settle merchandise trade in RMB, foreigners to hold offshore RMB deposits, and foreigners to issue offshore RMB bonds. In addition, a series of bilateral currency swap arrangements has been concluded between the People's Bank of China (PBOC) and foreign central banks to enable the latter to hold RMB and sell them to their importers who wish to pay for imports from the PRC in RMB.

Because of the rising economic importance of the PRC, its influence through expanding trade, and the RMB internationalization policy, the exchange rate policy of the PRC is likely to have significant implications for exchange rate regimes in emerging East Asian economies. Some experts (Eichengreen 2011) believe that the RMB will become a major international currency and rival—if not equal—the U.S. dollar relatively soon. Indeed, the RMB is now the world's eighth most actively used settlement currency and the world's ninth most heavily traded currency in foreign exchange markets. Some authors (Henning [2012], and Subramanian and Kessler [2013]) argue that the RMB has already begun to play the role of an anchor currency at least in emerging Asia. Others argue, however, that the RMB still has a long way to go to become a global reserve and anchor currency that other countries' central banks may use to stabilize the values of their currencies.

In this chapter we provide background information on the rising economic size of the PRC, the pace of RMB internationalization, and the capital account liberalization that is needed to support RMB internationalization. In the next section we discuss the evolution of the PRC's exchange rate regime and examine the behavior of the RMB exchange rate between 2000 and 2014 using the Frankel-Wei regression model. We then investigate the impact of RMB movements on those of other currencies in emerging East Asia, using the modified version of the Frankel-Wei regression model developed by Kawai and Pontines (2014). In the penultimate section we explore the potential for regional monetary and currency cooperation to achieve intra–East Asian exchange rate stability.

Rise of the People's Republic of China's Economy and Renminbi Internationalization

We will see in this section that alongside the expansion of the PRC economy, its trade has also increased rapidly until the PRC has become the world's largest trading nation. With the rise of the PRC as an important trade partner for most—maybe all—emerging economies in Asia, there is a good reason for these economies to track the RMB closely. Furthermore, since July 2009 the PRC has not only relaxed its restrictions on the use of the RMB for settling trade, it has also carefully and gradually eased some of its controls on the use of the renminbi for capital account transactions. Part of the reason for such official moves is the recognition that without adequate capital account liberalization, meaningful currency internationalization will not be achieved.

Rise of the People's Republic of China's Economy and Trade

The rapid pace of economic growth since the 1980s has made the PRC economy the world's second-largest economy, measured by nominal GDP at market exchange rates. It surpassed Japan in 2010 and is expected to become the world's largest economy, with a larger GDP than that of the United States, by the mid-2020s. The PRC's economic growth has important implications for exchange rate policies in other economies, particularly those in East Asia.

With the expansion of the PRC's economy, its trade has also increased rapidly. It has become the world's largest export nation, accounting for 14 percent of global exports in 2013 (see figure 6-1), and its imports have also risen and now account for 12 percent of the global total. The rising share of the PRC's exports in the global market suggests that its competitors may be concerned with their export competitiveness against the PRC and may wish to avoid the appreciation of their currencies against the RMB. The PRC's rising share of global imports also means that its expanding market is attractive for other economies as it provides an opportunity for economic growth. This suggests that these economies may wish to track the RMB closely.

Most emerging economies in East Asia have intensified their trade relationships with the PRC (table 6-1). Mongolia and Hong Kong, China have particularly high export dependence on the PRC, and Taipei,China; Australia; the Republic of Korea; Lao People's Democratic Republic (Lao PDR); and Myanmar have seen their export dependence rise in recent years. Myanmar, Mongolia, Viet Nam, Lao PDR, and Hong Kong, China have high import dependence on the PRC. It would not be surprising if most of these East Asian economies that have expanded trade with the PRC start to pay greater attention to the movement of the RMB in their exchange rate policies.

Renminbi Internationalization

Since the outbreak of the global financial crisis in the fall of 2008, the PRC authorities have been making significant efforts to internationalize the RMB. The U.S. dollar liquidity shortage caused by the crisis was considered to be a major deficiency of the existing international monetary system, and the PRC authorities believe that the creation of another international currency would make the global system more balanced and stable.

Since July 2009 the internationalization of the RMB has been pursued in finely calibrated phases. The PRC authorities started to allow exporters and importers to use RMB to settle merchandise trade. They then allowed RMB receipts by foreign exporters to be parked in Hong Kong, China as deposits. Banks and firms there were permitted to mobilize those RMB funds by issuing "dim sum bonds" so that they could use the funds to invest in mainland PRC. Issuance of RMB bonds in the Hong Kong, China offshore market has expanded. Furthermore, a

Figure 6-1. *Global Share of the People's Republic of China's Trade as Percentage of World Total*[a]

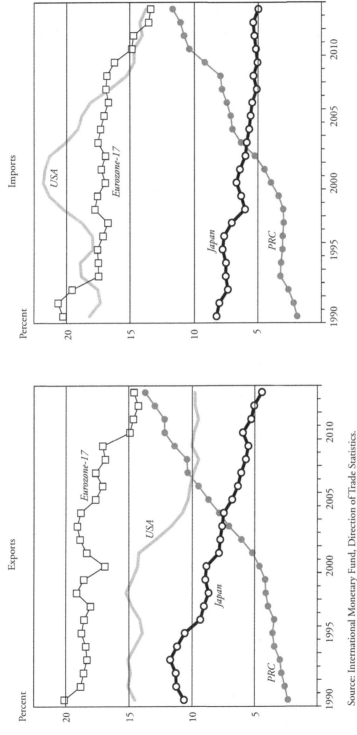

Source: International Monetary Fund, Direction of Trade Statistics.
a. Eurozone-17 exports and imports are net of intra-eurozone exports and imports.

Table 6-1. *Asian Economies' Share of Trade with the People's Republic of China as Percentage of Total Trade (Exports and Imports)*

	Exports to the PRC				Imports from the PRC			
	1990	2000	2010	2013	1990	2000	2010	2013
Australia	2.5	5.7	25.1	36.1	2.7	7.8	18.7	19.5
Bangladesh	1.5	0.2	1.2	1.7	3.4	7.4	16.8	21.9
Brunei Darussalam	0.1	1.8	7.0	0.8	2.7	1.2	12.9	22.1
Cambodia	0.4	2.1	1.2	3.7	5.9	7.9	24.2	22.0
Hong Kong, China	24.7	34.5	52.7	54.8	36.7	43.0	45.5	47.8
India	0.1	1.8	7.9	4.7	0.1	2.9	11.8	11.0
Indonesia	3.2	4.5	9.9	12.4	3.0	6.0	15.1	16.0
Japan	2.1	6.3	19.4	18.1	5.1	14.5	22.1	21.7
Republic of Korea	0.0	10.7	25.1	26.1	0.0	8.0	16.8	16.1
Lao PDR	9.1	1.5	23.3	25.1	10.7	5.5	14.7	26.1
Malaysia	2.1	3.1	12.5	14.1	1.9	3.9	12.6	17.0
Mongolia	11.4	49.8	81.6	90.0	21.5	17.8	41.7	37.8
Myanmar	8.1	5.7	13.5	24.5	20.6	18.0	38.5	40.0
New Zealand	1.0	3.0	11.2	20.8	1.2	6.2	16.0	17.5
Pakistan	1.2	2.7	7.4	11.0	4.6	5.0	17.4	22.5
Philippines	0.8	1.7	11.1	12.2	1.4	2.3	8.4	13.0
Singapore	1.5	3.9	10.4	11.8	3.4	5.3	10.8	11.7
Taipei, China	3.1	15.1	34.3	38.3	0.6	3.9	12.6	15.6
Thailand	1.2	4.1	11.1	11.9	3.3	5.5	13.2	15.0
Viet Nam	0.3	10.6	10.5	11.8	0.2	9.0	24.0	32.0

Source: IMF, *Direction of Trade Statistics.*
Lao PDR = Lao People's Democratic Republic.

series of bilateral currency-swap arrangements has been concluded between the People's Bank of China (PBOC) and foreign central banks to enable these foreign banks to hold RMB and sell the currency to their importers who wish to pay PRC exporters in RMB.

There is no question that the pace of RMB internationalization will be accelerated by these policy efforts. The rising economic size of the PRC and its expanding trade volume will also help the process of RMB internationalization, particularly in East Asia. These observations have led some experts (such as Eichengreen [2011] and Subramanian [2011]) to believe that the RMB, along with the euro, will become a major international currency rivaling the U.S. dollar relatively soon. It is highly desirable for the PRC as the world's second-largest economy to provide the RMB as an international currency not only for the PRC but also for global traders and investors.

An international currency plays several roles—as an invoicing currency for international trade, as a denomination currency for international investment, as a reference currency for other countries' exchange rate management, and as a foreign exchange reserve currency. The U.S. dollar, the euro, the Japanese yen, and the UK pound sterling are major international currencies today, and the Swiss franc, the Australian dollar, and the Canadian dollar are the next-tier international currencies (see table 6-2). These currencies are traded most frequently in international foreign exchange markets and are often held as foreign exchange reserves by the world's central banks.

Table 6-2 shows that the U.S. dollar is used for 87 percent of currency trading in global foreign exchange markets, followed by the euro (33 percent), the Japanese yen (23 percent), and the UK pound sterling (12 percent). The U.S. dollar is also the most preferred reserve currency, with 61 percent of the world's reserves being denominated in U.S. dollars, followed by the euro (25 percent), and sterling and the yen (4 percent each). Clearly, the U.S. dollar is by far the most dominant international currency, followed by the euro and then by the yen and sterling. The global presence of the RMB used to be very limited, but has been rapidly rising over the last few years. The RMB is the ninth most traded currency in the world's foreign exchange market and also the eighth most heavily used currency for payment.

The information presented in table 6-2 suggests that economies that provide international currencies tend to share several features:

1. They are the world's most advanced high-income countries (with the exception of Mexico).

2. They have eliminated capital flow restrictions and achieved full currency convertibility.

3. They have well-developed, liquid financial markets.

4. They have maintained social and political stability.

Once a country acquires these properties, its currency tends to become an international currency. Acquiring these properties is an important way for the PRC to make the RMB a truly international currency.

It is important to note that for a currency to become a *major* international currency, large economic size is essential. For example, the currencies of Singapore, New Zealand, and Hong Kong, China have achieved international currency status, but they are not major or even second-tier international currencies because of the economies' small economic size. Australia, Canada, and Switzerland cannot go beyond the second-tier international currency status for the same reason. The PRC's GDP is already the second-largest in the world and will likely catch up with the United States and the eurozone in less than ten years. In addition, the PRC's trade volume is now slightly larger than that of the United States. The currency of a large economy tends to be used frequently for trade invoicing, investment denomination, and reserve holding, and—if foreign investors and central banks find it easy and convenient to use the currency—as an anchor for exchange rate stabilization. This suggests that once the RMB achieves international currency sta-

Table 6-2. *Global Shares of Several International Currencies, Including the Currency of the People's Republic of China*[a]

Economy (currency)	Foreign exchange market turnover, 2013 (percent of total turnover)	Foreign exchange reserves held, 2013 (percent of total reserves)	World payment currency, Feb 2014 (percent of total payment)	GDP in $ trillion, 2013 (percent of world GDP)	GDP per capita, 2013 (US$)
United States ($)	87.0	61.2	38.9	16,800 (22.7)	53,101
Eurozone (€)	33.4	24.6	33.0	13,416 (17.2)	38,073
Japan (¥)	23.0	3.9	2.5	4,901 (6.6)	38,491
United Kingdom (£)	11.8	4.0	9.4	2,536 (3.4)	39,567
Australia (A$)	8.6	1.6	1.8	1,505 (2.0)	64,863
Switzerland (SwF)	5.2	0.2	1.5	651 (0.9)	81,324
Canada (Can$)	4.6	1.7	1.8	1,825 (2.5)	51,990
Mexico (Mex$)	2.5	—	0.3	1,259 (1.7)	10,630
PRC (CNY)	2.2	—	1.4	9,181 (12.4)	6,747
New Zealand (NZ$)	2.0	—	0.4	181 (0.2)	40,481

Sources: Bank for International Settlements; International Monetary Fund; Society for Worldwide Interbank Financial Telecommunication (SWIFT).

a. For foreign exchange market turnover data, the sum of the percentage shares of individual currencies totals 200 percent, as two currencies are involved in each transaction. GDP is at current prices and exchange rates.

Table 6-3. *State of Capital Account Liberalization in the People's Republic of China*

Type of cross-border transactions and items under control	Not convertible	Partially convertible (highly restricted)	Basically convertible (lightly restricted)	Fully convertible	Total
Capital and money market transactions	2	10	4	0	16
Derivatives and other instruments transactions	2	2	0	0	4
Credit instruments transactions	0	1	5	0	6
Direct investments	0	1	1	0	2
Liquidation of direct investments	0	0	1	0	1
Real estate transactions	0	2	1	0	3
Individual capital transactions	0	6	2	0	8
Subtotal	4	22	14	0	40

Source: People's Bank of China, Statistics and Analysis Section (February 2012).

tus, it has the potential to become a *major* international currency comparable to the U.S. dollar, the euro, and the yen.

Capital Account Liberalization

Progress toward capital account liberalization is essential to the internationalization of a currency—without adequate capital account liberalization, meaningful currency internationalization will not be achieved. The PRC has implemented a series of capital account liberalization measures since its adoption of economic reforms and opening in the late 1970s (see table 6-3).

According to the table, in the PRC, four capital account items out of forty are not convertible, twenty-two are partially convertible, and fourteen are basically convertible. No item has achieved full convertibility. Credit-instruments transactions and direct investments, which are essentially long-term capital flows, are the items that have been liberalized most, whereas capital and money market transactions, derivatives and other-instruments transactions, real estate transactions, and individual capital transactions are the least liberalized items.

The degree of financial market openness can be measured by indexes that show the extent of de jure as well as de facto capital account openness. Figure 6-2 plots such indexes for the PRC, using Japan as a reference. The index of de jure capital account openness was constructed by Chinn and Ito (2008) on the basis of information in the IMF's *Annual Report on Exchange Arrangements and Exchange Restrictions* (International Monetary Fund 2001 to 2013).[2] The index of de facto

2. Starting in 1950 the IMF's *Annual Report on Exchange Arrangements and Exchange Restrictions* (*AREAER*) database tracks exchange rate arrangements and exchange controls for all 187 IMF member countries. It is published annually and updated monthly.

Figure 6-2. *Indexes of Capital Account Openness for the People's Republic of China and Japan*

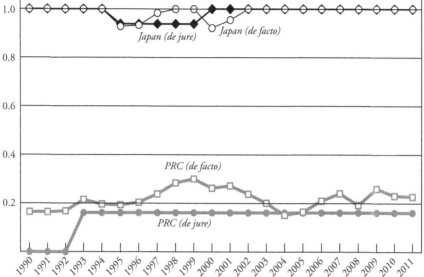

Index, 1.0 = fully open; 0.0 = completely closed

Sources: Chinn and Ito (2008; see also website: http://web.pdx.edu/~ito/Chinn-Ito_website.htm; Ito and Kawai (2012).

capital account openness has been developed by Ito and Kawai (2012), who use a country's external assets (excluding foreign exchange reserves) and liabilities relative to a combination of the country's GDP and trade values.

Figure 6-2 shows that the PRC achieved a certain degree of capital account openness in the first half of the 1990s but has not made any progress since then, according to the de jure index. Surprisingly, the de facto measure also suggests that the PRC has not made much progress on capital account liberalization in the 2000s, at least until 2011. In contrast, Japan had already achieved full capital account convertibility by 1990.[3] One of the reasons for the lack of progress on de facto capital account liberalization, despite the liberalization of various types of capital account restrictions (see table 6-3), is that the pace of regulatory liberalization has not been fast enough to catch up with the PRC's expanding GDP and trade volumes.

An internal document of the PBOC highlighted a three-stage plan to push forward capital account liberalization, hinting that it may take ten years for the PRC to achieve full capital account convertibility:

3. Although not shown in figure 6-2, the de jure and de facto indexes suggest that Japan achieved full capital account openness in 1983 (de jure) and 1989 (de facto). By 1970, Japan had achieved a level of de jure capital account openness that was far higher than the PRC's level in 2011. According to the de facto measure, the current level of the PRC's capital account openness is equivalent to Japan's in 1983.

—2012 to 2015: Relax flows associated with foreign direct investments, both inbound and outbound.

—2015 to 2017: Relax credit flows related to genuine trade to support the internationalization of the RMB.

—2017 to 2022: Strengthen the infrastructure of domestic financial systems; allowing inflows before outflows; and opening up real estate, equity, and bond markets for foreign capital investments.

PBOC Governor Zhou Xiaochuan also stated that the basic (not full or free) convertibility of the capital account would be achieved by 2015. However, figure 6-2 suggests that achieving a high degree of capital account liberalization within such a short time period would be a significant challenge.

Evolution of the People's Republic of China's Exchange Rate Regime

Although the PRC has since 2005 allowed some flexibility in its exchange rate against the U.S. dollar, the overriding preference of monetary authorities in the PRC, on both a de jure and de facto basis, is to adhere to the U.S. dollar as the anchor of the exchange rate policy. Based on the trilemma hypothesis, this has so far permitted the authorities to control tightly its capital account and enjoy the benefits of high monetary policy independence. Such preferred policy choices are being tested as the PRC slowly moves to greater exchange rate flexibility.

Exchange Rate Behavior

Until 1994 the PRC had a dual exchange rate system where the official exchange rate was set at a much higher level than the market rate. In early 1994 these rates were unified, with the official rate being devalued by about 30 percent from CNY5.8 to CNY8.48 per U.S. dollar (see figure 6-3). Thereafter, the exchange rate appreciated slightly to CNY8.28 per U.S. dollar and stayed there until July 2005. Although the PRC authorities defined the country's exchange rate regime as a managed float with a 0.3 percent daily fluctuation band, it was in reality a fixed exchange rate regime against the U.S. dollar. The regime was maintained rigidly during and after the Asian financial crisis of 1997–1998.

On July 21, 2005, the PRC authorities announced that they would revalue the RMB against the U.S. dollar by 2.1 percent, from CNY8.28 to CNY8.11, and move away from the long-standing U.S. dollar peg system to a managed float system with an undisclosed currency basket as a reference. They also added that the daily exchange rate against the U.S. dollar might fluctuate within the previously set band of ±0.3 percent around the announced central parity, and ±1.5 percent against non-U.S.-dollar currencies.[4]

4. On September 25, 2005, the daily fluctuation range of non-U.S.-dollar currencies was widened from ±1.5 percent to ±3 percent.

Figure 6-3. *Renminbi–U.S. Dollar Exchange Rate and the Renminbi's Real Effective Exchange Rate (REER), November 1990–January 2013*[a]

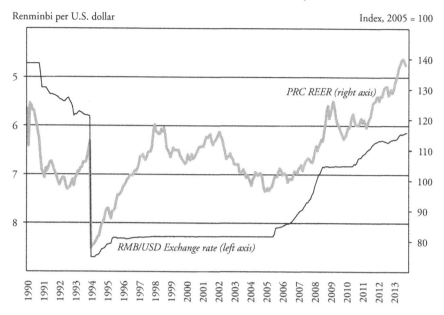

Renminbi per U.S. dollar   Index, 2005 = 100

Source: International Monetary Fund, *International Financial Statistics.*
a. An increase in the value means RMB appreciation.

Starting in July 2005, the authorities allowed the RMB to appreciate gradually, partly to tighten monetary policy in response to the domestic economy's overheating and partly to respond to the criticism by the United States and IMF that the PRC had maintained an undervalued currency, which led to rising current account surpluses and foreign exchange reserves. The pace of appreciation was slow and well controlled but persistent until the summer of 2008. The nominal RMB value against the U.S. dollar appreciated by 17.5 percent and the RMB real effective rate, by 15 percent between June 2005 and September 2008, when the RMB reached a peak before the world faced the grave consequences of the global financial crisis.

In the summer of 2008 the PRC authorities decelerated the pace of RMB appreciation and restored a U.S. dollar peg system for the RMB before the Lehman shock sent global financial markets into deep turmoil. These officials were concerned about the erosion of the PRC's export competitiveness and decided to stabilize the RMB rate against the U.S. dollar even before many of its export competitors in the region began to suffer from sharp depreciations of their currencies after the collapse of Lehman Brothers. The RMB exchange rate was set at CNY6.83 per U.S. dollar until May 2010. In June 2010 the PRC abandoned the peg once again, allowing RMB appreciation against the U.S. dollar to resume.

Figure 6-4. *The People's Republic of China's Current Account, Financial Account, and Reserves, 1990–2010*

Percent of GDP

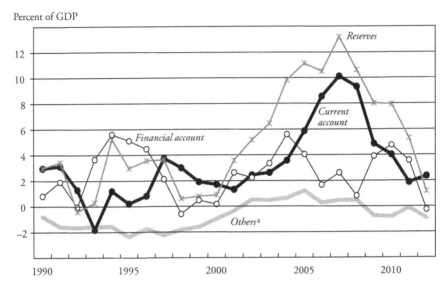

Source: International Monetary Fund, *International Financial Statistics.*
a. Refers to errors and omissions.

Figure 6-4 shows the PRC's balance of payments: the current account, the financial account, and reserve accumulation. The PRC ran a large current account surplus in the second half of the 2000s, reaching 10 percent of GDP in 2007, and rapidly shrank thereafter. The country's reserve accumulation was also notable, given the surpluses in both the current account and the financial account. Its stock of foreign exchange reserves reached US$3.8 trillion at the end of 2013.

IMF Classification of the PRC's Exchange Rate Regimes

East Asia exhibits a rich set of diverse foreign exchange rate regimes. The spectrum ranges from the U.S. dollar peg of Hong Kong, China's currency board system (and Brunei Darussalam's Singapore dollar peg under its own currency board system) at one end to the free–floating Japanese yen at the other (see table 6-4). In between, there are various types of intermediate regimes chosen by different economies (other conventional fixed-peg arrangements, stabilized arrangements, crawling-peg regimes, crawl-like arrangements, other managed regimes, managed floating arrangements, and floating regimes).

The first row of the table shows changes in the PRC's exchange rate regime as defined by the IMF. As explained earlier, the PRC had a dollar peg system until July 2005, defined by the IMF as "other conventional fixed peg arrangement (U.S. dollar)." The move to what the authorities called a managed float was recognized by the IMF as a move to a "crawling peg" only in August 2006 and was reported

Table 6-4. *International Monetary Fund's Classification of Exchange Rate Arrangements of East Asian Economies, 2000 to 2013*[a]

	Dec 2000	Dec 2001	Dec 2002	Dec 2003	Dec 2004	Apr 2006	Apr 2007	Apr 2008	Apr 2009	Apr 2010	Apr 2011	Apr 2012	Apr 2013
PRC	Other conventional fixed-peg arrangement (USD)					Crawling-peg (USD)			Stabilized arrangement (USD)		Crawl-like arrangement		
Japan		Independently floating							Free floating				
Rep. of Korea		Independently floating							Free floating	Floating			
Hong Kong, China	Currency board (USD)												
India	Managed floating[b]									Floating			
Mongolia	Independently floating		Managed floating				Other conventional fixed-peg arrangement (USD)			Floating			
Brunei Darussalam	Currency board (Singapore dollar)												
Cambodia	Managed floating (USD)					Managed floating			Floating		Stabilized arrangement (USD)		
Indonesia	Independently floating			Managed floating					Floating				Crawl-like arrangement
Lao People's Democratic Republic	Managed floating						Conventional pegged arrangement (USD)	Managed floating (USD)	Stabilized arrangement (USD)		Stabilized arrangement		
Malaysia	Other conventional fixed-peg arrangement (USD)					Managed floating				Other managed arrangement			
Myanmar	Other conventional fixed-peg arrangement (composite)			Managed floating				Managed floating (USD)	Other managed arrangement				
Philippines	Independently floating								Floating				
Singapore	Managed floating							Managed floating (composite)	Other managed arrangement (composite)	Crawl-like arrangement (composite)			
Thailand	Independently floating			Managed floating					Floating				
Viet Nam	Pegged exchange rate within horizontal bands		Managed floating			Other conventional fixed-peg arrangement (USD)			Stabilized arrangement (USD)			Stabilized arrangement (composite)	Stabilized arrangement (USD)

Sources: For 2001 to 2013: International Monetary Fund, Annual Report on Exchange Arrangements and Exchange Restrictions; for 2000: International Monetary Fund, *International Financial Statistics*.

a. Beginning in 2006, the IMF adopted new classifications based on de facto exchange rate arrangements which could be different from de jure arrangements.

b. "Managed floating" means floating with no predetermined path for the exchange rate.

as such in the April 2007 issue of the IMF's *Annual Report on Exchange Arrangements and Exchange Restrictions (AREAER).*[5] The reason for this delay was that the fluctuation in the RMB-U.S. dollar exchange rate was less than the 2 percent range (for a three-month period) used in the IMF's exchange rate classification system, so that initially the regime was classified as a conventional fixed-peg exchange rate arrangement. The return to a U.S. dollar peg in mid-2008 was immediately captured by the IMF, effective June 2008, as the RMB showed the characteristics of a stabilized arrangement. The table shows the change made in the April 2009 issue of *AREAER* to a "U.S. dollar stabilized arrangement," which lasted briefly. The authorities then began allowing RMB appreciation in mid-2010. In the April 2011 issue of *AREAER*, the IMF reclassified the PRC's exchange rate arrangement, effective June 2010, to a "crawl-like arrangement" because the RMB had gradually appreciated against the U.S. dollar, while the rate remained in a 2 percent crawling band. Previously, the RMB had been stable within a range of ±1 percent since mid-2008. This continues to be the PRC's current arrangement, according to the most recent IMF classification of exchange rate arrangements published in April 2013.

Changes in the People's Republic of China's Observed Exchange Rate Regimes

Although the IMF classification of exchange rate arrangements is useful, the question remains as to how clear-cut these definitions are, especially in those periods when the observed exchange rates appear to have tight links with the U.S. dollar. The way to ascertain this is to run the Frankel-Wei (1994) regression; that is, to regress changes in the value of the local currency, in this case the RMB against changes in the value of the U.S. dollar, euro, yen, and sterling that can exert a significant influence on the movements in the RMB. This has become the standard approach used to estimate the influence of important international currencies in the currency baskets of individual countries and thus identify "observed" exchange rate regimes. The equation to be estimated is expressed as:

$$(6\text{-}1) \quad \Delta\log\left(\frac{RMB}{NZD}\right) = \phi_0 + \phi_1\Delta\log\left(\frac{USD}{NZD}\right) + \phi_2\Delta\log\left(\frac{EURO}{NZD}\right) + \phi_3\Delta\log\left(\frac{JPY}{NZD}\right)$$
$$+ \phi_4\Delta\log\left(\frac{GBP}{NZD}\right),$$

where $\Delta\log\left(\frac{k}{NZD}\right)$, k = *RMB, USD, EURO, JPY,* and *GBP*, is the logarithmic change in the exchange rate of currency (the RMB, U.S. dollar, euro, yen and sterling, respectively) per New Zealand dollar.[6] The exchange rates are taken in logs

5. See International Monetary Fund (2007).
6. Here the New Zealand dollar is chosen as the numeraire currency. Previous studies have typically used either the Swiss franc or the special drawing rights (SDRs) as the numeraire currency. How-

Table 6-5. *Changes in Observed Exchange Rate Regimes for the Renminbi*[a]

Estimation period	U.S. Dollar	Euro	Yen	Pound sterling	R^2
Post-AFC period					
(January 3, 2000, to June 30, 2005)	0.999*** (0.000)	0.000 (0.000)	0.000 (0.000)	−0.000 (0.000)	0.999
Pre-Lehman period					
(July 21, 2005, to July 21, 2008)	0.934*** (0.009)	0.044*** (0.013)	0.028*** (0.007)	−0.017 (0.013)	0.979
GFC period					
(August 1, 2008, to May 31, 2010)	0.970*** (0.006)	0.023*** (0.008)	0.003 (0.004)	0.003 (0.005)	0.996
Post-GFC period					
(June 1, 2010, to March 31, 2014)	0.940*** (0.008)	0.034*** (0.007)	0.011** (0.005)	0.002 (0.008)	0.985

Source: Authors' calculations.

a.. The estimates for the baskets of the RMB are obtained from estimating equation 6-1. The values in parentheses are the estimated robust standard errors.

AFC = Asian financial crisis, GFC = global financial crisis.

* = $p < 10\%$; ** = $p < 5\%$; *** = $p < 1\%$.

and transformed into first differences. The important international anchor (or reference) currencies are on the right-hand side of this equation and the estimated coefficients of these anchor or reference currencies are their implied weights in the currency basket for the RMB.[7]

We have run equation 6-1 across four non-overlapping sub-periods: the post–Asian financial crisis (post-AFC) period (January 3, 2000, to June 30, 2005); the pre-Lehman period (July 21, 2005, to July 21, 2008); the global financial crisis (GFC) period (August 1, 2008, to May 31, 2010); and the post-GFC period (June 1, 2010, to March 31, 2014). Table 6-5 presents the estimation results of the Frankel-Wei regressions for the PRC's observed exchange rate regimes. The results in the sub-periods that correspond to the PRC as having operated a conventional

---

ever, there are problems with these numeraire currencies. The Swiss franc has been pegged to the euro since September 2011 and would be inappropriate to serve as a numeraire currency in the Frankel-Wei regression. The SDR on the other hand, comprises the same currencies that are included on the right-hand side of equation 6-1. The choice of the New Zealand dollar in our estimation is based on the fact that it is a freely floating currency of a small and open economy without capital and exchange controls, and one that we believe should not be accorded major importance or significant weight to the currency baskets of the Asian economies that we examine here.

7. We are not aware of any previous study besides Ogawa and Sakane (2006) that shows the RMB to depend on other East Asian currencies in a systematic manner. The Ogawa and Sakane (2006) study included the Republic of Korea's won on the right-hand side of equation 6-1, but, in all of the regressions, the won came out to be statistically insignificant.

fixed peg arrangement (post-AFC period) as well as a U.S. dollar stabilized arrangement (GFC period) are fully captured by the large and significant U.S. dollar coefficients that are close to unity.[8] The results in the sub-periods when the PRC was classified as having operated a U.S. dollar crawling peg and a crawl-like arrangement show lower weights on the U.S. dollar (0.934 in the pre-Lehman period; 0.940 in the post-GFC period) than in the sub-periods of the RMB's U.S. dollar peg or stabilization, although these estimated U.S. dollar weights are still quite high in value. In addition, the fit, measured by R^2, is still good even in the periods of relative exchange rate flexibility. For example, R^2 was almost 1 during the initial period of a fixed exchange rate regime (post-AFC) and the second period of a peg (GFC period), and declined marginally to 0.979 and 0.985 in the periods of relative exchange rate flexibility (pre-Lehman and post-GFC periods). These findings seem to indicate that the PRC's exchange rate management behavior reflected its willingness, thus far, to allow RMB appreciation against the U.S. dollar but not to let go of the U.S. dollar as its major anchor currency. In the pre-Lehman period and the post-GFC period, the euro and the yen took on some importance in the PRC's exchange rate management.

How stable are the estimates presented in table 6-5? One way to answer this is to carry out a series of "rolling" regressions of the Frankel-Wei type presented earlier. The way to implement such regressions is first to specify a window width of 260 daily trading observations (equivalent to a year) that begins on the first trading day of January 2000. This specified window width is then moved by estimating equation 6-1 at a step-size of one daily observation at a time and through the remaining observations that end on the last trading day of March 2014. In each of the rolling regressions using the specified window width of 260 days, we are able to arrive at a collection of point estimates of the coefficients (that is, weights) of the currencies on the right-hand side of the equation, including the U.S. dollar, euro, yen, and sterling (see figure 6-5). What is clear from the figure is that, while the U.S. dollar weights accorded by the PRC have dipped slightly following the move to introduce some relative flexibility to the RMB in July 2005, these U.S. dollar weights are still quite high in value and dominate those of the other international major currencies. However, the decision to introduce some flexibility to the RMB is associated with the rising weights of the euro and yen in the PRC's currency basket.

Factors behind a High Degree of Exchange Rate Stability in the People's Republic of China

An important question is why the PRC has maintained relatively high weights on the U.S. dollar and a high degree of exchange rate stability even though it has

8. In fact, in the post-AFC period, during which the PRC was classified as having operated a conventional fixed peg arrangement, the estimated U.S. dollar coefficient was equal to 0.999, and in the

Figure 6-5. *Estimated Weights of the U.S. Dollar, Euro, Yen, and Pound Sterling in the People's Republic of China's Currency Basket*

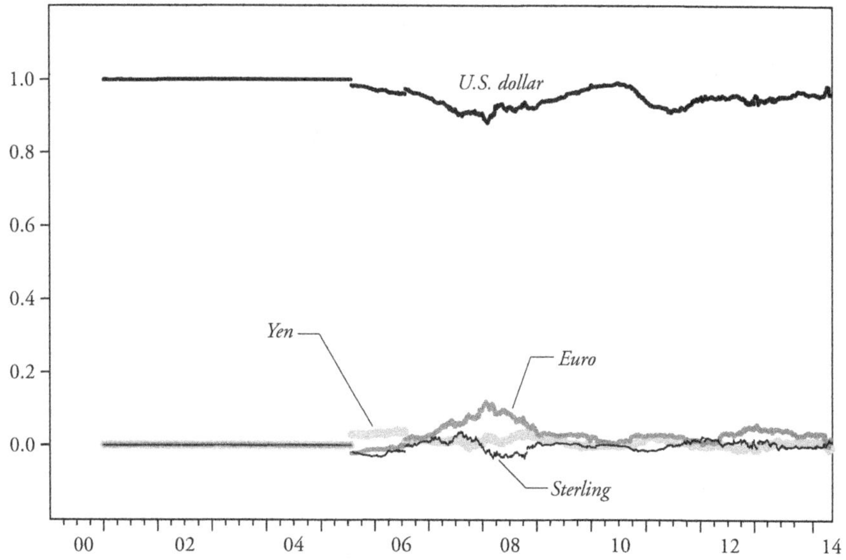

Source: Authors' calculations, based on rolling regressions of the Frankel-Wei regression model.

allowed substantial RMB appreciation since mid-2005. One important factor is its tight capital controls (see figure 6-2). Without significant capital account opening, the PRC authorities have been able to enjoy a high degree of monetary policy independence even under relatively stable exchange rate arrangements. This reflects the well-known "impossible trinity" or "trilemma" hypothesis in the choice of exchange rate regime for any economy. The hypothesis states that an economy may simultaneously choose any two, but not all, of three goals: exchange rate stability, capital account openness, and monetary policy independence.

Figure 6-6 depicts the Ito–Kawai (2012) index of monetary policy independence for the PRC and Japan as a reference. While the values of the index gyrate, the PRC appears to be enjoying an increasing degree of monetary policy independence (almost to the same extent as Japan). In the context of the trilemma hypothesis, Japan's choice has been to open its capital account fully and to allow free floating of the currency, thereby securing monetary policy independence. The PRC's trilemma choice has been to control its capital account tightly, to maintain stable exchange rates against the U.S. dollar (although allowing measured RMB appreciation), and to secure high degrees of monetary policy independence. Essentially, the

GFC period, when the PRC was classified as having operated a U.S. dollar stabilized arrangement, the estimated U.S. dollar coefficient was close to 1, at 0.970.

Figure 6-6. *Indexes of Monetary Policy Independence for the People's Republic of China and Japan, 1990 to 2011*

Index, 1 = complete monetary independence; 0 = no monetary independence

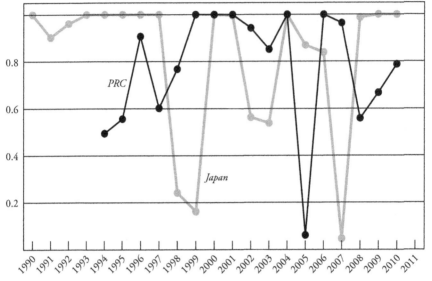

Source: Ito and Kawai (2012).

PRC authorities have been able to set the interest rate and stabilize the exchange rate under the tightly controlled capital account.

This suggests, however, that with planned progressive capital account liberalization (to be achieved by 2015 or 2020), the PRC authorities will have to make the RMB exchange rate much more flexible if they want to maintain monetary policy independence. Thus, the current policy of RMB internationalization, which would require significant capital account openness, calls for substantial exchange rate flexibility.

Role of the Renminbi in the Exchange Rate Regimes of Emerging Asian Economies

Have the East Asian economies attached any importance to the RMB in their exchange rate policies? We identify difficulties in estimating the weight of the RMB in the usual Frankel-Wei method and attempt to overcome such difficulties. Based on a new method, we document that the East Asian economies have assigned some importance to the RMB but not to the extent of concluding that a RMB bloc has emerged in Asia. This result is in contrast to several previous studies that claim that there is indeed a RMB bloc in Asia.

Exchange Rate Behavior of East Asian Currencies

The exchange rate movements of East Asian currencies during the period 2000–2014 are plotted in nominal effective terms in figure 6-7 and in real effective terms in figure 6-8.[9]

Figure 6-7 shows that at the beginning of the 2000s, most currencies except the Hong Kong dollar and RMB fluctuated and often depreciated to varying extents. This nominal depreciation quickly reversed, however, in most currencies—a trend that continued until the onset of the global financial crisis. The RMB began its gradual appreciation in mid-2005 when the PRC exited from the U.S. dollar peg, and this trend continued after the global financial crisis. The Republic of Korea's won, the Japanese yen, and to a lesser extent the New Taiwan (NT) dollar also experienced appreciating trends, though the won depreciated significantly during the global financial crisis of 2008–2009. The yen had already experienced a nominal depreciation just before the global financial crisis and was on a nominal trend appreciation at the time of the crisis. This nominal yen appreciation lasted for a few more years and only started to reverse in late 2012.

The Thai baht, Singapore dollar, Philippine peso, Indian rupee, and to a lesser extent the Indonesian rupiah also experienced depreciation trends in the early 2000s. The Malaysian ringgit appreciated after the authorities decided to loosen its fixed peg to the U.S. dollar (following the RMB's move to exit from its U.S. dollar peg) and also depreciated in nominal terms in 2008 and 2009. Eventually, most Association of Southeast Asian Nations (ASEAN) currencies recovered in nominal terms from the effects of the global financial crisis and have experienced relatively stable rates toward the end of the period of observation. The notable exceptions are the Indonesian rupiah and the Indian rupee, which experienced substantial nominal depreciations in the wake of discussions of the possible beginning of tapering off of U.S. quantitative easing monetary policy between May and September 2013.

Figure 6-8 depicts movements of real effective exchange rates (REERs), based on consumer price indexes, for East Asian currencies. The RMB began to appreciate in mid-2005 and has consistently trended this way since. Three currencies—the Hong Kong dollar, the NT dollar, and the Japanese yen—have experienced real depreciations to varying extents since the beginning of the 2000s. The yen experienced a real depreciation until the global financial crisis, sharply appreciated and remained strong during the 2008–2009 global financial crisis, and in recent years has again experienced a real depreciation. In contrast, the won, which had appreciated in real terms since the beginning of the 2000s, began to depreciate a year before the global financial crisis and remained steady in real terms.

9. BIS data on nominal and real effective exchange rates are available only for the Asian economies shown in figures 6-7 and 6-8. They are not readily available for Brunei Darussalam, Cambodia, Lao PDR, Mongolia, Myanmar, and Viet Nam.

Figure 6-7. *Nominal Exchange Rate Movements of Asian Currencies, January 2000 to April 2014*

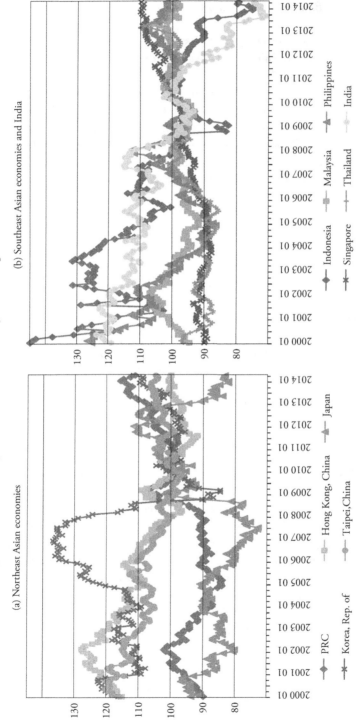

(a) Northeast Asian economies

(b) Southeast Asian economies and India

Indonesia   Malaysia   Philippines

Singapore   Thailand   India

PRC   Hong Kong, China   Japan

Korea, Rep. of   Taipei,China

Source: Bank for International Settlements (2001–13).
a. An increase denotes an appreciation; a decrease denotes a depreciation.

Figure 6-8. *Real Effective Exchange Rate Movements of Asian Economies, January 2000 to April 2014*

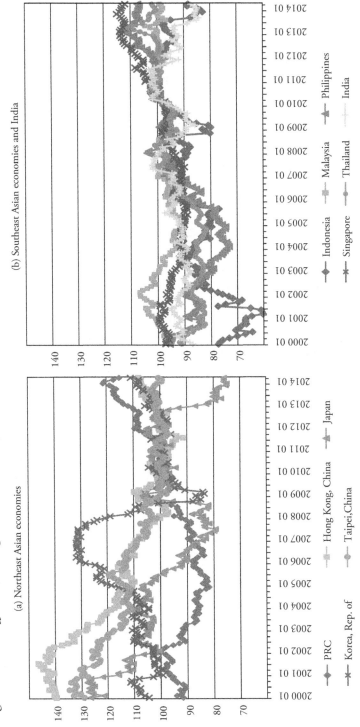

(a) Northeast Asian economies

(b) Southeast Asian economies and India

◆ PRC   ■ Hong Kong, China   ▲ Japan

✶ Korea, Rep. of   ● Taipei,China

◆ Indonesia   ■ Malaysia   ▲ Philippines

● Singapore   ✶ Thailand   ┼ India

Source: Bank for International Settlements.

a. Bank for International Settlements effective exchange rate (EER) indexes. An increase denotes an appreciation; a decrease denotes a depreciation.

The Indonesian rupiah, for most of the period of observation, experienced a real appreciation that was only briefly interrupted during the global financial crisis. In recent years the rupiah has started to depreciate in real terms. The Philippine peso initially experienced a real depreciation, started to appreciate in real terms in late 2004, and has continued on this path since then. The Malaysian ringgit, Indian rupee, Thai baht, and Singapore dollar were relatively steady in their movements in real terms for the most part, although in recent years the Singapore dollar has experienced a moderate real appreciation and the Indian rupee a moderate real depreciation.

Table 6-6 shows the correlation coefficients between pairs of currencies across the four non-overlapping sub-periods considered in the previous section. The correlation coefficients that are at least 0.70 in the table are shaded to show that they are high.

Focusing first on the post-AFC period, when the RMB was pegged to the U.S. dollar, one can see relatively high correlations between major international currencies (except the euro) and East Asian currencies (except the Indonesian rupiah). The RMB also exhibited high correlations with all East Asian currencies other than the rupiah and the yen, which may reflect the RMB's peg to the U.S. dollar—with the correlation coefficient between the RMB and the U.S. dollar being 1.0—and other East Asian authorities' preference to stabilize their currencies against the U.S. dollar. Turning to the pre-Lehman period, when the RMB steadily appreciated against the U.S. dollar, correlations between Asian currencies and major international currencies became much tighter than in the previous sub-period. The correlation coefficient between the U.S. dollar and the RMB for this sub-period declined slightly to 0.989, which was still high. The RMB continued to exhibit high correlations with other East Asian currencies, but these correlations tended to be lower than the U.S. dollar's correlations with these currencies except the NT dollar, Singapore dollar, and Thai baht. This suggests the possibility that at least the NT dollar, Singapore dollar, and baht began to move more closely to the RMB than in the previous sub-period. Looking at the GFC period when the RMB resumed its U.S. dollar peg, we observe that the strong correlations in the earlier sub-periods disappeared in a number of pairs of currencies. For instance, the pound sterling lost its strong correlations with other currencies and the correlations of the Cambodian riel also went below the threshold across almost all pairs of currencies. The currencies that exhibited stronger correlations with the RMB than with the U.S. dollar were the NT dollar, Singapore dollar, riel, Indian rupee, ringgit, and rupiah. Finally, with regard to the correlation coefficients during the post-GFC period, when the RMB again steadily appreciated against the U.S. dollar, we observe that the euro lost its strong correlation with most East Asian currencies. The East Asian currencies that exhibited higher correlations with the RMB than with the U.S. dollar were the won, Singapore dollar, ringgit, and baht.

*Evolution of International Monetary Fund–Defined Exchange Rate
Regimes in East Asia*

Table 6-4 shows the IMF's classification of exchange rate arrangements for East
Asian economies for the period 2000–13. The table shows that after the 1997–
1998 Asian financial crisis, almost all the crisis-affected economies, with the
exception of Malaysia, were reported to have adopted different varieties of
exchange rate flexibility. The Philippines and Republic of Korea adopted an independent float from 2000 to 2008, and then a floating regime from 2009 to 2013.
Indonesia and Thailand were briefly in an independent float from 2000 to 2001,
then both switched to a managed float regime from 2002 to 2008, and returned
to introducing more flexibility by adopting a floating regime from 2009 to 2012.
The only difference between these two countries is that Indonesia was recently
reported to have adopted a crawl-like exchange rate arrangement. Malaysia
implemented a conventional fixed peg arrangement in September 1998, and then
followed the PRC's exit from its U.S. dollar peg in July 2005 to adopt a managed
float regime.

The exchange rate arrangements of other Asian economies not directly affected
by the Asian financial crisis cover a wide spectrum of regimes, including the currency board systems of Hong Kong, China and Brunei Darussalam, as well as the
free-floating regime adopted by Japan. Japan, perhaps the best example of a floating currency in the region, had been on an independent float from 2000 to 2008
and a free-floating regime from 2009 to 2013.[10] Most countries not directly affected
by the Asian financial crisis, such as Cambodia, India, Mongolia, Myanmar, and
Singapore, switched back and forth for most of the 2000s to different forms of flexible exchange rate arrangements, such as between an independent float and managed floating. The only two exceptions were Lao PDR and Viet Nam, which for
most of the 2000s adopted stabilized arrangements with regard to the U.S. dollar.

Also evident in the region has been a significant buildup of foreign exchange
reserves. Although this reserve buildup slowed somewhat for the majority of the
East Asian economies during the 2008–2009 global financial crisis, owing to
exchange rate depreciation pressures caused by reversals in capital inflows, the
upward trend has nonetheless resumed in recent years (see figure 6-9). This trend
suggests that there has been a high degree of exchange rate management in the
region, which then points to the nature of the exchange rate regimes in the region
being managed floating. In other words, exchange rate movements in most
economies in the region should have otherwise displayed relatively greater flexibility in the absence, or lesser degree, of foreign exchange intervention.

---

10. A major difference between an independent floating regime and a free-floating regime is that
the former may allow frequent currency market interventions while the latter does not.

Table 6-6. *Correlation Coefficients between Nominal Exchange Rates of Currencies*[a]

	KRW	TWD	HKD	SGD	CAM	IDR	LAK	MYR
Post-AFC period: January 3, 2000, to June 30, 2005 (period of U.S. dollar-peg of the RMB)								
USD	**0.853**	**0.957**	**0.999**	**0.931**	**0.947**	0.634	**0.907**	**1.000**
EUR	0.571	0.646	0.634	0.682	0.641	0.376	0.584	0.633
JPY	**0.765**	**0.765**	**0.743**	**0.822**	0.680	0.528	0.648	**0.741**
GBP	0.674	**0.741**	**0.742**	**0.741**	**0.762**	0.475	0.685	**0.740**
RMB	**0.853**	**0.957**	**0.999**	**0.931**	**0.947**	0.634	**0.907**	**1.000**
Pre-Lehman period: July 21, 2005, to July 21, 2008 (period of relative flexibility of the RMB)								
	KRW	TWD	HKD	SGD	CAM	IDR	LAK	MYR
USD	**0.847**	**0.946**	**0.999**	**0.942**	**0.905**	**0.785**	0.959	**0.934**
EUR	**0.736**	**0.808**	**0.804**	**0.859**	**0.728**	0.679	**0.740**	**0.787**
JPY	0.686	**0.802**	**0.798**	**0.831**	0.668	0.651	**0.696**	**0.769**
GBP	**0.740**	**0.803**	**0.812**	**0.837**	**0.733**	0.689	**0.771**	**0.790**
RMB	**0.846**	**0.947**	**0.989**	**0.944**	**0.894**	**0.777**	**0.952**	**0.933**
GFC period: August 1, 2008, to May 31, 2010 (return to U.S. dollar-peg of the RMB)								
	KRW	TWD	HKD	SGD	CAM	IDR	LAK	MYR
USD	0.476	**0.973**	**1.000**	**0.958**	0.240	**0.778**	**0.978**	**0.940**
EUR	0.365	**0.761**	**0.753**	**0.817**	0.204	0.583	**0.744**	**0.757**
JPY	**0.334**	**0.859**	**0.886**	**0.877**	0.203	0.647	**0.853**	**0.822**
GBP	0.331	0.677	0.668	0.692	0.178	0.539	0.679	0.661
RMB	0.471	**0.974**	**0.998**	**0.960**	0.242	**0.780**	**0.977**	**0.943**
Post-GFC period: June 1, 2010, to March 31, 2014 (period of relative flexibility of RMB)								
	KRW	TWD	HKD	SGD	CAM	IDR	LAK	MYR
USD	**0.779**	**0.962**	**0.999**	**0.897**	**0.955**	**0.748**	**0.928**	**0.872**
EUR	0.553	0.653	0.635	**0.709**	0.619	0.504	0.646	0.624
JPY	0.581	**0.741**	**0.763**	**0.733**	**0.728**	0.579	**0.703**	0.644
GBP	0.644	**0.772**	**0.787**	**0.791**	**0.768**	0.607	**0.751**	**0.720**
RMB	**0.780**	**0.962**	**0.992**	**0.898**	**0.953**	**0.741**	**0.924**	**0.876**

Source: Authors' calculations.

a. All exchange rates are the logarithmic first-difference of the currencies with respect to the New Zealand dollar. Entries that are bold are correlation coefficients that exceed 0.7 in value.

AFC = Asian financial crisis; CAM = Cambodian riel; EUR = euro; GBP = pound sterling; GFC = global financial crisis; HKD = Hong Kong dollar; IDR = Indonesian rupiah; INR = Indian rupee; JPY = Japanese yen; KRW =

The choice of exchange rate regime for any economy must be made in relation to the trilemma hypothesis. Table 6-7 shows indexes of capital account openness and monetary policy independence. According to the index of de jure capital account openness, some East Asian economies—Japan, Singapore, and Hong Kong, China—already have relatively open capital accounts. For most economies—particularly Cambodia, the Republic of Korea, and Viet Nam—the index has trended upward (Indonesia and Malaysia are exceptions). The de facto index of capital account openness displays largely similar trends of rising openness

INR	MNT	PHP	THB	VND	USD	EUR	JPY	GBP	RMB
0.978	0.834	0.845	0.901	0.998	1.000				
0.632	0.562	0.551	0.627	0.632	0.633	1.000			
0.740	0.585	0.689	0.793	0.740	0.641	0.586	1.000		
0.739	0.606	0.618	0.701	0.738	0.640	0.648	0.621	1.000	
0.978	0.833	0.845	0.901	0.998	1.000	0.633	0.641	0.640	1.000

INR	MNT	PHP	THB	VND	USD	EUR	JPY	GBP	RMB
0.927	0.939	0.880	0.892	0.990	1.000				
0.774	0.746	0.724	0.770	0.790	0.699	1.000			
0.742	0.731	0.700	0.785	0.781	0.692	0.614	1.000		
0.784	0.769	0.735	0.767	0.797	0.608	0.670	0.645	1.000	
0.917	0.929	0.870	0.894	0.978	0.989	0.607	0.603	0.607	1.000

INR	MNT	PHP	THB	VND	USD	EUR	JPY	GBP	RMB
0.895	0.884	0.940	0.984	0.970	1.000				
0.712	0.662	0.722	0.774	0.723	0.652	1.000			
0.779	0.780	0.810	0.892	0.864	0.685	0.646	1.000		
0.619	0.591	0.649	0.670	0.649	0.667	0.685	0.599	1.000	
0.897	0.882	0.938	0.984	0.967	0.998	0.659	0.688	0.670	1.000

INR	MNT	PHP	THB	VND	USD	EUR	JPY	GBP	RMB
0.707	0.892	0.905	0.922	0.949	1.000				
0.529	0.559	0.641	0.661	0.605	0.634	1.000			
0.508	0.688	0.674	0.730	0.731	0.665	0.538	1.000		
0.599	0.690	0.750	0.765	0.743	0.687	0.652	0.653	1.000	
0.707	0.882	0.905	0.923	0.940	0.992	0.640	0.665	0.685	1.000

Republic of Korea won; LAK = Lao PDR kip; MNT = Mongolian togrog; MYR = Malaysian ringgit; PHP = Philippine peso; RMB = renminbi; SGD = Singapore dollar; THB = Thailand baht; TWD = NT dollar; USD = US dollar; VND = Viet Namese dong.

for many economies. In contrast to the de jure measure, Malaysia's de facto index suggests rising openness over time. The index for monetary policy independence suggests a generally high degree of monetary policy independence for many economies, with the exception of Hong Kong, China, although it is difficult to find a clear trend over time for individual economies. In summary, as capital account openness has increased over time, most East Asian economies seem to have chosen greater exchange rate flexibility to retain a certain degree of monetary policy independence under the trilemma constraint.

Figure 6-9. *Foreign Exchange Reserve Accumulation in East Asian Economies and Exchange Rate of Their Currencies against the U.S. Dollar, 2000 to 2013*

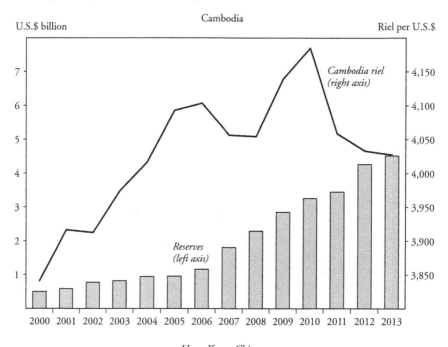

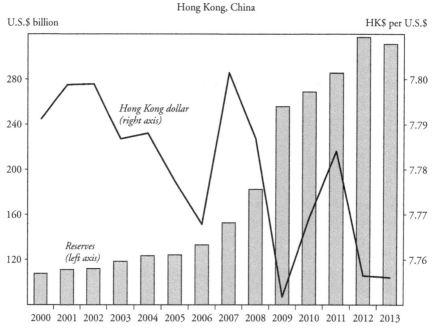

(continued)

Figure 6-9. *Foreign Exchange Reserve Accumulation in East Asian Economies and Exchange Rate of Their Currencies against the U.S. Dollar, 2000 to 2013 (Continued)*

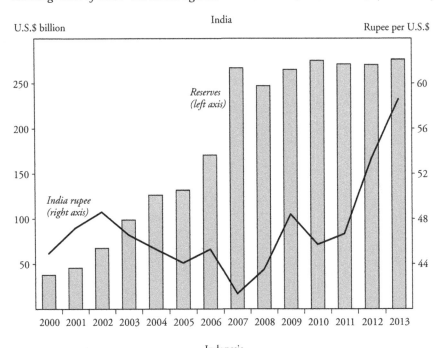

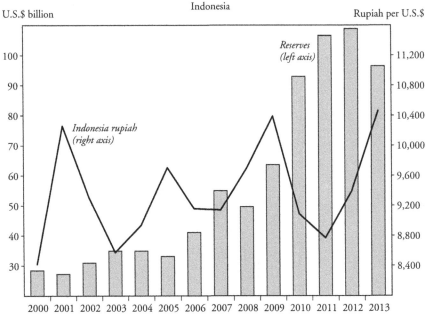

(continued)

Figure 6-9. *Foreign Exchange Reserve Accumulation in East Asian Economies and Exchange Rate of Their Currencies against the U.S. Dollar, 2000 to 2013 (Continued)*

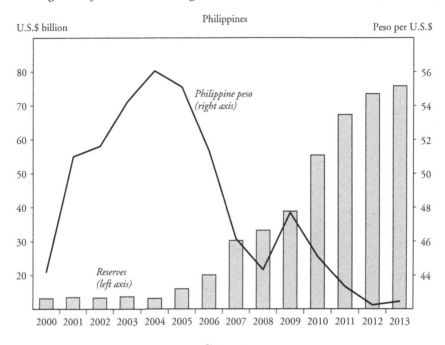

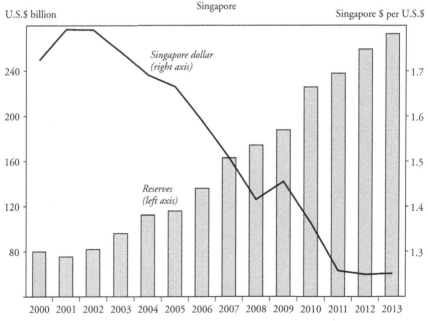

(continued)

Figure 6-9. *Foreign Exchange Reserve Accumulation in East Asian Economies and Exchange Rate of Their Currencies against the U.S. Dollar, 2000 to 2013 (Continued)*

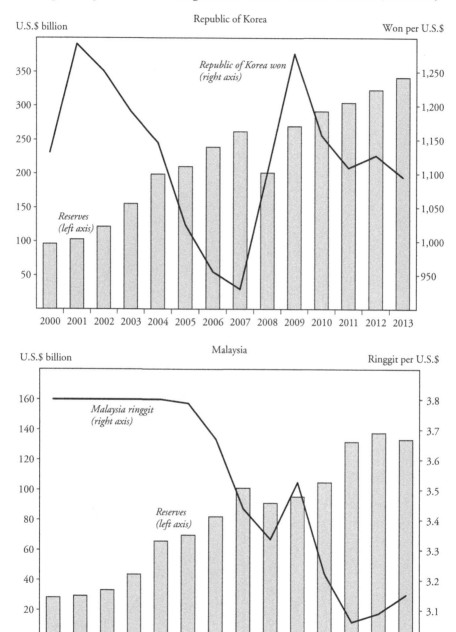

(continued)

Figure 6-9. *Foreign Exchange Reserve Accumulation in East Asian Economies and Exchange Rate of Their Currencies against the U.S. Dollar, 2000 to 2013 (Continued)*

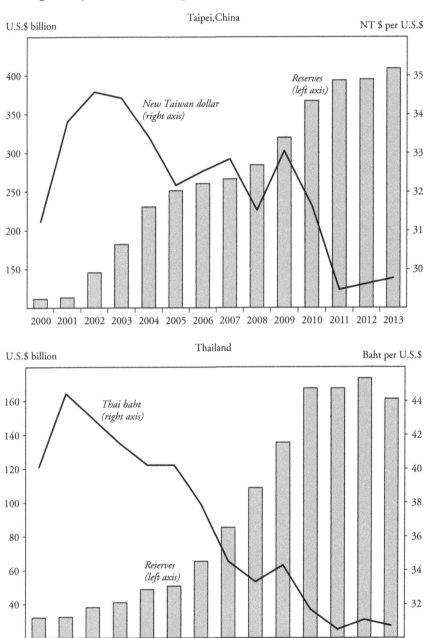

Table 6-7. De Jure and De Facto Indexes Showing Relative Capital Account Openness and Monetary Policy Independence[a]

| Economy | Capital account openness | | | | | | | | Monetary policy independence | | |
| | Chinn-Ito (de jure) | | | | Ito-Kawai (de facto) | | | | Ito-Kawai (de facto) | | |
	1990	2000	2010	2011	1990	2000	2010	2011	1990	2000	2010
People's Republic of China	0.00	0.16	0.16	0.16	0.17	0.26	0.23	0.23	—	1.00	0.79
Japan	1.00	1.00	1.00	1.00	1.00	0.92	1.00	1.00	1.00	1.00	1.00
Republic of Korea	0.41	0.41	0.59	0.65	0.04	0.20	0.29	—	1.00	1.00	1.00
Hong Kong, China	1.00	1.00	1.00	1.00	1.00	1.00	1.00	1.00	0.06	0.58	0.11
Taipei,China	—	—	—	—	—	—	—	—	1.00	0.00	1.00
India	0.16	0.16	0.16	0.16	0.29	0.18	0.25	0.19	1.00	0.54	1.00
Cambodia	—	0.00	0.71	0.71	—	0.34	0.39	0.40	—	—	—
Indonesia	1.00	0.69	0.69	0.41	0.32	0.40	0.30	0.25	1.00	1.00	1.00
Lao People's Democratic Republic	0.00	0.25	0.16	0.16	1.00	0.72	0.46	—	—	—	—
Malaysia	1.00	0.41	0.16	0.16	0.18	0.26	0.45	0.43	0.94	1.00	1.00
Philippines	0.16	0.45	0.16	0.16	0.34	0.29	0.26	0.25	1.00	1.00	0.56
Singapore	1.00	1.00	1.00	1.00	0.60	1.00	1.00	1.00	0.86	1.00	1.00
Thailand	0.41	0.41	0.16	0.16	0.11	0.25	0.27	0.25	1.00	1.00	1.00
Viet Nam	0.00	0.22	0.41	0.41	—	0.23	0.20	—	—	—	—

Sources: Chinn and Ito (2008; see also http://web.pdx.edu/~ito/Chinn-Ito_website.htm); Ito and Kawai (2012).

a. On the construction of the de jure measure of capital account openness, see Chinn and Ito (2008). On the development of the de facto measure of capital account openness and the monetary policy independence index, see Ito and Kawai (2012).

Estimating the Weight of the Renminbi in East Asian Currency Baskets

Several recent studies have examined whether the RMB has started to figure in the currency baskets of individual economies, particularly in the East Asian region (see, for example, Ho, Ma, and McCauley 2005; Balasubramaniam, Patnaik, and Shah 2011; Chow 2011; Fratzscher and Mehl 2011; Henning 2012; and Subramanian and Kessler 2013).

These studies also employed the Frankel-Wei model which was used in Section 3, except that this time the movement in the RMB is included on the right-hand side of the equation, which is expressed as

$$(6\text{-}2) \quad \Delta\log\left(\frac{x}{CHF}\right) = \phi_0 + \phi_1\Delta\log\left(\frac{USD}{CHF}\right) + \phi_2\Delta\log\left(\frac{EURO}{CHF}\right) + \phi_3\Delta\log\left(\frac{JPY}{CHF}\right)$$
$$+ \phi_4\Delta\log\left(\frac{GBP}{CHF}\right) + \phi_4\Delta\log\left(\frac{RMB}{CHF}\right) + u',$$

where $\Delta\log\left(\frac{k}{CHF}\right)$, $k = x$, *USD, EURO, JPY, GBP, RMB* is the logarithmic change in the exchange rate of currency k (a particular East Asian emerging currency x, U.S. dollar, euro, Japanese yen, pound sterling, and RMB) per Swiss franc. As mentioned earlier, the exchange rates are taken as log first differences. The estimated coefficient on the RMB measures the importance of the RMB assigned to the currency basket of a particular Asian currency x. The difficulty with this regression, as has been pointed out by previous studies, is that the correlation between changes in the U.S. dollar and the RMB—particularly during the periods in which the PRC pursued an official U.S. dollar peg—is remarkably high, that is, multi-collinearity is present.

THREE EARLIER APPROACHES TO MULTICOLLINEARITY. Earlier literature attempted to address the multicollinearity problem in three ways. The first was to estimate equation 6-2 at the two known periods in which the PRC authorities allowed the RMB to exhibit some flexibility against the U.S. dollar. For example, Henning (2012) estimated the Frankel-Wei regression with the RMB movements included on the right-hand side for the period from July 22, 2005, to July 2, 2009, and also for the period from June 18, 2010, to December 30, 2011. Subramanian and Kessler (2013) estimated the regression for the periods from July 2005 to August 2008 and July 2010 to July 2013. Adopting this approach, Henning (2012) obtained results that led him to conclude that Malaysia, the Philippines, Singapore, and Thailand had formed a loose but effective "RMB bloc" with the PRC, in which the Republic of Korea had participated since the global financial crisis. Subramanian and Kessler (2013) were more forthcoming in arriving at their conclusion that the RMB had become the dominant reference currency in East Asia, particularly for Indonesia, the Republic of Korea, Malaysia, the Philippines, Singapore, Thailand, and Taipei,China, eclipsing the U.S. dollar and the euro. They argued that an RMB bloc had emerged in a number of East Asian economies.

The second way of approaching the multicollinearity problem was to express all the exchange rates in terms of the U.S. dollar and place the RMB-U.S. dollar rate on the right-hand side of the regression equation. This approach removed the U.S. dollar movements from the right-hand side of equation 6-2, making the dollar the numeraire currency, and then used the movements in the RMB-U.S. dollar rate as one of the right-hand side variables. This method was expected to resolve the multicollinearity problem. The U.S. dollar weight was implied from the estimation of the modified Frankel-Wei regression. For instance, Ho, Ma, and McCauley (2005) employed this approach by using the movements in the RMB non-deliverable forward (NDF) rate per U.S. dollar as the RMB variable on the right-hand side of the equation for the 2003 and 2004 data.[11] They found that the role of the RMB had been significant even in the first half of the 2000s, that several Asian currencies (the rupiah, won, and NT dollar) had already tracked the RMB, and that the importance of the RMB rose in three currencies between 2003 and 2004.

The third way of surmounting the multicollinearity problem was to first purge the U.S. dollar component from the RMB movements and then incorporate the "independent" movements of the RMB in the Frankel-Wei model. This approach was suggested by several authors, including Balasubramaniam, Patnaik, and Shah (2011) and Fratzscher and Mehl (2011). The former study found that all the East Asian currencies they considered had attached importance to the U.S. dollar, and that beginning in October 2005 two Asian currencies—the ringgit (until June 2007) and the NT dollar (until February 2011)—had attached importance to the RMB. But in June 2007, the ringgit stepped away from giving importance to the RMB. In October 2009, movements in the RMB started to matter for the Viet Namese dong. Thus, at the end of their period of observation, only two Asian currencies, the NT dollar and the dong, were found to have accorded importance to movements in the RMB.

NEWER ESTIMATIONS.   In a recent study, Kawai and Pontines (2014) replicated these three approaches by conducting a series of "rolling" regressions of the Frankel-Wei model or its modifications and found that none of the three approaches just described provided adequate solutions to the issue of multicollinearity.[12] With regard to the first approach, Kawai and Pontines (2014)

11. In addition, Ho, Ma, and McCauley (2005) excluded the pound sterling from the right-hand side of the equation.

12. The rolling regression is carried out by first specifying a window width of 260 daily trading observations (equivalent to a year) that begins on July 22, 2005—the day following the announcement by the PBOC that it would allow relative flexibility in the RMB exchange rate against the U.S. dollar. This specified window width is then moved by estimating the Frankel-Wei type regression at a step-size of one daily observation at a time and through the remaining observations. The last observation was on March 31, 2014.

obtained two important results: First, the U.S. dollar weights moved in the opposite direction to the RMB weights, exhibiting highly negative correlations. Second, in almost all of the rolling regressions conducted, both the U.S. dollar and
RMB weights showed instability in the form of quite large or small coefficients.
With regard to the second approach, they found unstable and very large or small
values for both the implied U.S. dollar weights and the RMB weights. The implied
U.S. dollar coefficients behaved as if they had a multicollinear relationship with
the RMB coefficients, with highly negative correlations regardless of the period
examined, that is, the period when the RMB was pegged to the U.S. dollar or the
period when it was relatively flexible.[13] With regard to the third approach, they
found that the U.S. dollar weights had been more stable than in the previous two
approaches but the RMB weights had remained very volatile. That is, the estimated RMB weights exhibited unstable and very large or small values for almost
the whole period of observation.

Kawai and Pontines (2014) presented a new method of estimating the U.S. dollar and RMB weights in the Frankel-Wei regression model. A two-step regression
was conducted and followed at first the strategy of removing the "dependent"
components of the movements in the RMB from the movements of major international currencies, particularly the U.S. dollar, and obtaining the residuals from
the first-step regression, which was identical to equation 6-1. This was used to
determine the weights accorded by the PRC authorities to the major international
currencies in their currency basket.

Once the estimated residuals from the estimation were obtained, these residuals were used as a proxy for the actual RMB movements in equation 6-2 (except
that the numeraire currency of equation 6-2 is now the New Zealand dollar), and
these were subtracted from both sides of the equation under the condition that
the sum of the estimated coefficients was unity. This yielded the following, modified version of the Frankel–Wei regression for a particular East Asian emerging
economy currency, x:

$$(6\text{-}3) \qquad \Delta\log\left(\frac{x}{NZD}\right) - \hat{u} = \gamma_0 + \gamma_1 \left[\Delta\log\left(\frac{USD}{NZD}\right) - \hat{u}\right] + \gamma_2 \left[\Delta\log\left(\frac{EURO}{NZD}\right) - \hat{u}\right]$$

$$+ \gamma_3 \left[\Delta\log\left(\frac{JPY}{NZD}\right) - \hat{u}\right] + \gamma_4 \left[\Delta\log\left(\frac{GBP}{NZD}\right) - \hat{u}\right] + v.$$

Estimation of this modified Frankel–Wei regression equation 6-3 also yielded the
implied RMB coefficient as $\gamma_5 = 1 - \gamma_1 - \gamma_2 - \gamma_3 - \gamma_4$.[14]

13. In addition, Kawai and Pontines (2014) found that results were very similar even if the RMB
spot exchange rate was used instead of the RMB NDF rate.

14. Kawai and Pontines (2014) demonstrated the superiority of their method over the previous
approaches. First, conducting rolling regressions for equation 6-3, they found that their method produced much more stable and smoothly changing estimates of the U.S. dollar and RMB weights than
previous approaches. Second, by obtaining the goodness-of-fit measured by the constructed

Table 6-8 shows the estimation results for the four sub-periods that were earlier considered in previous subsections using the Kawai-Pontines estimation method. Several important observations can be made from the table.

First, throughout the whole period of observation, for all the emerging East Asian currencies considered, the U.S. dollar reigned supreme as the major anchor currency in view of its weights in the currency baskets. In addition to the official U.S. dollar peg of the Hong Kong dollar and the pre-July 2005 U.S. dollar peg of the Malaysian ringgit, in all four sub-periods the U.S. dollar was the most important anchor currency for all East Asian currencies, although the authorities in Indonesia, the Republic of Korea, Malaysia (after 2005), the Philippines, and Taipei,China have attached slightly less importance to the U.S. dollar than previously. Although in the case of the Indian rupee and Singapore dollar, the U.S. dollar's role has declined between the post-AFC period and the post-GFC period, it has not been replaced by the RMB.

Second, the RMB was already important for five currencies (the won, Singapore dollar, rupiah, Indian rupee, and baht) in the post-AFC period, and the number of Asian currencies according importance to the RMB and the average magnitudes of the RMB weights have increased over time. All currencies—with the exception of the riel, kip, togrog, and dong—had assigned statistically significant weights to the RMB by the post-GFC period. The size of the estimated RMB coefficients have risen in the case of the won, NT dollar, Singapore dollar, rupiah, ringgit, rupee, peso, and baht. For example, in the post-GFC period, India and the Republic of Korea assigned close to 30 percent weight to the RMB in their respective currency baskets. Singapore and Malaysia assigned more than 20 percent; and Indonesia, the Philippines, Taipei,China, and Thailand, more than 10 percent. However, these estimated weights are still smaller than those of the U.S. dollar and do not suggest that the RMB has supplanted the U.S. dollar in the currency baskets of these economies.

Third, the importance of the euro, yen, and pound sterling in the currency baskets of East Asian currencies has changed over time. The number of currencies that attach some importance to the euro has risen from two during the post-AFC period (the NT dollar and the Singapore dollar) to seven in the post-GFC period (the NT dollar, Singapore dollar, kip, ringgit, rupee, peso, and baht). Meanwhile, the importance of the yen and sterling has dropped. In the case of the yen, the number of currencies that attached some importance to it declined from seven during the post-AFC period (the won, NT dollar, Singapore dollar, rupiah, rupee, peso, and baht) to just one by the post-GFC period (the Singapore dollar). In the case of sterling the number of currencies that attached some importance to it had come down from four (the won, NT dollar, Singapore dollar, and rupee) in the

---

R-squared values of the new method and the Balasubramaniam-Patnaik-Shah approach, the constructed R-squared values are larger under the new method than under the Balasubramaniam-Patnaik-Shah method. These suggest an estimation outcome superior to those of the other approaches.

Table 6-8. *Estimation Results for the Currency Basket Weights Using the Kawai-Pontines Method, with Renminbi Spot Rate*[a]

	U.S. dollar	Euro	Japanese yen	Pound sterling	Renminbi	R^2
Rep. of Korea won						
Post-AFC period	0.638***	−0.022	0.270***	0.065**	0.048***	0.768
	(0.030)	(0.021)	(0.021)	(0.025)	(0.017)	
Pre-Lehman period	0.686***	0.140**	−0.036	0.096	0.112***	0.730
	(0.055)	(0.067)	(0.055)	(0.070)	(0.023)	
GFC period	0.684***	0.086	−0.265***	0.030	0.465***	0.231
	(0.096)	(0.105)	(0.076)	(0.075)	(0.083)	
Post-GFC period	0.638***	0.085*	−0.034	0.026	0.284***	0.608
	(0.043)	(0.032)	(0.027)	(0.047)	(0.027)	
NT dollar						
Post-AFC period	0.810***	0.031**	0.094***	0.045***	0.016*	0.924
	(0.017)	(0.014)	(0.011)	(0.012)	(0.010)	
Pre-Lehman period	0.737***	0.076**	0.079***	0.042	0.064***	0.908
	(0.027)	(0.032)	(0.020)	(0.031)	(0.014)	
GFC period	0.837***	0.040	−0.028	0.041*	0.109***	0.909
	(0.027)	(0.033)	(0.022)	(0.024)	(0.021)	
Post-GFC period	0.832***	0.073***	0.004	−0.013	0.103***	0.929
	(0.019)	(0.017)	(0.012)	(0.022)	(0.014)	
Hong Kong dollar						
Post-AFC period	0.988***	0.000	0.004***	0.004***	0.001	0.998
	(0.002)	(0.000)	(0.001)	(0.001)	(0.001)	
Pre-Lehman period	0.980***	0.007	0.010***	0.001	0.000	0.998
	(0.002)	(0.005)	(0.002)	(0.004)	(0.001)	
GFC period	0.992***	0.005*	0.002	−0.001	0.001	0.999
	(0.003)	(0.003)	(0.002)	(0.002)	(0.002)	
Post-GFC period	0.985***	0.002	−0.003*	0.001	0.015***	0.999
	(0.003)	(0.002)	(0.002)	(0.003)	(0.002)	
Singapore dollar						
Post-AFC period	0.611***	0.082***	0.219***	0.036***	0.049***	0.911
	(0.017)	(0.011)	(0.012)	(0.013)	(0.009)	
Pre-Lehman period	0.562***	0.196***	0.078***	0.049*	0.113***	0.925
	(0.022)	(0.024)	(0.019)	(0.025)	(0.013)	
GFC period	0.597***	0.196***	0.022	0.029	0.156***	0.913
	(0.022)	(0.027)	(0.019)	(0.018)	(0.020)	
Post-GFC period	0.478***	0.159***	0.049***	0.073***	0.240***	0.842
	(0.027)	(0.026)	(0.016)	(0.027)	(0.020)	
Cambodia riel						
Post-AFC period	0.992***	0.011	−0.022	0.036	−0.017	0.897
	(0.015)	(0.015)	(0.017)	(0.026)	(0.017)	
Pre-Lehman period	0.964***	0.037	−0.015	0.005	0.007	0.822
	(0.035)	(0.080)	(0.027)	(0.065)	(0.020)	
GFC period	1.013***	0.032*	0.005	−0.044**	−0.007	0.977
	(0.014)	(0.019)	(0.012)	(0.017)	(0.011)	
Post-GFC period	0.973***	−0.002	−0.009	0.032*	0.006	0.914
	(0.017)	(0.023)	(0.010)	(0.018)	(0.013)	

(continued)

Table 6-8. *Estimation Results for the Currency Basket Weights Using the Kawai-Pontines Method, with Renminbi Spot Rate*[a] *(Continued)*

	U.S. dollar	Euro	Japanese yen	Pound sterling	Renminbi	R^2
Indonesia rupiah						
Post-AFC period	0.779*** (0.052)	-0.101 (0.049)	0.180*** (0.041)	0.028 (0.050)	0.113*** (0.035)	0.411
Pre-Lehman period	0.664*** (0.081)	0.087* (0.048)	0.008 (0.042)	0.127** (0.059)	0.113*** (0.024)	0.631
GFC period	0.866*** (0.067)	0.020 (0.085)	−0.163*** (0.053)	0.081 (0.056)	0.195*** (0.053)	0.569
Post-GFC period	0.791*** (0.045)	0.035 (0.045)	−0.005 (0.035)	0.033 (0.051)	0.146*** (0.042)	0.558
Lao PDR kip						
Post-AFC period	0.996*** (0.016)	−0.029 (0.041)	−0.003 (0.019)	0.038 (0.033)	−0.000 (0.016)	0.821
Pre-Lehman period	1.032*** (0.023)	−0.073* (0.043)	0.004 (0.015)	0.008 (0.026)	0.027 (0.021)	0.920
GFC period	0.977*** (0.022)	0.061 (0.048)	−0.024 (0.023)	−0.003 (0.032)	−0.011 (0.028)	0.918
Post-GFC period	0.932*** (0.035)	0.119** (0.036)	−0.028 (0.026)	−0.020 (0.039)	−0.002 (0.015)	0.867
Malaysia ringgit						
Post-AFC period	0.999*** (0.000)	0.000 (0.000)	0.000 (0.000)	−0.000 (0.000)	0.000 (0.000)	0.999
Pre-Lehman period	0.752*** (0.029)	0.068 (0.042)	0.021 (0.025)	0.042 (0.042)	0.114*** (0.018)	0.879
GFC period	0.764*** (0.029)	0.104** (0.038)	−0.078*** (0.020)	0.034 (0.023)	0.176*** (0.024)	0.837
Post-GFC period	0.709*** (0.034)	0.110*** (0.026)	−0.049** (0.022)	0.018 (0.033)	0.212*** (0.020)	0.771
Philippine peso						
Post-AFC period	0.878*** (0.024)	0.012 (0.018)	0.144*** (0.039)	−0.055 (0.039)	0.019 (0.013)	0.723
Pre-Lehman period	0.801*** (0.041)	0.044 (0.046)	−0.021 (0.034)	0.059 (0.045)	0.115*** (0.022)	0.779
GFC period	0.849*** (0.044)	0.063 (0.045)	−0.117*** (0.031)	0.029 (0.031)	0.176*** (0.031)	0.804
Post-GFC period	0.760*** (0.033)	0.102*** (0.023)	−0.041** (0.021)	0.036 (0.032)	0.143*** (0.018)	0.828
Thai baht						
Post-AFC period	0.652*** (0.023)	0.033* (0.018)	0.231*** (0.018)	0.020 (0.022)	0.061*** (0.015)	0.847
Pre-Lehman period	0.681*** (0.035)	0.038 (0.041)	0.140*** (0.025)	0.057* (0.032)	0.082*** (0.023)	0.815
GFC period	0.786*** (0.024)	0.077** (0.024)	0.041*** (0.013)	0.018 (0.016)	0.078*** (0.014)	0.950
Post-GFC period	0.692*** (0.028)	0.110*** (0.021)	0.032* (0.017)	0.022 (0.024)	0.145*** (0.016)	0.862

(continued)

Table 6-8. *Estimation Results for the Currency Basket Weights Using the Kawai-Pontines Method, with Renminbi Spot Rate*[a] *(Continued)*

	U.S. dollar	Euro	Japanese yen	Pound sterling	Renminbi	R^2
Viet Nam dong						
Post-AFC period	1.000***	−0.003	0.001	0.003	−0.002	0.996
	(0.002)	(0.002)	(0.001)	(0.003)	(0.001)	
Pre-Lehman period	1.014***	0.006	−0.005	−0.013*	−0.002	0.980
	(0.010)	(0.009)	(0.009)	(0.007)	(0.004)	
GFC period	0.987***	−0.034	−0.003	0.014	0.037	0.912
	(0.026)	(0.038)	(0.023)	(0.020)	(0.025)	
Post-GFC period	0.977***	0.015	0.015	−0.020	0.014	0.890
	(0.030)	(0.011)	(0.019)	(0.012)	(0.013)	
Mongolia togrog						
Post-AFC period	1.026***	0.063	−0.025	−0.104	0.039	0.696
	(0.033)	(0.065)	(0.021)	(0.079)	(0.033)	
Pre-Lehman period	1.028***	−0.011	−0.018	0.012	−0.010	0.883
	(0.035)	(0.021)	(0.012)	(0.031)	(0.014)	
GFC period	1.024***	−0.071	−0.015	0.028	0.034	0.749
	(0.047)	(0.051)	(0.031)	(0.044)	(0.041)	
Post-GFC period	1.016***	0.001	0.019	−0.044	0.008	0.794
	(0.032)	(0.032)	(0.020)	(0.035)	(0.026)	
India rupee						
Post-AFC period	0.915***	0.007	0.024***	0.028***	0.023***	0.956
	(0.016)	(0.008)	(0.008)	(0.010)	(0.006)	
Pre-Lehman period	0.804***	0.058*	−0.023	0.080**	0.079***	0.866
	(0.030)	(0.034)	(0.023)	(0.036)	(0.021)	
GFC period	0.746***	0.113*	−0.129**	0.045	0.225***	0.667
	(0.060)	(0.059)	(0.039)	(0.042)	(0.038)	
Post-GFC period	0.604***	0.132***	−0.072**	0.045	0.290***	0.519
	(0.042)	(0.044)	(0.038)	(0.058)	(0.030)	

Source: Authors' calculations.

a. Numbers in parentheses are standard errors.

* = $p < 10\%$; ** = $p < 5\%$; *** = $p < 1\%$.

AFC = Asian financial crisis; GFC = Global financial crisis.

post-AFC period to just one by the post-GFC period (the Singapore dollar). One could say that the weights of the RMB in East Asian currency baskets rose at the expense of the yen and sterling.

Monetary and Currency Cooperation in East Asia

There is no doubt that an increasingly integrated East Asia will need more stable intraregional exchange rates. The region has created closely knit supply chains where capital goods, industrial materials, parts and components, semi-finished goods, and final products are traded across borders. The ever closer economic integration in the region means that each economy is increasingly affected by shocks and policies that originate in neighboring economies. At the same time, economies in the region compete among each other in markets within and outside the region, and therefore the potential of losing competitiveness against each other is treated with utmost sensitivity. Ultimately, the prospect of a beggar-thy-neighbor competitive depreciation strategy, which could be very costly to the region in terms of large and unnecessary reallocations of resources across the region, always looms large (Kawai and Takagi 2012). Despite the paramount importance of the achievement of intraregional exchange rate stability, there has been limited progress in moving toward a regional framework for exchange rate policy coordination.

In East Asia, there are potentially three ways in which intraregional exchange rate stability could be achieved:

—Choosing a single currency, such as the U.S. dollar, the RMB, or the yen, as the region's monetary anchor

—Selecting a currency basket that includes major international and/or regional currencies as the region's monetary anchor

—Establishing a coordinated arrangement of choosing a mutually acceptable currency or currency basket as the region's common currency.

The U.S. Dollar, the Renminbi, or the Yen as Anchor for East Asia?

The experience of the global financial crisis and Asia's diverse economic relationship with the major economies of the world suggest that the traditional practice of choosing the U.S. dollar as the region's monetary anchor is no longer the best policy. The East Asian economy will continue to grow and far exceed the U.S. economy in size, and the region cannot simply continue to depend on the monetary policy of the U.S. Federal Reserve for its monetary and financial stability.

For the RMB to play an anchor currency role in East Asia, the PRC must create enabling environments for global investors to freely hold and utilize the RMB by fully liberalizing its capital account, dismantling exchange controls, and building deep and liquid financial markets. The RMB's international role will clearly expand over time, supported by the PRC's strong growth performance, trade and investment expansion, and currency internationalization policy. Nonetheless, decades may have to pass before the RMB becomes a fully convertible international currency that is functionally equivalent to the U.S. dollar, the euro, or the yen.[15] More to the point, it may take a long time for the PRC to establish a truly independent, credible central bank, to put in place effective prudential and supervisory frameworks governing its financial systems, and to implement rule of law through independent judicial systems.

---

15. For the RMB to become equal to or exceed the functionality of these major international currencies, the PRC economy must become fully open with respect to trade, investment, and finance. It was the openness and liquidity of U.S. financial markets after all that heightened the U.S. dollar's

The Japanese yen is a fully convertible international currency and fulfills all the conditions for becoming a regional anchor currency. Japan is Asia's second-largest economy, with massive amounts of savings. It has a fully open capital account, deep and liquid financial markets, systems for international clearance for yen financial instruments, transparent rules-based institutions, and a strong tradition of rule of law coupled with independent judicial systems. Tokyo is one of the top five global financial centers. Despite these strengths, the yen has not yet achieved its full potential as the region's anchor currency. Because of Japan's two decades of economic stagnation, its large government debt, and its aging population, which places further constraints on the country's growth potential and fiscal capacity, Japan is economically struggling. If "Abenomics" is successful in revitalizing the economy, however, Japan may be able to enhance the international role of the yen significantly—yet it will be hard for the yen to play an anchor currency role in East Asia on its own.

Furthermore, other East Asian economies, however robust their economic policies, are too small for their currencies to take on a meaningful leadership role as anchor currencies, although collectively they can be important. Thus, no single East Asian currency is capable of playing a dominant monetary anchor role in the near future. This makes it desirable—even necessary—to introduce a mechanism for intraregional currency stability based on a currency basket or a regionally coordinated framework.

A Case for Currency Basket Systems

A currency basket system is an attractive and viable direction to suggest for emerging East Asian economies. Both the RMB and yen need to play prominent roles in the currency baskets of emerging Asian economies. Three options may be considered for the region's currency baskets:

—The IMF special drawing rights (SDRs) comprising the U.S. dollar, euro, pound sterling, and yen

—An SDR+ currency basket comprising the U.S. dollar, euro, pound sterling, yen, and emerging East Asian currencies

—An Asian currency unit (ACU) consisting of a basket of East Asian currencies, including the RMB, yen, won, baht, ringgit, and possibly other currencies.

---

international role and that made foreign investors willingly hold dollar-denominated assets. In addition, the United States provided transparent, rules-based institutions that protected private property and enabled market participants to resolve any disputes in the courts. If the RMB is to play a significant role as an anchor currency, the PRC must fully liberalize its capital account and build deep, broad, and liquid financial markets. In addition, it needs to significantly improve the quality of domestic institutions. Practically speaking, this is not going to happen anytime soon. A precondition for capital account convertibility is that the country must complete its transition to a market economy and establish a sound and resilient financial sector. The PRC is still far from a free market economy, with extensive problems in its banking and shadow banking system and underdeveloped capital markets. At a minimum, completing this transition will require another ten to twenty years, although some degree of capital account liberalization might be achieved by 2020.

The first two options would not require a substantial degree of policy coordination because they rely on external nominal anchors. The third option requires either a certain degree of currency cooperation or a few major country central banks pursuing a form of inflation targeting, together with soft exchange rate stabilization, in order to establish a regional nominal anchor. The first option is the simplest and the third option, the most complex. One of the advantages of the second option is that once it is introduced, moving to the third option at a later stage would be easy since it would require only reducing the weights of the dollar, euro, and pound sterling to zero.[16]

As implied from the evidence in the section on the PRC's currency basket weights, at this point the PRC appears to have chosen the first option, a type of SDR basket system with a very large weight assigned to the U.S. dollar. This choice is reasonable, as the PRC does not have to adopt a freely flexible exchange rate regime in the presence of capital controls, and wishes to tightly manage the exchange rate. Until now, the U.S. dollar-skewed SDR basket system has served the PRC well in maintaining a high degree of exchange rate stability while allowing gradual RMB appreciation against the U.S. dollar—particularly given the need to rebalance the current account. However, to cope with the process toward greater capital account opening and RMB internationalization, it will be increasingly important for the PRC to shift to more loosely managed floating with a more balanced SDR basket system that assigns a much smaller weight to the U.S. dollar.

The second option, the SDR+ currency basket system, appears to have been adopted by many emerging East Asian economies. A typical example is Singapore, which has been managing its exchange rate in an SDR+ basket framework, which includes the U.S. dollar, euro, sterling, yen, and RMB.[17] Other economies— including India, Indonesia, the Republic of Korea, Malaysia, the Philippines, Thailand, and Taipei,China—also assign varying weights to the U.S. dollar, euro, and RMB. By pursuing managed float exchange rate systems, these emerging economies can enhance the degrees of extraregional exchange rate flexibility and intraregional stability. National monetary authorities can maintain policy independence by combining an appropriately defined inflation targeting policy and a basket-based managed floating policy (Kawai and Takagi 2012). One advantage of this approach is that it does not require significant economic and structural convergence among the economies.

The third option, the introduction of an ACU, would be useful in at least four ways (Kawai 2009). It would provide

---

16. An SDR+ currency basket is also defined as a basket of the U.S. dollar, euro, sterling, and an ACU, which is a currency basket of the yen and other East Asian currencies. If the weights on the dollar, euro, and sterling become zero, the SDR+ basket becomes an ACU.

17. It is often claimed that other regional currencies are also included in the currency basket for the Singapore dollar. The estimation results in table 6-8 for Singapore did not include other regional currencies but they may be partly represented by the U.S. dollar, euro, yen, and RMB to the extent that these affect other regional currencies.

1. A statistical indicator summarizing the collective movement of Asian currencies
2. An accounting unit for operations of regional financial cooperation mechanisms
3. A currency basket used by the market
4. An official unit of account for exchange rate policy coordination

Given that there is currently no consensus about whether the region should embark on exchange rate policy coordination, the creation of an ACU could support the ongoing process of market-driven economic integration in several ways.[18]

First, an ACU index could be used for intensive policy discussions on exchange rate policy as a part of regional economic and financial surveillance. The end objective would be to cultivate a culture that views the exchange rate not merely as a national concern but also as a regional matter. The means of getting there would be to work in a gradual and calibrated fashion in which policy dialogue and surveillance take center stage. An ACU index could be used as a benchmark, a tool to measure the value of East Asian currencies as a whole against external currencies such as the U.S. dollar and the euro, as well as to track the degree of divergence of each currency's value from the regional average set by the ACU.

Second, the ACU could be used for informal currency policy coordination in order to achieve both greater exchange rate flexibility vis-à-vis external currencies (particularly the U.S. dollar) and improve exchange rate stability within East Asia. As mentioned earlier, most emerging East Asian economies have adopted a managed floating regime based on an SDR+ basket system. The PRC may reduce the U.S. dollar's weight in its SDR basket system, while economies with sufficient rate flexibility, such as Japan and the Republic of Korea, may continue to allow their currencies to float. To achieve a degree of intraregional rate stability, greater convergence of exchange rate regimes would be desirable, starting with similar managed floating regimes based on an SDR or SDR+ basket and then moving to an ACU basket once sufficient economic and structural convergence has been achieved among the economies. With these developments, countries with floating currencies, such as Japan and the Republic of Korea, may also eventually move to ACU-based systems.

Financial Cooperation

Despite the importance of achieving intraregional exchange rate stability, there has been limited progress toward establishing a regional framework for exchange rate

---

18. A group comprising the ASEAN+3 (the ten ASEAN member states—Brunei Darussalam, Cambodia, Indonesia, Lao PDR, Malaysia, Myanmar, Philippines, Singapore, Thailand, and Viet Nam—plus the PRC, Japan, and the Republic of Korea) and Hong Kong,China is a natural starting point for constructing an ACU because of the group's existing financial cooperation efforts. Given that India will continue to grow and its currency, the rupee, can also play an important role in South Asia, the country may well be included in this group. The ACU could be used as an index to monitor exchange market developments; as an accounting unit to denominate the operations of regional institutions; in the private sector to denominate Asian bond issues, bank deposits and loans, and trade invoicing; and as an official unit for currency market intervention. For more information on the ACU, see papers included in Chung and Eichengreen (2009) and Pontines (2013).

policy coordination. This represents a major disconnect in the area of monetary and financial cooperation, given that several financial cooperation mechanisms have been developed in the region under the auspices of ASEAN+3 finance ministers and central bank governors.

The PRC, Japan, and other emerging East Asian economies can introduce a more coordinated approach to intraregional currency stability. A starting point could be to enlarge the use of local currencies for international trade invoicing and settlement, issuance of local currency bonds in counterparts' markets, mutual holding of sovereign debt as foreign exchange reserves, and activation of direct trading of currencies. Other efforts could include collaboration of financial authorities and supervisors to monitor cross-border financial risks; intensive policy dialogue on exchange rate policies, including reducing large bilateral exchange rate volatility through the use of the ACU; and convergence of exchange rate regimes toward managed floating arrangements within emerging East Asia.

At the same time, it is vital that the important strides toward financial cooperation achieved by the region in recent years be strengthened. This could include measures such as expanding substantially the size of financial resources available to individual countries under the Chiang Mai Initiative Multilateralization (CMIM); over time, reducing the CMIM link with the IMF, ultimately to zero, by making the ASEAN+3 Macroeconomic Research Office (AMRO) and the Economic Review and Policy Dialogue more effective; and providing sufficient resources and more solid funding and institutional arrangements for AMRO. It is important that CMIM and AMRO work with the IMF, as the East Asian financial safety net may not be sufficient to cope with a large-scale financial crisis in the region on its own, and the CMIM facility needs to be supplemented by IMF resources. In addition, the ASEAN+3 authorities may consider enlarging membership of CMIM and AMRO to include India, Australia, and New Zealand. Once these measures are achieved, a de facto Asian monetary fund will have been created.

Deepening Asian bond markets remains an important challenge so that the large accumulated savings in the region, currently invested in major international markets in the United States and Europe, can be invested in East Asia. For this purpose it would be useful to strengthen the Asian Bond Markets Initiative (ABMI). In addition, a new Asian Bond Fund-3 could be launched to encourage corporate bond markets, possibly with the help of the Credit Guarantee and Investment Facility (CGIF), established by ASEAN+3 and the Asian Development Bank. Finally, more policy dialogue on Asian financial stability among the region's financial authorities would help to promote the stability of the regional financial system.

Conclusion

In this chapter we have examined the evolution of exchange rate regimes in the PRC and other emerging East Asian economies, including India. Since 2000, the

PRC authorities and those of most East Asian currencies have increased their exchange rate flexibility against the U.S. dollar (with a few exceptions, such as Brunei Darussalam and Hong Kong, China, which have kept their currency board systems). The RMB exited from a U.S. dollar peg in July 2005 and has since appreciated against the U.S. dollar. The Singapore dollar and the currencies of the founding-member countries of ASEAN have also become more flexible and exhibited similar movements with each other over time.

To preserve monetary policy independence, policymakers need to make exchange rates more flexible as they open their financial markets. Greater exchange rate flexibility would serve as a cushion against shocks and events in the global and regional financial markets and allow greater policy independence for central banks.

We have shown that since July 2005 the RMB has become more flexible in the sense that the U.S. dollar's weight in the Frankel-Wei regression equation has become smaller and the R^2 of the regression has declined. But these changes are still marginal for the RMB, reflecting a limited degree of capital account liberalization in the PRC. In a sense, tight capital controls have meant that a high degree of exchange rate flexibility has not been required to preserve monetary policy independence. Once the authorities attempt to pursue significant capital account liberalization to promote RMB internationalization, however, a high degree of exchange rate flexibility is clearly needed for the PBOC to maintain policy independence.

Other East Asian currencies exhibit greater exchange rate flexibility, reflecting the underlying trend toward more open financial markets. In addition, the role of the RMB in the exchange rate policies of East Asian emerging economies has become increasingly important as the PRC's economy, its trade volumes, and its economic influence on these economies have grown. On the basis of Kawai and Pontines (2014), we have here argued that the RMB weight in the modified Frankel-Wei regression model has risen for many East Asian economies. For example, in the post-GFC period India and the Republic of Korea have assigned close to 30 percent of their respective currency baskets to the RMB; Malaysia and Singapore, more than 20 percent; and Indonesia, the Philippines, Taipei,China, and Thailand, more than 10 percent. Although there is as yet no RMB bloc—contrary to some authors' assertions—the RMB has gained importance in the exchange rate policies of the region's emerging economies. This seems to have taken place at the expense of the yen and pound sterling. It remains to be seen whether this trend will lead to the emergence of the RMB as the most dominant anchor currency in East Asia and one of the global currencies in the future.

We then explored how greater regional monetary and currency coordination could help to achieve intra–East Asian exchange rate stability. This could be a challenge, for the RMB is to operate on an SDR basket system (comprising the U.S. dollar, euro, pound sterling, and yen) and most other East Asian currencies are to operate on an SDR+ basket system (the same currencies plus an emerging East Asian currency such as the RMB). For a start, as the PRC achieves significant capital account liberalization, it must reduce the weight of the U.S. dollar in its dollar-dominant SDR basket system and increase exchange rate flexibility substantially. We suggest that a transition to greater convergence of exchange rate regimes would begin with similar managed floating regimes based on an SDR or SDR+ basket and then move to an ACU basket once sufficient economic and structural convergence has been achieved among the economies. The Indian rupee may also be included in an ACU because of its potential to grow as another important international currency.

It goes without saying that the region's economic future is a matter of speculation. A stronger form of economic policy coordination such as the eventual establishment of a regional monetary union would depend on getting political support from the region's political leaders and on their readiness to create the needed institutions at every stage of the process. The recent euro area crisis has shown that if monetary unions are to function properly, institutions must be stronger than previously thought.

References

Balasubramaniam, Vimal, Ila Patnaik, and Ajay Shah. 2011. "Who Cares about the Chinese Yuan?" NIPFP Working Paper No. 89. New Delhi: National Institute of Public Finance and Policy.

Bank for International Settlements. 2000–13. *BIS Statistics*. Basel: BIS.

Chinn, Menzie, and Hiro Ito. 2008. "A New Measure of Financial Openness." *Journal of Comparative Policy Analysis* 10, no. 3: 309–22.

Chow, Hwee-Kwan. 2011. "Towards an Expanded Role for Asian Currencies: Issues and Prospects." ADBI Working Paper No. 285. Tokyo: Asian Development Bank Institute.

Chung, Duck-Koo and Barry Eichengreen, eds. 2007. *Toward an East Asian Exchange Rate Regime*. Brookings Institution.

Eichengreen, Barry. 2011. *Exorbitant Privilege: The Rise and Fall of the Dollar and the Future of the International Monetary System*. Oxford University Press.

Frankel, Jeffrey, and Shang Jin Wei. 1994. "Yen Bloc or Dollar Bloc? Exchange Rate Policies of the East Asian Economies." In *Macroeconomic Linkages: Savings, Exchange Rates and Capital Flows*, edited by T. Ito and A. Krueger. University of Chicago Press.

Fratzscher, Marcel, and Arnaud Mehl. 2011. "China's Dominance Hypothesis and the Emergence of a Tri-Polar Global Currency System." ECB Working Paper No. 1392. Frankfurt: European Central Bank.

Henning, Randall. 2012. "Choice and Coercion in East Asian Exchange Rate Regimes." Working Paper 12-15. Washington: Peterson Institute for International Economics.

Ho, Corinne, Guonan Ma, and Robert N. McCauley. 2005. "Trading Asian Currencies." *BIS Quarterly Review* (March): 49–59.

International Monetary Fund. 2000–13. *International Financial Statistics*. Washington, D.C.: IMF.

International Monetary Fund. 2001 to 2013. *Annual Report on Exchange Arrangements and Exchange Restrictions*. Washington: International Monetary Fund (www.imf.org/external/pubs/cat/longres.cfm?sk=20272.0).

Ito, Hiro, and Masahiro Kawai. 2012. "New Measures of the Trilemma Hypothesis: Implications for Asia." ADBI Working Paper No. 381. Tokyo: Asian Development Bank Institute.

Kawai, Masahiro. 2009. "An Asian Currency Unit for Regional Exchange Rate Policy Coordi-
nation." In *Fostering Monetary and Financial Cooperation in East Asia*, edited by D.-K. Chung
and B. Eichengreen, pp. 73–112. Singapore: World Scientific.
Kawai, Masahiro, and Victor Pontines. 2014. "Is There Really a RMB Bloc in Asia?" ADBI
Working Paper No. 467. Tokyo: Asian Development Bank Institute.
Kawai, Masahiro, and Shinji Takagi. 2012. "A Proposal for Exchange Rate Policy Coordination
in East Asia." In *Monetary and Currency Policy Management in Asia*, edited by M. Kawai,
P. Morgan, and S. Takagi. Cheltenham, U.K.: Edward Elgar.
Ogawa, Eiji, and Michiru Sakane. 2006. "Chinese Yuan after Chinese Exchange Rate System
Reform." *China and the World Economy* 14, no. 6: 39–57.
Pontines, Victor. 2013. "How Useful Is an Asian Currency Unit (ACU) Index for Surveillance
in East Asia?" ADBI Working Paper No. 413. Tokyo: Asian Development Bank Institute.
Society for Worldwide Interbank Financial Telecommunication. 2014. "RMB Swift Tracker."
February.
Subramanian, Arvind. 2011. *Eclipse: Living in the Shadow of China's Economic Dominance.*
Washington: Peterson Institute for International Economics.
Subramanian, Arvind, and Martin Kessler. 2013. "The Renminbi Bloc Is Here: Asia Down,
Rest of the World to Go?" Working Paper 12-19. Washington: Peterson Institute for Inter-
national Economics.

PART **III**

The Process

7

The Role of Offshore Financial Centers in the Process of Renminbi Internationalization

YIN-WONG CHEUNG

Financial crises highlight the vulnerability of economic systems and feed on the weakness of market designs. One of the lessons from the global financial crisis of 2008–09 is the danger of building the international monetary architecture around a single dominating global currency. Specifically, the shortage of the U.S. dollar that occurred in the midst of the recent crisis has led to turmoil in the global financial market, and the resulting contraction of global liquidity has severely hampered international trade and financial transactions. The cataclysmic effects of the dollar shortage have alarmed the world that the current dollar-dependent international monetary system could be very risky.

In response to this experience, the People's Republic of China (PRC) has launched a number of initiatives to reduce its reliance on the U.S. dollar and to facilitate the use of its own currency, the renminbi (RMB), in conducting international transactions. In light of the PRC's growing economic prowess in the global market, it seems quite natural for it to push the RMB into the international arena. An International Monetary Fund (2010) study considered the RMB one of the three national currencies that could compete with the U.S. dollar in the global market, the other two being the euro and the yen. The international acceptance of the RMB is partly made possible by calls for the U.S. dollar to play a less prominent global role, the occurrence of the European sovereign debt crisis, and Japan's two "lost decades."

The author would like to thank the Hung Hing Ying and Leung Hau Ling Charitable Foundation for its support.

Policymakers and academics are interested in unraveling the motivation behind these RMB internationalization initiatives. Some suggested motivations are that it is driven by economic pragmatism in the midst of a dollar shortage crisis; it is a disguised component of the PRC's financial development policy; and it is an attempt to undercut the U.S. dollar's supremacy in the global market. Quite apart from possible motivations, it is generally agreed that the integration of the RMB into the global monetary system would greatly change the international economic and geopolitical landscapes.[1]

The world is watching the way the PRC is seeking to internationalize the use of its currency. In the last few years, the PRC has pursued a seemingly unorthodox approach. One main component of the general policy has been to establish offshore RMB markets, especially the one in Hong Kong, China. That offshore RMB market was conceived in 2004, but it made relatively slow progress in the few years immediately following its inception. Since the recent global financial crisis, however, efforts to widen and deepen the offshore RMB market have intensified. Since 2012 the PRC has been working with other financial centers, including London and Singapore, to promote offshore RMB businesses.

Does the presence of offshore markets help establish the global status of a currency? It is hard to imagine that the U.S. dollar could achieve and maintain its prominent global role without the support of fully developed U.S. dollar markets around the globe. At the minimum, offshore markets allow a currency to perform its potential as an international currency outside the country in which it is issued.

In the case of the RMB, it is natural to ask to what extent the process of internationalization will be facilitated by the newly developed offshore RMB market. Clearly, there is an optimal demand on the part of nonresidents for international transactions conducted in the PRC's currency. The establishment of an offshore market allows nonresidents to conduct transactions in RMB. Nevertheless, will the level of RMB activity go beyond what is justified by overseas demand for such activity?[2] Will the offshore market push the RMB to the level of existing world demand that is warranted by the global demand?

The role of offshore RMB markets deserves some attention. By and large, an offshore market and the international role of a currency are believed to be determined by market forces and to exhibit economies of scale. In the case of the RMB, however, the PRC assumes an active policy stance in establishing offshore RMB markets, and in orchestrating and promoting its use overseas.

This unconventional strategy has drawn both praise and skepticism. Some analysts believe that the offshore-market approach is a clever maneuver in view of the relatively underdeveloped domestic financial market and the strong domestic

---

1. See, for example, Eichengreen (2013), McCauley (2011), and Yu (2012) for recent discussions on RMB internationalization.

2. For simplicity, we ignore the possible ambiguities arising from the transition to the optimal level.

resistance to the liberalization of financial markets. The offshore experiences could be brought back to the domestic market to further the liberalization policy. Thus, the offshore market approach functions as a backdoor to advance financial market reforms domestically. The PRC's 2001 accession to the World Trade Organization is often cited as an example of the country's efforts to affirm and deepen its domestic economic reforms by opening up to world trade.

Skeptics of this strategy note that without a well-functioning domestic finance sector, offshore RMB markets could create unbalanced growth forces in the domestic and offshore markets, and the unbalanced growth could lead to adverse economic consequences in the medium to long run. In the short run, arbitrage across domestic and offshore markets imposes significant costs on the PRC. Furthermore, the prevailing capital control practices confine the scope of integrating successful experiences from offshore markets to the underdeveloped and heavily regulated domestic finance sector, and limit the growth of offshore RMB businesses.

Against this backdrop, in this chapter I assess the role of offshore RMB markets in promoting the international use of the RMB, and some related issues. Besides providing a marketplace for the RMB to play the role of an international currency, could the offshore market "force" the PRC to deepen reform of its domestic finance sector and capital account policy? Will the PRC respond to the feedback from the newly developed offshore RMB markets? Or is the PRC able and willing to direct and dictate the process of financial liberalization and the related RMB internationalization policy?

In the next section, I provide a general overview of offshore currency markets and global currencies. The following section focuses on the offshore RMB markets, paying special attention to the one in Hong Kong, China. Next I discuss recent developments in the PRC, including the launching of the Qianhai initiative in Shenzhen and the Pilot Free Trade Zone program in Shanghai, and offer some views on the limited roles of offshore markets in the RMB internationalization process. In my concluding remarks I sum up the prospects of offshore markets and the internationalization of the currency.

Offshore Currency Markets and Global Currencies

There is no exact, straightforward definition of an offshore financial center.[3] For the purposes of this discussion, an offshore currency market is a market that facilitates and specializes in transactions of products denominated in currencies not issued by that offshore market. An offshore currency market is not limited to foreign exchange transactions; and owing to the nature of offshore business, it serves a disproportionately large nonresident population.

---

3. For discussions on the conceptual and operational definitions of offshore financial centers, see International Monetary Fund (2000) and Zoromé (2007).

A main feature of an offshore currency market is that it separates the currency risk from the country risk. The currency risk becomes combined with the risk of the country in which the offshore market is located. Usually, an offshore market is established in a country with a good reputation for the rule of law, sound financial market infrastructure, and favorable regulatory and tax policies on offshore transactions.

The pros and cons of an offshore currency market can be summarized as follows: All else equal, an offshore market adds overall liquidity to a currency. Besides separating the currency risk and the country risk, an offshore currency market offers a means to bypass rules and regulations that apply in the onshore market. Participants may also enjoy diversification and management advantages related to the time zone and location, language, and business environment of an offshore center. Because of differential regulatory requirements, especially those related to reserve requirements, pricing is typically quite competitive in offshore markets as compared to onshore ones.

The usual concern on the cost is that a loosely regulated offshore market could induce monetary and financial instability because it amplifies market risk and undermines authorities' ability to conduct domestic policy and manage capital flows. A different cost view is that the global status facilitated by offshore currency markets promotes the privilege that an international currency enjoys. In fact, the U.S. dollar is commonly referred to as the global currency that enjoys an "exorbitant privilege" because it profits handsomely from its power as an international currency while simultaneously imposing costs on other economies.[4]

London, New York, and Tokyo are the renowned offshore currency markets in Europe, North America, and Asia. Each market offers a rich menu of products denominated in a wide array of foreign currencies. In addition to these main offshore currency centers, some centers are known for more regional currencies. For instance, Singapore was known for its role as an offshore currency market for the Malaysian ringgit before 1997 and is still a major offshore currency market for Southeast Asian currencies.

The offshore dollar markets (commonly known as eurodollar markets) constitute the largest segment of the global financial market and greatly facilitate the use of the U.S. dollar in international trade and investment transactions across different time zones and geographic locations. Some argue that the sprawling presence of offshore U.S. dollar markets is a reflection of the prominence of the U.S. dollar in the international monetary architecture. The network dollar usage effect generated by these markets that enhances the global status of the dollar should not be underestimated.

The evolution of offshore U.S. dollar markets reflects the changes in the perceptions of offshore currency markets and currency internationalization. When

---

4. *Exorbitant Privilege* is the title of Eichengreen's (2011) book, which describes the path of the dollar to international prominence and its future prospects.

these markets first started to develop in the 1950s, the general perception of them was quite skeptical. Over time, with the expansion of offshore market activity, the sentiment has become quite positive, even though reservations remain.[5]

Could the U.S. dollar experience offer some hints on the nascent offshore RMB markets? Despite the temptation to draw a lesson from history, we note that in the 1950s, when the U.S. dollar began its ascent as an international currency, its status was quite different from the current status of the RMB. One main difference is that when the eurodollar market emerged in the late 1950s and early 1960s, the U.S. dollar was already quite widely accepted as a global reserve currency. The U.S. dollar was essentially in strong demand by both public and private sectors outside the United States. Furthermore, in the first few decades of the eurodollar market, U.S. policies discernibly leaned toward the domestic economy and were not swayed by these policies' possible adverse effects on the rest of the world. For example, in 1971, Treasury Secretary John Connally told U.S. allies, "The dollar is our currency, but it is your problem." (Later in the chapter, the background to U.S. policies in the early phase of the eurodollar market is discussed in more detail and compared to the background of the RMB and recent developments in the PRC.)

Like other financial markets, a well-functioning offshore currency market has to offer both convenience and confidence. Convenience requires a sizable market with depth and breadth. This convenience is enhanced by an established trading and clearance infrastructure, a well-connected transactional network, and a good set of investment and funding alternatives. Confidence relies on the rule of law governing the offshore currency market and the government's attitudes toward offshore transactions.

The convenience and confidence of an offshore market could be affected by the policy stance of the country that issues the currency being traded. For instance, fund flows associated with offshore transactions ultimately have to be cleared in the onshore banking system. Governments can directly and indirectly affect the attractiveness of offshore currency markets by managing and enforcing rules and regulations on clearing balances of foreign financial institutions being held with onshore banks.[6]

Hong Kong, China: The First Offshore Renminbi Market

So far, Hong Kong, China is the principal offshore market for the renminbi, but others are eyeing the potential to become offshore RMB markets.

5. Dufey and Giddy (1994) offer a textbook description of the evolution of euro-currency markets. The efforts by some countries to restrict offshore trading of their currencies after the 1997 financial crisis are reported in Ishii, Ötker-Robe, and Cui (2001).

6. The reluctance of the Bundesbank was perceived as a reason of the limited degree of the internationalization of the deutsche mark before the euro era (Franke 1999).

Background Information on Hong Kong, China as an Offshore Currency Market

The offshore RMB market in Hong Kong, China is an archetypical example of the existing offshore RMB trading centers. Both its inception and evolution reflect the PRC's concerted efforts to shape the development of an offshore RMB market and guide the process of introducing the RMB to the global stage. At the risk of stating the obvious, two reasons of focusing on the offshore RMB market in Hong Kong, China are that it is the first of its kind and has always accounted for the lion's share of offshore RMB business, and that its special status allows the PRC to design specific policy measures to control and manage the process of RMB internationalization.

Hong Kong, China is the PRC's first testing ground for the international use of the RMB. Since its inception in 2004, the offshore RMB market in Hong Kong, China has evolved from a primitive market that was dominated by RMB bank deposits to an increasingly sophisticated RMB trading center that offers a wide range of RMB-denominated products. Other offshore centers—including London, Singapore, and Taipei,China—are making headway to compete for offshore RMB businesses, yet Hong Kong, China has maintained its leading position, accounting for about 80 percent of global offshore RMB payment volumes.[7] In addition to the first-mover advantage, the PRC's policy support plays an important role in Hong Kong, China's accomplishment.[8]

The PRC's choice is closely related to Hong Kong, China's unique economic and political status. Even before the sovereignty change in 1997, when the British handed over the city to the PRC, it was a renowned international financial center with well-regarded rule of law practices as well as a world-class financial market infrastructure that had extensive economic ties with the PRC. Now a special administrative region of the PRC, Hong Kong, China maintains its own legal structure and financial system. Specifically, it has its own currency, the Hong Kong dollar, and imposes no capital controls.

The differences in the PRC and Hong Kong, China legal and financial systems make it relatively straightforward for the former to institute specific rules and procedures to regulate cross-border RMB transactions with the latter. Although Hong Kong, China is part of its territory, the PRC treats Hong Kong, China as an offshore market in terms of RMB trading. Indeed, market practitioners view the RMB transacted in Hong Kong, China as different from the RMB in the PRC; they coined the trading symbol CNH for RMB traded in Hong Kong, China (the usual designation is CNY, for Chinese yuan, which is still the official International

---

7. Society for Worldwide Interbank Financial Telecommunication, "Efficiency for Offshore Chinese Yuan (RMB) Settlement," July 25, 2011 (www.swift.com/news/standards/chinese_Yuan_projects).

8. For instance, the policy of developing Hong Kong, China into a prime offshore RMB center was affirmed in the PRC's Twelfth Five-Year Plan (2011–15).

Organization for Standardization currency code in international settlement practice).[9]

Hong Kong, China commands an advantage over other offshore RMB financial centers. In accordance with its usual gradualist approach to reform, the PRC has followed a measured strategy to experiment with offshore RMB transactions. Despite the PRC's strong preference for establishing the use of the RMB overseas, it is not likely to give up capital controls outright. Thus, in addition to establishing clearing and settlement systems and market liquidity, the authorities have to work out the nitty-gritty of regulatory cooperation. These regulatory cooperation arrangements offer the PRC some leverage to assess the implications of intermediating international transactions in the RMB. For instance, the PRC could dictate the pace and the means by which offshore RMB capital is remitted back to the domestic market and thus evaluate the effectiveness of its capital control measures and its ability to manage the PRC economy. As a special administrative region of the PRC, Hong Kong, China is relatively pliable. The PRC could dictate both the growth and the evolution of the offshore market via necessary legislation. This potential for regulatory cooperation gives Hong Kong, China an insurmountable advantage over other international financial centers.

Offshore Renminbi Deposits, Trade Settlements, and Dim Sum Bonds

To set the stage for launching overseas RMB business activity, the PRC in 2003 appointed the Bank of China (Hong Kong, China) as the first clearing bank for RMB transactions outside the mainland of the PRC. Hong Kong Interbank Clearing Limited provides a real-time gross settlement system for the RMB, an important infrastructure to support RMB clearing services in Hong Kong, China and to facilitate RMB transactions in other overseas financial centers.[10]

Indicators show that the first-mover advantage and the PRC's policy support have allowed the offshore RMB market in Hong Kong, China to expand in its size and offering of RMB-denominated products. Figure 7-1 plots the total offshore RMB (CNH) deposits in Hong Kong, China. The growth pattern of CNH deposits mirrors the anecdotal evidence that the PRC has accelerated its efforts to promote the international use of its currency. The volume of CNH deposits has been on a steep ascent since July 2010, when the PRC expanded the scheme for

9. See Society for Worldwide Interbank Financial Telecommunication, "Efficiency for Offshore Chinese Yuan (RMB) Settlement," July 25, 2011 (www.swift.com/news/standards/chinese_Yuan_projects). With the establishment of offshore RMB markets beyond Hong Kong, China, the H in CNH could be understood as standing for "overseas" (*haiwai*, in Chinese). See Cheung and Rime (2014) on the interrelationships between the CNY and the CNH.

10. The settlement system operates from 8:30 a.m. to 11:30 p.m., Hong Kong, China time, which overlaps partly with business hours in London and New York. See Hong Kong Monetary Authority, "Renminbi Cross-Border Trade Settlement and Net Open Position" (www.hkma.gov.hk/media/eng/doc/key-functions/monetary-stability/rmb-business-in-hong-kong/hkma-rmb-booklet.pdf), for some quick facts about the system, including the list of participating banks.

Figure 7-1. *Renminbi Deposits in Hong Kong, China*

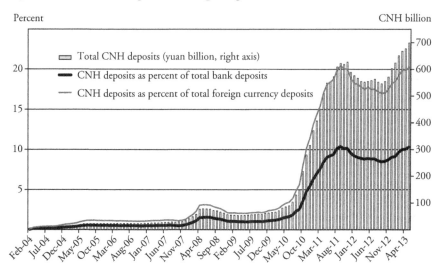

Source: CEIC database.
CNH = offshore renminbi.

cross-border RMB trade settlement and the signing of the Supplementary Memorandum of Co-operation between the Hong Kong Monetary Authority and the People's Bank of China on RMB businesses.[11] Between July 2010 and November 2011, CNH deposits grew by 500 percent, from RMB103.4 billion to RMB627.3 billion. The phenomenal growth rate makes the CNH the second most popular foreign currency, after the U.S. dollar, in the Hong Kong, China market.

The decline of CNH deposits in the first half of 2012 triggered concern about the prospects of the offshore market, but anxiety was allayed in the middle of 2012, when the PRC reaffirmed the role of Hong Kong, China, and the volume of CNH deposits regained its upward trajectory. This instance highlights the PRC's influential role—for example, to increase confidence—in the development of the offshore RMB market.

International trade settlement is an officially encouraged international use of the RMB. Figure 7-2 presents the volume of trade settled in RMB conducted via Hong Kong, China. In April 2009, the PRC's State Council approved a pilot scheme for cross-border trade settlement in RMB.[12] In June 2010 the scheme was

11. The supplementary memorandum (2010) essentially allows a rich menu of RMB trading activities in Hong Kong, China, including spot and forward RMB trading and RMB-linked structural products. See Hong Kong Monetary Authority, "Renminbi Cross-Border Trade Settlement and Net Open Position" (www.info.gov.hk/hkma/eng/guide/circu_date/20111223e1.pdf; subscription needed).

12. The use of the RMB to settle cross-border trade could be traced back to at least 2003. See, for example, the directives issued by the PRC's State Administration of Foreign Exchange (SAFE) on using the RMB in settling trade (see at www.safe.gov.cn/wps/portal). Before 2009, RMB trade set-

Figure 7-2. Monthly Volume of Cross-Border Trade Settled in Renminbi via Hong Kong, China

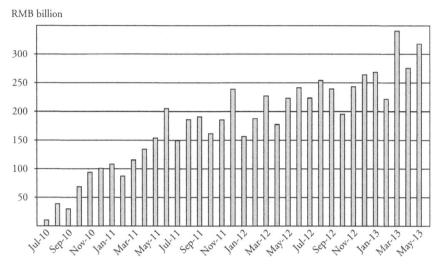

Source: Hong Kong Monetary Authority.

expanded to cover twenty of the thirty-one mainland PRC provinces and in August 2011, to cover the entire PRC.

The value of RMB trade settlement has been growing strongly since 2010. The official efforts have paid off quite well: the monthly volume has surged from CNY10 billion in July 2010 to CNY318 billion in May 2013, a thirty-fold increase in less than three years. Even allowing for possibly misclassified transactions related to arbitrage between onshore and offshore markets via trade invoicing, the growth of the volume of trade settled in RMB is quite phenomenal.

Another concerted effort is to establish an offshore RMB bond market in Hong Kong, China. The first issuance of RMB-denominated bonds—called dim sum bonds—issued in Hong Kong, China by the China Development Bank in 2007 started a new chapter in the history of the offshore RMB market (see figure 7-3). The typical monthly issuance volume is still under RMB10 billion, but this represents a steady established flow of supply to the dim sum bond market.

Among all the issuers, the PRC's Ministry of Finance plays a special role. Every year since 2009, the Ministry of Finance has issued its RMB sovereign bonds in Hong Kong, China. Issuances are usually large, ranging from the CNY6 billion offer in 2009 to the CNY23 billion offer in 2013.[13] Unlike other dim sum bond

tlement mainly occurred for trade taking place along the PRC's borders, with Cambodia, Mongolia, the Russian Federation, and Viet Nam. Very little data are available on these early cross-border trade settlements, so the discussion in this chapter focuses on the post-2009 era.

13. The 2013 issuance was offered in two slots: one of CNY13 billion and the other of CNY10 billion.

Figure 7-3. *Monthly Issuance of Dim Sum Bonds*

RMB billion

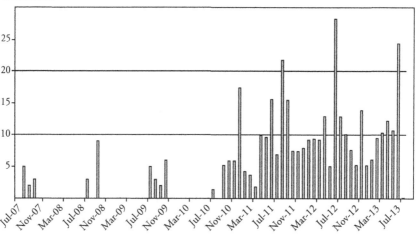

Source: Bloomberg.

issuances, Ministry of Finance sovereign bonds cover long tenors, up to a maturity of thirty years. The issuance of long-term RMB-denominated bonds is seen as an effort to set up an offshore market yield curve, which is essential for the operation of a full-fledged offshore RMB bond market.

Dim sum bonds and onshore RMB bonds are governed by different legal systems, leading to significant differences between them. The dim sum bond covenants are typically covered by the laws of Hong Kong, China, not those in the mainland of the PRC. In general, the legal system in Hong Kong, China is considered as an internationally recognized legal framework. Thus, the dim sum bond market is attractive to individual and sovereign investors who are concerned about, say, possible covenant violations and insolvency proceedings. Furthermore, trading in the dim sum bond market is not subject to the regulations and disclosure requirements in the onshore market.

An Interim Assessment of the Hong Kong, China Offshore RMB Market

The offshore RMB market in Hong Kong, China has undergone some significant developments since 2004. This subsection offers a brief assessment of the nascent offshore RMB market.

GENERAL DEVELOPMENT. Most of the actions in the offshore RMB market have taken place in the wake of the recent global financial crisis. Since 2008–09, a variety of financial products denominated in RMB–RMB-denominated equities and exchange-traded funds, RMB-denominated certificates of deposit, Renminbi Kilobar Gold, foreign exchange options, futures and related RMB-linked structural products, and insurance plans and products—have been introduced in

Hong Kong, China. These RMB-denominated products are available in retail and corporate banking, capital and currency markets, and the insurance sector.[14]

There is no denying that the nascent offshore RMB market has been progressively expanding in size and product offerings. In general, the offshore market provides a physical platform for the PRC to assess the implications of using the RMB to intermediate international transactions and for the rest of the world to become familiar with the RMB via real-life business activities.

The PRC's domestic finance sector is relatively underdeveloped and has limited experience with modern financial transactions. The PRC authorities can use the Hong Kong, China market as a setting to gain needed experience and expertise. They can use the offshore market activity to assess the responses of domestic and overseas participants to RMB exchange rate flexibility and convertibility and their implications for authorities' ability to manage the local economy. Similarly, PRC corporations and financial institutions can gain practical experience conducting international business using the RMB in a legal environment that is recognized by international participants but that is different from the one in the PRC, and recognizing trading partners' currency concerns. They can also experiment with using various RMB-denominated products in offshore markets to manage their funding and investment needs.

Anecdotal evidence emerging from conferences, seminars, and workshops offered by financial institutions, professional bodies, and commercial entities suggests that corporations and investors domiciled outside the PRC have tremendous interest in the offshore RMB markets. For these overseas participants, sourcing and investing in the RMB is uncharted territory. The offshore RMB market in Hong Kong, China presents an attractive alternative to the costs of accessing the local RMB market. The absence of capital controls means that Hong Kong, China can allow individuals to move funds in and out of the offshore market to assess the costs and benefits of working with the RMB.

For instance, for a corporation to adopt the RMB as a settlement currency, it has to set up the corresponding internal and external arrangements, including guidelines for cash management, exchange rate risk management, fund transfers, and banking facilities. Even though the common principles are assumed to be common knowledge, individual corporations have their own idiosyncratic practices that are implemented and evolved according to management philosophy and local regulations. The offshore RMB market offers a testing ground for them to work out and fine-tune the practical aspects of including the RMB in their menus of operating currencies. Similarly, overseas investors can learn the trading and settlement details of moving RMB funds in and out of the market.

---

14. See, for example, Hong Kong Monetary Authority, "Renminbi Cross-Border Trade Settlement and Net Open Position" (www.hkma.gov.hk/media/eng/doc/key-functions/monetary-stability/rmb-business-in-hong-kong/hkma-rmb-booklet.pdf), for a list of available RMB-denominated products.

In principle, these experiences help domestic and foreign corporations and investors set up similar systems in their operations in the PRC.

OTHER ISSUES. Despite the healthy development in the last few years, the offshore RMB market is quite far from a full-fledged offshore market such as the eurodollar market and still lacks some basic features. For instance, the dim sum component of the offshore RMB market is expanding quite rapidly, yet credit ratings of dim sum bonds are lacking—which could dilute the issuer's quality. The presence of low-quality issuers raises the concern about dim sum bonds lacking explicit clauses in their covenants to protect investors. The availability of objective credit ratings and improved investor protection will nurture the dynamic growth of the dim sum bond market.

Only recently, in June 2013, did the Treasury Markets Association in Hong Kong, China offer CNH Hong Kong Interbank Offered Rate (HIBOR) fixing. The fixing covers tenors from overnight to one year and its purpose is to facilitate the pricing of offshore RMB-denominated loans and related structural products for risk management. Its overall effect is yet to be seen.

Despite its rapid growth, the scale of the offshore RMB market is still small. For instance, even though the volume of CNH deposits had jumped to CNY698.5 billion as of May 2013, it is less than 1 percent of the PRC's domestic deposit balance of CNY99.3 trillion in the same period. Since the other offshore RMB markets are much smaller than the one in Hong Kong, China, the total offshore RMB deposits are likely to be less than 2 percent of domestic deposits.[15]

The PRC's extensive trade network justifies its policy of using the trade settlement channel to promote the use of the RMB on the global stage. It has been reported that PRC corporations offer price concessions to encourage their overseas trading partners to conduct their import and export transactions in RMB, which complements the official stance of promoting the use of RMB overseas. Since the scheme was first introduced in 2009, the value of cross-border PRC trade settled in RMB has increased from a minuscule amount to an aggregate monthly volume of CNY364.3 billion as of May 2013, which represents 16.9 percent of the PRC's aggregate trade volume in the same period.

This is an impressive development, yet the current fraction of trade settled in RMB is far less than the one third predicted by Chen and Peng (2007). Furthermore, Japan settles about 40 percent of its trade in the yen (Goldberg and Tille 2008) and the eurozone invoices more than one half of its international trade in its own currency, even in the midst of the sovereign debt crisis (European Central Bank 2013). Achievement of the goal of one third depends on economic and political developments in both the PRC and the global economy.

---

15. The comparable RMB deposit figures in Taipei,China and London are estimated to be less than CNY70 billion and CNY6 billion, respectively.

Another important attribute of an international currency is its use as a vehicle currency, the currency used to invoice an international trade transaction. Even though the PRC has made impressive strides in using RMB to settle its trade with the rest of the world, the RMB has played a limited role as a vehicle currency. Additional efforts have to be made to enhance its vehicle currency function.

Regarding the dim sum bond market, first, both the monthly issuance value and outstanding volume of the dim sum bond market are small compared with the bond market in the PRC. This relative size is not surprising, given the short history of the offshore market.

But it is discouraging to observe that, despite the increase in market size, dim sum bond issuance is dominated by the PRC's Ministry of Finance and policy banks (banks are responsible for financing economic and trade development and state-invested projects). If these banks do not issue bonds, the monthly issuance is typically less than CNY10 billion. The PRC institutions and their affiliates in Hong Kong, China together are estimated to account for well over one half of the value of outstanding offshore bonds (Cheung and Hui 2013). Despite the policy intention to promote offshore market activities and the lower RMB funding cost in the offshore market compared to the onshore market, not all PRC corporations are allowed to issue dim sum bonds. PRC corporations have to obtain official approval and financial guarantors before they can issue dim sum bonds in Hong Kong, China. The procedures result in reducing the default risk and managing the inflow of offshore RMB capital.

The lack of active nonresident issuers undermines the international nature of the dim sum bond market and limits its funding and investment opportunities. The dominance of PRC issuers reflects the PRC's policies. For instance, overseas issuers have limited ways to deploy the RMB capital raised via dim sum bond issuance. Investment opportunities in offshore markets are constrained by the limited investment products denominated in the RMB, and those in the onshore market are hampered by administrative regulations for foreign issuers to remit offshore RMB capital back to the PRC.

In addition to the international characteristic of the currency, the presence of nonresidents has implications for the benefit of promoting the use of the RMB overseas. With its trade surplus and capital inflows, the PRC's external assets are mostly in foreign currencies and predominantly in U.S. dollars, yet most of its international liabilities are in RMB. By allowing nonresidents to borrow in RMB, the PRC increases its RMB-denominated claims and shares the exchange rate risk arising from its dollar-biased international assets and liability position with the rest of the world (Cheung, Ma, and McCauley 2011). The current composition of the dim sum bond issuers does not offer much risk-sharing benefit to the PRC.

Other Possible Offshore RMB Markets

The offshore RMB business's enormous potential has attracted considerable attention from financial centers around the world. These cities are eager to explore the possibility of setting up the infrastructure to compete for a share of the global offshore RMB business. London, Singapore, and Taipei,China are considered as serious contenders. Dubai, Frankfurt, Luxembourg, San Francisco, and Tokyo are reportedly at different stages of preparing themselves to claim a slice of the global RMB market.

Despite all the buzz, Hong Kong, China so far has maintained its competitive edge and accounts for over 80 percent of overseas RMB payment flows (Society for Worldwide Interbank Financial Telecommunication 2012).[16] Hong Kong, China's prominence reflects the policy-driven nature of the offshore RMB market. It is hard for other financial centers to expand their RMB activities if they do not get the PRC's endorsement and support. For example, prior to 2013, the offshore RMB settlement and clearing infrastructure was only available to Hong Kong, China.[17] Taipei,China and Singapore had their own authorized RMB clearing banks by the first half of 2013, but London does not, relying on Hong Kong, China's settlement and clearing facility—and still realizing profits. So Hong Kong, China is currently the major player, but the offshore RMB business is likely to take root gradually in other financial centers. Indeed, it is in the PRC's interest to support additional RMB trading markets and work with other financial centers to develop offshore RMB businesses. The presence of more established offshore RMB centers across different geographic locations and time zones will increase global RMB liquidity and business opportunities, and these developments help to increase the RMB's international acceptance.

For example, Taipei,China and Singapore, both with a local RMB clearing bank, are in a position to compete for a spot in the global offshore RMB market. Both saw their offshore RMB activities grow quickly after their authorized local RMB clearing services were launched in early 2013. The offshore business in Taipei,China is underpinned by its special political relationship and economic ties with the mainland of the PRC. Singapore, by contrast, a major financial hub in Southeast Asia, operates an active offshore RMB market by leveraging its well-established financial market infrastructure and links with neighboring countries.

London has a huge potential as an offshore RMB market. As a premium international financial center, London could provide critical RMB business services in

16. Society for Worldwide Interbank Financial Telecommunication, "RMB Internationalisation: Perspectives on the Future of RMB Clearing," SWIFT white paper, October 29, 2012 (www.swift.com/news/press_releases/SWIFT_shares_new_perspectives_on_RMB_clearing).

17. Hong Kong, China also benefits from the swap arrangement it established with the PRC. The CNY400 billion swap line is the largest of the currency swap lines the PRC has arranged so far and provides the needed RMB liquidity to operate and expand the offshore market smoothly.

the Western Hemisphere and beyond. Even without a local RMB clearing bank, London signed a three-year swap agreement of CNY200 billion with the PRC in June 2013. The swap line is the first that the PRC signed with a Group of Seven country. The symbolic meaning for London's role in offshore RMB business may be more than the RMB liquidity available through the swap line. London's potential to be a significant hub of the global RMB business is enhanced with the promise of the Renminbi Qualified Foreign Institutional Investor (RQFII) quota of CNY80 billion announced in October 2013. London's current status is confirmed by the SWIFT statistics, which show that the United Kingdom accounts for over 50 percent of RMB foreign exchange transactions (excluding the PRC and Hong Kong, China).[18]

London's good relationship with Hong Kong, China may blunt the possible drawbacks of using Hong Kong, China's RMB clearing facility to develop its offshore RMB business.

New York, another important international financial center, is mysteriously missing from most discussions surrounding offshore RMB business. Even though the PRC launched trading of its currency in the United States in January 2011, New York seldom publicly expresses its interest in establishing an offshore RMB market.[19] Whether this is due to political considerations or regulatory concerns, New York appears to be unenthusiastic or not aggressive in developing RMB businesses. In fact, New York appears to be behind in the game of securing offshore RMB business.[20] The United States accounted for 14 percent in 2012 and 13 percent in 2013 (up to September) of the offshore RMB foreign exchange transactions outside Hong Kong, China and the PRC. These numbers are much smaller than the corresponding ones of the United Kingdom.[21]

Evidently, the PRC has been strategically guiding the development of the offshore RMB market in Hong Kong, China. With its efficient financial infrastructure, relative pliability, and track record on implementing the offshore RMB strategies, Hong Kong, China is likely to maintain its considerable lead in the

18. The United Kingdom accounted for 54 percent in 2012 and 62 percent in 2013 (up to September). See Society for Worldwide Interbank Financial Telecommunication, "RMB Tracker–September 2013" (www.swift.com/assets/swift_com/documents/products_services/RMB_Tracker_September_2013_Slides.pdf).

19. The scope of trading is restricted; the purchase of RMB for an individual U.S. customer is limited to the equivalent of $4,000 a day (see Lingling Wei, "New Move to Make Yuan a Global Currency," *Wall Street Journal*, January 12, 2011). However, there is no limit on converting RMB back into dollars. There are also no conversion limits on businesses that are engaged in international trading.

20. In February 2013, San Francisco, the third largest financial center in the United States, was reported to be planning to become a center for offshore RMB trading (Andrew S. Ross, "SF Seeks to Be Hub for Chinese Currency," *San Francisco Chronicle*, February 16, 2013).

21. Society for Worldwide Interbank Financial Telecommunication, "RMB Tracker–September 2013" (www.swift.com/assets/swift_com/documents/products_services/RMB_Tracker_September_2013_Slides.pdf).

global offshore RMB business in the near future. If the currency is increasingly used overseas and people become more familiar with the offshore market, the acceptance of the RMB will improve and additional demand will be created. The RMB could support the existence of multiple active offshore RMB markets when it realizes its potential as an international currency. Overall offshore growth of the RMB business will benefit Hong Kong, China and other financial centers. In the meanwhile, Hong Kong, China is leading the pack in offshore RMB business, followed by London, Singapore, and Taipei,China.

Developments within the People's Republic of China

Skeptics regarding the effectiveness of the PRC's outsourcing approach to internationalize the RMB cite the extreme impediments and controls in the onshore market. Their worry is that if the PRC maintains the status quo and does not implement changes in the domestic market to complement the changes made offshore, the offshore experiences will have only limited implications for the overall acceptance by the international community.

Anecdotal evidence does indicate that the PRC has been progressing along its path of reform. Opinions may differ as to whether the pace of reform is too slow or appropriate, but there is no sign that the process has stopped. Since the beginning of 2013, the PRC has introduced policies to simplify regulatory requirements regarding cross-border RMB payments for large international corporations and the deployment of onshore and offshore funds by foreign firms. These changes help to improve the efficiency of the domestic system and thus complement the effort of promoting the overseas use of the currency. Also, on July 19, 2013, the People's Bank of China announced the removal of controls on lending rates, which is the latest policy move toward interest rate liberalization.

Capital Controls

When the PRC switched to an aggressive mode to promote the RMB, there was a serious debate on the necessity of removing capital controls before internationalizing the currency. Despite the PRC's relaxing its regulatory policy over time, a strong view is that it is premature to push for the international use of the RMB before liberalizing local financial markets. A counterargument is that the pound sterling and the U.S. dollar acquired their prime international currency status in an era when capital controls were the norm. For instance, in the early period of the eurodollar market, the United States imposed restrictions on the inflow of the dollar from overseas. Indeed, the United States only removed the deposit interest rate ceilings, with the exception of the demand deposit rate, in the 1980s.[22] These

---

22. These interest rate ceilings were eliminated between 1981 and 1986. The payment of interest on demand deposits was allowed (but not required) in 2011.

experiences undermine the causal link between capital controls and currency internationalization.

Nevertheless, the effects of capital controls for the overseas use of the RMB could be stronger now than they were in the 1950s. To gain a share in the international market, the RMB has to compete with the U.S. dollar and other international currencies that are subject to few capital controls. Will people choose to use a currency that is subject to capital controls?

Despite the existence of capital controls in the PRC, the offshore RMB market in Hong Kong, China has developed quite quickly in the last few years. The development has also attracted the interest of a few other financial centers to join the offshore RMB venture. As noted earlier, the arrangement for foreign financial institutions to clear cross-border trade and investment transactions through the appointed local RMB clearing banks makes the offshore business possible. The PRC, by offering the means to foreign financial institutions to manage their RMB clearing balances, effectively creates a form of convertibility for designated cross-border RMB transactions. The arrangement is similar in spirit to the one adopted by the United States before the era of convertible capital accounts (He and McCauley 2013).

What are the implications of the nascent offshore RMB market for the PRC's capital controls? Ma and McCauley (2008) and Cheung and Herrala (2014) show that the PRC's capital controls have not been watertight but remain substantially binding. The evidence based on offshore RMB (CNH) and onshore RMB (CNY) exchange rates give a different impression. The percentages of daily CNH–CNY premiums are plotted in figure 7-4.

If we use the premium of CNH over CNY to gauge the market price of capital controls, the price appears less volatile and converging. When the CNH was introduced in late 2010, it enjoyed a premium that reflected the market's preference for the RMB in Hong Kong, China, where no capital controls are imposed. The negative premium observed in September 2011 was attributed to a policy crackdown on mis-invoicing of CNH transactions and to a decline in risk appetite due to heightened market volatility in that period. Since then, the premium has fluctuated mainly in the range of –0.5 to 0.5 percent. The circumstantial evidence thus suggests (1) that the PRC's capital controls are becoming less effective, (2) that the market is placing a smaller value on convertibility of the CNH market over time, (3) that the market anticipates that over time, the PRC's ongoing policy reform will reduce the cost of capital controls on business, or (4) that the CNH exchange rate follows the CNY exchange rate because the trading volume of the latter is much larger than that of the former.[23]

23. According to Bank for International Settlements (2013), Hong Kong, China accounted for 16 percent of the total global RMB foreign exchange trading and the onshore market accounted for 59 percent of the trading volume.

Figure 7-4. *Offshore (CNH)/Onshore (CNY) Renminbi Premiums*

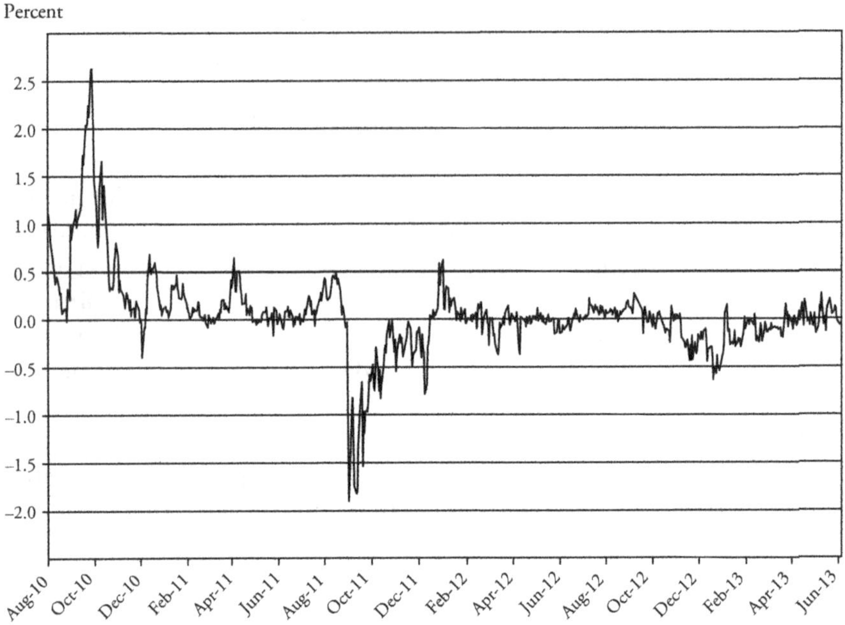

Percent

Source: Bloomberg.

A Domestic Offshore Market

On June 27, 2012, the PRC unveiled a bold economic reform initiative to create a special economic zone within the first special economic zone Shenzhen in the PRC. In essence, the central government approved the plan to develop Qianhai, a port district of Shenzhen, into a modern service industry cooperation zone that would enjoy pilot policy preferences beyond those available in the rest of Shenzhen.[24] Most commentators lauded the initiative as a confirmation of the PRC's commitment to liberalize its capital account and boost the international use of the RMB.

The Qianhai area is set for completion by 2020. Although the reform initiative goes beyond the finance sector, the hype surrounds the provisions related to offshore RMB business.[25] One key theme of the experimental zone is that offshore

24. See "Official Reply of the State Council on Policies Concerning the Development and Opening of Qianhai Shenzhen–Hong Kong Modern Service Cooperation Zone of Shenzhen," released by the State Council. The approved plan for Qianhai is based on the one outlined in the document "Overall Development Plan for Qianhai Shenzhen–Hong Kong Modern Service Industry Cooperation Area," approved in August 2010.

25. The modern service industries covered by the development plan include the financial and securities industries, legal and professional services, education and medical services, and telecommunication services. Preferential tax incentives will be offered to qualified enterprises and workers.

RMB capital could be sent back to Qianhai. Possible arrangements include that eligible enterprises and banks in Qianhai could borrow RMB loans from banks in Hong Kong, China; issue dim sum bonds; and extend offshore RMB loans. Such arrangements would convert Qianhai into an offshore RMB center within the PRC. The exact policies and terms governing these cross-border RMB-based transactions are still unfolding.

At first glance, the creation of a hub to recycle offshore RMB back to the PRC would seem to benefit the offshore RMB market in Hong Kong, China by enriching its investment opportunities. However, there may be some unintended consequences. Currently there is a legal firewall between the offshore and onshore markets. One concern is the leakage of offshore RMB capital back into the domestic PRC economy. If offshore RMB could be lent to enterprises in Qianhai, should the PRC institute some regulatory oversight of Qianhai to preserve the existing capital controls for the rest of the country?

The leakage effect may not be a critical matter in the beginning, since the initial loans for the pilot were relatively small—mostly for financing the development and construction of the Qianhai district. But the leakage effect will aggravate quickly once business borrowing and lending activities pick up as the project nears finalization and after its completion, in 2020. Unless the PRC eradicates its capital control policy and modernizes its finance sector by 2015 or 2020—the target dates that are sporadically mentioned in the media—one has to consider the challenges of damming the spillovers to the domestic economy from Qianhai.

In principle, the influence of offshore transactions on the domestic offshore market can be contained via the creation of offshore market settings that are actually located within a country's borders (Dufey and Giddy 1994; He and McCauley 2013). A good example of this is the U.S. international banking facilities (IBFs) set up in December 1981. Similarly, Japan established the Japan Offshore Market in Tokyo in December 1985 to accommodate offshore yen transactions within Japan. These facilities require banks to keep separate books and follow different regulations for onshore and offshore transactions. A well-functioning domestic offshore market such as an IBF can create a symbiotic relationship between offshore and onshore markets.

Policy measures designed to establish an onshore-offshore market may not always have the desired effects, however. The Japan Offshore Market was established in response to foreign pressure and did not contribute significantly to the liberalization of Japan's capital account and the international use of the yen (Osugi 1990; Takagi 2011). Indeed, an offshore-onshore market can backfire. Krongkaew (1999) asserted that the Bangkok International Banking Facility established in 1993, which allowed enormous capital inflows, is one of the causes of the 1997 crisis in Thailand.

The real issue is the cost for the PRC to implement a set of operationally efficient regulations to insulate the domestic sector from possible adverse impacts of offshore RMB capital. Some related issues are the implications of the presence of segregated onshore and offshore accounts for tax, regulatory, and risk management policies. Given the PRC's relatively unsophisticated financial system, the administrative cost of setting up effective barriers to contain the spillovers from an offshore market that is physically located within the country is quite high.

The financial innovation of recycling offshore RMB capital could give a short-term boost to the offshore RMB market in Hong Kong, China, but at the expense of impeding the long-term growth potential of the international use of the RMB. Cross-border trade settlement is a main component of the current extraterritorial use of the RMB. The global function of the RMB, however, goes beyond the settlement of the PRC's exports and imports.

Along the path to become an international currency, the RMB should evolve to be a vehicle currency that facilitates transactions among nonresidents, which is the case with the prime global currency, the U.S. dollar: a large proportion of international transactions denominated in the U.S. dollar do not involve U.S. entities. Currently the liquidity in the offshore RMB market is still quite low on the international scale. If the RMB recycle program works too well, it will constrain the offshore RMB liquidity available to nonresidents and thus stifle the use of the RMB as a vehicle currency. This in turn will inhibit the growth of the offshore RMB market. Thus, in the absence of a progressive scheme to provide RMB to nonresidents, a RMB recycle program may work against the objective of promoting the overseas use of the currency.

The Shanghai Free Trade Zone

Shanghai is one of the main economic centers in the PRC. The selection of Qianhai as the designated hub connecting the offshore market in Hong Kong, China and the domestic market raises the question of the role of Shanghai in promoting the overseas use of the RMB. It is conceivable that Shanghai will stay its course for a short period to become a global center for onshore RMB business, but not a base of domestic offshore RMB activity. However, the approval of the establishment of the Shanghai Free Trade Zone by the State Council in July 2013 has reasserted the role of Shanghai in the PRC's reform agenda. The zone was officially inaugurated on September 29, 2013.

Similar to the Qianhai initiative, the official plan for the Shanghai Free Trade Zone encompasses reform measures in several service industries.[26] The official document that created the zone states that the Shanghai Free Trade Zone, assuming risk controllability, could be the testing ground of capital account RMB convertibility, market-determined interest rates, and cross-border RMB transactions.

---

26. These include financial services, shipping services, trade-related services, professional services, cultural services, and social services. See www.shftz.gov.cn/WebViewPublic/item_page.aspx?newsid =635158957941988294&coltype=8.

There are considerable overlaps between financial reform measures of the Qianhai project and the Shanghai Free Trade Zone.

As we went to press, these reform measures were mostly cast in general terms. The lack of specifics makes it difficult to assess the actual impacts of these measures on exchange rate flexibility, capital account convertibility, and interest rate liberalization. Nevertheless, the administrative challenges of implementing financial reforms on a restricted domestic physical area and preventing the spillovers to the domestic financial market discussed below are relevant to both cases. One serious challenge is that of reining in the effect of offshore RMB capital inflows while retaining an effective grip on capital controls in the rest of the PRC.

Implications of Developments in the Domestic Market

Both the Qianhai initiative and the Shanghai Free Trade Zone reassure the global community that the PRC is on course to open up its economy in general and deepen its financial reform in particular, albeit in its usual gradualist style.

Announcement of the Qianhai project and the Shanghai Free Trade Zone have triggered discussions on the future of the offshore RMB market in Hong Kong, China. One view is that Hong Kong, China will be marginalized and lose out in the process. The assumption is that two reform experiments conducted in small physical areas would trigger and speed up financial reforms at the national level. The Shanghai Free Trade Zone has been officially in operation since September 2013, and the construction of the Qianhai region will be completed in 2020. Will Shanghai—the PRC's commercial heavyweight and designated international financial market—with its free trade zone provision undermine its archetypical competitor, Hong Kong, China?

The implicit rivalry between Hong Kong, China and Shanghai depends crucially on how fast the PRC could revamp its financial market regulations, tax policies, and the related governance practices. The history of international finance shows that the process of capital account liberalization is usually laden with financial and economic crises. Indeed, the PRC is quite concerned about the adverse effects of hot money flows. Such a concern is reinforced by a recent study showing that capital account liberalization in the PRC may trigger net portfolio outflows (Bayoumi and Ohnsorge 2013). Thus, the PRC must carefully navigate the minefield of capital account liberalization as it undergoes the process of opening up and modernizing.

Against this backdrop, it is expected that the PRC is likely to follow its typically gradualist approach in reforming the domestic finance sector. For the time being Hong Kong, China is likely to enjoy its comparative advantages in brokering financial transactions. The PRC, in promoting onshore financial centers, can diversify its financial business within the country.

As noted earlier, Hong Kong, China has been designated as the premier offshore RMB market, but it has to compete and, more important, cooperate with other overseas international finance centers and onshore financial centers to promote international use of the RMB. With its first-mover advantages in offshore businesses and settlement facilities, Hong Kong, China is well positioned to meet the challenge of increased competition in the foreseeable future. But the question remains: What will Hong Kong, China's role become when the PRC has removed capital controls and instituted capital account convertibility?

Barring unexpected developments, Hong Kong, China, with its established financial market infrastructure, well-regarded legal system, and extensive international network, will retain its position as a renowned international finance center. The global offshore RMB market will be much larger than its existing size when the PRC has achieved capital account convertibility and has realized the potential of the RMB as a global currency that is commensurate with its economic and political strengths. When the pie grows bigger, Hong Kong, China will benefit, too. Looking into the future, Hong Kong, China is likely to enjoy a healthy volume of offshore RMB activity, although not necessarily the same large share it currently enjoys.

When one looks at the experiences of the offshore U.S. dollar markets, it is not unreasonable to anticipate that the growing global RMB activity will support multiple financial centers conducting offshore RMB businesses. Given the PRC's geographic diversity and economic size, it could support more than one domestically located offshore-onshore financial center.

Multiple offshore currency markets likely are not seen as inevitable competitors in the PRC. Rather, the PRC may be taking a holistic approach in establishing the offshore RMB market in Hong Kong, China and implementing the Qianhai and the Shanghai Free Trade Zone initiatives, whereby these three efforts are integral to its overall financial development strategy. Since 2011 the PRC has used Hong Kong, China's experiences to develop offshore RMB businesses in other financial centers overseas and to guide the two domestic initiatives. According to official documents, both domestic initiatives initially are to be confined to the designated geographic regions, but the successful financial reform practice that emerges will be transplanted to other parts of the country so as to broaden the financial account liberalization policy to the national level. In short, the PRC is following a two-pronged approach that involves both offshore and onshore markets to promote the international use of the RMB and to implement its financial development policy—an interpretation that is in line with the PRC's gradualist trial-and-error approach.

Offshore Markets as a Facilitator

What is the role of offshore markets in promoting the international use of the RMB? The answer depends on the factors that affect the international demand for the currency. The following subsections discuss the international demand from the perspectives of economic factors, possible lessons from history, and political considerations.

Canonical Economic Factors

A fair assessment of the role of offshore RMB markets has to consider possible factors that affect the global status of a currency. The most important factors considered in the literature are the following:

1. Size of the economy and the trade sector
2. Size and quality of the financial market
3. Capital account openness
4. Economic and political stability

These factors are largely affected by domestic economic policies and are not directly influenced by an offshore market policy. The PRC scores quite well on factors 1 and 4—the size of the economy and general stability—but not on capital account openness and financial markets. Capital account openness is a hotly debated issue. As noted earlier, complete capital account openness is not a necessary precondition for the international use of the RMB. The extant offshore and cross-border RMB activities are evidence that the PRC's policy of allowing foreign financial institutions to manage their RMB balances that are (directly or indirectly) held in the domestic banking system presents a form of convertibility that facilitates the international use of the RMB.

Still, a full-fledged global RMB requires the support of an open capital account. Despite the usual hyperbolic rhetoric on how far and how fast the PRC could liberalize its capital account and transform its finance sector, the PRC has to take the time to put in place the hardware and, more important, the software required to establish and maintain a robust finance sector and the related regulatory framework. Evidently the PRC is continuing with its financial development policy. Given the finance sector's close links with other segments of the economy, modernizing it requires accompanying policy changes in other sectors and even in politics. In view of the PRC's usual incremental reform style, there is good reason to expect that it will take government a long time to implement changes that lead to a deep and efficient finance sector. In this context, a fully internationalized RMB is a distant goal.

Subject to the level that is allowed by the PRC's policy, the ultimate overseas demand is determined by nonresidents' perception of the desirability of the RMB as a global currency. One could say that an offshore market policy can help a currency attain its level of acceptance overseas warranted by its economic fundamentals, but not more than that.

Lessons from the Eurodollar Market

Might the advances in the offshore RMB market induce changes to the domestic markets, including policies of capital controls, and thus force the progress of the

RMB internationalization process? Do U.S. responses to the evolution of the eurodollar market offer some insights?

As noted earlier, the U.S. dollar was a reserve currency when the eurodollar market emerged in London during the late 1950s. Reserve currency status is an important organic growth factor of the eurodollar market. Furthermore, the U.S. economic and military reach helps to further spread the use of the U.S. dollar around the world. The RMB, by contrast, is still in its early stage as a reserve currency and a global currency. The difference in the status of these two currencies makes it quite difficult to transfer lessons from the U.S. dollar experience to the RMB.

The scale of the eurodollar activity appears to have had a material impact on business conditions in the United States. In the early phase of the eurodollar market, the U.S. policy was to protect the onshore market from the offshore one. Commonly cited U.S. policy responses include the Interest Equalization Tax (1963), which narrowed the U.S. dollar funding costs of domestic and offshore bond issuers; the Voluntary Foreign Credit Restraint Program (1964), which limited the onshore banks' lending to nonresidents; and Regulation D (1969), which imposed marginal reserve requirements on U.S. bank borrowings from the offshore dollar market.[27]

The United States devised these policy measures to isolate and divert the adverse effects of the offshore U.S. capital. That is, at that time the United States imposed implicit and explicit restrictions on cross-border capital movement. Interestingly, it is now commonly perceived that these restrictions, by limiting the dollar flow, actually fostered the growth of the eurodollar market.

As these measures were being phased out in the late 1970s and the 1980s, the U.S. IBFs were introduced in 1981 to create a level playing field for onshore domestic financial institutions to compete directly with those offshore. Arguably, the motivation behind the IBFs was different from that behind the PRC's Qianhai initiative, which is dubbed a Chinese version of an offshore-offshore market. Specifically, the IBFs aimed at equalizing the competition between onshore and offshore banks, whereas the Qianhai initiative focuses on financial reforms.

These developments are quite different from those observed in the recently developed offshore RMB market and the PRC's policy initiatives on promoting the use of the RMB overseas. The RMB faces different domestic and overseas conditions than the U.S. dollar did then. The PRC is experimenting with financial (currency) internationalization, whereas the United States tried to rein in the offshore market influences on its domestic economy. Not only the difference in the global status of the two currencies but also the differences in the scope and scale of the offshore dollar and RMB markets explain dissimilar responses.

Over the last few years, the PRC has made some concerted effort to push the RMB onto the global stage, and to convince the rest of the world to adopt its cur-

---

27. The reserve requirement was increased from 10 to 20 percent in November 1970.

rency for international transactions, albeit in a controlled manner. Despite its rapid growth, the offshore RMB market is still quite small compared with the onshore market; this large size difference constrains the ability of the offshore market to affect the development of the onshore market. The limited feedback from the offshore market is ascribed to the PRC's tight grip on its own finance sector and the offshore market. There is no indication that the PRC will change its reform policies under the pressures of offshore RMB activities, including cross-border arbitrage.

Political Factors in the Expansion of the Offshore RMB Market

Notwithstanding official policies and good intentions, the economic quality of the currency itself is not the sole factor determining the acceptance of the RMB in the global market. The PRC not only must make some fundamental structural changes in its finance sector but also must convince other countries to conduct international trade and financial transactions in its currency. More than economic reasoning is needed to do this, as shown by Japan's attempt to internationalize its currency in the late twentieth century (Japanese Ministry of Finance 2003; Takagi 2011). Political considerations, especially in East Asia, play a non-negligible role in the adoption of an international currency. Overall, to facilitate the global use of the RMB, offshore markets have to overcome limits defined by economic and political factors.

The region is wary of any perceived hegemonic threats. In this context the PRC's communist political structure, military buildup, and recent territorial disputes with its neighboring countries could seriously impede the acceptance of the RMB abroad and be a drag on its efforts to internationalize the RMB. The PRC has often reaffirmed its commitment to peaceful development, the noninterference foreign policy, and the Five Principles of Peaceful Coexistence, but its neighbors may not find these reassurances completely convincing, especially in light of the PRC's expansion of its military capacity and its ongoing territorial disputes with Japan, the Philippines, and Viet Nam.[28] In this context the PRC will have to make some extra efforts to promote the acceptance of the RMB in Asia and in the global market.

Recently there have been some apparent international efforts to contain the PRC's influences. The Trans-Pacific Partnership is a treaty whose ostensible purpose is to enhance trade and investment activities between the United States and major trading countries on both sides of the Pacific Ocean. Yet the PRC is not part of the negotiations. It is hard to conceive that this is a coincidence. The PRC is the world's second-largest economy and the largest trading nation in the region.

28. The Five Principles of Peaceful Coexistence: mutual respect for sovereignty and territorial integrity, mutual nonaggression, noninterference in each other's internal affairs, equality and mutual benefit, and peaceful coexistence. They were the result of negotiations between the PRC and India and were formally included in the agreement forged between the two countries in 1956.

It is likely that one purpose of the TPP is to wall out the PRC and create a barrier to its commercial expansion and inhibit its influence in the Pacific Basin.[29]

Conclusions

The history of international finance affords many glimpses of the potential role of an offshore market. Active offshore markets such as the eurodollar markets are essential for a currency to realize its role in the international money system. It is hard to imagine that a currency could maintain its significant presence as a global currency without the backing of a fully functional offshore market network.

The launch of offshore RMB business in Hong Kong, China in 2004 was the beginning of a grand economic experiment. The PRC's approach to build the architecture to promote the international status of the RMB almost from scratch is quite deliberate and elaborate and differs markedly from the policies that were used in the past by various countries—in particular, the United States.[30]

The evolution of the offshore RMB market in Hong Kong, China illustrates both potentials and limitations of the policy-driven approach to promoting the extraterritorial use of the RMB. So far, the offshore market has advanced to the PRC's tune and experienced no major disruptions. Between 2010 and 2013, global RMB activity has increased quite noticeably: The RMB was the seventeenth most actively traded currency in the 2010 triennial central bank survey, but ranked ninth in the 2013 survey (Bank for International Settlements 2013). The expansion of both onshore and offshore RMB trading have contributed to the advance in the ranking.

Despite this strong momentum, the scale of RMB use in the global market is still minute compared with the size of the PRC economy and with the volume of U.S. dollar use. Global RMB trading accounted for 2.2 percent (out of a total of 200 percent) of the global trading volume, as compared to 87.0 percent for the U.S. dollar and 39.1 percent for the euro (Bank for International Settlements 2013). Furthermore, the international currency functionalities undertaken by the RMB are quite limited and the level of nonresident participation is relatively low (Chen and Cheung 2011).

As of summer 2014, anecdotal evidence substantiates the positive effect of the offshore market on the international use of the RMB, and the view that the road that the RMB takes to become a full-fledged global currency is likely to be a fairly long, if not a winding, one. One encouraging sign is that the PRC has been adjusting and reforming domestic policies and offshore strategies on promoting and enhancing overseas RMB markets and RMB businesses.

29. The website of the Trans-Pacific Partnership is www.ustr.gov/tpp.
30. Eichengreen and Flandreau (2012) pointed out the U.S. policy support that helps the U.S. dollar gain prominence in the global market. The official efforts to internationalize the Japanese yen in the 1990s are documented in Takagi (2011).

Offshore markets play a constructive role and offer scope for corporations and governments to work together to explore opportunities of using the currency in an efficient manner. With improved liquidity and enhanced investment opportunities, they offer opportunities to nonresidents to experience business dealings using the RMB and to the PRC authorities to assess the implications of intermediating international transactions without eradicating capital controls. Yet we must be realistic in our assessment of their potential influence. The PRC can be expected to maintain its usual gradualist approach to liberalizing its economy, including its finance sector; to retain its grip on critical policy matters; and to respond mainly to domestic rather than to foreign considerations.

I anticipate that the offshore RMB market will grow at a healthy pace in the foreseeable future, a pace that is directed and dictated by the PRC authorities. Emphasizing stability, the PRC will assume an active role in designing the offshore market development and be very sensitive to any adverse influences on its underdeveloped finance sector.

The offshore market policy is used to improve the RMB's overseas acceptance but is subordinate to the overall financial liberalization policy. It generates information to make changes but not to force domestic regulatory reform. That is, the role of offshore markets is complementary in the sense that it helps the RMB achieve its potential as a global currency, but offshore market conditions or requirements will not be allowed to force changes in domestic policies.

Alternatively, the observed developments could be interpreted through the lens of the "feel the rock, wade across the river" strategy, whereby general policies are designed, and the operational specifics are introduced and implemented in small incremental steps, taking market responses into consideration, to guard against large negative surprises. Indeed, the PRC has initiated changes to accommodate and complement developments in the market since the adoption of the open-door policy. The case of RMB offshore markets is no exception. Specific policies that do not threaten stability are introduced to promote the overall international use of the RMB in a gradual manner.

The experience of, say, the eurodollar market suggests that the offshore market could create pressure on domestic policy. Since the offshore RMB market is relatively small, it is unlikely to generate any noticeable pressure on the PRC's domestic market and, hence, its domestic policy. The PRC's capital control policy also helps to insulate its domestic sectors from the offshore market. Should the offshore RMB market become quite large relative to the onshore one and should the PRC's capital control policy become so lax that it allows offshore financial institutions to compete directly with and challenge onshore financial institutions, then the domestic policy will have to respond to these overseas developments. It is not unreasonable to assume that the PRC is aware of the potential shock and risk to its underdeveloped finance sector if overseas financial institutions are allowed to compete head-on with the domestic institutions. Given the usual emphasis on stability and political reality, it is unlikely that the PRC will allow the offshore market to exert any material pressure on domestic policy in the near future.

In sum, the PRC has made some good efforts in preparing for full convertibility and the internationalization of its currency. Although the PRC's accomplishment in the last few years is quite admirable, the RMB is still quite far from being a full-fledged international currency. To move forward, the PRC has to continue its financial market reform, liberalize the capital account, and enhance the efficiency and governance of the finance sector. The effort of promoting the international use of the RMB will be reinforced by engaging with the world in a responsive and responsible manner.

A well-designed network of offshore markets will advance the overseas acceptance and solidify the international status of the RMB. However, the ultimate acceptance of and demand for the RMB as a global currency will be determined by the underlying economic forces shaped by the PRC's economic fundamentals, and global political dynamics. Offshore RMB markets by themselves cannot raise the RMB's status beyond what is justified by its economic and political attributes.

References

Bank for International Settlements, Monetary and Economic Department. 2013. "Foreign Exchange Turnover in April 2013: Preliminary Global Results." Basel: Bank for International Settlements.

Bayoumi, Tamim, and Franziska Ohnsorge. 2013. "Do Inflows or Outflows Dominate? Global Implications of Capital Account Liberalization in China." IMF Working Paper WP/13/189. Washington: International Monetary Fund, August 28.

Chen, Hongyi, and Wensheng Peng. 2007. "The Potential of the Renminbi as an International Currency." *China Economic Issues* No. 7/07. Hong Kong, China: Hong Kong Monetary Authority.

Chen, Xiaoli, and Yin-Wong Cheung. 2011. "Renminbi Going Global." *China & World Economy* 19, no. 2: 1–18.

Cheung, Yin-Wong, and Risto Herrala. 2014. "China's Capital Controls—Through the Prism of Covered Interest Differentials." *Pacific Economic Review* 19, no. 1: 112–34.

Cheung, Yin-Wong, Guonan Ma, and Robert N. McCauley. 2011. "Renminbising China's Foreign Assets." *Pacific Economic Review* 16, no. 1: 1–17.

Cheung, Yin-Wong, and Hui Miao. 2013. "The Offshore RMB Market in Hong Kong and RMB Internationalization." In *Oxford Handbook of the Economics of the Pacific Rim*, edited by Inderjit Kaur and Nirvikar Singh, pp. 649–66. Oxford University Press.

Cheung, Yin-Wong, and Dagfinn Rime. 2014. "The Offshore Renminbi Exchange Rate: Microstructure and Links to the Onshore Market." *Journal of International Money and Finance* 24: 1150–75 (DOI: 10.1016/j.jimonfin.2014.05.012).

Dufey, Gunter, and Ian Giddy. 1994. *The International Money Market*. 2nd edition. Englewood Cliffs, N.J:. Prentice-Hall International.

Eichengreen, Barry. 2011. *Exorbitant Privilege: The Rise and Fall of the Dollar and the Future of the International Monetary System*. Oxford University Press.

———. 2013. "Renminbi Internationalization: Tempest in a Teapot?" *Asian Development Review* 30, no. 1: 148–64.

Eichengreen, Barry, and Marc Flandreau. 2012. "The Federal Reserve, the Bank of England, and the Rise of the Dollar as an International Currency, 1914–1939." *Open Economies Review* 23, no. 1: 57–87.

European Central Bank. 2013. *The International Role of the Euro*. Brussels: European Central Bank, July.

Franke, Günter. 1999. "The Bundesbank and the Markets." In *Fifty Years of the Deutsche Mark: Central Bank and the Currency in Germany since 1948*, edited by the Deutsche Bundesbank, pp. 219–67. Oxford University Press.

Goldberg, Linda S., and Cédric Tille. 2008. "Vehicle Currency Use in International Trade." *Journal of International Economics* 76, no. 2: 177–92.

He, Dong, and Robert N. McCauley. 2013. "Offshore Markets for the Domestic Currency: Monetary and Financial Stability Issues." In *The Evolving Role of China in the Global Economy*, edited by Yin-Wong Cheung and Jakob de Haan, pp. 301–37. MIT Press.

International Monetary Fund. 2000. "Offshore Financial Centers." IMF Background Paper. Washington: June 23 (www.imf.org/external/np/mae/oshore/2000/eng/back.htm#I).

———. 2010. "Reserve Accumulation and International Monetary Stability: Supplementary Information." Washington: International Monetary Fund, Strategy, Policy and Review Department (www.imf.org/external/np/pp/eng/2010/041310a.pdf).

Ishii, Shogo, Inci Ötker-Robe, and Li Cui. 2001. "Measures to Limit the Offshore Use of Currencies: Pros and Cons." IMF Working Paper WP/01/43. Washington: International Monetary Fund.

Krongkaew, Medhi. 1999. "Capital Flows and Economic Crisis in Thailand." *The Developing Economies* 37, no. 4: 395–416.

Ma, Guonan, and Robert N. McCauley. 2008. "The Efficacy of China's Capital Controls— Evidence from Price and Flow Data." *Pacific Economic Review* 13, no. 1: 104–23.

McCauley, Robert N. 2011. "Renminbi Internationalization and China's Financial Development Model." CGS-IIGG Working Paper. New York: Council of Foreign Relations.

Osugi, K. 1990. "Japan's Experience of Financial Deregulation since 1984 in an International Perspective." BIS Economic Papers No. 26. Basel: Bank for International Settlements.

Takagi, Shinji. 2011. "Internationalizing the Yen, 1984–2003: Unfinished Agenda or Mission Impossible?" In *Asia and China in the Global Economy*, edited by Yin-Wong Cheung and Guonan Ma, pp. 219–44. Singapore: World Scientific Publishing.

Yu, Yongding. 2012. "Revisiting the Internationalization of the Yuan." ADBI Working Paper No. 366. Tokyo: Asian Development Bank Institute.

Zoromé, Ahmed. 2007. "Concept of Offshore Financial Centers: In Search of an Operational Definition." IMF Working Paper WP/07/87. Washington: International Monetary Fund.

8

Regional Settlement Infrastructure and Currency Internationalization: The Case of Asia and the Renminbi

CHANGYONG RHEE AND LEA SUMULONG

Notwithstanding its success over the last decades, the international monetary system (IMS) has shown symptoms of fragility. Persistent and recurrent crises, global imbalances, volatility in exchange rates and capital flows, and the accumulation of large foreign exchange reserves are often cited as manifestations of such weaknesses. Indeed, the global financial crisis of 2008–09 revealed vulnerabilities in the IMS that led to the instability of world financial markets and the subsequent contraction of the world economy. Consequently, possible reforms to strengthen the IMS are being discussed more widely than previously, not only in academia but also in political circles.

One proposal is to build a global safety net, defined by the International Monetary Fund (IMF) as "a set of crisis prevention and resolution instruments, encompassing self-insurance (reserves); bilateral arrangements (e.g., swap lines between central banks during periods of stress); regional arrangements such as those in Asia, Europe, and Latin America; and multilateral arrangements with the IMF at their center" (International Monetary Fund 2011). This would certainly help, but it would not solve the problem. Despite significant efforts by the IMF, it is manifest that the available resources will not be sufficient to address another crisis of the same magnitude as the recent global financial crisis. The stigma attached to countries that seek help from the IMF also constrains the effectiveness of the IMF crisis-prevention toolkit because it is a disincentive for asking for help, so countries are

An earlier version of this paper was published as an ADB-CIGIHKIMR working paper.

likely to continue to self-insure against crises by accumulating foreign exchange reserves. This is not good for the global economy because it aggravates the problem of the global imbalance between the external positions of surplus and deficit countries.

Two other popular options that have emerged are the shift to a system based on special drawing rights (SDRs) and the move to a multiple-currency system. However, markets seem skeptical about the feasibility of these options. There are current political constraints in raising the allocation of SDRs, but even if allocations were allowed to increase, it would take some time before the SDR could be widely used in private markets. Also, under existing conditions, high transaction costs between non–U.S. dollar currencies are the prime reason for a triangular transaction of non–U.S. dollar currencies through the U.S. dollar. In light of the high transaction costs, it is hard to imagine that some other currency, including SDRs, could replace the role of the U.S. dollar as a global reserve currency in the near future.

An interim solution could be to establish regional settlement infrastructure for regional currencies, and could actually make a practical contribution to reform of the IMS. Using regional currencies to settle intraregional transactions does not mean that some Asian currencies will become international reserve currencies soon. Rather, the use of Asian currencies for regional trade and investment could be gradually promoted by providing proper infrastructure, even before they become reserve currencies with full convertibility.

The best example of such a regional solution is the renminbi (RMB) trade settlement scheme initiated by the People's Republic of China (PRC). The pilot scheme, launched in July 2009, allowed the settlement in RMB of trade transactions between five cities in the PRC and selected trade partners. It also permitted banks in PRC partner locations to provide RMB services, such as deposit taking, currency exchange, remittance, trade finance, and check issuance, to enterprises choosing to settle trade transactions in RMB. The scheme was promoted by the PRC monetary authorities in the expectation that it would benefit the PRC economy by reducing exchange rate risks, shrinking trade transaction costs, improving the funding efficiency of financial institutions, and diminishing the need to hold the U.S. dollar as a medium of exchange and store of value. The logic is that the increase in import settlement denominated in RMB, coupled with policies that encourage RMB recycling, will result in larger cross-border RMB flows and a larger stock of RMB held by nonresidents (Yu 2012b).

Indeed, the value of RMB trade settlement transactions has massively increased, from just CNY3.6 billion in the second half of 2009 to nearly CNY1.3 trillion in the first half of 2012 and over CNY2.0 trillion in the first half of 2013 (People's Bank of China 2011a, 2012b, 2013c). The volume of non-trade transactions has also risen tremendously. RMB deposits have swelled from CNY62.7 billion at end-2009 to CNY730.0 billion by end-September 2013 (Hong Kong Monetary

Authority 2013b). According to Bloomberg data, RMB-denominated bond issuance has grown from only CNY10 billion in 2007 to CNY281.9 billion in 2012. "Dim sum bond" issuance is projected to grow even bigger this year–the value of these bonds issued reached CNY305.4 billion in the first ten months of 2013.[1]

This rapid expansion demonstrates that the issue of the relatively larger costs of bilateral currency transactions compared with triangular transactions is a "chicken and egg" question: building infrastructure can make a difference. Transaction costs of using non–U.S. dollar currencies are high because adequate infrastructure has not been built, but these costs could be significantly reduced if proper infrastructure were set up. This experience also shows that full liberalization of the capital account or full deregulation of capital markets is not required to build necessary infrastructure. Expanding the local currency trade settlement scheme into a regional trade settlement system does not need to be led by the PRC alone. As a practical solution for IMS reform, Asian economies could introduce a bilateral or multilateral trade-related payment settlement scheme. This does not mean that all regional currencies will be internationalized or used for the settlement of trade transactions. As Deng Xiaoping famously said, "It doesn't matter whether a cat is black or white as long as it catches mice." Markets are likely to determine which currencies will be more widely used for trade settlements. But irrespective of the markets' choice, the emergence of regional currencies as trade settlement currencies will reduce Asia's dependence on the U.S. dollar and contribute to the diversification of international settlement currencies.

To expedite this process, building efficient payments and securities settlements is the key to success. Depositors' incentives to hold RMB deposits in Hong Kong, China would have been lower if they had not been able to find diverse opportunities to manage their RMB-denominated assets. The availability of other investment opportunities for RMB—such as bonds, and investment and asset management products—is an important aspect of the system that promoted the wider use of the RMB. This investment opportunity would have developed more slowly if a securities settlement system had not been in place. Thus, the expansion of the offshore RMB market is largely due to the efficient securities trading and settlement system in Hong Kong, China, where infrastructure for payment versus payment was available together with infrastructure for delivery versus payment for RMB securities.

In this chapter we propose the promotion of more bilateral trade settlement systems or a multilateral trade settlement system in Asia, together with a govern-

---

1. Needless to say, this unprecedented increase in trade settlement values and the expansion of the offshore capital market in Hong Kong, China is partly due to RMB exchange rate appreciation expectations (Li, Wu, and Pei 2012; Yu 2012a). But the persistent hike in RMB trade settlement transactions shows that this trend will continue despite the recent moderation in exchange rate appreciation expectations (He 2012).

ment securities settlement scheme. As most central banks are securities depositories of government bonds anyway, combining trade settlement with government securities settlement could have large synergistic effects without substantial extra costs. It would also help to promote the development of local currency bond markets in Asia, as envisioned by the Association of Southeast Asian Nations (ASEAN)+3 members' Asian Bond Markets Initiative (ABMI) after the Asian financial crisis in 1997.[2]

In the next section we look at the existing RMB trade settlement scheme involving the PRC; Hong Kong, China; and Macao, China, focusing on the system, progress, impacts on the offshore RMB market, and prospects. In the following section we present a proposal to expand the current bilateral systems to other economies and deepen the scheme by combining the trade settlement system with government bond settlement systems. Such a scheme would help solve the "third time zone problem" and develop financial markets in Asia (Asia is considered the "third time zone"—the United States and Europe being the first two time zones). The "third time zone" problem arises because real-time settlement of Asian bonds is not possible due to the time difference between the U.S. and European time zones, where securities settlement takes place, and Asian ones, where payment settlement takes place. Then we discuss the relationship of this proposal with other regional initiatives such as the ABMI, in particular the issues of building a Regional Settlement Intermediary (RSI) and strengthening the regional financial safety net.

The Renminbi Trade Settlement System

On July 6, 2009, the People's Bank of China (PBOC) marked a significant milestone in the development of offshore RMB business by launching a pilot scheme for the cross-border settlement in RMB of trade involving approved areas in the PRC and selected areas outside the PRC. Yu (2012b) succinctly summarized the main objectives of this new initiative: promoting RMB internationalization, reducing exchange rate risks, shrinking trade transaction costs, improving the funding efficiency of financial institutions, and diminishing the need to hold the U.S. dollar as a medium of exchange and store of value. Ma, Liu, and Miao (2012) identified other benefits from RMB internationalization, including raising seigniorage income, insulating the PRC from changes in U.S. macroeconomic policies, and enhancing the PRC's influence in reforming the international financial system. The pilot scheme initially allowed the settlement in RMB of trade

---

2. ASEAN Secretariat, "Chairman's Press Release on the Asian Bond Markets Initiative" (www.asean.org/communities/asean-economic-community/item/chairman-s-press-release-on-the-asian-bond-markets-initiative). ASEAN+3 comprises ten members of ASEAN—Brunei Darussalam, Cambodia, Indonesia, the Lao People's Democratic Republic, Malaysia, Myanmar, the Philippines, Singapore, Thailand, and Viet Nam—plus the PRC, Japan, and the Republic of Korea.

transactions between five cities in the PRC (Shanghai, Guangzhou, Shenzhen, Dongguan, and Zhuhai) and selected partners (Hong Kong, China; Macao, China; and ASEAN members).

To gain eligibility, enterprises in the PRC needed to secure endorsement from provincial authorities and approval from central authorities. Commercial banks in selected PRC partner locations were permitted to provide RMB-related services to enterprises choosing to settle trade in RMB. Specifically, commercial banks could engage in deposit taking, currency exchange, remittance, trade finance, and check issuance. These transactions are facilitated by the relevant clearing and settlement services. Participating banks outside the PRC can engage banks in the PRC as correspondent banks or the clearing bank, or both, for RMB business in Hong Kong, China and Macao, China to handle the associated settlement of RMB funds at the wholesale level. This implies that these banks can get RMB funding through the clearing bank, PRC correspondent banks, other participating banks outside the PRC, or RMB deposits (Hong Kong Monetary Authority 2009).

On June 22, 2010, the pilot scheme was expanded to cover eighteen provinces and cities plus Guangdong and Shanghai, and the trade partners were no longer limited to Hong Kong, China; Macao, China; and ASEAN members. The scheme was in effect extended to all trading partners of the selected twenty PRC provinces and cities. In addition, the scope of the settlement scheme was enlarged to include services and other current account transactions. A further expansion of the RMB trade settlement scheme was implemented in August 2011, making coverage nationwide. Eligibility to settle trade in RMB was also offered to all licensed importers and exporters in good standing in March 2012. This basically repealed the system of having to enlist as a mainland designated enterprise before getting access to the platform.

Moreover, the PRC authorities relaxed the country's capital restrictions. In October 2011, RMB-denominated foreign direct investment (FDI) had been allowed from Macao, China and Taipei,China to the PRC. In particular, enterprises in the two economies were permitted to use offshore RMB proceeds for onshore FDI subject to certain restrictions.[3] Qualified Foreign Institutional Investors (QFIIs), using offshore RMB, were likewise allowed to invest in PRC stock markets as of December 2011. Although equity inflows were initially capped at CNY20 billion, this was raised to CNY70 billion in April 2012 (de Silva and

---

3. RMB FDI applications valued at a minimum of CNY300 million must be approved by the Ministry of Commerce. Placement of cross-border RMB direct investment in securities, derivatives, and entrusted loans within the PRC is still not permitted. However, legitimately acquired offshore RMB funds can be utilized to assign or transfer stocks of PRC-listed companies subject to approval by the Ministry of Commerce. Moreover, if inward RMB funds are intended to finance mergers and acquisitions or related purposes, an application for a special RMB mergers and acquisitions account will have to be submitted. Any FDI funds received by the foreign invested enterprise's onshore entity thereafter will also be subject to the Ministry of Commerce approval and registration guidelines (Ministry of Commerce 2011; HSBC 2011).

Tan 2012). To provide a support mechanism to the buildup of RMB capital overseas, the PRC government has likewise aggressively negotiated swap agreements with a number of central banks. As of October 2013, active RMB swap lines with twenty-one partners totaled about CNY2.5 trillion (US$410 billion).

The introduction of the RMB trade settlement pilot scheme and its subsequent expansion has led to the establishment of an offshore RMB market in Hong Kong, China and to a lesser extent in Macao, China. Although the original intent of the pilot scheme was to promote trade settlement, the legal, regulatory, and financial infrastructure in Hong Kong, China also significantly encouraged non-trade-related financial transactions.

The growing international acceptance of the RMB, coupled with recent liberalization measures, has inspired other financial centers such as London, Singapore, and Taipei,China to develop offshore RMB capabilities as well. Paris has also expressed its desire to catch up with the other financial centers. In addition, a number of central banks have showed interest in including RMB in the composition of their foreign reserves.[4]

The Trade Settlement Framework

An overview of the RMB trade settlement scheme platform in Hong Kong, China is provided in figure 8-1. Initially the system required participating enterprises to be accredited by the PBOC and the Hong Kong Monetary Authority (HKMA) in their respective jurisdictions.[5] But the scope of the framework now includes all trading firms that import to and export from the PRC, regardless of the location. Once an RMB-based transaction between onshore and offshore parties has been agreed, there are two possible alternatives for making cross-border payments.

Take the case of an offshore importer. One way to move funds is by coursing the payment through an authorized participating overseas bank that will then have to transmit it to the designated offshore clearing bank. If the cash transaction poses no concerns regarding PBOC and HKMA regulations, the offshore clearing bank will have to channel the funds to the onshore settlement bank before it reaches the onshore exporter's RMB account. The other way is to have a domestic commercial bank function as an agent of the overseas participating bank by virtue of a binding agreement. In this case, the domestic commercial bank will have to open an onshore interbank RMB fund-transfer account for the overseas participating bank. The domestic agent bank will also be the one to settle the cross-border transaction and will have to report transaction details to the local PBOC office.

Notably, overseas participating banks, onshore settlement banks, and domestic agent banks have to be approved by HKMA (offshore) and PBOC (onshore)

---

4. Banco Bilbao Vizcaya Argentaria, "RMB Internationalization Gains Momentum from Liberalization Steps," November 19, 2013 (www.slideshare.net/BBVAResearch/131119-china-watchrmb internationalizationentcm348411506).

5. The Monetary Authority of Macao, in the case of Macao, China.

Figure 8-1. *The PRC–Hong Kong, China Renminbi Settlement Scheme*

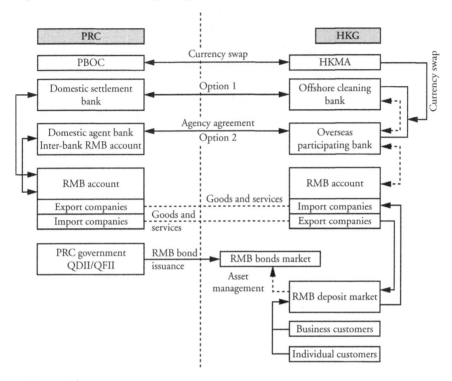

Source: Authors.
HKG = Hong Kong, China; HKMA = Hong Kong Monetary Authority; PBOC = People's Bank of
China; PRC = People's Republic of China; QDII = qualified domestic institutional investors; QFII = qual-
ified foreign institutional investors.

to gain eligibility in mediating RMB cross-border trade settlements. Offshore
banks are given the option either to participate directly in the platform or to
conduct business indirectly via their subsidiaries in Hong Kong, China. Moreover, the scheme allows any bank outside the PRC to take part in the system (in
other words, participation is not confined to banks based in Hong Kong,
China). As of March 2013, a total of 208 banks were participating in the scheme
in Hong Kong, China alone, forming a network that covers over thirty countries and six continents. HKMA also estimates that these participating banks
handle over 1,500 RMB correspondent accounts (Hong Kong Monetary
Authority 2013a).

RMB trade settlement in Macao, China practically follows the same model,
with the Monetary Authority of Macao as the supervising institution. The Bank
of China (Hong Kong, China) Limited (BOCHK) and the Bank of China Macao
Branch were designated as the offshore clearing banks in Hong Kong, China and

Macao, China, respectively.[6] Essentially, the two aforementioned Bank of China affiliates were authorized to convert foreign currencies into RMB and to utilize credit lines with the interbank foreign exchange and interbank borrowing market in the PRC in accordance with the parameters set by the PBOC (People's Bank of China 2009). In addition to the onshore credit sources of the clearing bank, the swap line between the PRC and Hong Kong, China (which currently amounts to CNY400 billion), also stands ready to lend offshore RMB liquidity support.

One noteworthy change arising from the inception of the RMB trade settlement scheme infrastructure is that offshore parties that agree to settle trade transactions with PRC firms in RMB now have the facility to convert RMB to other major currencies with relative ease if the need arises. That significantly contributed to the increase in the demand for RMB deposits in Hong Kong, China and consequently in the rise of non-trade-related financial transactions such as RMB-denominated bond issuance and asset management. This trend is helped by the efficient payment and securities settlement systems in Hong Kong, China, including its multicurrency Real Time Gross Settlement (RTGS) system (something that Macao, China still does not have).[7] Thus, the aversion to conducting trade business in RMB, which had previously been strongly reinforced by difficulties related to convertibility, has been reversed in recent years. Increases in RMB trade transactions resulting from the pilot scheme have led to a tremendous growth in offshore RMB deposits, which in turn fed the development of the offshore RMB bond and asset management market.

The Ensuing Results of the Renminbi Trade Settlement Scheme

From an initial 365 mainland designated enterprises approved to take part in the pilot RMB trade settlement scheme during its inception in 2009, the number had soared to over 67,000 by the end of 2011 (AHK Greater China 2011). Since March 2012, however, registration as a mainland designated enterprise had no longer been necessary. Monthly cross-border RMB trade settlements (RTS) rose from an average of CNY42.2 billion in 2010 to CNY244.8 billion in 2012, while the RTS share of total PRC trade with the world nearly quintupled from 2.5 percent to 12.0 percent. During the first nine months of 2013, the RTS value further increased to an average of CNY351.1 billion, raising the RTS share of total PRC trade to 16.6 percent (table 8-1).

In terms of the PRC's trade with Hong Kong, China, RTS facilitated by the BOCHK accounted for just 22.2 percent in 2010. Since 2011, however, the share has exceeded 100 percent, implying that some of the PRC's trade with other economies has also been settled in RMB that were cleared through Hong Kong,

---

6. The Clearing Agreement between the PBOC and the Bank of China affiliates in relation to RMB business was signed in July 2009.

7. Macao, China launched its RTGS for the Macao pataca and U.S. dollar in March 2013, but authorities are also looking to extend the facility to the PRC RMB (Society for Worldwide Interbank Financial Telecommunication 2013c).

Table 8-1. *Cross-Border Renminbi Trade Settlement (RTS)*[a]

Period	Total RTS, CNY Bn	HKG RTS, CNY Bn	MAC RTS, CNY Bn	Total RTS, Mo. Ave, CNY Bn	HKG RTS, Mo. Ave, CNY Bn	MAC RTS, Mo. Ave, CNY Bn
Jul–Dec 2009	3.6			0.6		
Jan–Dec 2010	506.3	342.1	6.0	42.2	28.5	0.5
Jan–Dec 2011	2,080.8	1,914.5	62.8	173.4	159.5	5.2
Jan–Dec 2012	2,938.2	2,632.5	97.2	244.8	219.4	8.1
Jan–Sep 2013	3,160.0	2,616.6	108.9	351.1	290.7	12.1

Period	HKG RTS, percentage of total RTS	MAC RTS, percentage of total RTS	Residual RTS, percentage of total RTS	Total RTS, percentage of PRC total trade	HKG RTS, percentage of PRC trade with HKG	MAC RTS, percentage of PRC trade with MAC
Jul–Dec 2009				0.04		
Jan–Dec 2010	67.6	1.2	31.2	2.5	22.2	39.3
Jan–Dec 2011	92.0	3.0	5.0	8.8	104.5	386.8
Jan–Dec 2012	89.6	3.3	7.1	12.0	122.1	516.1
Jan–Sep 2013	82.8	3.4	13.8	16.6	156.2	741.4

Sources: CEIC, PBOC, HKMA, Monetary Authority of Macao, and authors' calculations.

a. RTS covers goods and services trade, whereas total trade refers to merchandise trade only. For consistency, all trade data were sourced from the PRC statistics.

Ave = average; Bn = billion; CNY = yuan; HKG = Hong Kong, China; MAC = Macao, China; Mo. = monthly; PRC = People's Republic of China; RMB = renminbi.

China. Indeed, the Philippines; the Gulf Cooperation Countries; Singapore; Taipei,China; the Republic of Korea; France; the United Kingdom; Thailand; Italy; and the Russian Federation have recently seen a strong uptake in the use of RMB for trade payments. Of the 160 countries that settled payments with the PRC and Hong Kong, China in April 2013, 47 had used RMB as the settlement currency for at least 10 percent of their total payments (see Society for Worldwide Interbank Financial Telecommunication 2013b).

Activity in Hong Kong, China currently dwarfs the turnover in Macao, China. Based on data for the first nine months of 2013, RTS in Macao, China is just about 4.2 percent of the business in Hong Kong, China. One obvious reason is that when the pilot platform was launched, Hong Kong, China already had a substantially deeper financial market, a more sophisticated infrastructure, and a much broader international linkage. But looking at the growth of the RTS and the ratio of RTS to bilateral trade, Macao, China undoubtedly shows a promising potential. Between 2010 and 2012, RTS in Macao, China rose more than sixteen-fold and is likely to register a growth rate of about 50 percent in 2013. RTS from January to September 2013 stood at CNY108.9 billion, 60 percent higher than the CNY68.0 billion recorded in the first nine months of 2012. The RTS ratio to bilateral trade of Macao, China and the PRC had likewise ballooned to over 700 percent by the end of September 2013 from less than 40 percent in 2010, also suggesting clearing through Macao, China of PRC's trade with other partners.

Initially, trade settlements had been largely import-oriented (that is, RMB flows were biased in favor of settling PRC imports as opposed to invoicing PRC exports). The receipt-to-payment ratio by the end of 2010 was 1:5.5 (People's Bank of China 2012a). But the ratio seems to be headed gradually toward a more balanced RMB flow. In 2011, the ratio improved to 1:1.7, and as of the end of 2012 it stood at 1:1.2 (People's Bank of China 2013a).

This trend is inevitably related to market expectations of RMB appreciation and arbitrage opportunities between the onshore RMB (CNY) and offshore RMB (CNH) markets. Zhang and Xu (2011) show that the RMB receipt-to-payment ratio is highly correlated with the CNH–CNY spread. But despite the recent narrowing of the CNH–CNY spread, the growth in RTS has remained robust. RTS in 2012 still grew year-on-year by 41.2 percent (and by 54.4 percent in the first nine months of 2013), albeit substantially slower than the 311 percent year-on-year expansion registered in 2011. Certainly, the absence of a reversal in the RTS growth path and receipt-to-payment ratio in light of the generally weaker RMB appreciation expectations and the tapering cross-RMB market arbitrage opportunities indicates that growing RMB utilization is not only due to currency speculations.[8]

---

8. He (2012) concludes that as the PRC's economic power continues to grow, non-PRC residents will have an incentive to increase their exposure to RMB assets and liabilities. Such an incentive is likely to remain strong and not easily reversed by the cyclicality of RMB exchange rate expectations.

One immediate result of the expansion of RMB-based cross-border trade settlement is the swelling of RMB deposits in Hong Kong, China and Macao, China. As traders are secure in their ability to convert their RMB deposits into reserve currencies, whenever they want to or need to, they have an incentive to increase their holdings of offshore RMB deposits. This expedites the growth of RMB-denominated financial products, which in turn increases RMB-denominated lending and borrowing to offshore investors who have no trade linkages with PRC corporations.

From about CNY62.7 billion at end-2009, the total RMB deposit value in Hong Kong, China had ballooned to CNY603.0 billion at end-2012, and further to CNY730.0 billion by end-September 2013 (figure 8-2). Overseas banks' RMB correspondent accounts increased more than five times over 12 months—from 187 in 2010 to 968 the following year before breaching the 1,500 mark in March 2013. RMB amounts due to and from overseas banks (banks based outside the PRC and Hong Kong, China) rose considerably, from CNY30.5 billion at the start of 2011 to CNY216 billion two years later (Chan 2013). And the number of institutions authorized to conduct RMB business (deposit taking, remittances, and cross-border trade settlement) in Hong Kong, China had risen from 49 at the end of July 2009 (Sekine 2011), right after the RMB trade settlement scheme was put in place, to 187 at the end of 2011 (KPMG 2012) to 208 at the end of the first quarter of 2013 (Hong Kong Monetary Authority 2013a).

Similarly, in Macao, China, RMB deposits increased by a factor of over 700 in less than nine years—from CNY82 million at the end of 2004, they swelled to almost CNY62.3 billion nine months into 2013. Accordingly, the RMB deposit share of total deposits in Macao, China has risen dramatically, from 0.06 percent in 2004 to 12.3 percent, based on the most recent data. A majority of the twenty-nine banks in Macao, China have signed clearing agreements with the clearing bank for relevant RMB businesses.

The rapid expansion of RMB trade settlement and the accompanying measures that recalibrated other capital flow policy regulations, such as the circulars relaxing FDI and equity investment regulations, have bolstered the growth of the RMB bond market in Hong Kong, China (also known as the dim sum bond market).[9] From only CNY10 billion in 2007—the year when the first dim sum bond was issued—RMB-denominated bond issuance in Hong Kong, China increased

9. Ministry of Commerce (2011), which became effective on October 12, 2011; People's Bank of China (2011b), which became effective on October 13, 2011. The Renminbi Qualified Foreign Institutional Investor scheme is governed by the Pilot Scheme for Domestic Securities Investment. Previously, a foreign company could only participate in the PRC's securities market via the qualified foreign institutional investor program whereby the company can convert foreign currency to RMB to take part in the trading. The (People's Republic of) China Securities Regulatory Commission has to approve the application while the State Administration of Foreign Exchange determines the allocation of quotas.

Figure 8-2. *Outstanding Renminbi Deposits in Hong Kong, China and Macao, China*

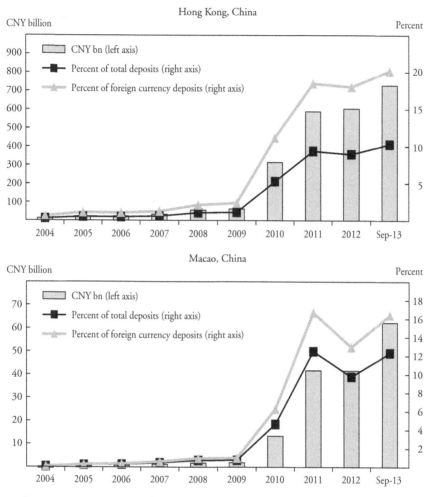

Sources: CEIC; Hong Kong Monetary Authority; Monetary Authority of Macao.
CNY = yuan.

significantly, to CNY189.5 billion in 2011 and CNY281.9 billion in 2012 (figure 8-3).[10] In the first ten months of 2013, bond issuance swelled to CNY305.4 billion. The number of bond issuances has likewise climbed steeply,

10. Initially, bond issuers were limited to sovereign entities and PRC banks, but they now include multinational corporations such as Caterpillar, McDonald's, Tesco, Unilever, and Volkswagen and multilateral organizations such as the Asian Development Bank, the World Bank, and the International Finance Corporation.

Figure 8-3. *Renminbi Bond Issuance in Hong Kong, China*

Number of dim sum bond issuers and issuances

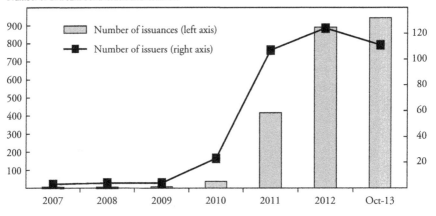

Dim sum bond issuance by country of issuer, CNY billion

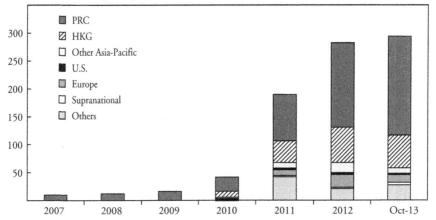

Source: Authors' calculations, based on Bloomberg data.
CNY = yuan; HKG = Hong Kong, China; PRC = People's Republic of China; U.S. = United States.

from just 5 in 2007 to 417 in 2011 and to 891 as of end-2012,[11] whereas the number of bond issuers increased from just 3 in 2007 to 107 by the end of 2011, and 124 in 2012. From January to October 2013, 943 bonds were issued by 111 issuers.

The RMB capital market in Hong Kong, China also saw sizable corrections in key indexes as a result of the gradual opening of the PRC's capital account. For

11. In May 2012, the National Development and Reform Committee decided to allow nonfinancial corporations on the mainland to issue RMB bonds in Hong Kong, China (ANZ Research 2012).

instance, sovereign yield spreads (CNY–CNH) narrowed from a range of 1.9 to 3.8 percentage points in June 2011 to less than half a percentage point in October 2012 (on average) before settling around 1.0 percentage point beginning in June 2013.[12] Deposit rate spreads (CNY–CNH) swung from a positive margin of 2.0 to 3.0 percentage points in June 2011 to below zero in June 2013, but turned positive again (at around 1.0 percentage point) at the end of August 2013. Similarly, the Hang Seng China AH Premium Index,[13] which had been trading at a premium of over 100 percent, favoring stock prices of PRC companies' A-shares at one point in 2008, declined considerably from mid-2010 (that is, the prices of H-shares caught up with the prices of A-shares and even exceeded the latter on some trading days).[14] With the increase in offshore liquidity, RMB clearing transactions also surged, from CNY39.3 billion in 2009 to CNY43.2 trillion in 2012, while the cumulative value as of September 2013 was already about CNY57.6 trillion, indicating favorable conditions for RMB businesses offshore.

In Macao, China, the resulting business synergies are not as pronounced as in Hong Kong, China, despite the phenomenal growth in RTS and RMB deposits. Nevertheless, local authorities are looking to up the ante in the years ahead by repackaging their RMB hub as the gateway for Portuguese-speaking trading partners of the PRC. The target markets include Angola, Brazil, Cape Verde, Timor-Leste, Guinea-Bissau, Mozambique, Portugal, and São Tomé and Príncipe (Teng 2013). The chairman of the Monetary Authority of Macao has noted the increasing economic ties between the PRC and the Lusophone (Portuguese-speaking) countries over the years. IMF Direction of Trade Statistics indicate that bilateral trade growth between the two blocs averaged 39.4 percent annually from 2000 to 2012 (International Monetary Fund 2014).

Recent developments suggest that the interest in RMB business is gaining headway outside the two pioneer offshore RMB locations. In the first half of 2013, Taipei, China and Singapore were permitted to operate their own RMB hubs after successfully negotiating clearing agreements with the PRC. The local branch of the Bank of China and the Industrial and Commercial Bank of China (ICBC) were designated as clearing banks in Taipei,China and Singapore, respectively (People's Bank of China 2013b). This decision makes business sense since these

---

12. This refers to the differential of yuan government Bloomberg Fair Value curve and offshore yuan (People's Republic of) China Government Bond curve (per Bloomberg's definition).

13. Some companies trade in the stock markets in both Shanghai and Hong Kong, China. A-shares refer to the stock price of the company in Shanghai, whereas H-shares refer to the stock price of the same company in Hong Kong, China. The Hang Seng China AH Premium Index ("HSAHP") measures the absolute price premium (or discount) of A-shares over H-shares for the largest and most liquid PRC companies with both A-share and H-share listings (Hang Seng Indexes, http://www.hsi.com.hk/HSI-Net/HSI-Net).

14. The index spiked briefly starting end-September 2011, when there were speculations about Asia's ability to absorb external weakness, but the differential in the stock prices quickly declined over the next two to three weeks.

two economies occupied the second and third spots in the list of the biggest RMB remitters to the PRC and Hong Kong, China as of April 2013 (Society for Worldwide Interbank Financial Telecommunication 2013a).

Taipei,China's participation in the PRC's efforts to promote the RMB overseas can be traced back to the signing of the Cross-Straits Banking Supervision Memorandum of Understanding in November 2009 (Subacchi and Huang 2013). Notably, as of 2013, the PRC accounts for close to a quarter of Taipei,China's total trade, making it the economy's biggest trading partner. Taipei,China does not appear to be interested in challenging Hong Kong, China's primordial role in the region in terms of RMB business, but it has aspirations of making it big as an intermediary (Subacchi and Huang 2013).

Within around four months of the RMB platform being formalized in Taipei, China, RTS had risen to CNY240 billion, as reported by the Bank of China.[15] RMB clearing in Taipei,China had been participated in by sixty-four agent banks, which had processed 36,000 RMB settlement and clearing transactions as of July 5, 2013. Moreover, members of the local financial circles saw the commencement of Taipei,China's version of dim sum bonds. The first RMB bonds in Taipei, China—locally known as the "bao dao," or "Formosa," bonds—were issued by Chinatrust Financial Holding on February 25, 2013. The notes had a three-year tenor worth CNY1 billion at a yield of 2.9 percent. Deutsche Bank became the first foreign institution to tap Taipei,China's RMB bond market after completing a CNY1.1 billion debt sale on June 5, 2013. The fund-raising comprised CNY1 billion three-year bonds at 2.45 percent and CNY100 million five-year non-call one bonds at 2.65 percent. After a series of successful tenders (five in all, totaling CNY3.9 billion as of June 2013), some of China's well-known finance brands (China Development Bank, ICBC, Barclays, HSBC, and Standard Chartered) were seen to be following suit (Wong 2013).[16] Outstanding RMB deposits in Taipei,China stood at CNY98.7 billion at end-September 2013, from practically nil when local banks started accepting RMB deposits seven months earlier.[17]

Singapore aims to corner the growing PRC transaction volume of Southeast Asian countries, which to a certain extent would put it toe-to-toe with Hong Kong, China. The market did not disappoint when Singapore opened its bid to challenge Hong Kong, China's dominance in facilitating RMB dealings. Two business days after the release of the circular regarding the conduct of RMB business in Singapore, HSBC and Standard Chartered issued the first "Lion City" RMB

15. Bank of China, May 7, 2013 (www.boc.cn/en/bocinfo/bi1/201307/t20130707_ 23490 61.html).

16. Based on data from Bloomberg.

17. Based on a media release of the Bank of China (2013), sixty-four banks are currently taking part in RMB intermediation in Taipei,China. This indicates that nine in every ten banks in Taipei, China offer RMB facilities. According to the statistics posted on the Web site of the central bank of Taipei,China, there are a total of sixty-nine banking institutions in Taipei,China, of which forty-one are domestic and twenty-eight are foreign bank affiliates based in Taipei,China.

bonds totaling CNY1.5 billion. Standard Chartered rolled out a three-year CNY1 billion bond at 2.62 percent, which was oversubscribed by a factor of 3. HSBC, on the other hand, floated CNY500 million worth of debt papers yielding 2.25 percent. RMB deposits in Singapore have built up to over CNY60 billion a month after the RMB platform began to function—about the same RTS value recorded by ICBC during the period.[18]

In Europe, the City of London, with the support of some of the biggest banks in the world (collectively called the City of London Initiative), has also been campaigning quite strongly to have its own clearing bank and to effectively become the RMB corridor of the continent.[19] According to the SWIFT RMB tracker (Society for Worldwide Interbank Financial Telecommunication 2013a), the United Kingdom (UK) is the largest RMB remitter to the PRC and Hong Kong, China. Thus, it makes sense for the City to lobby for its own platform. With the PRC trying to ramp up its business interests outside Asia, the wide-ranging London financial sector stands to capitalize on the massive potential of RMB-based international flows.[20] In October 2013, the UK and the PRC reached an agreement granting London-based institutional investors a CNY80 billion quota to invest in PRC domestic securities through the Renminbi Qualified Foreign Institutional Investor scheme. The following month London also played host to the first RMB bond issuance of a PRC institution outside of PRC juridical territory when the ICBC successfully negotiated CNY2 billion worth of debt notes with investors based in the English capital, cementing London's stature as Europe's leading RMB hub.[21]

Indeed, with the establishment of RTS and the implementation of the associated deregulation measures, offshore liquidity circulation and competition have improved, the gaps between the fundamental onshore market indexes and their offshore counterparts have narrowed, and offshore RMB-related business has flourished.[22]

18. As of 2014 some fifty banks participate in the RMB business in Singapore, according to information provided by the Monetary Authority of Singapore (MAS) to the authors. This number represents roughly a quarter of the total number of banking institutions in the country, but it is only reasonable to expect that involvement of banks in the new market will broaden in the coming years as RMB liquidity increases. There are generally no restrictions on banks conducting RMB business and any bank may opt to conduct RMB business as long it complies with existing regulations (Monetary Authority of Singapore 2013).

19. The list of banks includes Bank of China, Barclays, China Construction Bank, Citi, Deutsche Bank, HSBC, ICBC, JP Morgan, Royal Bank of Scotland, and Standard Chartered.

20. In addition to London, Frankfurt and Sydney are also reportedly crafting strong cases to become RMB hubs.

21. The first RMB bond issuance in London was done by HSBC Holdings in April 2012. The bond offer raked in CNY2 billion. This was followed by a bond tender by the Australia and New Zealand Banking Group Limited amounting to CNY1 billion in August 2012 (see City of London 2012).

22. Eichengreen (2012) argues that the PRC's plan for the RMB to rival the U.S. dollar depends on how PRC officials deal with the following challenges in the long run: (1) building more liquid financial markets; (2) opening the capital account; (3) handling the growth slowdown; and (4) making credible commitments to develop deep and liquid financial markets.

Lessons Learned

The pilot RMB trade settlement scheme provides a few lessons for Asia concerning its role in reforming the IMS.

First, it shows that building the necessary monetary and financial infrastructure can make a difference. Lack of infrastructure and high transaction costs between non–U.S. dollar currencies are the prime reasons for the triangular transaction of non–U.S. dollar currencies through the U.S. dollar and the skepticism that no currency can replace the role of the U.S. dollar as a global reserve currency in the near future. But the RMB trade settlement scheme shows that this can be a "chicken and egg" question. It is a good example of how proper infrastructure can facilitate trade transactions and generate new demand. This experience implies that, rather than focusing on what the new global reserve currency should be, building the necessary monetary and financial infrastructure and letting markets determine the winner may be an appropriate approach in reforming the IMS. It is true that markets, not governments, determine settlement currencies, but policy also plays a role. Asia's development experience in particular demonstrates that governments can build infrastructure to affect markets' choice. Asia has not yet invested in cross-border financial infrastructure and if Asia continues to avoid doing so, high transaction costs and risks will remain the order of the day.

Second, another important implication from this experience is that full liberalization of the capital account or full deregulation of capital markets is not required for a currency to be internationalized. Full convertibility may be necessary to be a reserve currency, but establishing regional settlement currencies may not require full liberalization. The cases of the Japanese yen and the former German mark demonstrate that a currency can be used for settlement and reserve holdings while remaining subject to certain capital controls. Similarly, the RMB trade settlement scheme is a highly restrictive and controlled system, but it can still contribute to reducing U.S. dollar dependence and to diversification of international settlement currencies in the medium term. The fear of risks involved in capital market liberalization and deregulation cannot be an argument against the internationalization of local currencies. One can argue that the RMB trade settlement scheme can cause more speculation and volatility as it contributes to increased offshore activities (Yu 2012b; Mallaby and Wethington 2011). However, this view is somewhat exaggerated. Even without the RMB trade settlement scheme, the non-deliverable forward (NDF) market can flourish and affect domestic monetary policy management and volatility in a similar way to the RMB trade settlement scheme. The recent experience of the Republic of Korea's own NDF market is a case in point. Other examples include the Australian dollar and the Mexican peso, where offshore capital market developments preceded local markets. It is true that the RMB trade settlement scheme can increase offshore deposits and thus offshore RMB borrowings, which can be used for leveraged speculative attacks. However, the beauty of the current system is that the PRC government is liable only up to some multiple value of settlement of trade-related payments, limiting the possibility of speculative attacks. On the other hand, it spurs the development of selected capital market instruments in offshore markets. Compared with its long-term benefits, such as local currency–denominated offshore capital market development and a gradual learning experience for managing capital market opening, the cost does not seem large. This is even more accurate if we consider that the NDF market for the RMB would have developed much faster anyway.

Third, to be effective, payments and securities settlement systems should go hand in hand. People would not own RMB deposits if the opportunities for managing their assets were limited. In other words, the availability of other investment opportunities for RMB, such as RMB bonds and RMB investment and asset management products, is an important aspect of the system that has promoted the wider use of the RMB. This investment opportunity would not have arisen if a securities settlement system had not been in place. The early success of the RMB trade settlement system is partly due to the efficient securities trading and settlement system in Hong Kong, China, where infrastructure for payment versus payment is available together with infrastructure for delivery versus payment for RMB securities. A joint payments settlement and securities settlement infrastructure can also address the cross-border securities settlement risks, the so-called third time zone problem, as will be discussed in the next section.

Expanding and Deepening the Regional Currency Settlement System

Considering the initial success of the RMB trade settlement system, one can think of two options for further promotion of RMB internationalization. One is to expedite capital market liberalization and allow more repatriation of the RMB in overseas markets to the PRC (Ma, Liu, and Miao 2012). An alternative approach would be further expansion of the trade settlement scheme to neighboring economies. Unlike what occurred during the first phase of yen internationalization,[23] both options are consistent with the apparent policy willingness of the PRC authorities to push the RMB up the reserve currency ladder in the long run.[24]

---

23. The process of the internationalization of the yen can be divided into two phases. The first phase was from the 1970s to the mid-1980s, when the international use of the yen was a popular market strategy but not a popular government policy. The second phase started sometime in the mid-1990s, when the government's perception about the supposed international status of the yen changed but the market was no longer as willing as it had been to accommodate the yen as a portfolio currency in the face of less rosy prospects for the Japanese economy (Frankel 2011; Maziad and Kang 2012).

24. Mallaby and Wethington (2011) discuss the political economy behind the unorthodox sequencing of RMB internationalization.

With the volume of offshore RMB deposits increasing, there has been and will be more outside pressure on the PRC to allow the deregulation of capital markets through the repatriation of RMB offshore to the PRC. Allowing more repatriation and capital market liberalization will definitely accelerate the internationalization of the RMB and is inevitable in the long run. But deregulation will complicate exchange rate and monetary policy management and will also pose risks of capital volatility in the short run. Even though more deregulation is called for, the PRC government needs to carefully distinguish between the policy objective of ensuring an orderly capital market deregulation and the objective of developing offshore capital markets and promoting RMB internationalization. It may need to consider first expanding the current trade settlement scheme to other regional economies such as Japan, ASEAN, and the Republic of Korea. This way the PRC can continue with its RMB internationalization plan while gradually deregulating and deepening RMB-denominated financial markets.

Expansion of the Bilateral Trade Settlement System

Expanding the local currency trade settlement scheme into a regional trade settlement system does not need to be led by the PRC alone. As a practical solution for IMS reform, Asian economies could introduce a bilateral or multilateral trade-related payment settlement scheme such as that between the PRC and the current offshore hubs. Extending the trade settlement scheme to regional economies does not imply that all regional currencies will be internationalized or used for settlement of trade transactions. Markets will determine which currencies will be more widely used for trade settlements, and the RMB will most likely dominate. But irrespective of which currency will be used more often or chosen by the market, the emergence of regional currencies as trade settlement currencies will reduce developing Asia's dependence on the U.S. dollar and contribute to the diversification of international settlement currencies. Indeed, these agreements do not even have to be limited to Asian economies. Trade among emerging economies is on the rise, and local currency trade settlements could facilitate the integration of interregional emerging markets more broadly.

Intraregional trade has grown tremendously since 1990. In that year, annual trade within developing Asia was only $284 billion. By 2012, intra-Asian trade had risen to $4,371 billion (equivalent to an average annual growth rate of 12.4 percent). Considering the rising middle-income class in Asia and the protracted slowdown in advanced economies, Asian traders are likely to look more to their neighbors as alternative destinations of the goods they produce. Asian economies' vulnerabilities will increase if regional traders continue to use the U.S. dollar to settle transactions.

As noted earlier, RMB cross-border trade settlement in Hong Kong, China and Macao, China has already exceeded 100 percent of their bilateral trade with the PRC. If we assume that all intraregional trade within developing Asia is settled in local currencies, the use of the U.S. dollar for trade transactions could potentially be reduced by over $4 trillion per year.

Data from the Hong Kong Interbank Clearing System suggest that RMB clearing transactions have also risen very strongly. When it started operations in 2006, the monthly average transaction value was only CNY352 million. In the first ten months of 2013, average RMB clearing transactions in Hong Kong, China reached CNY6,326 billion. This is more than twenty-one times the monthly average PRC trade settled in RMB due to the rapid rise in non-trade-related RMB transactions. This factor of 21 demonstrates the huge potential of reducing U.S. dollar usage in developing Asia through local-currency intraregional clearing transactions.[25]

The PRC can learn from the experience of the United States during the early part of the twentieth century. The prime position of the U.S. dollar in the international monetary system today was achieved mainly as a result of a combination of timely circumstances.[26] Of particular importance was the development of the U.S. dollar–denominated trade acceptances market resulting from the passage of the Federal Reserve Act (FRA) of 1913 and the subsequent supporting measures of the Federal Reserve (the Fed). The dramatic expansion of U.S. dollar–denominated trade acceptances proved to be a pivotal factor that underpinned the transformation of the U.S. dollar from a marginal currency to the most dominant unit of money in the world. Until then, despite the United States' enormous trade linkages, U.S. traders, along with most traders in other countries, had been heavily reliant on the London market to finance their trade negotiations, and at a higher cost.[27]

In essence, the FRA gave the U.S. domestic financial market much-needed stability with the creation of the Fed as the central monetary regulator and as a lender of last resort. Having such an institution lessened market volatilities and improved the investment climate. The FRA also did away with restrictions on foreign bank branching as well as trade financing and provided a structure for U.S. banks to expand their overseas operations, especially the promotion of U.S.

25. To illustrate, if 100 percent of intraregional trade transactions in developing Asia were settled in local currency, U.S. dollar usage could be reduced by over $4 trillion per year. If local currency intraregional clearing transactions could amount to twenty-one times this value, it would run up to over US$90 trillion per year, which is a significant improvement but still only a small fraction of the over US$200 quadrillion annual (or more than US$800 billion a day) over-the-counter foreign exchange turnover in U.S. dollars in the 10 Asian economies (the PRC; Hong Kong, China; India; Indonesia; the Republic of Korea; Malaysia; the Philippines; Singapore; Taipei,China; and Thailand) included in the BIS Triennial Central Bank Survey (Bank for International Settlements 2013). The proposal presented in this chapter should be regarded as a first small step toward establishing regional settlement currencies.

26. These include a dramatic growth in the global economic reach of the United States beginning in the mid-1800s, well-grounded forward-looking domestic regulations following a series of financial crises by the turn of the century, and the unfortunate turn of events that hobbled its European rivals in the first half of the twentieth century.

27. The United States surpassed the economic size of the United Kingdom in 1870, and the value of U.S. merchandise exports exceeded the UK's in 1912 (Eichengreen 2011).

dollar–denominated trade credits.[28] Authorities initially viewed the promotion of U.S. dollar trade acceptances overseas as a way to smoothe "interest rate spikes and market seizures" (Eichengreen 2011).

With the trade acceptances market in place, the unfolding of World War I provided an important avenue for the United States to elevate the U.S. dollar's international position.[29] The war, which disjointed both the flow of commodity and trade financing in Europe, resulted in increased international demand for U.S. commodities and U.S. dollar trade credit. After the war, no country in Europe was in a position to compete with the United States economically or financially. Rather, postwar reconstruction broadened the trade and financial dependence of Europe on the United States and placed the U.S. dollar much more firmly at the center of the international monetary system. At some point in the mid-1920s, even imports and exports between countries that neither bordered the United States nor involved U.S. enterprises already made use of U.S. dollar trade acceptances.

The increasing role of the U.S. dollar in international trade finance spilled over to other financing arrangements. The stability in the value of the U.S. currency that resulted from a much stronger domestic financial market made it an attractive vehicle to do business and move money across borders. It was not just a case of Europeans reaching out to the U.S. markets; the U.S. authorities also aggressively promoted U.S. dollar financing in Europe. At the same time, the war undermined the international standing of the then reigning de facto global currency, the UK's pound sterling, as a result of a deterioration in the UK's public finances.

---

28. The National Bank Act of 1863 that preceded the Federal Reserve Bank Act of 1913 had strict branching restrictions. National banks were not allowed to have branches in other countries, nor at times even in other states. National banks were also prohibited from entering into trade credit transactions. The only national bank not covered by the regulation was the International Banking Corporation—a specialized institution that was created to focus on overseas banking but was not allowed to deliver banking services domestically, on antitrust grounds. Although trust companies were permitted to branch out overseas, only a handful of institutions did erect branches on foreign soil. Some big U.S. private banks that were outside the scope of national regulations and had overseas offices could have easily entertained trade credit transactions, but incentives to do so were low. They were largely hampered by their cost disadvantage compared with their European counterparts. The United States, in the absence of a central financial market regulator and a lender of last resort, constantly succumbed to highly volatile market swings, making investment activities (even reserve placement) very risky. The United States at that time also had an underdeveloped financial market that made it difficult to re-sell the acceptances.

29. A shallow investor pool, a lack of familiarity of U.S.-based creditors with the trade acceptances, and the difficulty of liquidating the instruments initially hampered full-blown development of trade financing business in the United States. But the Fed responded by directing its regional offices to take on the trade-financing responsibilities in their own accounts, which lowered the discount rates on trade acceptances. The Fed's actions organized the trade acceptances credit flow and gave credibility to such notes with its regional branches serving as the primary counterparty that made them easier to trade. The resulting ease with which U.S. dollar trade acceptances could be intermediated provided an incentive for its usage. Subsequently, the U.S. dollar trade acceptances market began to attract more investors, not just domestically but also foreign central bank surpluses in the United States, thus paving the way for the considerable expansion of the instrument's utilization.

Internal disruptions affecting the UK's production lines added to the growing loss of confidence in the UK currency.

Expansion of the RMB trade settlement scheme into a multilateral system could be based on the settlement system that was initially put in place when the euro was launched. Before the introduction of the euro, eurozone member countries had their own independent Real Time Gross Settlement (RTGS) systems for their national currencies. With their adoption of the single currency in 1999, these independent systems were linked together via the Trans-European Automated Real-Time Gross Settlement Express Transfer (TARGET) system following the definition of harmonized standards for cross-border sending and receiving of payments. Central banks continued to handle the settlement of payments for their domestic banking community.

At that time, transaction fees were not harmonized and were individually set by each central bank. The decentralized nature of the system also multiplied the costs. To better harmonize service and cost, as well as to improve cost-efficiency (since revenues were insufficient to cover costs), the Governing Council of the European Central Bank agreed in 2002 to establish the second-generation TARGET system, TARGET2. The new system offers harmonized services delivered on a single technical platform—the "Single Shared Platform"—at uniform cost. Fees were set at levels that allow the system to fully recover costs. TARGET2 went live in November 2007, but replaced the first generation system only in May 2008.

In general, TARGET2 facilitates the settlement of euro payments in central bank money with immediate finality. Currently, TARGET2 is considered to be one of the top three global wholesale payment systems and settles transactions the size of the annual eurozone gross domestic product (GDP) in just over three days. At the local level, the decentralized nature of TARGET2 is maintained, and the relationship between central banks and their counterparties is preserved, including those for monetary policy and lender of last resort.

Combining the Regional Trade and Government Bonds Settlement Systems

One lesson from the RMB trade settlement scheme experience of Hong Kong, China is that having an efficient payments and securities settlement system could simultaneously have strong synergy effects in terms of promoting internationalization of regional currencies. As such, the regional trade payment settlement system could be combined with a government securities settlement scheme. This could be an effective way to both reduce U.S. dollar dependence and promote local-currency-denominated bond markets in Asia.

After the Asian financial crisis in 1997, the ASEAN+3 economies tried hard to promote the development of local-currency-denominated bond markets. There was a strong realization that the underdevelopment of bond markets in the region greatly exacerbated, or perhaps even caused, the crisis. The idea of regional bond markets was promoted as a means of overcoming the double mismatch problem

Figure 8-4. *Local-Currency Bonds Outstanding in Asia*

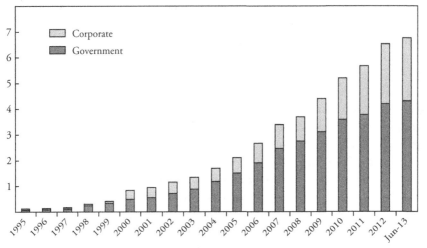

US$ trillion

Source: AsianBondsOnline.

that most Asian borrowers face when they try to raise funds abroad. The double mismatch refers to the currency mismatch and the maturity mismatch, and it is also considered to be the root cause of the 1997 Asian financial crisis.

Supported by these policy initiatives, local-currency bond market issuance in developing Asia has expanded rapidly since the Asian financial crisis. From only US$126 billion by the end of 1995, outstanding local currency bonds in Asia had ballooned to US$6,532 billion by end-2012, and US$6,762 billion by June 2013 (figure 8-4).

Corporate bond issuance has likewise increased, but government bonds still account for close to two thirds of this amount. It is worth noting that cross-border holdings of portfolio securities among ASEAN+3 economies have sharply increased as well. Intra-ASEAN+3 cross-border holdings of debt securities were US$29 billion in 2001 and amounted to US$130 billion at end-2012 (figure 8-5). Since bonds originating from Asia are predominantly government securities, these cross-border holdings are perhaps mostly government bonds too. This implies that there are tremendous new business opportunities for cross-border trading and settlement of government bonds in Asia. So combining the regional trade payment settlement system with a government securities settlement scheme could make good business sense as well.

In fact, as a part of the ASEAN+3 Asian Bond Markets Initiative (ABMI), discussions are currently under way to set up a Regional Settlement Intermediary (RSI) for securities, in particular cross-border bond transactions (ABMI Group of Experts, Asian Development Bank 2010). This is a very important initiative and

Figure 8-5. *Intra-ASEAN+3 Cross-Border Holdings of Debt Securities*[a]

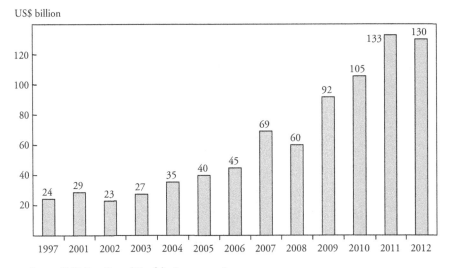

US$ billion

Source: IMF Coordinated Portfolio Investment Survey.

a. ASEAN+3 = Association of Southeast Asian Nations (Brunei Darussalam, Cambodia, Indonesia, the Lao People's Democratic Republic, Malaysia, Myanmar, the Philippines, Singapore, Thailand, and Viet Nam) plus the People's Republic of China, Japan, and the Republic of Korea.

some limited progress has been made. Building a full business model for securities settlement would require large fixed costs and full liberalization of capital markets. Progress with the realization of this initiative has slowed since the global financial crisis, partly reflecting increasing unwillingness of regional governments to expedite capital market liberalization.

For the time being, instead of trying to develop a full-scale RSI with full capital market liberalization, it may be better to focus on a government bond trading and settlement system together with a trade-related payment settlement system (see figure 8-6).

Similar to the RMB trade settlement scheme between the PRC and Hong Kong, China, Asian central banks could enter into bilateral agreements with other regional central banks—just like the one between PBOC and HKMA—to allow the settlement of trade transactions in regional currencies. In addition, using the same platform, trading and settlement of government bonds could be included in these bilateral trade settlement agreements. Having an efficient payments and securities settlement system simultaneously could produce strong synergies in promoting internationalization of regional currencies as demonstrated by the RMB trade settlement scheme in Hong Kong, China. To make this proposal work, central banks must ensure that there is sufficient supply of their local currencies in partner countries to facilitate payment of trade as well as government bond transactions. In other words, as long as traders are able to provide evidence that their

Figure 8-6. *The Proposed System for Clearing and Settlement*

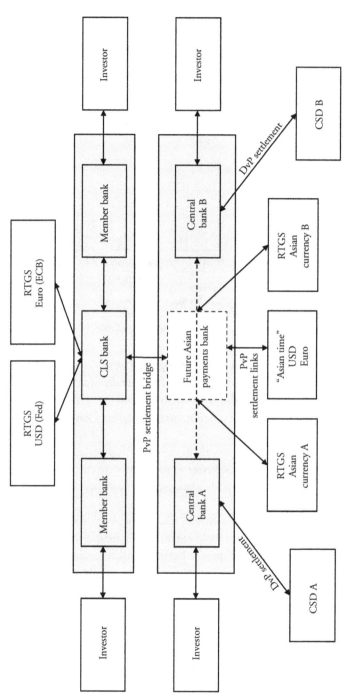

Source: Authors.

CLS = continuous linked settlement; CSD = central securities depository; DvP = delivery versus payment; ECB = European Central Bank; PvP = payment versus payment; RTGS = real-time gross settlement; USD = U.S. dollar. Broken line (- - -) indicates potential future additions.

holdings of regional currencies result from trade or government bond transactions, central banks could guarantee the convertibility of these regional currencies into international currencies anytime. Opening of bilateral currency swap lines is thus vital to addressing these liquidity considerations where trade and government bond transactions are concerned.

However, unlike in trade transactions where actual delivery of goods is outside the scope of the settlement infrastructure, bond transactions require an additional dimension in terms of custodians and central securities depositories, which can be provided by central banks either directly or indirectly.

Fortunately, most central banks in Asia function as government bond securities depositories and settlement institutions anyway (see table 8-2).[30] Since expanding the bilateral trade payment settlement system regionally requires linkages between central banks, adding a government bond settlement system with securities depositories will not cost a large amount of new fixed investment. Yet it will promote additional business and expedite the internationalization of currencies. Once this model has generated sufficient business, it can be privatized later as the RSI and expanded for other securities such as corporate bonds or equity depository and settlement.

This model could parallel Euroclear and Clearstream, international central securities depositories (ICSDs) that were established in the late 1960s and early 1970s, respectively.[31] The experience of these ICSDs in intermediating stateless Eurobond issuances, although not entirely comparable to the Asian case with respect to financial feasibility, indicates that defragmenting clearing and settlement of securities is a high-potential business.[32] Moreover, it was also seen in the case of

30. Starting with a government bond settlement scheme makes sense from business feasibility perspectives, too. After the launch of ABMI, there has been significant progress in the development of government bond markets in the region, but less so in corporate bonds. At the start of 2003, the value of outstanding government bonds in developing Asia was only US$711 billion, and corporate bonds, US$456 billion. By June 2013, the size of outstanding government bonds had risen more than six times, but that of corporate bonds by just over five times.

31. Euro-clear (the hyphen was dropped in 1989) was launched by Morgan Guaranty on December 2, 1968. It was the first ICSD to break ground with a client list comprising more than fifty banks and dealers at its start. In one year its client base increased to 150. Euro-clear quickly made a hefty fortune—both from the value of services and from their investments funded by the huge deposits in the cash accounts of their clients. Much of the business is anchored on the market's appreciation of the delivery versus payment capability of the infrastructure. The establishment of Euro-clear also prevented the Eurobond market from seizing up. But at this early stage, a sense of the necessity to break away from the flagship U.S. bank Morgan Guaranty, whether for technical or political reasons, was already palpable. On September 28, 1970, Centrale de Livraison de Valeurs Mobilières (Cedel), a company that is co-owned by seventy-one banks from eleven countries, was inaugurated. It had an initial capital of US$1.15 million. Cedel was later bought by Deutsche Börse Clearing and is presently known as Clearstream.

32. In July 1963, the very first Eurobond issuance by the Italian firm Autostrade was offered to European investors and was received warmly with strong participation from the "Belgian Dentists" (a reference to European investors who finally managed to set aside some savings during postwar reconstruction). One factor considered in the Autostrade issuance was the size of the offshore dollar

Table 8-2. *Clearing and Settlement Institutions for Government Bonds in Asia*

Economy	Clearing	Securities settlement	Deposits	Payment settlement
Australia	Austraclear	Austraclear	Austraclear	RBA
New Zealand	NZClear	NZClear	NZCSD	RBNZ
Hong Kong, China	CMU	CMU	CMU	HKMA
Indonesia	KPEI	BI-SSSS	BI-SSSS	BI
Malaysia	SSDS	SSDS	SSDS	BNM
Thailand	BOT	TSD	TSD	BOT
Philippines	BTr	BTr	BTr	BSP
Japan	JGBCC	BOJ	BOJ	BOJ
Republic of Korea	KRX	KSD	KSD	BOK
PRC	CGSDTC	CGSDTC	CGSDTC	
Taipei,China	CBC	TSCD	TSCD	CBC
Singapore	MAS	MAS	CDP	
India	CCIL	RBI	RBI	NDS/SSS
Pakistan	State Bank of Pakistan			

Sources: Bank for International Settlements (2011, 2012); Executives' Meeting of East Asia Pacific Central Banks (2012).

BI = Bank Indonesia; BNM = Bank Negara Malaysia; BOJ = Bank of Japan; BOK = Bank of Korea; BOT = Bank of Thailand; BSP = Bangko Sentral ng Pilipinas; BTr = Bureau of the Treasury; CBC = Central Bank of China; CCIL = Clearing Corporation of India Limited; CDP = Central Depository Pte Ltd; CGSDTC = China Government Securities Depository Trust and Clearing Co., Ltd.; CMU = Central Moneymarkets Unit; HKMA = Hong Kong Monetary Authority; JGBCC = Japan Government Bond Clearing Corporation; KPEI = PT Kliring Penjaminan Efek Indonesia (Securities Underwriting Clearing Indonesia); KRX = Korea Exchange; KSD = Korea Securities Depository; MAS = Monetary Authority of Singapore; NDS/SSS = Negotiated Dealing System/Securities Settlement System; NSDL = National Securities Depository Limited; NZCSD = New Zealand Central Securities Depository Limited; PRC = People's Republic of China; RBA = Reserve Bank of Australia; RBNZ = Reserve Bank of New Zealand; SSDS = Scripless Securities Depository System; SSSS = Scripless Securities Settlement System; TSCD = Taipei, China Securities Central Depository Co., Ltd.; TSD = Thailand Securities Depository.

Eurobonds that the existence of a centralized interface for multiple issuances available in multiple markets lowered the cost of intermediation, and thus encouraged greater transaction volume.

However, if the securities settlement system in the eurozone is any indication, integrating securities infrastructure may take a long time. In 2006, the TARGET2–Securities (T2S) project was introduced to integrate euro securities infra-

---

pool that European countries had accumulated since the late 1800s. Another factor that resulted in essentially the second expansionary phase of the offshore dollar bond market was the levy slapped by the U.S. government on bond issuance of foreign companies in the United States–the interest equalization tax (IET) imposed in July 1963. U.S. authorities at that time were worried about the strain on the U.S. balance-of-payments position brought about by its spending on the Korean and the Viet Nam wars. The IET, which was approved by Congress the following year with retroactive effect from the president's announcement, imposed a 15 percent tax on the cost of foreign shares bought by U.S. citizens and a graduated tax on foreign bonds from 2.75 percent for those with a maturity of less than 3.5 years to 15 percent on long-dated bonds (Norman 2007). A pilot securities settlement scheme, structure, but progress has not been as fast as with TARGET2. The T2S aims to provide a single pan-European platform for securities settlement in central bank money at low cost. Just like TARGET2, uniform rules, standards, and tariffs will apply to all transactions in all T2S markets when it begins operation in June 2015.

In any case, a combined trade settlement and securities settlement system would create various synergies across the financial market. First, government bonds deposited in central banks could be used as collateral, which could efficiently reduce risks in trade and non-trade-related cross-border securities transactions. Indeed, the system in Europe also provides collateral management services, in which eligible counterparties mobilize collateral for use in credit operations. But one of the most important benefits of this joint payments and securities settlement infrastructure is to alleviate "the third time zone" problem (Park and Rhee 2006).

The lack of an Asian securities settlement system causes Asian investors to lose liquidity or pay more transaction costs, even though they can settle their payment transactions with each other in the same time zone. That is, payment and settlement systems are in different time zones. Currently, when Asian investors trade securities with each other, payment transactions can be made instantly or nearly instantly as the business hours of most central banks in Asia are in a similar time zone. But securities settlement has to wait until the settlement hours in the United States or Europe as most of the international securities are deposited in Europe and the United States with time zones quite different from Asia. By having payment and settlement systems in the same Asian time zone, this third time zone problem could be solved.

To illustrate the third time zone problem, consider the settlement process of an Asian bond that is denominated in Hong Kong dollars. Hong Kong, China is seven hours ahead of Brussels, where Euroclear is located. Assume that the settlement date of the bond is October 2 in Brussels. In order to finalize the settlement by that date, Euroclear currently mandates that a buyer and a seller deposit money and security in a common depository of Euroclear in Hong Kong, China—HSBC bank—by October 1, which is a day before the settlement date. After getting notification from HSBC overnight, Euroclear Bank in Brussels completes the security settlement by 9 a.m. on October 2 (4 p.m. in Hong Kong, China), after which the seller in Hong Kong, China can withdraw Hong Kong dollars, and the settlement could be finished by October 2.

Now imagine that instead of depositing money and securities a day before the settlement date, if the buyer and seller want to settle securities by using the RTGS system on October 2 in Belgium, the seller may not be able to withdraw money by October 2. For example, by the time the RTGS settlement is completed by

spearheaded by the U.S. banking giant Morgan Guaranty Trust Company and launched on July 21, 1967, largely as a response to the burgeoning Eurobond market, facilitated the establishment of European ICSDs.

3 p.m. on October 2, it is already 10 p.m. in Hong Kong, China and the bond seller would have to wait until the next day to withdraw her money. This is one reason why Euroclear mandates that traders deposit money and securities a day in advance of settling bonds that are denominated in Asian currencies. Otherwise, it cannot secure a settlement date.

If bonds are denominated in European currencies or the U.S. dollar, security and payment settlement can be completed on the same day through the RTGS system because the time difference between the Americas and Europe works in favor of the security settlement and payment settlement. The third time zone problem implies that investors have to bear the extra cost of losing liquidity for a day when trading Asian currency–denominated bonds. If there were a regional securities depository within Asia, investors would not face this extra cost. The benefit of solving the third time zone problem could be significant, considering that major investors for Asian currency–denominated bonds are institutional investors located in Asia.

In addition to solving the time difference problem, establishing a combined trade and government bond settlement system through the cooperation of Asian central banks could be a catalyst for the gradual opening of domestic markets and regulatory harmonization across the region. Existing ICSDs such as Euroclear and Clearstream are private entities, and it would be hard for Asian governments to provide incentives to ease regulations to increase business flows for them unless doing so would benefit their national interests. On the other hand, the central banks' network of trade and government bond settlement systems would encourage them to discuss greater financial policy coordination among Asian governments. It would also promote government bond market dealers, custodians, and pricing agencies, which are all necessary infrastructure for the development of a full-fledged local currency capital market in Asia.

Related Regional Initiatives

Over the years, several initiatives were created to build infrastructure for local bond markets on the back of calls for greater regional integration. The idea to establish a regional-currency-denominated bond market and a regional central securities depository (CSD) was first put forward in the early 1990s. However, the early initiatives advocating such propositions were "merely talk without action" (see Oh and others 2003). Factors that were cited for the non-action of most stakeholders include reluctance to liberalize local capital markets and the absence of the requisite institutions.

Most Asian countries, following their debilitating experience during the 1997 Asian financial crisis, focused on strengthening their balance-of-payments positions and started piling up foreign exchange reserves. The rising reserves impelled national authorities to renew discussions concerning regional bond market development to recycle their savings within the region and simultaneously reduce their foreign currency exposure. One of the major movements spearheading the creation of the regional bond market infrastructure is the ABMI. The planning stage of ABMI began in November 2002, before it was formally launched during the ASEAN+3 Finance Ministers Meeting in Manila in August 2003. ABMI came after the Chiang Mai Initiative was formalized in May 2000, also by the ASEAN+3 group, and was later complemented by the Executives' Meeting of East Asia Pacific Central Banks with the launch of the Asia Bond Fund initiative in June 2003 and the Asia Bond Fund 2 initiative in December 2004.[33]

ABMI and RSI

Under ABMI, ASEAN+3 initially launched six working groups to study various aspects of regional bond markets including securitization, regional credit rating agencies, regional clearing and settlement systems, and regional credit guarantee agencies.[34] Regarding the clearing and settlement infrastructure component of ABMI, two studies were undertaken to examine the relevant factors and dimensions. The first of these reports is "Bond Market Settlements and Emerging Linkages among Selected ASEAN+3 Countries," published in 2005.[35] Essentially, the reports pointed out that over-the-counter securities trading in many Asian countries mostly uses central bank–operated settlement systems that are not linked with a clearing company or a central counterparty. While European ICSDs extended linkages to some economies in Asia for cross-border issuances, the differences in settlement cycles and time zones naturally bring with them inefficiency costs and risks. The study noted that, as in the cases of Clearstream and Euroclear, it may take some time before such regional settlement infrastructure has fully developed. Instead, in the interim, it proposed to focus on improvements in fundamental matters such as individual markets' compliance with international standards to have better links with the global settlement system, especially in terms of legal certainty, delivery versus payment facility, and so on.

The follow-up study, titled "Minimizing Foreign Exchange Settlement Risk in ASEAN+3 Region" and released in 2007, was the second research cycle on bond market infrastructure under ABMI.[36] It assessed the settlement costs and risks

33. The Executives' Meeting of East Asia Pacific Central Banks is composed of the Reserve Bank of Australia, the People's Bank of China, the Hong Kong Monetary Authority, Bank Indonesia, the Bank of Japan, the Bank of Korea, Bank Negara Malaysia, the Reserve Bank of New Zealand, Bangko Sentral ng Pilipinas, the Monetary Authority of Singapore, and the Bank of Thailand.

The primary goal of the Asia Bond Fund and Asia Bond Fund 2 is to boost the demand for local currency bonds (Hyun and Jang 2008).

34. This section draws heavily on Park and Rhee (2006).

35. "Bond Market Settlements and Emerging Linkages among Selected ASEAN+3 Countries" (http://asianbondsonline.adb.org/regional/documents/ABMI_WG_FETS_Regional_Settlement_Linkage_Nov2005.pdf).

36. "Minimizing Foreign Exchange Settlement Risk in ASEAN+3 Region" (www.adb.org/sites/default/files/projdocs/2012/39312-012-reg-tcr.pdf).

accompanying the settlement systems in the region in greater detail. It proposed to establish the RSI and suggested its possible architecture. As one of the rationales for establishing the RSI, the report discussed the lack of regional infrastructure and how this can exacerbate the foreign exchange settlement risks (the "third time zone" problem explained earlier). The suggested types of RSI architecture include the Asia ICSD model, the Pan-Asia CSD model, the Asian Payment Bank model, and the CSD Linkage option.[37]

Building on the findings of these reports, the ABMI Group of Experts with representation from ASEAN+3 members was formed in April 2008 to evaluate the financial and legal viability of designs of the Asian RSI previously proposed. For reasons of "practicality, the Group of Experts' report assessed only the Asian ICSD model and the CSD linkage model in terms of operational and legal feasibility." In a nutshell, the report is geared toward supporting the creation of an Asian ICSD model over the CSD linkage model, but it clearly pointed out that in most Asian economies, trimming down legal and regulatory barriers is more daunting for the Asian ICSD model than for the CSD linkage model.

Needless to say, the proposal put forward here is to build bilateral trade and government bond settlement infrastructure that is closer to, or a subset of, the CSD linkage model. Theoretically, creating a multilateral RSI would be the first best option, as pointed out by the Group of Experts report. However, the report's observation that regulatory controls and legal barriers need to be trimmed down significantly for the RSI to take form does not seem to bode well for the current prospects that a number of sovereign monetary authorities will undertake such measures—particularly after the global financial crisis. That is why, although RSI is arguably the best option to remedy the infrastructure limitations in the region, perhaps it would be more pragmatic to just harness the current trade settlement scheme between Hong Kong, China and the PRC and extend its coverage to government bonds, as mentioned in the previous section. Financial viability may be a concern, too, in the short term in building regional settlement infrastructure. Euroclear and Clearstream also did not make money at first—infrastructure was built first to attract private investors, similar to the plot of Asia's growth story. The same logic should apply to the development of regional capital markets in Asia.

---

37. The Asian ICSD model proposes a similar platform to the European ICSDs such as Clearstream and Euroclear with direct linkages to local central securities depositories (CSDs) as well as to the other ICSDs. The Pan-Asian CSD model indicates that a regional depository for ASEAN+3 debt securities will be established—the Pan Asian CSD, where all national CSDs could be subdepositories. A link between the Pan-Asian CSD and other ICSDs will be created and settlement will be in central bank money. The Asian Payment Bank model proposes to have a multilateral payments bank supported by Asian countries. It envisions having a payment versus payment linkage to the national payments systems and the Continuous Link Settlement (CLS) Bank in Europe, and final settlement will be based on the Asian time zone. Finally, the CSD linkage model suggests that instead of creating a central body, it would be easier to just link the national CSDs patterned after the Link Up Markets initiative that was originally participated in by seven European CSDs.

ASEAN+3 Local Currency Trading System

The push for a more extensive cross-border local-currency-based trading system was further boosted following the conclusion of the fifteenth ASEAN+3 Finance Ministers and Central Bank Governors' Meeting in Manila on May 3, 2012. Recognizing the need to advance the agenda of regional financial integration at a higher level, the caucus called for the ABMI to undertake further study on the use of local currencies for regional trade settlement, and put forward concrete policy recommendations. Such an endorsement shows the political will of ASEAN+3 members to reduce the region's heavy reliance on the U.S. dollar for trade settlement. The proposal set forth here—combining the expanded trade settlement scheme with a government bond payment and settlement scheme—could be one option to achieve this end. So far, Asian policymakers have continued to complain about rising financial vulnerabilities of their economies resulting from the greater interconnectedness of the global economy. To help the region reduce the risks from these vulnerabilities without requiring substantial startup costs, authorities should show strong political will in establishing central banks' linkages for trade and government bond settlement.

Bilateral Swaps and Regional Financial Safety Nets

As part of the effort to create regional safety nets, many Asian economies are entering into bilateral swap agreements with other countries to guard against liquidity crises. It is ironic that during the 2008 global financial crisis, which started with the financial crisis in the United States, it was its currency swap with the U.S. Federal Reserve that helped the Republic of Korea overcome its liquidity constraints. Although bilateral swaps of Asian central banks with the U.S. Federal Reserve have been valuable in mitigating the impacts of past financial crises, this option is simply not politically sustainable, and these swaps are not provided on a regular basis. Hence, it is vital for Asian economies to expand intraregional swap lines to strengthen the regional insurance mechanism and to increase their capabilities to appropriately address crisis scenarios in the future. And this is happening. For example, the PRC had twenty-one active local currency bilateral swap agreements as of October 2013, with a total size of about CNY2.5 trillion.

Another facet of the safety net is the Chiang Mai Initiative, introduced in 2000 as a series of bilateral swap agreements to manage the region's short-term liquidity problems. In 2007, the ASEAN+3 members agreed to improve it and turn it into a multilateral agreement, the Chiang Mai Initiative Multilateralization (CMIM). When the global financial crisis erupted in 2008, the massive contraction in global liquidity underscored the urgent need to strengthen the CMIM as a regional financial safety net and the total fund has recently been doubled to $240 billion. The IMF delinked portion was also increased, to 30 percent in 2012, and was targeted to be further raised to 40 percent in 2014. Following the IMF's crisis-prevention toolkits, a crisis prevention facility called the CMIM Precautionary Line was introduced as well.

Although ASEAN+3 countries have made significant progress in building these bilateral and multilateral safety nets, much more still needs to be done. In particular, the committed funds under CMIM continue to remain in each individual country's coffers, and the mechanism for funds disbursement remains unclear. In addition, a well-functioning independent surveillance unit needs to be put in place to monitor and assess the vulnerability of each country so that remedial action can be implemented swiftly. This task has been assigned to the ASEAN+3 Macroeconomic Research Office (AMRO), with inputs from each country's central bank. However, building AMRO's surveillance capacity will take a lot of time and effort.

The IMF conditionality connection is a disincentive for countries in securing assistance. Programs must be designed in such a way that the stigma effect of obtaining CMIM funds is reduced. Several ideas have been put forward to deal with this stigma effect, including simultaneously offering programs to a group of countries with similar macroeconomic indicators, rather than to just a single country, and setting prequalification criteria for program eligibility. One could consider implementing a clear, rules-based, and automated prequalification process via a set of transparent "Maastricht-like" criteria, and having offers of liquidity extended simultaneously to all qualified countries, which could possibly reduce the stigma effect.

The existence of bilateral and regional safety nets does not obviate the proposed trade and securities settlement system. The former is an insurance mechanism. The latter is a mechanism to reduce U.S. dollar dependence. The existing bilateral and regional safety-net mechanisms can supplement the proposed combined trade and government bond settlement system. For example, CMIM funds may be used as a credit guarantee for the trade settlement transactions of countries with lower credit ratings to expedite the bilateral linkages among Asian central banks.

Conclusion

The global financial crisis has once again stimulated discussion about reform of the international financial architecture. In this paper, we argue that establishment of regional settlement currencies can contribute positively to this reform agenda. In particular, extending the local currency trade settlement schemes such as the RMB trade settlement scheme between the PRC and Hong Kong, China to the rest of Asia, and combining it with a government securities payment and settlement scheme, can be a practical solution.

The proposal is based on the idea that building proper infrastructure first can make a big difference. Bilateral transactions between non–U.S. dollar currencies are less common since adequate infrastructure has not been built. With proper infrastructure, these transactions could be facilitated and costs could be significantly reduced. Proper infrastructure could also bring new demand for business. The role of Asian governments in helping to put this proposal into practice is extremely important. As Eichengreen (2011) noted, in the early twentieth century U.S. policymakers undertook domestic financial reforms to encourage the internationalization of the U.S. dollar. One of these reforms was the establishment of the Federal Reserve System and infrastructure for overseas U.S. dollar transactions, which was influenced by pressure from domestic financial firms seeking denomination rents and exporters seeking to reduce transaction costs (Broz 1997). Without this effort to build new infrastructure, the U.S. dollar would not have been able to dethrone the U.K. pound sterling as the key international currency. The legal framework that established the Eurosystem also facilitated the links among eurozone central banks that enabled euro settlement.

Asian policymakers could follow this path. Building proper settlement infrastructure should be the first step. This strategy is consistent with the Asian development experience in the last half century—which underlines the importance of building infrastructure—and it could be a practical way of reducing U.S. dollar dependence without the risks associated with rapid capital market opening. It would also contribute to capital market development in Asia.

References

ABMI Group of Experts, Asian Development Bank. 2010. "Final Report, Part II: Evaluation of the Feasibility of Regional Settlement Intermediary Options for the ASEAN+3." June. Manila: Asian Development Bank.

AHK Greater China. 2011. "The Long March of the Renminbi: Internationalization of China's Currency via Hong Kong." Newsletter article, May.

ANZ Research. 2012. "CNH Market Monitor." Newsletter article, May 9.

Bank for International Settlements. 2011. *Payment, Clearing and Settlement Systems in the CPSS Countries*. Volume 1. Basel: BIS.

———. 2012. *Payment, Clearing and Settlement Systems in the CPSS Countries*. Vol. 2. Basel: BIS.

———. 2013. *Triennial Central Bank Survey 2013*. Basel: Bank for International Settlements.

Broz, J. Lawrence. 1997. *The International Origins of the Federal Reserve System*. Cornell University Press.

Chan, Norman T. L. 2013. "Development of Offshore Renminbi Business in Hong Kong: Review and Outlook." *InSight* (online journal), February 21, 2013 (www.hkma.gov.hk/eng/key-information/insight/20130221.shtml).

City of London. "FAQs: City of London Renminbi Series," November 28, 2012 (www.cityoflondon.gov.uk/business/support-promotion-and-advice/promoting-the-city-internationally/china/Documents/renminbi_faqs.pdf).

De Silva, A., and P.-R. Tan. 2012. "China Bonds: Increase in QFII and RQFII Quotas." HSBC Global Research Flash Note. April.

Eichengreen, Barry. 2011. *Exorbitant Privilege: The Rise and Fall of the Dollar and the Future of the International Monetary System*. Oxford University Press.

———. 2012. "The Renminbi Challenge." Project Syndicate (Web site), October 9, 2012 (http://www.project-syndicate.org/commentary/can-china-have-an-international-reserve-currency-by-barry-eichengreen; requires registration).

Executives' Meeting of East Asia Pacific Central Banks. 2012. "Payment, Clearing and Settlement Systems in EMEAP Economies," 2012 (www.emeap.org/emeapdb/upload/Publications/Payment,_Clearing_and_Settlement_Systems_in_EMEAP_Economies_(August_2012)_.pdf).

Frankel, Jeffrey. 2011. *Historical Precedents for Internationalization of the RMB*. New York: Council on Foreign Relations.

He, Dong. 2012. *Renminbi Internationalisation: A Primer*. Hong Kong, China: Hong Kong Institute for Monetary Research.

Hong Kong Monetary Authority. 2013a. *Hong Kong: The Premier Offshore Renminbi Business Centre*. Hong Kong, China: HKMA.

———. 2013b. *Monthly Statistics*. Hong Kong, China: HKMA.

HSBC. 2011. "RMB FDI Formalization: A Structural Boost for CNH Market." October 14.

Hyun, Suk, and Hong Bum Jang. 2008. "Bond Market Development in Asia." Unpublished manuscript (www.academia.edu/4446995/BOND_MARKET_DEVELOPMENT_IN_ASIAHYUN_Suk_and_JANG_Hong_Bum).

International Monetary Fund (IMF). 2011. "Global Financial Safety Nets: How Can Countries Cooperate to Mitigate Contagion and Limit the Spread of Crises?" *Reforming the International Monetary System* (IMF blog), November 7.

———. 2014. Direction of Trade Statistics database. Washington, D.C.

KPMG. 2012. "Hong Kong Banking Survey 2012." Hong Kong, China.

Ma, Jun, Linan Liu, and Hui Miao. 2012. "Roadmap for RMB Internationalization." Hong Kong, China: Deutsche Bank Global Market Research.

Mallaby, Sebastian, and Olin Wethington. 2011. "The Future of the Yuan." *Foreign Affairs*, January–February.

Maziad, Samar, and Joong Shik Kang. 2012. "RMB Internationalization: Onshore/Offshore Links." International Monetary Fund Working Paper WP/12/133. Washington: International Monetary Fund.

Ministry of Commerce (People's Republic of China). 2011. "Circular on Issues Concerning Cross-Border RMB Direct Investment." Circular 2011–889. Beijing.

Monetary Authority of Singapore. 2013. "Conduct of Renminbi ('RMB') Business in Singapore." FSG Circular No. BD 04/2013. Singapore: May 23.

Norman, Peter. 2007. *Plumbers and Visionaries: Securities Settlement and Europe's Financial Market*. Chichester, UK: Wiley.

Park, Daekeun, and Changyong Rhee. 2006. "Building Infrastructure for Asian Bond Markets: Settlement and Credit Rating." *BIS Papers* No. 30. Basel: Bank for International Settlements.

People's Bank of China. 2009. "Administrative Rules on Pilot Program of Renminbi Settlement of Cross-Border Trade Transactions." Beijing: July 2.

———. 2011a. *The People's Bank of China Annual Report 2010*. Beijing.

———. 2011b. "Document No. 23. Administrative Measures on Renminbi Settlement for Foreign Direct Investment." Beijing.

———. 2012a. "China Monetary Policy Quarter 4–2011." Beijing: February 15.

———. 2012b. "RMB Financial Statistics, H12012." Beijing: July 129.

———. 2013a. "China Monetary Policy Quarter 4–2012." Beijing. February 6.

———. 2013b. "The PBC Signed an RMB Clearing Agreement with the Singapore Branch of Industrial and Commercial Bank of China." Press release. Beijing: April 8.

———. 2013c. "RMB Financial Statistics, H12013." Beijing: July 18.

Sekine, Eiichi. 2011. "Renminbi Trade Settlement as a Catalyst to Hong Kong's Development as an Offshore Renminbi Center." *Nomura Journal of Capital Markets* 3, no. 1 (Summer): 1–14.

Society for Worldwide Interbank Financial Telecommunication. 2013a. "RMB Swift Tracker." April.

———. 2013b. "RMB Swift Tracker." May.

———. 2013c. "RTGS Systems Go Live in Macau and Taiwan on SWIFT," March 25 (http://www.swift.com/about_swift/shownews?param_dcr=news.data/en/swift_com/2013/PR_RTGS_Macau_Taiwan.xml).

Subacchi, Paola, and Helena Huang. 2013. "Taipei in the Renminbi Offshore Market: Another Piece in the Jigsaw." Briefing Paper IE BP 2013/01. London: Chatham House, International Economics, June (www.chathamhouse.org/sites/files/chathamhouse/public/Research/International percent20Economics/0613bp_taipei.pdf).

Teng, Anselmo. 2013. "Internationalization of the RMB and the Role of Macao as a Financial Platform." Speech. 2013 Internationalization of RMB Global Forum. Shanghai, May 26.

Wong, Nethelie. 2013. "Heavyweight Issuers Target Bao Dao Bonds." *International Financing Review* 11 (July).

Yu, Yongding. 2012a. "Rattling the Renminbi." Project Syndicate (website), January 30 (www.project-syndicate.org/commentary/rattling-the-renminbi).

———. 2012b. "Revisiting the Internationalization of the Yuan." ADBI Working Paper 366. Tokyo: Asian Development Bank Institute.

Zhang, Bin, and Qiyuan Xu. 2011. "RMB Internationalization in the Context of Exchange Rate and Capital Account Control." Unpublished paper. Beijing (www.cf40.org.cn/uploads/111116/20124248.pdf).

9

Are the People's Republic of China Financial Markets Deep and Liquid Enough for Renminbi Internationalization?

PRINCE CHRISTIAN CRUZ, YUNING GAO, AND LEI LEI SONG

Domestic financial market development is a key determinant of a currency's international status (Tavlas 1990; Chinn and Frankel 2007; Forbes 2009; International Monetary Fund 2011). For a currency to be used internationally to settle financial transactions, international traders and investors must have access to a wide array of financial assets denominated in that currency. To provide such access, that country must have broad, deep, and liquid financial markets. The pace of internationalization of the People's Republic China's (PRC) currency, the renminbi, will be closely related to its financial market development. Moreover, to be a reserve currency the renminbi must be readily available with necessary abundance. A reserve currency must be a reliable store of value, with assets denominated in the currency being held by both the private sector as currency substitution and investment, and by the public sector as international reserves (Chinn and Frankel 2007).

There are three aspects of financial market development: breadth (availability of financial instruments and markets for various transaction purposes), depth (volume of financial instruments in the markets), and liquidity (ease of carrying out transactions for market participants). Without reasonably broad, deep, and liquid financial markets, the renminbi will not be creditably used in international transactions and will not be attractive to international investors. Institutional investors, including central banks, will not hold renminbi-denominated assets if they cannot convert these assets easily when needed. Furthermore, international traders and investors will not be able to hedge their exchange rate risks. Three further essential attributes for an international currency to be used in private, commercial, and financial transactions and held as official reserves are scale, stability, and liquidity (Eichengreen 2013).

Scale refers to international transactions between the country issuing the currency and the rest of the world, which is essentially linked to the breadth and depth of domestic financial markets. Stability refers to the fact that a currency holding stable values will help build users' confidence.

Liquidity plays a central role in the functioning of financial markets, and is believed to improve resource allocation and information efficiency. One dimension of liquidity is referred to as *funding liquidity:* the availability of credit, or the ease with which institutions can borrow or take on leverage. Another dimension is *market liquidity:* the ability of markets to absorb large transactions without there being much impact on prices. These two types of liquidity are connected and often are mutually reinforcing. This is because abundant funding liquidity can finance trading positions that smooth price movements and make markets liquid. Relative abundance of the supply of a currency and assets denominated in that currency are also key features of a reserve currency. Without adequate liquidity, international investors and traders will not be able to settle their transactions efficiently, making it difficult for them to hold the currency-denominated assets as investments or international reserves. A wide array of assets with different yields, maturities, and risk levels is required to match the needs of different investors abroad. Therefore, liquidity is closely linked to financial market breadth and depth.

Although there are few studies of the PRC's financial market breadth, depth, and liquidity from the perspective of currency internationalization, there is wide agreement that the PRC's financial markets are relatively shallow and underdeveloped and must develop further to support renminbi internationalization.[1] In this chapter we discuss the status of the PRC's financial markets and their liquidity conditions, and compare them with those in other economies, contemporaneously and historically. The contemporaneous comparison compares the PRC with both major developed economies issuing international currencies and major emerging economies that are at a similar stage of development as the PRC.

The historical comparison looks at the PRC now and at some developed economies in the past when they were at a similar level of development as the PRC is now and whose currencies are international now. Japan and Germany are chosen as the economies for historical comparison, because these two economies developed their financial markets rapidly and internationalized their currencies since the early 1970s. The Republic of Korea is also used for historical comparison as its currency is in the process of being internationalized. Comparisons with

1. See, for example, Prasad and Ye (2012).

the United States are included as a benchmark, although the circumstances surrounding the development of the U.S. dollar as a global currency are unique.
Based on data from the World Bank's *World Development Indicators* (WDI), the
PRC's gross domestic product (GDP) per capita (purchasing power parity [PPP],
current international dollars basis) of US$9,233 in 2012 was at par with that of
the United States in 1977, Germany in 1980, Japan in 1981, and the Republic of
Korea in 1992.[2] As well, the Russian Federation in 2003 and Brazil in 2006 were
at a similar level of GDP per capita (PPP, current international dollars).[3]

The time period of historical comparison can also be based on the time when
the economies "internationalized" their currencies. The exact year that a currency
is internationalized may be subject to interpretation. Frankel (2011) points to
1973 as the start of the rise of the deutsche mark and 1978 for the yen. Takagi
(2009) identifies 1984 as the year Japan was forced to internationalize the yen with
the release of the report by the ad hoc Yen/Dollar Working Group, whose members came from the Japan's Ministry of Finance and the United States' Treasury
Department. Kim and Suh (2011) show that the internationalization of the won
is an ongoing process, with the start date difficult to pinpoint, and propose that
2001 be used as an arbitrary benchmark, since several liberalization measures were
approved that year.. The PRC's income level in 2012 is lower than Japan's was in
1984 (US$12,000) and the Republic of Korea's in 2001 (US$18,000), but higher
than Germany's in the early 1970s (below US$5,000).[4]

We shall not only discuss the PRC's financial system, market structure, and
characteristics but also make some inferences regarding renminbi internationalization. In the next section we discuss the depth of the PRC's financial system—
the size of its financial institutions and markets. Money markets and other
emerging financial markets are not included in the discussion of the PRC's
financial depth, because it is difficult to compare these markets internationally.
In the following section we examine the PRC bond market and after that, the
PRC stock market. Then we turn our attention to foreign participation in the
PRC's securities markets and provide an overview of the money market and
some emerging markets in the PRC. Finally, we explore the main obstacles to
further deepening and development of the PRC's financial markets for renminbi
internationalization.

2. Data for Germany do not include the German Democratic Republic (East Germany) up to
1990; data after 1991 refer to the unified Germany.
3. All GDP per capita (PPP, current international dollars) figures are from *World Development
Indicators*, World Bank (accessed October 17, 2013).
4. Data for GDP per capita for Germany at PPP, current international dollars, are not available
prior to 1980. Using current U.S. dollars, Germany's GDP per capita rose from $2,672 in 1970 to
$4,884 in 1973 and $11,746 in 1980. Even adjusting for PPP, GDP per capita of Germany in 1973
is clearly lower than the PRC's in 2012, using current international dollars.

The Depth of the People's Republic of China's Financial System

Since the PRC opened up its economy in the late 1970s, the evolution of its financial system has been shaped by its institutional features. After more than thirty years of transformation, the PRC's financial depth has increased significantly. Yet it is still dominated by big state-owned commercial banks, and business funding is mainly provided by bank lending, with bond and equity markets not well developed. As of the end of 2012, banks provided 54 percent of total domestic financing, which exceeds equity and debt financing combined (figure 9-1).[5] By maintaining low interest rates and directly allocating credit, the financial system has played a critical role in the PRC's growth. Equity and debt financing, although relatively smaller than bank credit, have grown significantly since 2000, yet the government has continued to maintain substantial controls, including controls on entry to the capital markets. The decision by the recent Third Plenum of the Central Committee of the Communist Party of China in late 2013 to let the market play a decisive role in allocating resources, including capital, indicates that the authorities are determined to reform the financial system.[6] As a result, the PRC's financial sector may start to transform again, much more significantly than it has since the economy opened up.

The absolute size of the PRC's financial system is already the fourth largest in the world, after those of the United States, the eurozone, and Japan (figure 9-2). Excluding bank lending, the PRC's capital markets are in fifth place, after those of the United States, the eurozone, Japan, and the United Kingdom. The PRC's domestic financial system seems big enough to support an international currency. Yet even though market size matters, more important for a currency to be accepted internationally are confidence, convenience, ease, and costs. The PRC's financial sector as compared with the size of the economy is deeper than the depth of some major emerging economies such as Brazil, India, and Indonesia, but it is shallower than the depth of developed economies and such emerging economies as Thailand, South Africa, and Malaysia (figure 9-3).

Comparing the depth of the PRC's financial sector with that of developed countries at a similar stage of development, the PRC's financial sector in 2012 was deeper than Germany's in the late 1980s and the Republic of Korea's in the early 1990s (figure 9-4). The PRC was on par with Japan in the early 1980s. However, if the "currency internationalization" year is used as a benchmark, the PRC's financial sector was relatively larger than Germany's in 1973, was on par with the Republic of Korea's in 2001, but lags behind Japan's in 1984. Excluding bank lending, the

---

5. The surge in stock market capitalization in 2007 was largely due to the rise in stock prices by 200 percent in that year.

6. *China Daily*, "Party Sets Course for Next Decade," November 16, 2013.

Figure 9-1. *Financial Depth of the People's Republic of China*

Percent of GDP

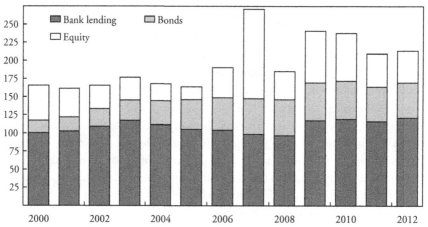

Source: Authors' calculations, using data from CEIC (www.ceicdata.com) and Asian Bonds Online (http://asianbondsonline.adb.org).

Figure 9-2. *The Top Six Financial Sector and Capital Markets as of 2012*[a]

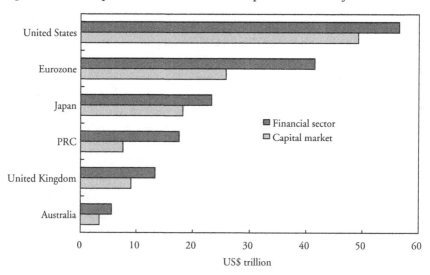

US$ trillion

Source: Authors' calculations, using data from CEIC (www.ceicdata.com); Asian Bonds Online (http://asianbondsonline.adb.org); Bank for International Settlements (www.bis.org); World Federation of Exchanges (www.world-exchanges.org); and national sources (Bank of England, Bank of Japan, European Central Bank, People's Bank of China, Reserve Bank of Australia, and United States Federal Reserve Board).

a. Capital market = the sum of stock market capitalization and bonds outstanding. Financial sector = the sum of capital market and bank lending.

Figure 9-3. *Financial Depth, 2012*

Percent of GDP

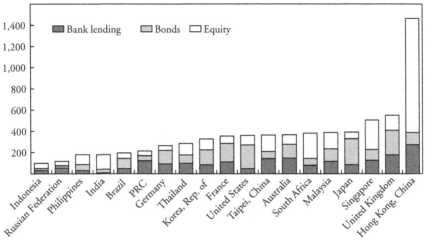

Source: Authors' calculations, using data from CEIC (www.ceicdata.com); Asian Bonds Online (http://asianbondsonline.adb.org; Bank for International Settlements (www.bis.org; World Federation of Exchanges (www.world-exchanges.org; International Monetary Fund, World Economic Outlook Database (www.imf.org).

PRC's capital markets as a ratio to GDP were smaller than Germany's, Japan's, and the Republic of Korea's in the years when their currencies started to internationalize. Given that the economies need increasingly more financing now than they did decades ago as a result of globalization and specialization, the PRC's financial sector appears not yet deep enough to support currency internationalization. The financial sector is one of the few important sectors in the PRC that are not as open and liberalized as the rest of the economy. The shallow financial sector is a major obstacle to renminbi internationalization.

The PRC's financial sector is dominated by banks. The share of bank lending in domestic financing is the highest among major economies and is higher than in other emerging economies at a similar stage of development. Furthermore, central and local government agencies and large state-owned entities have maintained significant shareholdings and interests in most commercial banks (Martin 2012). Although foreign investors have established a significant presence as strategic investors in the PRC's major financial firms, particularly commercial banks, foreign investments usually remain limited to 25 percent of the firm's total shares, and in most cases do not play a management role (Herd, Pigott, and Hill 2010). Bank and public sector dominance may help currency internationalization in the short run, since banks facilitate the use of renminbi in trade settlements, and banks can also help channel foreign capital flows to the PRC economy through their vast networks. However, indirect financing through banks is more restrictive and

Figure 9-4. *Financial Depth, Historical Comparison*

Percent of GDP

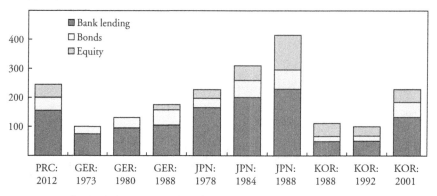

Source: Authors' calculations, using data from CEIC (www.ceicdata.com); Asian Bonds Online (http://asianbondsonline.adb.org); World Bank, World Development Indicators (http://data.worldbank. org/data-catalog/world-development-indicators); Bank of Korea (http://ecos.bok.or.kr/EIndex_en.jsp).
   GER = Germany; JPN = Japan; KOR = Republic of Korea.

expensive than direct financing through bonds and equities. Bonds and equities will be more attractive to foreign investors, and so in the long run, capital markets are much more important than banks to currency internationalization.

The People's Republic of China's Bond Market

In general, bond market development is more important for currency internationalization than the stock market. Given uncertain future earnings and the possibility of bankruptcy, equities are more risky than bonds, and therefore their prices are more volatile than those of bonds. Moreover, the participation of the public sector (government and other public agencies) in the bond market—but usually not in the stock market—anchors the bond market by providing a variety of assets to suit different investor preferences, and extra liquidity to ease market trading. These factors are true for domestic and foreign investors. By offering cheaper financing, bonds are also attractive to issuers.

   Since the 1990s the PRC's bond market has grown from being almost nonexistent to becoming one of the largest in the world. As the PRC is promoting renminbi internationalization while maintaining capital controls, an offshore renminbi-denominated bond market has also emerged. Yet in 2012, the PRC's bond and equity markets were the same size, whereas in international-currency-issuing economies, such as the eurozone, Japan, and the United States, bond markets are significantly larger than equity markets.

   The domestic bond market grew by around 40 percent annually from 2002 to 2008, before slowing to less than 20 percent annually from 2009 to 2011. The

Figure 9-5. Bonds Outstanding, 2012[a]

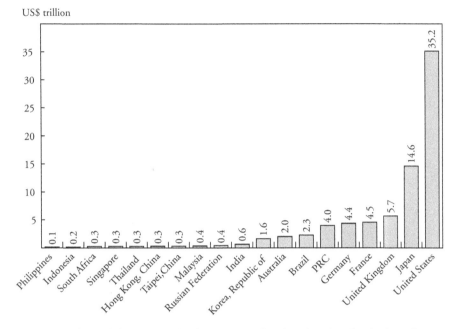

US$ trillion

Source: Authors' calculations, using data from Asian Bonds Online (http://asianbondsonline.adb.org; Bank for International Settlements (www.bis.org).

a.Outstanding bonds is the sum of local-currency- and foreign-currency- denominated bonds from Asian Bonds Online (PRC; Hong Kong, China; Indonesia; Republic of Korea; Malaysia; Philippines; Singapore; and Thailand), the sum of domestic and international debt securities from Bank for International Settlements (Brazil, India, Japan, and Taipei,China), or the total debt securities from Bank for International Settlements (Australia, France, Germany, Russian Federation, United Kingdom, and United States).

PRC has developed a large and increasingly diverse bond market that includes both public and private debt. As of December 2012, the amount of outstanding local currency bonds reached CNY24.6 trillion (US$4 trillion), which is about 48 percent of GDP. In dollar terms, the PRC's bond market is already the sixth largest in the world, yet it still lags behind economies with major international currencies (figure 9-5). As a percentage of GDP, the PRC's bond market is modest, compared not only to those with international currencies but also to those of many emerging economies such as South Africa, Thailand, Brazil, and Malaysia (figure 9-6).[7]

The depth of the PRC's bond market is similar to that of economies at similar levels of income, such as Japan in 1981 and Brazil in 2006 (figure 9-7), but deeper than that in the Republic of Korea. But if the currency internationalization year

7. For the development of the PRC's bond market, see, for example, Asia-Pacific Finance and Development Center and Asian Development Bank (2010) and Bae (2012). The bond market statistics used in this paper are from Asian Development Bank (2013).

Figure 9-6. *Bonds Outstanding as Percentage of GDP, 2012*[a]

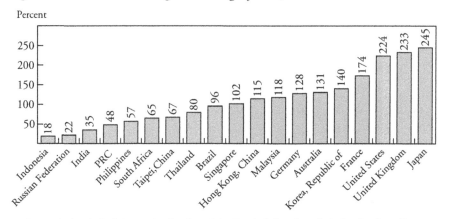

Percent

Source: Authors' calculations, using data from Asian Bonds Online (http://asianbondsonline.adb.org); Bank for International Settlements (www.bis.org); International Monetary Fund, World Economic Outlook Database (www.imf.org).

a. Outstanding bonds refer to sum of local-currency- and foreign-currency-denominated bonds from Asian Bonds Online (PRC, Indonesia, Republic of Korea, Malaysia, Philippines, Singapore, Thailand, and Hong Kong, China), sum of domestic and international debt securities from BIS (Brazil, India, Japan, and Taipei,China), or total debt securities from BIS (Australia, France, Germany, Russian Federation, United Kingdom, and United States).

Figure 9-7. *Bonds Outstanding and GDP per Capita*[a]

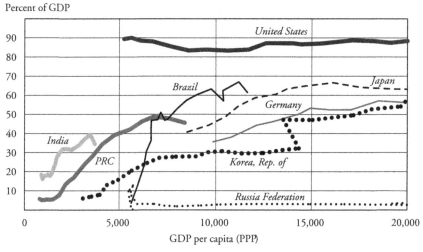

Percent of GDP

Source: Authors' calculations, using data from Asian Bonds Online (http://asianbondsonline.adb.org); Bank of Korea (http://ecos.bok.or.kr/EIndex_en.jsp); CEIC (www.ceicdata.com); United States Federal Reserve Board (www.federalreserve.gov); World Bank, World Development Indicators (http://data.worldbank.org).

a. For the United States, outstanding liabilities of corporations, the financial sector, and federal, state, and local governments are based on Flow of Funds data from 1970 to 1987.

PPP = purchasing power parity, current.

benchmarks are used, the PRC's bond market as a ratio to GDP is much smaller than that of Japan in 1984 and of the Republic of Korea in 2001, though bigger than Germany's in 1973. The U.S. bond market was more advanced, even in the earlier years of its economic development, with the bond market at about 40 percent of GDP in the early 1930s. Although the development of the PRC's bond market is comparable in its stage of economic development to those of Japan and the Republic of Korea, the scale has not reached those countries' depth when they started their currency internationalization. This suggests that the PRC's bond market has some way to go before it can support renminbi internationalization.

The government plays a large role in the PRC's domestic bond market: 73 percent of outstanding local currency bonds are government-issued, valued at US$2.77 trillion in 2012. The remaining 27 percent (US$1.0 trillion) are corporate bonds, which are also dominated by state-owned companies (defined as majority-owned by the government). Government bonds include treasury bonds (issued by the Ministry of Finance), central bank bonds issued by the People's Bank of China (PBOC), and policy bank bonds (issued by three state-owned policy banks and fully guaranteed by the central government).[8] About a third of bonds outstanding are treasury bonds (US$1.3 trillion), while another third are policy bank bonds (US$1.26 trillion). Central bank bonds were relatively small at US$215 billion at the end 2012.

The corporate bond market, on the other hand, can be seen as an extension of the lending activities by commercial banks that dominate this market. In 2012 corporate bonds were mainly composed of middle-term notes (US$400 billion), local corporate bonds, commercial bank bonds, state-owned enterprise (SOE) bonds, and others (figure 9-8).[9] The role of the government in the corporate bond market is significant because the biggest issuers are state-owned enterprises and big commercial banks that are also majority-owned by the government, despite the fact they are listed in the stock markets in the PRC and Hong Kong, China.

There are signs that corporate bonds are expanding faster than government bonds, because the share of treasury and policy bank bonds in total bond issuance has fallen to 57 percent in 2012 from more than 80 percent in 2010 (figure 9-9). The PRC's US$937 billion bond issuance in 2012 was the fifth largest in the world, after those of the United States, France, Japan, and Germany (figure 9-10), but the issuance of corporate bonds in these five economies is usually larger than

8. The three policy banks, the China Development Bank, the Export-Import Bank of China, and the Agricultural Development Bank of China, were created to raise funds and support specific sectors such as infrastructure (China Development Bank), agriculture (Agricultural Development Bank of China), and exports (Export-Import Bank of China).

9. Middle-term notes are issued by nonfinancial corporations in the interbank bond market with maturities ranging from two to ten years. Issuance requirements for middle-term notes are less rigid than for other bonds (Asia-Pacific Finance and Development Center and Asian Development Bank 2010).

Figure 9-8. *PRC's Composition of Local Currency Bonds Outstanding, 2012*

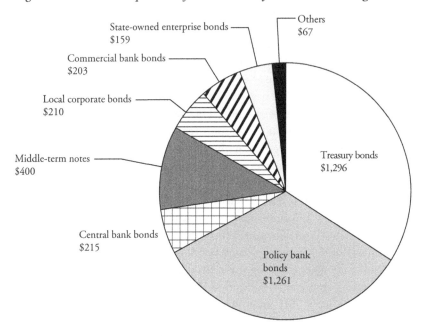

State-owned enterprise bonds
$159

Commercial bank bonds
$203

Local corporate bonds
$210

Middle-term notes
$400

Central bank bonds
$215

Others
$67

Treasury bonds
$1,296

Policy bank
bonds
$1,261

Source: Asian Development Bank (2013).

that of government bonds. From an almost negligible level in 2004, corporate bond issuance accounted for 36 percent of the total bond issuance, reaching US$336 billion in 2012. Yet a small number of issuers dominate the PRC's corporate bond market—the top thirty issuers accounted for 60 percent of the market. As in bonds outstanding, state-owned companies dominate corporate bond issuance. Only seven of the top thirty corporate issuers are not government-owned, and all seven are banks (Asian Development Bank 2013).

Bond investors, too, are not diverse, for commercial banks hold most of the bonds, although insurance companies hold most of the commercial bank bonds. For government bonds, commercial banks hold 75.6 percent of outstanding volume; special members hold 10.5 percent; and insurance and fund institutions and "others" hold the remaining 13.9 percent (figure 9-11).[10] Of the total government bonds, foreign banks hold 1.1 percent. Ownership is more diverse for corporate bonds: commercial banks hold 38.3 percent; fund institutions, 28.5 percent; insurance companies, 18.4 percent; and "others," 13.9 percent. Since most of the

10. Special members include the PBOC, Ministry of Finance, policy banks, the Shanghai and Shenzhen stock exchanges, and other government regulatory and financial institutions. "Others" include exchanges, credit cooperative banks, securities companies, non-bank financial institutions, nonfinancial institutions, and individuals.

Figure 9-9. *Composition of the PRC's Local Currency Bonds Issuance, 2012*

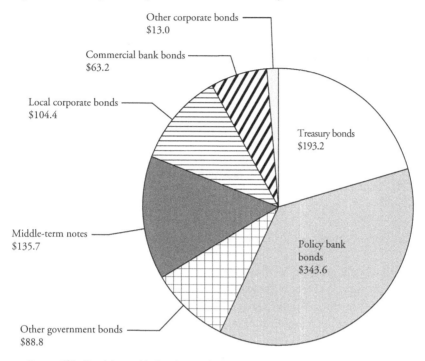

Other corporate bonds
$13.0

Commercial bank bonds
$63.2

Local corporate bonds
$104.4

Treasury bonds
$193.2

Middle-term notes
$135.7

Policy bank
bonds
$343.6

Other government bonds
$88.8

Source: ChinaBond (www.chinabond.com.cn).

Figure 9-10. *Government and Corporate Bonds Issuance as Percent of GDP, 2012*

Percent of GDP

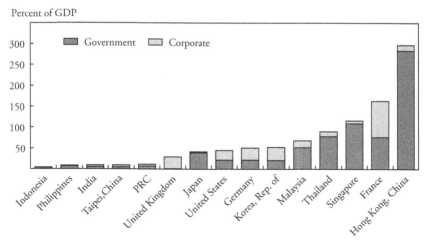

Source: Authors' calculations, using data from CEIC (www.ceicdata.com); Asian Bonds Online (http://asianbondsonline.adb.org); Bank for International Settlements (www.bis.org); International Monetary Fund, World Economic Outlook Database (www.imf.org).

Figure 9-11. *Investor Profile of Bond Holders in the PRC, 2012*

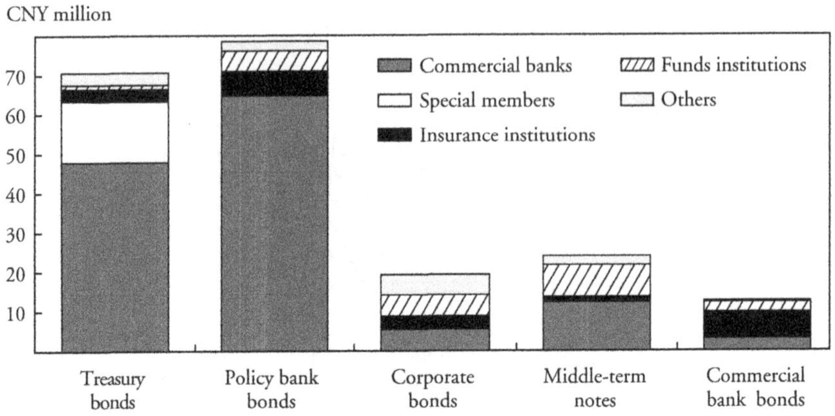

CNY million

Source: Authors' calculations, using data from ChinaBond (www.chinabond.com.cn).

commercial banks are government-owned, the government is in effect lending to itself and its projects through the issuance of bonds.

The disproportionate dominance of the public sector in the domestic bond market in terms of outstanding amount and issuance may actually help renminbi internationalization in the short term. This is because public sector bonds are safer as a result of explicit or implicit guarantees from the government. Public sector bonds are also less diverse because they have fewer issuers than corporate bonds. Given the PRC's weaker bond market infrastructure, particularly lacking in creditable rating agencies, public sector bonds are more attractive to foreign investors, and foreign central banks tend to hold such bonds as foreign exchange reserves. However, there is a limit to the volume of bonds that the public sector can issue, and without corporate bonds the development of the PRC's domestic bond market would be constrained. A key to increasing the use of the renminbi internationally is to facilitate the holding of renminbi-denominated assets by foreign investors, and deepening and broadening the PRC's corporate bond market is essential in creating these assets.

Although trading in the PRC's bond market has been increasing since 2000, it is not as active as bond markets in developed economies.[11] Based on the limited data from other countries, bond market turnover in the PRC is much lower than

11. The PRC's domestic bonds are traded mainly in the interbank bond market (or the over-the-counter market) and the exchange market. Regulated by the PBOC, the over-the-counter market is the main market where more than 90 percent of bond transactions occur. It is quota-driven where major institutional investors trade bonds; mainly treasury bonds, policy bank bonds, middle-term notes, and commercial bank bonds. The over-the-counter market is transparent, for bond transactions are registered and settled centrally (www.chinabond.com.cn). The exchange market, on the other hand, is regulated by the China Securities Regulatory Commission. Listed company corporate bonds are traded in the exchange market where small- and medium-sized institutional investors and

Figure 9-12. *Bond Market Turnover Ratio*[a]

Percent

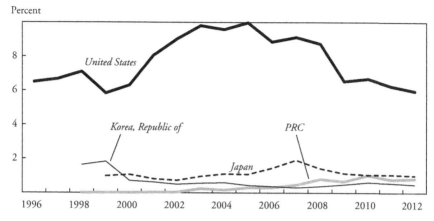

Source: Authors' calculations, using data from the Securities Industry and Financial Markets Association (www.sifma.org); Asian Bonds Online (http://asianbondsonline.adb.org).

a. Annual U.S. market turnover ratio is the sum of treasuries, municipal bonds, corporate debt, agency mortgage-backed securities, non-agency mortgage-backed securities, asset-backed securities, and federal agency securities. Market turnover ratios for the PRC, Japan, and the Republic of Korea refer to the sum of government and corporate bonds. Data started in 1999 for Japan and 1998 for the Republic of Korea and the PRC.

in the United States (figure 9-12). The lower level can be explained by the less diversified investor profile as well as the dominance of commercial banks in the bond markets. Yet the current level of bond market turnover in the PRC is also lower than, but not far from, the levels of Japan and the Republic of Korea in the earlier years when they started to internationalize their currencies. The commercial banks dominated the bond markets in Japan and the Republic of Korea in the 1990s.

The turnover ratio (defined as the value of bonds sold or purchased within the year divided by the total bonds outstanding by the end of the year) for the PRC's government bonds was at 2.7 in 2012, lower than those of the economies with international currencies, though on par with or higher than those of other developing economies (table 9-1). The turnover for U.S. government bonds was the highest in 2012, reflecting a highly liquid market. The volume of bonds bought or sold in secondary markets in other developed economies (including the Republic of Korea) is more than three times outstanding volumes. However, the turnover ratio for the PRC corporate bonds was higher than that of government bonds and those in developed economies, including the United States, with its large and liquid corporate bond markets. Compared to government bonds, corporate bonds

---

individuals trade bonds through the concentrated matchmaking method. Until July 2012, qualified foreign institutional investors (QFII) were only allowed access to the smaller exchange market.

Table 9-1. *Government and Corporate Bond Turnover, 2012*[a]

Economy	Government			Corporate		
	Amount outstanding (US$ billion)	Turnover (US$ billion)	Turnover ratio	Amount outstanding (US$ billion)	Turnover (US$ billion)	Turnover ratio
Newly industrialized economies						
Hong Kong, China	93	679	7.29	83	51	0.61
Korea, Republic of	538	2,216	4.12	833	500	0.60
Singapore	115	267	2.33	178	n.a.	n.a.
Taipei,China	167	60	0.36	89	64	0.72
ASEAN-4[b]						
Indonesia	87	106	1.22	19	9	0.45
Malaysia	192	476	2.48	127	53	0.41
Philippines	78	154	1.97	18	n.a.	n.a.
Thailand	214	622	2.91	55	13	0.24
BRICS						
Brazil	1,436	n.a.	n.a.	857	n.a.	n.a.
Russian Federation	436	n.a.	n.a.	157	n.a.	n.a.
India	641	1,736	2.71	227	127	0.56
China, People's Rep. of	2,725	7,356	2.70	1,176	4,329	3.68
South Africa	251	n.a.	n.a.	100	n.a	n.a
Developed economies						
Australia	493	1,820	3.69	798	613	0.77
France	1,781	n.a.	n.a.	2,484	n.a.	n.a.
Germany	2,121	6,902	3.25	2,100	n.a.	n.a.
Japan	11,537	55,040	4.77	1,079	356	0.33
United States	10,921	130,774	11.97	9,088	4,214	0.46
United Kingdom	2,139	7,876	3.68	3,459	n.a.	n.a.

Source: Authors' calculations, using data from CEIC (www.ceicdata.com); Asian Bonds Online (http://asianbondsonline.adb.org); Bank for International Settlements (www.bis.org); Securities Industry and Financial Markets Association (www.sifma.org); Australian Financial Market Association (www.afma.com.au); Gre Tai Securities Market (www.gretai.org.tw); Germany Finance Agency (www.deutsche-finanzagentur.de).

a. Turnover ratio is computed by dividing the annual turnover by the amount outstanding (figures are not available for all countries, for all dimensions). For the United States, "government" refers to treasuries. Other government-related bonds include municipal bonds (turnover ratio of 0.7). "Corporate" refers to corporate debt. Mortgage-related securities have a turnover ratio of 8.7 (outstanding amount of US$8.2 trillion and turnover of US$70.7 trillion). Other corporate-related bonds have a lower turnover ratio: asset-backed securities (0.2) and federal agency securities (1.2).

b. ASEAN = Association of Southeast Asian Nations; ASEAN-4 = Indonesia, Malaysia, the Philippines, and Thailand.

n.a. = not available.

are more diverse in terms of maturity, coupon, default risk, and bond covenants. This diversity tends to lead to corporate bonds' being held until maturity, which leads to low turnover ratios.[12] Government bonds, on the other hand, have much more standardized instruments available, leading to easier trades.

The high turnover for corporate bonds in the PRC does not necessarily mean that the market is liquid. Similar to the investor profile for bond holdings, commercial banks and funds institutions dominate the market for corporate bonds. The corporate bond market, serving mainly as an extension of the commercial banks' lending activities, might become active as banks extend loans. The turnover volume might be inflated, because it is used as one of the criteria for the PBOC's annual evaluation of banks. It is also possible that the corporate bond market turnover may be inflated by banks to circumvent regulations and supervision. Some banks and brokerage firms use bond trades to shift bonds from their balance sheets and to hide the bonds from the scrutiny of regulators trying to control the surge in domestic credit.[13] The government has recently launched investigations of certain bond trading activities that heighten the risks in the fast-growing debt market.

Liquidity in secondary bond markets is better captured by bid-ask spreads. The PRC's bid-ask spread for ten-year government bond yields was relatively stable at four basis points, higher than most developed economies but on par with most emerging economies (figures 9-13a–d). The higher bid-ask spreads reflect the lower level of liquidity of the PRC's secondary government bond market than those in more developed bond markets, which implies that the current level of liquidity in the PRC's bond market may not be attractive to active foreign investors. However, introducing more institutional investors, both domestic and foreign, should enhance liquidity and therefore help renminbi internationalization.

In addition to the domestic bond market, an offshore bond market has also emerged as the PRC has started to internationalize its currency. In 2003, offshore renminbi bonds appeared in Hong Kong, China with the formation of offshore settlement infrastructure and personal renminbi banking services. In June 2007, PRC-based financial institutions were officially allowed to issue renminbi bonds in Hong Kong, China. With relatively small bond offerings (averaging CNY2 billion) and short maturities (2.4 years on average), these offshore renminbi bonds were commonly called "dim sum bonds." Dim sum bonds were assigned the CNH code to distinguish them from the onshore bond market, which uses the CNY

12. An exception to this low turnover for corporate bonds is the mortgage-backed securities in the United States. Figures from the Securities Industry and Financial Markets Association show that with an outstanding amount of US$8.2 trillion and turnover of US$70.7 trillion, the turnover ratio was 8.7 in 2012. Mortgage-backed securities are guaranteed explicitly or implicitly by the U.S. government through the nationalized mortgage firms (Vickery and Wright 2013).

13. See news reports, such as L. Wei, "China Probe Focuses on Trading of Bonds," *Wall Street Journal*, April 24, 2013.

Figure 9-13a. *Bid-Ask Spreads of Generic Ten-Year Government Bond Yields in the PRC and Newly Industrialized Economies*

Basis points

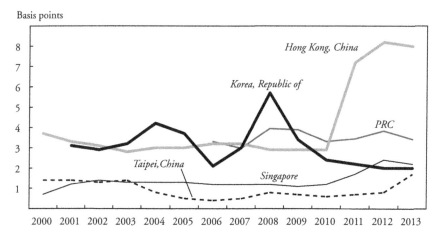

Source: Authors' calculations, using data from Bloomberg (www.bloomberg.com).

Figure 9-13b. *Bid-Ask Spreads of Generic Ten-Year Government Bond Yields among ASEAN-4*

Basis points

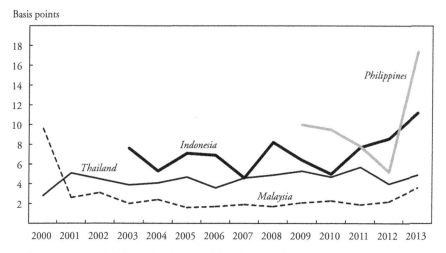

Source: Authors' calculations, using data from Bloomberg (www.bloomberg.com).

Figure 9-13c. *Bid-Ask Spreads of Generic Ten-Year Government Bond Yields in the BRICS*

Basis points

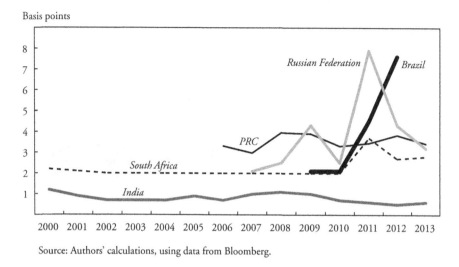

Source: Authors' calculations, using data from Bloomberg.

Figure 9-13d. *Bid-Ask Spreads of Generic Ten-Year Government Bond Yields in Developed Economies*

Basis points

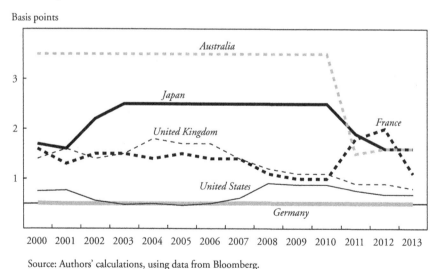

Source: Authors' calculations, using data from Bloomberg.

Figure 9-14. *Dim Sum Bonds (CNH) Outstanding, by Issuer, 2007–13*[a]

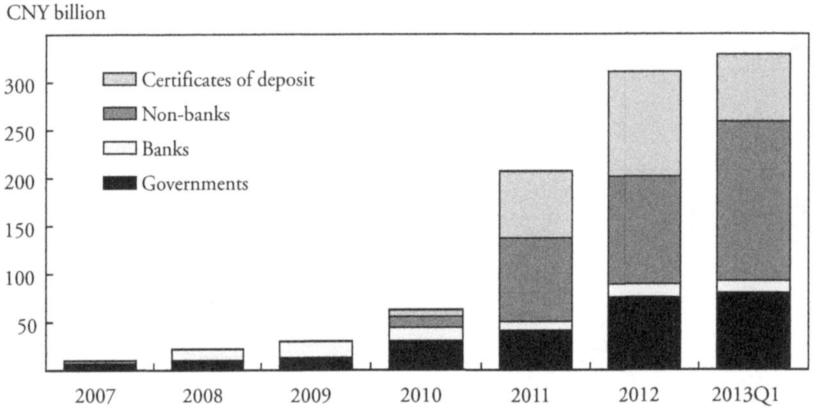

CNY billion

Source: Hong Kong Monetary Authority (www.hkma.gov.hk).
a. Governments include policy banks of the People's Republic of China, such as the China Development Bank.

(yuan) code.[14] The China Development Bank, the biggest of the PRC's three policy banks, issued the first CNH bond, worth CNY5 billion, with a tenor of two years.

Before 2010, growth of the offshore bond market was relatively slow even after the PRC's Ministry of Finance entered the market in October 2009. From CNY10 billion in 2007, outstanding CNH bonds were only CNY30 billion in the second quarter of 2010 (figure 9-14).

Several measures were introduced in 2010 to liberalize and expand the CNH market. In February 2010, nonfinancial corporations were allowed to issue CNH bonds. Certificates of deposit (CDs) were also introduced and all participating banks in Hong Kong, China could issue CDs without prior approval. As short-term debt products, CDs provide additional liquidity and trading activities to the CNH market. In July 2010, major deregulatory measures such as the removal of restrictions on issuer, investor, and amount of bond issuance were introduced. Corporations were also allowed to freely convert renminbi and transfer funds between accounts. These measures boosted offshore bond issuances to CNY42.7 billion in the second half of 2010, larger than the total amount of issuances since 2007. The total outstanding reached CNY62.6 billion by the end of 2010.

Since then, the offshore bond market has continued to expand, with total issuances reaching CNY170 billion in 2011 and CNY219 billion in 2012 (fig-

14. For details of the PRC offshore bond markets, see, for example, Fung, Ko, and Yau (2014) and Craig, Hua, Ng, and Yuen (2013).

Figure 9-15. *Volume of Dim Sum Bonds (CNH) Issuance, by Issuer, 2007–13*[a]

CNY billion

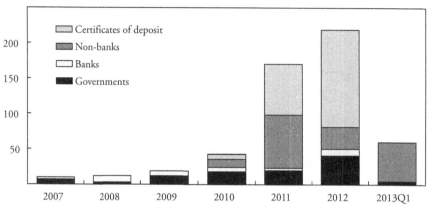

Source: Hong Kong Monetary Authority (www.hkma.gov.hk).
a. Governments include policy banks of the People's Republic of China such as the China Development Bank.

ure 9-15). Non-bank corporations accounted for 44 percent of issuances in 2011 and CDs accounted for 42 percent. In 2012, CDs accounted for 62 percent of issuances and official institutions (mainly the PRC's Ministry of Finance and policy banks) accounted for 18 percent of issuances. In the first quarter of 2013, issuances amounted to CNY60 billion, with CNY55.5 billion (92 percent) issued by non-bank corporations. This pushed the size of the CNH market to CNY330 billion in March 2013. Yet, most issuers are from the PRC and Hong Kong, China. While the amount of dim sum bonds launched by companies with headquarters outside the PRC and Hong Kong, China reached CNY42.5 billion in 2012, up by 40 percent from a year earlier (Hong Kong Monetary Authority 2013), it was less than 20 percent of the total amount of dim sum bonds issued that year.

The CNH bond market, dominated by non-bank corporate bonds, is more liquid than the domestic corporate bond market (figure 9-16). In mid-2011 the quarterly turnover was CNY117 billion, 80 percent of the CNY143 billion outstanding in the secondary market. The quarterly turnover increased to CNY155 billion in the first two quarters of 2012 before dropping to CNY121 billion in the second half. In the first half of 2013, the quarterly turnover grew to an average of CNY173 billion. With the rapid increase in the outstanding amount of dim sum bonds, the quarterly turnover ratio was 0.5 in the first half of 2013.

The PRC's dim sum bond market is shallow and less liquid than more mature offshore bond markets. Demand for CNH bonds is driven primarily by high yields and the expectation of renminbi appreciation. With yields currently falling, ongoing concerns regarding the PRC's economic slowdown, and anticipated tightening

Figure 9-16. *Dim Sum Bonds (CNH) Outstanding and Quarterly Turnover Ratio*[a]

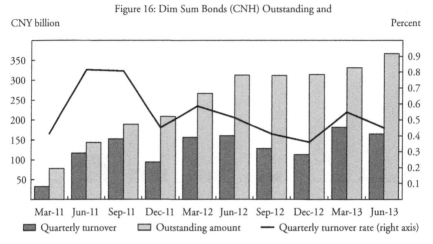

Figure 16: Dim Sum Bonds (CNH) Outstanding and

Quarterly turnover · Outstanding amount · Quarterly turnover rate (right axis)

Source: Authors' calculations, using data from the Hong Kong Monetary Authority (www.hkma. gov.hk).

a. Turnover ratio is computed by dividing the quarterly turnover value by the outstanding amount. Data refer to renminbi-denominated Central Moneymarkets Unit issues in the secondary market (remaining tenor).

of global liquidity, demand for dim sum bonds has waned. One of the problems facing the development of the PRC's offshore bond market is the weak demand for dim sum bonds from long-term investors such as central banks. Barclays Research (2012) reported that dim sum bonds were mainly bought by private banks (35 percent), asset managers (30 percent), and banks (23 percent). Insurance companies bought the remaining 8 percent and others, 4 percent.

Taipei,China is likely to be the second offshore trading center, given the economic and financial links between it and the PRC. In August 2012, the monetary authorities from the PRC and Taipei,China signed a memorandum, "Currency Clearing Cooperation across the Straits," in which the two parties agreed to establish a cross-straits currency clearing mechanism, paving the way for a currency clearing system to help facilitate trade and investment. Singapore is likely to become another offshore center; a renminbi clearing bank was authorized in February 2013. Singapore's strategic location means that it can serve as a hub for renminbi transactions in Southeast Asia. London is hoping to be the first renminbi trading center outside Asia. In April 2012, the first dim sum bond outside Asia was issued by HSBC in London with CNY2 billion worth of bonds and a maturity of three years.

The offshore bond market helps facilitate the international use of renminbi by offering convenience and confidence (Yin-Wong Cheung provides a detailed discussion of this topic in chapter 7 of this volume). The offshore market allows foreign investors to invest in renminbi-denominated bonds without dealing with the laws and regulations of the PRC. It also channels offshore renminbi back to the PRC, increasing the acceptance of renminbi overseas. Nevertheless, there were substantial unexplained arbitrage opportunities between the offshore and onshore bond markets, implying that the offshore market does not function as a close substitute for the domestic bond market (Craig and others 2013). This highlights the important role of capital account liberalization in renminbi internationalization.

The People's Republic of China's Stock Market

The PRC's stock market started in the early 1990s with the establishment of stock exchanges in Shanghai and Shenzhen. Since then the PRC's stock market has grown substantially in terms of issuances, participation, turnover, and liquidity. Although the stock market's size (volume) is modest as a proportion of GDP, it is the second largest in the world (figure 9-17). It would provide a significant class of assets for foreign investors if they were allowed access. Yet like the bond market, it is highly regulated and foreign participation is limited, both of which hamper its development as well as its supporting role in renminbi internationalization.

Three types of shares are issued in the PRC's stock market: normal domestic A-shares; B-shares, traded in foreign currency domestically; and H-shares, denominated in Hong Kong dollars (HK$) issued in the Hong Kong, China market. The peak of A-share issuances appeared in 2010, one year after the PRC's stimulus plan in the wake of the 2008–2009 global financial crisis, when there was strong encouragement of the initial public offering in order to finance investment and thus promote domestic demand. The capital raised from A-share issuances reached CNY887 billion, which pushed the total share issuances to a record high of CNY1.2 trillion in 2010 (figure 9-18). Higher issuing prices in 2007 due to peaking stock prices pushed the issuance amount to unusually high levels. The peak of H-share issuances was in 2006, before the global financial crisis; CNY313 billion was raised and H-shares contributed 73 percent of the total capital raised. The accumulation of the number of shares issued took a leap forward after 2005, with the annual issuance increasing more than five-fold, from 0.6 trillion shares to 3.2 trillion shares in 2012.

Stock market capitalization peaked in 2007 as PRC stock prices reached record levels (figure 9-19). Stock market capitalization of CNY32.7 trillion was 123 percent of GDP in 2007, three times the percentage of the previous year. By 2012, this percentage dropped back to 44.4 percent, close to the level in 2006. The PRC's stock market capitalization can be divided into negotiable and non-negotiable shares. Negotiable shares are the normal exchange-tradable shares, whereas non-negotiable shares are state-owned non-tradable shares. There was a structural shift after the global financial crisis, during which the proportion of the capitalization of non-negotiable shares fell from 63 percent in 2008 to 38 percent

Figure 9-17. *Stock Market Capitalization, 2012*

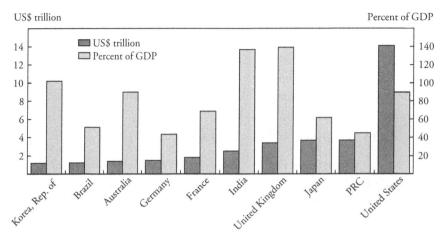

Source: Authors' calculations, using data from CEIC (www.ceicdata.com); World Federation of Exchanges (www.world-exchanges.org).

Figure 9-18. *Stock Market Capital Raised and Share Issuance in the PRC*

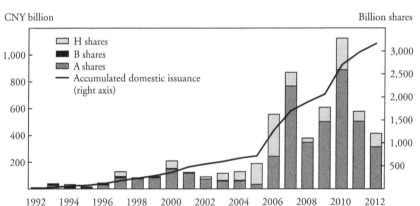

Source: *PRC Securities and Future Statistical Yearbook*, 2012.

in 2009, and 21 percent in 2012. This suggests that the market capitalization of the state-owned non-negotiable shares decreased sharply from its peak of 88 percent of GDP in 2007 to just 9.4 percent in 2012. This is partly due to the fall of stock prices and partly due to non-negotiable shares' becoming negotiable shares after a freeze of a few years.

The PRC's stock market capitalization is larger than other economies at a similar level of development: Japan in the early 1980s, the Republic of Korea in the early 1990s, the Russian Federation in 2003, and Brazil in 2006 (figure 9-20). The

Figure 9-19. *Stock Market Capitalization of the PRC*

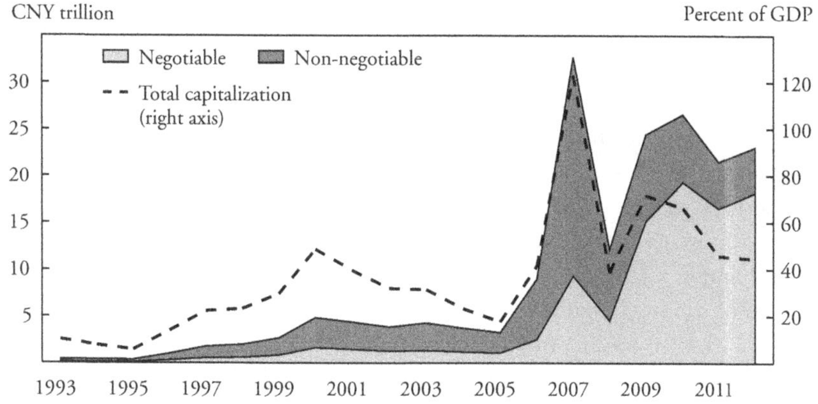

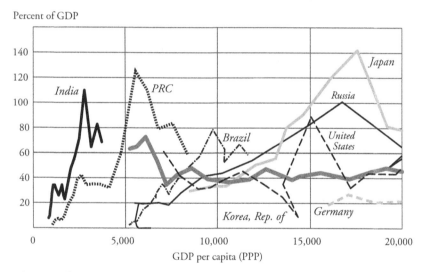

Source: PRC Securities and Future Statistical Yearbook, 2012.

Figure 9-20. *Stock Market Capitalization and GDP per Capita in the PRC*

Source: Authors' calculations, using data from CEIC (www.ceicdata.com); United States Securities and Exchange Commission, *Annual Report* (www.sec.gov); World Bank, World Development Indicators (http://data.worldbank.org).

PPP = purchasing power parity, current.

ratio of the PRC's stock market to GDP is close to that of Japan and the Republic of Korea when they started to internationalize their currencies. Market capitalization in both countries experienced a rapid ascent after they opened their financial markets, although it fluctuated with the business cycle. This suggests that stock markets and currency internationalization may support each other. But currency internationalization may also be linked to the asset bubble in Japan in the late 1980s, when stock market capitalization reached a peak of 142 percent of GDP.

The sizable stock market is attractive to foreign investors and may boost the international use of the renminbi. The A-share market is mostly closed to foreign investment, and this is the reason A-shares are sometimes called the world's last great untapped stock market. As the capital account is gradually being liberalized, foreign investors might hold more renminbi in order to invest in the PRC's stock market. However, the coexistence in dual-listed companies of A- and H-shares, denominated in renminbi and Hong Kong dollars, respectively, might hamper investment in PRC stocks. The differences in the market characteristics of the stock markets of the PRC and Hong Kong, China—such as different market environments, different groups of investors, and the inconvertibility between A- and H-shares—usually leads the A-share and H-share prices of the same company to diverge. The spread between them persists, with A-shares trading at a premium before mid-2010, and at a discount recently. To facilitate investment in PRC stocks, it might be necessary to have H-shares denominated in renminbi.

The turnover ratio of the PRC's stock market is among the highest in the world. Before the 2008–2009 global financial crisis, the turnover ratios of the two main boards in the Shanghai and Shenzhen stock exchanges were fluctuating from as low as 2 to nearly 10 in 2007. As share prices fell from their highest levels, share trading slowed significantly and the turnover ratio declined, with the turnover ratio in the Shanghai Main Board reaching 1.25 in 2011 and 1.02 in 2012 (figure 9-21). In contrast, the setup of the Small and Medium Enterprises Board and later the Growth Enterprise Market ChiNext Board, both based in the Shenzhen Stock Exchange, raised the turnover of the Shenzhen Stock Exchange because the two are much more active; especially the ChiNext Board, which reached a record high turnover ratio of 18 in 2011.

Comparisons with other countries' stock market turnovers yield inconclusive results. Stock market turnover data are available from the World Bank's *World Development Indicators* as far back as 1989. During that year, Germany had the highest turnover rate, which was twice as much as in other countries. After the PRC's stock market was reopened in 1992, turnover ratios were always among the highest in the world (figure 9-22). The high turnover does not mean high liquidity, as the stock markets are heavily regulated with numerous entry barriers. The PRC's stock turnover ratio is similar to that of the Republic of Korea in 1992, which had a similar level of GDP per capita as the PRC does now. It should be noted that turnover ratios peaked for the Republic of Korea in 2000 (as the Republic of Korea started to internationalize its currency in 2001). From 1989 to 2012, turnover ratios for Japan were usually the lowest among the seven economies considered.

The PRC's stock market is more active and more liquid than its bond market, and the participation of retail investors is higher. Yet the stock market, particularly

Figure 9-21. *Stock Market Turnover Ratio in the PRC*

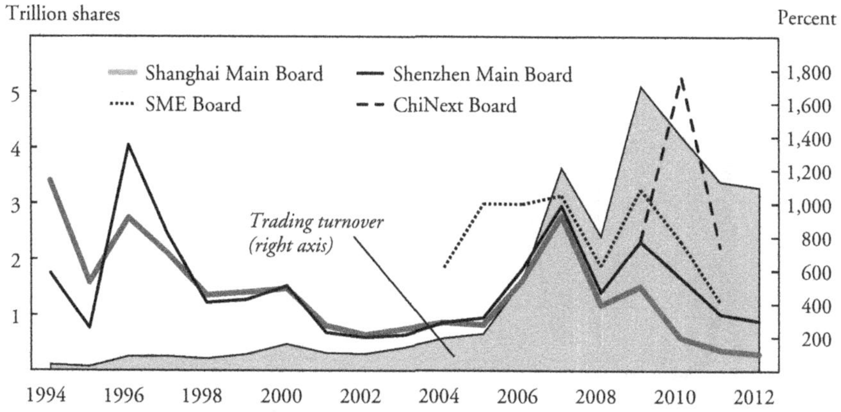

Trillion shares   Percent

Legend:
— Shanghai Main Board   — Shenzhen Main Board
···· SME Board   – – ChiNext Board

Trading turnover (right axis)

Source: *PRC Securities and Future Statistical Yearbook*, 2012.
SME = small and medium enterprise.

the approval of share issuances, is still regulated heavily by the authorities. Before 2000 the PRC adopted a quota system for share issuances in the stock market. A company had to obtain a certain amount of share quotas from the authorities before it was allowed to apply for a public listing or an increase in its shares. In principle, the new post-2000 system allows any company to apply for public listing, and once the China Securities Regulatory Commission (CSRC) approves its application, the company can go ahead with a listing. Although it is an improvement over the previous quota system, the present approval-based system still involves too much government planning, intervention, and regulation. To some extent, the authorities appear to use new listings to regulate share prices by controlling the supply of new shares to the market. When market conditions worsen, the authorities do not approve new listings, which supports share prices by limiting the number of shares available to be traded. When share prices rise too fast, more new listings are approved to create more competition in share prices and drive them down. The authorities' relaxing their control over the stock market would facilitate renminbi internationalization. The recent decision to move to a registration-based system in share issuances is a step in the right direction.

Foreign Participation in the People's Republic of China's Securities Markets

To fulfill its function as a store of value and a medium of exchange, an international currency requires foreign participation in the domestic financial markets. Increasing foreign participation is therefore an important step in currency internationalization (Chinn and Frankel 2007). International experience shows that

Figure 9-22. *Stock Market Turnover Ratio as Percent of GDP per Capita*[a]

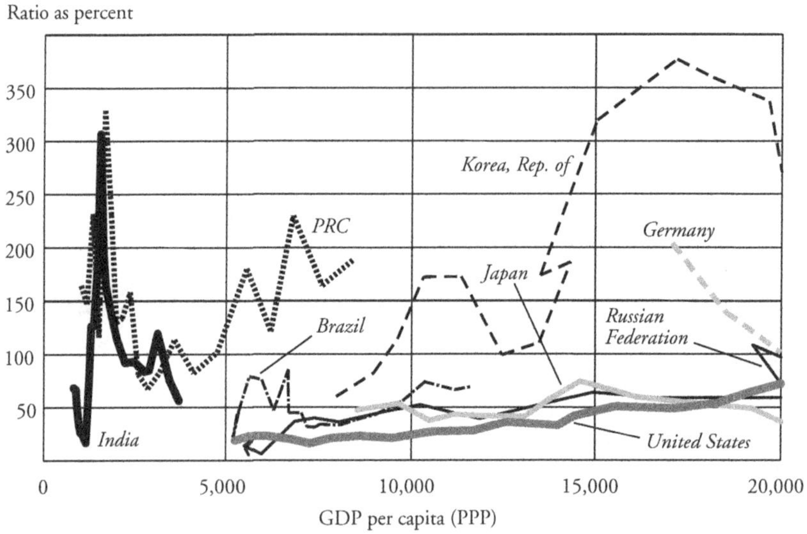

Ratio as percent

GDP per capita (PPP)

Sources: Authors' calculations, using data from CEIC (www.ceicdata.com); Haver Analytics (www. haver.com); United States Securities and Exchange Commission, *Annual Report* (www.sec.gov); World Bank, World Development Indicators (http://data.worldbank.org).

a. United States data are based on New York Stock Exchange data from 1970 to 1987.

PPP = purchasing power parity, current, current.

foreign participation can also boost the growth of the domestic securities markets and enhance liquidity.[15]

Unfortunately, foreign ownership of PRC securities remains negligible. Since 2002 the PRC has launched three programs to facilitate the participation of foreign investors in its securities markets. The first is the Qualified Foreign Institutional Investor (QFII) program, introduced in 2002, which aims to give foreigners limited access to the renminbi-denominated securities markets. QFIIs are allowed to invest in stocks (B-shares excluded) and exchange traded treasury bonds, convertible bonds, corporate bonds, and funds approved by the CSRC. Regarding bond investments, QFIIs were only allowed access to the much smaller and restricted exchange market, where only around 10 percent of transactions occurred. Only in July 2012 did the CSRC open the interbank bond market to QFIIs. As of mid-2013, there were 207 qualified foreign institutional investors with an approved quota of US$43.5 billion, less than 1 percent of the entire bond market. By comparison, for-

15. Caruana (2011) and Cassola and Porter (2011) find that interbank treasury and policy bank bond yields deviate from efficient pricing of shorter maturities, although they are relatively the most efficient in terms of pricing. They suggest that the introduction of foreign participants, including central banks, in the interbank bond market may improve bond market liquidity.

eign ownership of local currency bonds was around 30 percent for Indonesia and Malaysia; 15 percent for Thailand; 10 percent for Japan; and 10 percent for the Republic of Korea (Asian Development Bank 2013). In July 2013, quotas placed under the QFII program were increased from US$80 billion to US$150 billion.

The second program, launched in 2010, is a pilot program to allow access to the interbank bond market for three types of financial institutions: foreign central banks or monetary authorities, clearing banks for renminbi business in Macao, China and Hong Kong, China, and overseas participating banks for renminbi settlement of cross-border trade. These institutions are allowed to use the renminbi to invest in the interbank bond markets.

This program was later expanded to create the third program, Renminbi Qualified Foreign Institutional Investors (RQFII). Also a pilot program, it allows qualified investors to invest in the PRC securities markets using the renminbi from the offshore markets. It was started in late 2011 as a measure to strengthen the position of Hong Kong, China as a major international financial center and support for renminbi internationalization. It had an initial quota of CNY20 billion for RQFIIs to channel renminbi funds raised in Hong Kong, China to invest in the PRC securities markets. RQFII holders may issue public or private funds or other investment products using their RQFII quotas. The new regulation released in March 2013 does not restrict the investments of RQFII funds, though the initial regulations stipulated that bonds had to consist of at least 80 percent of the fund's assets. The RQFII program was extended to Taipei,China, Singapore, and London as these cities joined the renminbi settlement program. As of mid-2013, there were thirty RQFIIs with approved quotas of CNY104.9 billion.

In all three programs, foreign access to the securities markets is still strictly regulated. Liquidity is also hampered by concerns of foreign investors on the ease of repatriating profits from their investments. Although the PRC's bond and stock markets have developed quickly since the 1990s and become sizable world markets, the PRC lacks active and liquid secondary markets and foreign investments in domestic securities needed for vibrant and efficient markets in support of renminbi internationalization.

The People's Republic of China's Money Market and Other Emerging Markets

The PRC's financial system is evolving rapidly with the creation of new financial instruments and the emergence of new markets. New instruments and markets have broadened and deepened the PRC's financial markets, reducing transaction costs and making the markets more efficient. Moreover, they help accelerate renminbi internationalization by creating a vibrant and efficient market foundation.

Money market development is important to renminbi internationalization. In addition to satisfying the economy's short-term financing needs, the money market

Table 9-2. *Basic Indicators of the PRC's Money Market*

	Issuance (CNY billion)		Outstanding Balance (CNY trillion)		Turnover (CNY trillion)	
	2007	2013	2007	2013	2007	2013
Central bank bill	4,072.13	536.20	3.66	0.55	9.21	1.06
Treasury bill	226.15	228.78	n.a.	n.a.	n.a.	n.a.
Commercial paper[a]	493.91	1,885.60	0.32	1.38	1.34	1.70
Bank acceptance	5,867.63	21,267.10[b]	2.44	9.00[b]	15.97[c]	21.30
Discount	...	...	1.21	1.96	n.a.	35.30[b]
Bond repo	...	...	0.76	2.60	44.07	151.98
Interbank lending	...	...	0.13	0.00	10.65	33.29

Sources: Central Depository and Clearing Co. Ltd. Monthly Statistics; Shanghai Clearing House Monthly Statistics; People's Bank of China Monetary Policy Execution Report; *China Financial Yearbook.*
a. 270 to 360 days included.
b. Authors' estimate.
c. Bank acceptance and discount.
n.a. = not available.

is a market of liquidity and can greatly enhance liquidity in the financial system. Liquidity is stored in the money market by investing in money market instruments, and liquidity can also be bought by issuing money market instruments. Therefore money market development is necessary for an international currency, which relies on a liquid and efficient financial market.

The PRC's money market is developing fast, is undergoing fundamental changes, and has become much more active in recent years. The money market mainly relies on secondary markets such as bond repurchases and on an uncollateralized basis such as interbank lending because of the lack of primary market tools (table 9-2). Unlike bank interest rates, yields in the money market are not regulated but determined by market forces. Currently, central bank bills play the role of treasury bills as the PRC's treasuries are dominated by medium- and long-term bonds. The peak of central bank bill issuance of CNY996 billion was in March 2007, when the PBOC countered the record-high foreign exchange inflows early that year by issuing bonds to commercial banks to prevent the expansion of money supply due to the PBOC's purchase of foreign exchange to limit renminbi appreciation, a process called sterilization. Unlike in the United States, in the PRC commercial paper plays only a small role in the money market; even promissory notes from financial institutions are included. As an alternative instrument under the dominance of indirect finance from commercial banks, bank acceptance (BA, mostly eligible bills) also plays an important role in the PRC's money market. The total issuance of BA rose from CNY6 trillion in 2007 to CNY21 trillion in 2013, contributing around 90 percent of the basic instruments issued that year.

Figure 9-23. *The PRC Overnight Interbank Rate, Weighted Monthly Average*

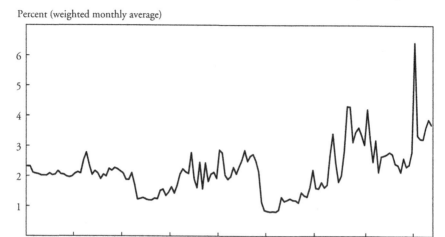

Percent (weighted monthly average)

Source: Haver Analytics (www.haver.com).

The turnover of the PRC's money market grew tenfold in the past ten years, from CNY22.3 trillion in 2003 to CNY253 trillion in 2013, with interbank lending, bank acceptance and discount, and bond repurchase contributing the most. The rapid expansion of interbank lending and bond repo was triggered by the launch of one-day repo in January 2006 and the sharp rise of overnight interbank lending from 2007 as many non-bank financial institutions rely on the money market for financing. The launch of the fiscal stimulus after the collapse of Lehman Brothers in 2008 led to a surge in credit in 2009 and 2010 and resulted in a significant expansion of the money market. The active money market is also related to "shadow banking activities," which often rely on wholesale financing through the money market. While exhibiting some seasonal patterns, the money market rates have been rising in the past few years, as the demand for liquidity is increasing (figure 9-23).

As in the capital market, foreign participation in the PRC's money market is also limited. Currently, thirty-eight foreign banks have joined the National Association of Financial Market Institutional Investors. They are qualified to trade in the interbank bond and money markets and authorized to underwrite central bank bills, treasury bills, and later commercial paper. The main impediment for foreign participation in the PRC's interbank money market is the lack of a "recycling mechanism" for the offshore renminbi, since the repatriation of the renminbi in the Hong Kong, China market back to the mainland needs approval from the regulatory authorities on a case-by-case basis. According to the PBOC, the renminbi used to invest in the interbank market should be those from central bank currency swaps, cross-border trade, and investment settlement.

Many new instruments are being introduced to manage liquidity, maturity, and risk, and to boost returns. Some instruments are also aimed to circumvent regulations, interest rate controls, and regulatory requirements. Below is a brief discussion of two of these new instruments—wealth management products (WMPs) and interest rate derivatives—that have increased liquidity in the financial markets and contributed to the development of the PRC's financial sector.

The PRC's commercial banks started to offer WMPs to clients in 2005, sometimes jointly with trust companies. WMPs usually are investments in securities, properties, and loans to new startups and other firms with limited access to formal financing channels and other financial products, such as trust funds. Not subject to deposit rate regulations, WMPs offer higher yields than deposits, and usually are short-term, which is why WMPs became popular immediately after they appeared and took off after 2010. By offering higher returns, a WMP is a de facto liberalization of interest rates. WMPs are thought to be the main element of the PRC's shadow banking system.[16] Although some WMPs are on the bank's balance sheet, WMPs are not as strictly regulated as deposits and lack transparency. Their investments concentrate in properties and other high-risk assets, and therefore increase the systemic risk of the financial system. Official statistics show that WMPs rose from about CNY2 trillion in 2010 to more than CNY10 trillion in late 2013 (figure 9-24), which alarmed authorities because of these products' exposure to the property market.[17] Falling property prices and stalling transactions could bring significant risks, including maturity mismatch, drying up of liquidity, and insolvency to WMPs.

The PRC's interest rate derivative market includes bond forwards, interest rate swaps, and forward interest rate agreements (table 9-3). Before 2009 bond forwards were the main products, but by the end of 2012 the trading turnover of interest swaps had increased six-fold, to CNY2.9 trillion, from CNY461.64 billion in 2009. Furthermore, the average size of the swap agreements also rose steadily, from CNY114 million to CNY139 million. Although the National Association of Financial Institutional Investors announced a plan of issuing interest rate options at the end of 2010, as of 2014 it is still under discussion, and so is relaunching interest rate futures. The authorities are cautious about the derivative

16. The Financial Stability Board (2011, 4–7) defines the shadow banking system as the subset of non-bank credit intermediation where there are (1) developments that increase systemic risk (in particular maturity/liquidity transformation, imperfect credit risk transfer and/or leverage), and/or (2) indications of regulatory arbitrage that is undermining the benefits of financial regulation.

17. Market estimates of wealth management products are much higher. For example, Sang's estimate of CNY13 trillion in mid-2013 was about 24 percent of the PRC's GDP and 9 percent of the total assets of the PRC's banking sector (X. Sang, "Game with PRC's Shadow Banking Sector," *Financial Times* [PRC edition], July 17, 2013).

Figure 9-24. *Wealth Management Products (WMP) of the PRC*

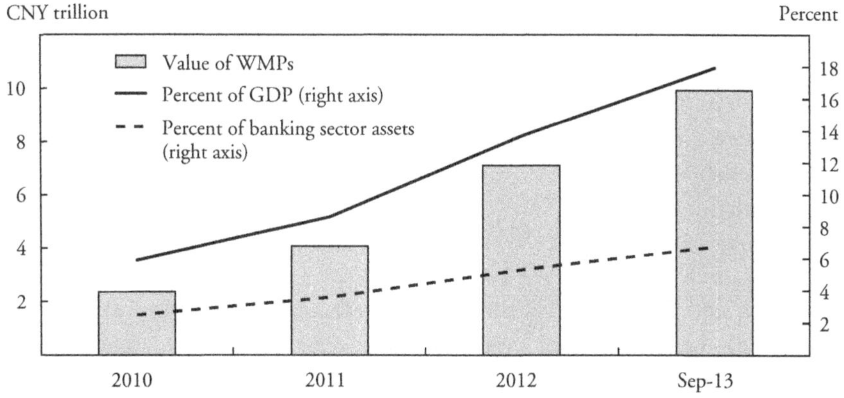

Source: Authors' calculations, using data from CEIC (www.ceicdata.com).

Table 9-3. *Summary of Interest Rate Derivatives*

	Bond forwards		Forward rate agreements		Interest rate swaps	
	Trading amount (no. deals)	Turnover (CNY billion)[a]	Trading amount (no. deals)	Nominal principle (CNY billion)	Trading amount (no. deals)	Nominal principle (CNY billion)
2006	398	66.45	n.a.	n.a.	103	35.57
2007	1,238	251.81	14	1.05	1,978	218.69
2008	1,327	500.55	137	11.36	4,040	412.15
2009	1,599	655.64	27	6.00	4,044	461.64
2010	967	318.34	20	3.35	11,643	1,500.34
2011	436	103.01	3	0.30	20,202	2,675.96
2012	56	16.61	3	0.20	20,945	2,902.14

Source: People's Bank of China, Monetary Policy Analysis Group (2013, table 7).
a. From 2009, the turnover of bond forwards was calculated by the amount of settlement.
n.a. = not available.

markets, and it is expected that the scale of the PRC's interest rate derivative markets will remain more limited than other markets in the near future.

Conclusion

In this chapter we have discussed the status of the PRC's financial markets, including the offshore bond markets, and their liquidity conditions, and compared them with other developed and emerging economies, contemporaneously and historically. The PRC's financial markets have grown rapidly since the 1990s and their financial depth and liquidity have increased dramatically. The PRC's financial depth is similar to those of other economies such as Japan, the Republic of Korea, Brazil, and the Russian Federation when they were at a similar level of economic development as the PRC is now. However, the PRC's financial markets are not as deep and liquid as were Germany's, Japan's, and the Republic of Korea's when they started to internationalize their currencies; and they are shallow and much less liquid than are the financial markets in such economies with international currencies as Germany and Japan. In particular, capital market development lags far behind the international-currency economies, contemporaneously and historically.

We also find that the PRC's financial markets are still reliant on the banking system, with the bond market serving as a mere extension of bank lending activities. The financial system lacks the transparency that would allow foreign investors to hold a substantial amount of renminbi-denominated assets. The involvement of the government in the financial market is unclear and is complicated by the interweaving ownership of state-owned banks and state-owned enterprises that dominate the financial sector.

To support renminbi internationalization, the PRC's financial markets have to be further developed and strengthened. From the market perspective, the PRC's authorities need to further deregulate the financial sector and ensure financial stability. To further deepen the financial markets and develop market liquidity, several major obstacles relevant to renminbi internationalization need to be overcome. The authorities seem determined to remove some of these major obstacles in the coming years, as the Third Plenum decided that the market would play a decisive role in resource allocation.

Regulated interest rates, particularly deposit rates, are hampering financial market development. Market-determined interest rates may be one of the most important preconditions for a well-functioning and developed financial market. The PRC's deposit rates are still subject to ceilings on benchmark rates set by the authorities, despite steady progress in interest rate liberalization in favor of a market-driven system in recent years. The PBOC removed the lending rate floor in July 2013, which makes the benchmark lending rate no longer binding, although banks had already been able to charge higher interest rates against the benchmark rates. Allowing banks to set their own lending rates is an important step toward interest rate liberalization and will help reduce financing costs. Yet without deregulated deposit rates, other interest rates would still be tied to the deposit rates and markets have a limited role in determining interest rates. The authorities have argued that it is essential to have a proper deposit rate pricing mechanism and a deposit insurance scheme in place before the liberalization of deposit rates.

Controls over entry to the capital market remain a major hurdle for further developing market liquidity in the PRC. The stock- and bond-issuing processes in the PRC have been relaxed dramatically since the 1990s. In the 1990s and early 2000s, the central government had an annual plan with quotas for initial public offerings and bond issuances that were allocated to provinces and sectors. The quota system was abolished in 2000. The first amendment of the Securities Law in late 2005 stipulates that securities issuances are subject to approval by the CSRC, which is a ministry-level unit directly under the State Council. The approval process could last several years, and the authorities have also adjusted the approval process to suit market conditions. This has distorted the supply and demand and artificially inflated valuations of new security offerings. The decisions by the Third Plenum promised to turn the current approval-based system of security offerings into a "registration-based" one, thus finally removing the stumbling block.

Restricted entry of private and foreign capital to the financial sector is another factor that hinders deepening financial markets and developing market liquidity. The banking sector is dominated by major state-owned commercial banks (although these banks are listed in the stock exchanges in the PRC and Hong Kong, China). Moreover, foreign financial institutions have had limited market access and domestic institutions are protected from foreign competition. With the state playing a dominating role in the financial sector, the degree of competition in the PRC's financial sector has been low and does not support market development. The recent decision allowing qualified private capital ventures to set up small and medium banks is an encouraging sign of further opening up of the financial sector.

Other factors limiting the development of financial depth and market liquidity are heavily managed exchange rates, the administrative nature of financial regulation and supervision, and interventions by the authorities in financial institutions and markets. The financial sector is considered a "strategic" sector, hence it is subject to many controls and interventions by the authorities, and market forces have not been able to play the role that they could. Financial deepening and market liquidity suffer because these controls and interventions distort incentives and prices as well as the supply of and demand for financial instruments.

The future progress of the PRC's financial markets will increasingly depend on the enactment of broader economic reforms. The PRC authorities have recently decided that the market should play a decisive role in resource allocation: market forces should be allowed to determine financial prices, such as interest rates, exchange rates, and bond yields. Private and foreign capital will be encouraged to enter strategic sectors, including financial services, and the arrival of new entrants will bring more competition, and thus greater efficiency and innovation. These will greatly deepen the financial markets and enhance market liquidity. The new round of economic reforms in the coming years is expected to build a solid market foundation for renminbi internationalization.

References

Asia-Pacific Finance and Development Center and Asian Development Bank. 2010. "The Growth of China's Inter-Bank Corporate Bond Market" (www.afdc.org.cn/UploadFile/20108938829093.pdf).

Asian Development Bank. 2013. *Asia Bond Monitor*. Manila.

Bae, K.-H. 2012. "Determinants of Local Currency Bonds and Foreign Holdings: Implications for Bond Market Development in the People's Republic of China." ADB Working Paper Series on Regional Economic Integration No. 97. Manila: Asian Development Bank.

Barclays Research. 2012. "CNH Market Primer: Casting a Wider Net." Cross Asset Research Report. London: Barclays Capital, September.

Caruana, J. 2011. "Foreign Participation and Bond Market Development in Asia and the Pacific." Closing Remarks at the Bank of Japan–BIS High-Level Seminar on the Development of Regional Capital Markets. Yokohama, Japan, November 20–22 (www.bis.org/speeches/sp111209.pdf).

Cassola, N., and N. Porter. 2011. "Understanding Chinese Bond Yields and Their Role in Monetary Policy." IMF Working Paper WP/11/225. Washington: International Monetary Fund.

Chinn, M., and J. A. Frankel. 2007. "Will the Euro Eventually Surpass the Dollar as Leading International Reserve Currency?" In *Current Account Imbalances: Sustainability and Adjustment*, edited by R. H. Clarida. University of Chicago Press.

Craig, R. S., C. Hua, P. Ng, and R. Yuen. 2013. "Development of the Renminbi Market in Hong Kong SAR: Assessing Onshore-Offshore Market Integration." IMF Working Paper WP/13/268. Washington: International Monetary Fund.

Eichengreen, Barry. 2013. "ADB Distinguished Lecture: Renminbi Internationalization: Tempest in a Teapot?" *Asian Development Review* 30, no. 1: 148–64.

Financial Stability Board. 2011. "Shadow Banking: Scoping the Issues." A Background Note of the Financial Stability Board. Basel: April 12.

Forbes, K. 2009. "Financial Deepening and Global Currency Usage." In *The Euro at Ten: The Next Global Currency?*, edited by J. Pisani-Ferry and S. A. Posen. Washington: Peterson Institute of International Economics.

Frankel, J. A. 2011. "Historical Precedents for Internationalization of the RMB." Center for Geoeconomic Studies and International Institutions and Global Governance Working Paper. New York: Council on Foreign Relations.

Fung, Hung-Gay, Glenn Ko, and Jot Yau. 2014. *Dim Sum Bonds: The Offshore Renminbi (RMB)-Denominated Bonds.* Hoboken, N.J.: Wiley (http://onlinelibrary.wiley.com/doi/10.1002/9781118839591.fmatter/pdf).

Herd, R., C. Pigott, and S. Hill. 2010. "China's Financial Sector Reforms." OECD Economics Department Working Papers No. 747. Paris: OECD Publishing.

Hong Kong Monetary Authority. 2013. "Half-Yearly Monetary and Financial Stability Report." Hong Kong, China: March.

International Monetary Fund. 2011. "Internationalization of Emerging Market Currencies: A Balance between Risks and Rewards." IMF Staff Discussion Note SDN 11/17. Washington: IMF, October 19.

Kim, Kyungsoo, and Young Kyung Suh. 2011. "Dealing with the Benefits and Costs of Internationalization of the Korean Won." BIS Papers 61, pp. 151–71. Basel: Bank for International Settlements, December (www.bis.org/publ/bppdf/bispap61.pdf).

Martin, M. F. 2012. *China's Banking System: Issues for Congress.* Washington: Congressional Research Service.

People's Bank of China, Monetary Policy Analysis Group. 2013. "China Monetary Policy Report, Quarter Four, 2012." Beijing: People's Bank of China, February 6.

Prasad, E., and L. Ye. 2012. *The Renminbi's Role in the Global Monetary System.* Brookings Institution.

Takagi, S. 2009. "Internationalizing the Yen, 1984–2003: Unfinished Agenda or Mission Impossible?" Paper presented at the Bank for International Settlements–Bank of Korea seminar, Currency Internationalization: Lessons from the Global Financial Crisis and Prospects for the Future in Asia and the Pacific. Seoul, March 19–20.

Tavlas, G. 1990. "On the International Use of Currencies: The Case of the Deutsche Mark." IMF Working Paper 90/3. Washington: IMF, January.

Vickery, J., and J. Wright. 2013. "TBA Trading and Liquidity in the Agency MBS Market." *FRBNY Economic Policy Review* 19, no. 1: 1–18.

PART IV

The View from the People's Republic of China

10

Paths to a Reserve Currency: Renminbi Internationalization and Its Implications

YIPING HUANG, DAILI WANG, AND FAN GANG

Around mid-2008 at the height of the global financial crisis, the People's Bank of China (PBOC) made two important decisions with regard to its currency policy: one was to significantly narrow the trading band of the renminbi–U.S. dollar exchange rate and the other was to promote the international use of the renminbi (RMB) in trade settlement, especially trade with neighboring economies. The former was similar to what the PBOC did during the Asian financial crisis to stabilize investors' currency expectations. The latter, however, was likely motivated by the ambition to make the RMB an international currency.

Many policymakers in the People's Republic of China (PRC) believe that the international monetary system dominated by a national currency, the U.S. dollar, is logically inconsistent and unsustainable. The outbreak of the subprime crisis in the United States was evidence of the problem. A possible long-term solution is to create a supranational currency, such as a revamped special drawing right (SDR) of the International Monetary Fund (IMF) (see, for example, Zhou 2009). In the short run, however, the subprime crisis could lead to weakening demand for the U.S. dollar and create room for the RMB to play some kind of international role.

Although policies to internationalize the RMB picked up the pace in late 2008, in fact, the People's Bank of China's planning of this effort started much earlier. In 2006, a study group of the PBOC, the central bank, published an article titled "The Timing, Path and Strategies of RMB Internationalization," in which it argued that "the time has come for promotion of the internationalization of the

RMB" (People's Bank of China Study Group 2006). The study group also suggested that internationalization of the RMB could enhance the PRC's international status and competitiveness and would increase the country's influence in the world economy.

The PRC's strategy of RMB internationalization is sometimes characterized as a two-track approach (Subacchi 2010). The first track aims at increasing the international use of the currency, starting with regional use for trade and investment settlement and establishment of the offshore currency market in Hong Kong, China. The second track tackles the capital account convertibility issue, allowing greater cross-border capital mobility, encouraging holding of RMB assets by nonresidents, and providing instruments for hedging currency risks. Since 2009, the PRC authorities have made significant progress in all these areas and will probably move ahead more rapidly in the coming years.

How likely is it that the RMB will become a global reserve currency? This is the central question we attempt to address in this chapter. To shed light on this subject we tackle four specific issues. First, what has the PRC accomplished so far in terms of RMB internationalization? Second, what are the main obstacles for it to become an international reserve currency? Third, what can the PRC authorities do to promote the international role of the country's currency? And finally, what are the implications for the PRC and the world if the RMB becomes a reserve currency?

What Has the PRC Accomplished So Far?

Chinn and Frankel (2005) provide a good analytical framework for organizing the PRC's policy efforts in internationalizing its currency (see table 10-1). An international currency should possess three important cross-border functions: store of value, medium of exchange, and unit of account. Each of these functions may be further decomposed into public and private purposes. Gao and Yu (2012) confirm that nonresidents have started using the RMB as a vehicle currency in trade and financial settlement; and Li and Liu (2008) sketch a promising future for it to serve as a reserve currency.

Public Sector and Private Sector Uses

Due to the long-existing legal and administrative barriers, the PRC's capital market features apparent segmentation. The nonequivalence of the offshore currency (CNH) market with the official or onshore currency (CNY) generates nonnegligible benefits for foreign investment: whereas investing in the offshore market generates payoffs equivalent to that in most states of the world, investing in the onshore market could yield returns as much as 100 to 150 basis points higher than the global benchmark (Maziad and Kang 2012). As a result, RMB-denominated assets greatly appeal to foreign central banks that seek high-yield yet safe investments to diversify their asset portfolio. In 2010, the PRC began allow-

Table 10-1. *International Use of the Renminbi*

Function	Purpose	Date	Event
Store of value	International reserves (public)	Jul 2012	Indonesia's central bank allowed to invest in the People's Republic of China interbank bond market
		Apr 2013	Reserve Bank of Australia plans to invest 5 percent of its foreign reserves in renminbi
	Currency substitution (private)	Dec 2002	Provisional Measures on Administration of Domestic Securities Investments of Qualified Foreign Institutional Investors
		Feb 2004	Banks in Hong Kong, China allowed to open renminbi deposit accounts
		Jun 2007	First renminbi-denominated bond issued
		Dec 2012	Qianhai cross-border renminbi loan rules published by the People's Bank of China
Medium of exchange	Vehicle currency (public)	n.a.	n.a.
	Invoicing currency (private)	Jul 2009	Pilot program for renminbi settlement of cross-border trade transactions
		Jan 2011	Domestic enterprises allowed to invest renminbi overseas
		Aug 2011	Cross-border trade settlement in renminbi extended to the whole country
Unit of account	Anchor for pegging (public)	n.a.	n.a.
	Denominating currency (private)	n.a.	n.a.

Source: Chinn and Frankel (2005), updated by authors.
n.a. = Not available.

ing foreign central banks to invest directly in its domestic interbank bond market without going through the Qualified Foreign Institutional Investor (QFII) program, which allows foreign investors to buy onshore stocks and bonds under a quota system. On July 23, 2012, Bank Indonesia and the PBOC announced they had reached an agreement allowing the Indonesian central bank to invest in the PRC interbank bond market.

Clearly, foreign central banks' interest in the PRC bond market is driven by at least two considerations. First, most central banks with large foreign exchange reserves struggle with the only major option of investing in the U.S. Treasury market, so the PRC bond market offers a useful option for diversification. This makes sense, especially as the PRC is on the way to becoming a dominant economic power in the world. Second, the PRC bond market offers somewhat higher yields than similar markets in the developed world. It is also helped by the expectation that the onshore currency market could show a longer-term trend of appreciation.

In terms of functioning as a medium of exchange, the PRC started signing currency swap agreements with other countries under the framework of the Chiang Mai Initiative (CMI) following the Asian financial crisis. The purpose of such agreements is to improve future financial stability by functioning as an alternative to the individually accumulated foreign exchange reserves, and to promote trade and investment with these countries. As a result of the PRC's involvement in the buildup of the regional financial architecture, the RMB is used as a vehicle currency via the swap agreements and as a denominating currency in the issuance of Asian bonds under the Asian Bond Fund II scheme.

The PBOC has subsequently also signed other currency swap agreements beyond the CMI framework (table 10-2). For instance, in December 2008, the PRC signed its first swap agreement with the Republic of Korea. This was a serious move by the PRC in response to the widespread financial crisis. Since then, the PRC has signed swap agreements with central banks of nineteen economies. The latest was signed between the PBOC and the Bank of England in late June 2013 for a total of 200 billion yuan. It is possible that France may also follow the United Kingdom (UK) to sign such an agreement with the PRC. According to our count, the total value of currency swap agreements is more than 2.2 trillion yuan.

At the private level, the authorities took various steps to use the RMB for settlement of international trade and investment in order to partially replace traditional invoicing currencies such as the U.S. dollar and yen. In July 2009, the PBOC and other government departments introduced the first pilot program for using RMB in the settlement of cross-border trade. This program aims at facilitating trade and investment for 67,000 enterprises in sixteen provinces. Two years later, in August 2011, the authorities issued a notice extending the geographical coverage of RMB trade settlements to the whole country. The PBOC issued the Administrative Rules on RMB-Denominated Foreign Direct Investment in October 2011 and announced in June 2012 that all PRC companies with an import-export license can use RMB to settle cross-border trade.

RMB settlement has grown very rapidly during the past years. According to PBOC data, international trade and foreign direct investment settled in RMB amounted to 1 trillion yuan (US$161 billion) and 85.4 billion yuan (US$13.7 billion), respectively, during the first quarter of 2013.[1] One caveat needs to be made,

---

1. See People's Bank of China, "Financial Statistics Q1 2013" (www.pbc.gov.cn/publish/english/955/2013/20130417083528793671703/20130417083528793671703_.html).

Table 10-2. *Bilateral Swap Agreements Signed since 2008*

Economy	Date	Amount (CNY billions)	Economy	Date	Amount (CNY billions)
Republic of Korea	Dec 12, 2008	180	Uzbekistan	Apr 19, 2011	0.7
	Oct 26, 2011	360	Mongolia	May 6, 2011	5
Hong Kong, China	Jan 20, 2009	200		Mar 20, 2012	10
	Nov 22, 2011	400	Kazakhstan	Jun 13, 2011	7
Malaysia	Feb 8, 2009	80	Thailand	Dec 22, 2011	70
	Feb 8, 2012	180	Pakistan	Dec 23, 2011	10
Belarus	Mar 11, 2009	20	United Arab Emirates	Jan 17, 2012	35
Indonesia	Mar 23, 2009	100	Turkey	Feb 21, 2012	10
Argentina	Apr 2, 2009	70	Australia	Mar 22, 2012	200
Iceland	Jun 9, 2010	3.5	Ukraine	Jun 26, 2012	15
Singapore	Jul 23, 2010	150	Brazil	Mar 26, 2013	190
	Mar 7, 2013	300	United Kingdom	Jun 22, 2013	200
New Zealand	Apr 18, 2011	25	Total		2,206

Source: People's Bank of China. (www.pbc.gov.cn/publish/huobizhengceersi/3135/index.html).

which is that while RMB settlement has increased exponentially, most cross-border activities are still invoiced in other hard currencies such as U.S. dollars. Therefore, the RMB is not yet being used as a true international currency.

The development of the offshore currency market in Hong Kong, China made a unique contribution in encouraging private nonresident holding of RMB. The offshore market offers a useful laboratory for strengthening RMB outbound circulation and appealing to nonresident investors. As early as 2004, the Hong Kong Monetary Authority launched the RMB Business Scheme, allowing banks in Hong Kong, China to open RMB deposit accounts for individuals and some enterprises. However, the offshore deposit market did not really take off until mid-2010 when new rules were issued to relax restrictions on RMB activities of banks in Hong Kong, China. By March 2013, the total value of CNH deposits had reached 668 billion yuan (US$107 billion), almost 745 times the value of when the market was first established in February 2004 (figure 10-1). In addition, the number of institutions engaging in RMB business has increased to 140 from the original 32, quadrupling within less than 10 years.

Development of an offshore market for RMB-denominated bonds began in mid-2007, when selected mainland banks were permitted for the first time to raise funds by issuing such bonds in Hong Kong, China. The China Development Bank was the first to issue RMB-denominated bonds in Hong Kong, China, in July 2007. Later on, London was selected as another offshore market by some Chinese companies who intended to issue RMB-denominated instruments. The

Figure 10-1. *Renminbi Deposits in Hong Kong, China Offshore Markets, 2004–13*

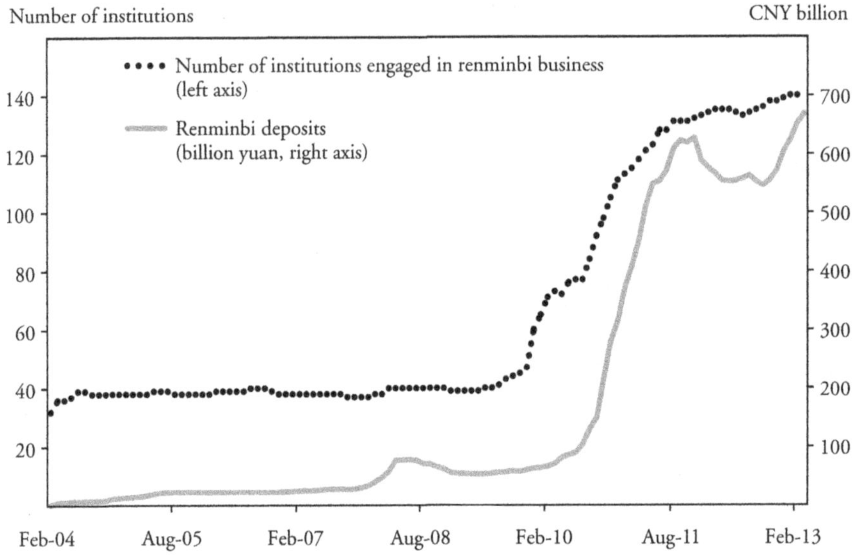

Number of institutions   CNY billion

•••• Number of institutions engaged in renminbi business (left axis)

▬▬▬ Renminbi deposits (billion yuan, right axis)

Source: Hong Kong Monetary Authority.

China Construction Bank became the first PRC bank to issue them in London in November 2012.

In 2010, bond issuance permission was extended to nonfinancial firms and foreign multinationals doing business in the PRC. McDonald's, the well-known fast-food chain, and Caterpillar, the United States–based maker of construction equipment, were in the first group of foreign companies to tap into the "dim sum" bond market. HSBC became the first non–Hong Kong, China institution to issue RMB bonds in London, in April 2012. Despite its short history, the size of the offshore bond market has expanded rapidly since 2012, with continuous relaxation of restrictions imposed by PRC regulators and strong expectations of RMB appreciation.

The international significance of the currency has increased rapidly, and some foreign central banks have started to hold RMB as part of their foreign reserves. However, this activity remains primitive, mainly because the currency is not yet convertible under the capital account, and internationally available RMB-denominated assets remain scarce. One recent significant step occurred in June 2013 when the Reserve Bank of Australia decided to invest $2 billion in RMB, about 5 percent of its foreign reserves, in Chinese securities.

Is the Renminbi Already a De Facto Anchor for Regional Currencies?

Economists have long argued that some fundamental factors are driving implicit or explicit regional currency arrangements in Asia (Kawai 2002). The U.S. dollar has in the past been the most significant anchor currency for the region, although in the last decade of the twentieth century the yen also played an important role for some regional currencies such as the won and the NT dollar. Given the PRC's capital account controls and the inflexibility of the RMB exchange rate, as yet no explicit arrangement links foreign exchange rates to the RMB. However, Ito (2008) suggested that, implicitly, the RMB was probably already serving as one of the anchors for regional currencies.

To assess this possibility, especially with respect to changes over time, we conduct some statistical analyses by applying the framework of Frankel and Wei (1994). Specifically, the following model is estimated:

$$\Delta e \, \frac{AsianCurrency}{SDR} = \alpha_0 + \alpha_1 \Delta e \, \frac{USD}{SDR} + \alpha_1 \Delta e \, \frac{EUR}{SDR} + \alpha_1 \Delta e \, \frac{JPY}{SDR} + \alpha_1 \Delta e \, \frac{CNY}{SDR}.$$

On the left is the dependent variable, which is the daily return of exchange rates of Asian economies. The daily return of the U.S. dollar, the euro, the yen, and the RMB are placed on the right side of the equation as explanatory variables. All the exchange rates are expressed relative to the IMF's SDR, as suggested by Fratzscher and Mehl (2011). Moreover, to ensure that all the factors are exogenous and circumvent the potential multicollinearity arising from the fact that the RMB is to some extent pegged to the U.S. dollar, the RMB factor is orthogonalized with respect to the U.S. dollar factor by regressing the former on the latter and taking the residuals as the new explanatory factor.[2]

All daily data are drawn from the IMF database for the period between January 1, 1999, and June 10, 2013. In the empirical estimation, we use the date of the exchange rate policy reform on July 21, 2005, to divide the whole sample period into two subperiods.

Estimation results using pre-reform data confirm that the exchange rates of all seven Asian currencies are significantly influenced by the U.S. dollar (top half of table 10-3). Among them, the Hong Kong dollar and the ringgit are strict dollar pegs. The Indian rupee, the Indonesian rupiah, and the Korean won are heavily affected by the U.S. dollar with a weight of more than 0.85. The U.S. dollar's influence on the Singapore dollar and the baht, however, is slightly smaller, with a weight of around 0.55 to 0.65. Influences of the yen are noticeably smaller but present in a number of cases, such as the Singapore dollar and the baht. The euro does not have a noticeable effect and the RMB exerts no significant influence on other Asian currencies.

The story changed significantly after the July 2005 exchange rate reform (bottom half of table 10-3). The overall impacts of the U.S. dollar, the yen, and the

---

2. The empirical findings discussed hold when conducting a similar regression on euro and yen. The results are available upon request from the authors.

Table 10-3. *Asian Currency Regimes with Rise of the Renminbi*

Currency	Hong Kong dollar	Rupiah	Indian rupee	Won	Ringgit	Singapore dollar	Baht
Before the renminbi reform (Jan 1, 1999, to Jul 20, 2005)							
U.S. dollar	0.994***	0.858***	0.875***	0.978***	1.000***	0.570***	0.619***
	(0.0162)	(0.0737)	(0.091)	(0.235)	(0.0002)	(0.0954)	(0.177)
Euro	0.0103	0.0309**	0.197	0.0192	−3.83E-05*	−0.0185	−0.0133
	(0.0116)	(0.0144)	(0.136)	(0.0388)	(2.32E-05)	(0.0195)	(0.0354)
Yen	0.00996*	0.0150*	0.243***	0.0317	−5.2E-06	0.171***	0.164***
	(0.00555)	(0.00876)	(0.0732)	(0.0232)	(1.3E-04)	(0.0133)	(0.0231)
Yuan	0.00555	0.00139	1.913	0.144	0.0066	1.452	1.244
	(0.0348)	(0.00155)	(2.111)	(0.515)	(0.00417)	(2.033)	(3.888)
Constant	−4.2E-04	5.06E-05	0.00128	3.03E-04	5.08E-07	0.000133	−5.6E-05
	(2.74E-04)	(1.18E-04)	(1.7E-03)	(4.09E-04)	(3.28E-07)	(1.67E-04)	(3.0E-04)
Observations	1,340	1,205	1,089	1,026	1,348	1,286	1,108
R-squared	0.951	0.738	0.131	0.4	0.99	0.502	0.368
After the reform (Jul 20, 2005, to Jun 10, 2013)							
U.S. dollar	0.966***	0.673***	0.714***	0.919***	0.717***	0.592***	0.836***
	(0.0106)	(0.0725)	(0.104)	(0.114)	(0.0489)	(0.0406)	(0.0369)
Euro	0.00119	0.0677	−0.0216	−0.15	0.0595	0.0792**	−0.0471
	(0.0072)	(0.0608)	(0.0638)	(0.117)	(0.0408)	(0.0342)	(0.0301)
Yen	−0.00215	−0.205***	−0.248***	−0.0186	−0.127***	−0.0593***	−0.00608
	(0.00359)	(0.0253)	(0.0511)	(0.0623)	(0.018)	(0.0151)	(0.0149)
Yuan	0.0403**	0.749***	0.954***	0.526**	1.227***	1.185***	0.444***
	(0.018)	(0.163)	(0.177)	(0.229)	(0.136)	(0.111)	(0.126)
Constant	−4.3E-06	−3.18E-04**	−1.7E-04	−2.9E-04	−5.8E-05	1.94E-05	2.57E-05
	(1.63E-05)	(1.27E-04)	(2.17E-04)	(1.93E-04)	(9.20E-05)	(7.51E-05)	(8.24E-05)
Observations	1,525	1,382	1,453	1,489	1,457	1,526	1,329
R-squared	0.957	0.186	0.09	0.164	0.286	0.26	0.468

Source: International Monetary Fund, International Financial Statistics; CEIC.

* = $p < 10$ percent; ** = $p < 5$ percent; *** = $p < 1$ percent.

euro are similar to those before July 2005. Yet the RMB shows important influences on its neighbors' currencies. Specifically, whereas the U.S. dollar seems to dominate in the case of the Hong Kong dollar, the won, and the baht, the RMB affects the Indian rupee, the Indonesian rupiah, the ringgit, and the Singapore dollar more, although this finding is still slightly odd given that it is not yet fully convertible and the exchange rate is not yet freely floating. It is, nonetheless, consistent with the fact that Asian central banks pay close attention to the movement of the RMB exchange rate.

Recently, however, Kawai and Pontines (2014) challenged the validity of this type of exercise by arguing that there could be a serious multicollinearity problem between the U.S. dollar and RMB exchange rates (as indicated, our analyses first take out the influences of the U.S. dollar exchange rate on the RMB and then use the residual of the RMB exchange rate to estimate its influence on Asian currencies). By proposing and applying a new two-step estimation method, Kawai and Pontines found that although the RMB's influence was on the rise, there was not yet a RMB bloc in East Asia. This issue needs to be explored further.

Summary

Within a relatively short period, the PRC authorities have made meaningful progress in internationalizing the country's currency. The amount of international trade and direct investment settled in RMB is growing very rapidly. RMB deposits have already reached a relatively high level in Hong Kong, China and are growing quickly in other markets. RMB-denominated assets, mainly bonds, are already on offer both in Hong Kong, China and London. In addition to large volumes of currency swap agreements, some foreign central banks have also started holding RMB as part of their foreign exchange reserves. The RMB even exerts important influences on exchange rates of some other Asian currencies.

Assessing such progress in the framework proposed by Chinn and Frankel (2005), we find that RMB internationalization has advanced most remarkably in its use as a medium of exchange for both the public and private sectors. International functions lag most clearly as a unit of account for the private sector and store of value for the public sector. The significant achievements are attributable to two important factors: one is the relative decline of the U.S. dollar following the global financial crisis and consequent new demand for an alternative international currency; and the other is the PRC government's well-planned and well-executed policies. Some even argue that the main driving force behind the impressive growth of the offshore RMB market is the strongly held view that the RMB will inevitably and substantially appreciate against other major currencies. In other words, speculative desire has overwhelmed other fundamental demand, such as risk hedging, in driving the growth of the offshore currency market (Garber 2011).

What Are the Main Obstacles?

Despite the progress the PRC authorities have made in internationalizing the currency, the RMB is not yet an international currency. Is it realistic to expect it to become an international currency in the perceivable future? Academic assessment may lead to very different conclusions. Some may suggest that given that the PRC is already the world's second-largest economy and one of the most important global trading partners, it is only a matter of time before the RMB ascends to international-currency status. Meanwhile, others may argue that it is very hard for the international market to accept the RMB as a global currency because of the PRC's primitive financial markets, unique monetary policy mechanism, capital account controls, and underdeveloped legal system.

Brief Review of International Experiences

What are the main obstacles for the RMB to become an international currency? We try to shed some light on this question. First, we take a brief look at the rise of the U.S. dollar, the deutsche mark, the yen, and the euro to global reserve currency status and draw some simple lessons. Second, we adopt some quantitative methods to identify key determinants of the shares of existing international currencies in global currency reserves. The estimates are then applied to predict the likely shares of the RMB under different sets of assumptions. One key message appears to be clear and consistent: size of gross domestic product (GDP) and size of trade are necessary preconditions for producing international currencies, but on their own they do not suffice: quality of markets, policies, and institutions are by far more important.

During the twentieth century, three national currencies rose to international-currency status: the U.S. dollar in the first half of the century, and the deutsche mark and the yen over the two decades following the 1971–1973 collapse of the Bretton Woods system. The first decade of the twenty-first century witnessed the ascendancy of a supranational currency, the euro. By looking at the circumstances in which each of the currencies became an international currency, we may be able to infer some useful lessons for the internationalization of the RMB.

At the beginning of the twentieth century the pound sterling reigned supreme. Although the United States was already the world's largest economy, its currency was still relatively unimportant in global financial markets. In retrospect, the main reason the U.S. dollar did not rule the world economy before World War I was its lack of a deep, liquid, and open financial market. Another important reason was the absence of a credible central bank, which is often considered a prerequisite for development of financial markets and financial instruments (Frankel 2011). These reasons suggest that although size of the economy is an important condition for creating an international currency, it is far from a sufficient condition.

The situation changed in 1913 when President Woodrow Wilson ratified the establishment of the Federal Reserve; the onset of World War I accelerated the U.S.

Figure 10-2. *Currency Composition of Official Foreign Reserves*

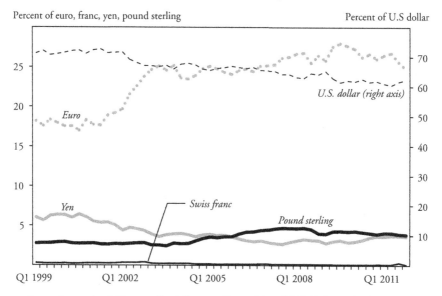

Source: International Monetary Fund Currency Composition of Official Foreign Exchange Reserves database.

dollar's rise. Large-scale wartime lending by the United States to Britain reversed the long-established creditor-debtor relationship, positioning the dollar as a strong global currency. Even though the pound sterling made a slight comeback later in the 1930s after the Great Depression, by 1944 the dollar had sealed its top position through the establishment of the Bretton Woods system. The new position of the U.S. dollar relative to the pound sterling was also clearly reflected in the composition of foreign-owned liquid assets around that time. Since 2002 the dollar's share in international reserves has trended down gradually but has stayed above 60 percent (see figure 10-2).

The deutsche mark emerged from Ludwig Erhard's currency reform in 1948, but the German central bank, the Bundesbank, was not founded until 1957. Despite its relative youth, the mark continued to gain status throughout the 1980s. The main contributor to this was the growing size of the German economy and the impeccable reputation that the Bundesbank established in keeping the value of the mark high. In 1989, the deutsche mark saw its peak performance in the international monetary system when the currency reached almost 20 percent of world foreign exchange reserves. Following that peak, the deutsche mark started a long decline, owing to a slowdown of the economy and the collapse of the Berlin Wall. The Maastricht Treaty, signed in 1992, came to fruition in January 1999 and the deutsche mark, together with the French franc and nine other continental currencies, went out of existence in the historic creation of the euro.

The story of the rise of the yen began as Japan's export-driven economic miracle enabled the country's currency to meet the first criterion for internationalization: Japan's economic weight. After the collapse of the Bretton Woods system in 1973, central banks around the world began to hold yen as a substitute foreign exchange reserve. Nevertheless, since Japanese financial markets remained uncompetitive, highly regulated, and mostly closed to foreigners, the actual extent of yen internationalization was low. International use of the yen accelerated in the late 1980s and the share of world foreign exchange reserves denominated in yen reached its peak at 9 percent in 1991. Since the bursting of the real estate and equity bubbles at the start of the 1990s, the country slowly yet painfully spiraled into a long-lasting recession. By the end of 2003, it had become clear that any further attempt to internationalize the yen would be futile without a fundamental change in the economic might of Japan (Takagi 2011).

At the end of the twentieth century, a supranational regional currency came into existence. The motivation of creating the euro was mainly political: it was deemed an indispensable step toward realizing the ambition of a united Europe. Naturally the euro started with two advantages: it was the home currency for a bloc that resembled the United States in terms of economic scale, and it seemed likely to inherit the credibility of the deutsche mark. As a result, it advanced quickly into the ranks of the top reserve currencies in its first decade and was expected to pose a challenge to the long global supremacy of the greenback.[3]

Experiences of the dollar, deutsche mark, yen, and euro suggest that to assume international status, a currency needs to be supported by at least three key factors: the *scale of the economy*, which leads to the extensiveness of the issuing country's transactional networks (Eichengreen 2005); the *stability of the currency value*, which is believed to be linked to sound macroeconomic fundamentals in the issuing country (Chen, Peng, and Shu 2009); and the *existence of well-developed and open financial markets*, which guarantees the liquidity and convertibility of the currency (Cohen 2009). But these may still not be sufficient. As Helleiner (2008) suggested, confidence and power in a currency may derive not only from economic fundamentals but also from social institutions. Further, as Krugman (1984) noted, there is a kind of circular causation encouraging a leading international currency to become even more prominent over time, since people find benefits in using a currency that is used by others.

Determinants of a Currency's Share of Global Reserves

To verify these suggestions and illustrate the importance of the various factors for RMB internationalization, we apply a quantitative framework to identify the determinants of shares of individual currencies in total global reserve holdings,

---

3. Whether the euro will displace the U.S. dollar as the main international currency is unclear. See Kenen (2002), Chinn and Frankel (2008), and McNamara (2008) for a detailed discussion.

using data compiled for existing reserve currencies. Potential explanatory variables include scale of the economy, stability of the currency, and development of financial markets and social institutions. After estimation of the model using data for existing international reserve currencies, we also carry out a series of counterfactual exercises to identify some of the main obstacles for the RMB in becoming a reserve currency.

Several studies in the literature look at the same question. Previous models, such as those adopted by Chen, Peng, and Shu (2009) and Li and Liu (2008), considered the three traditional economic fundamentals in determining currency shares in global foreign reserve holdings. This is a reasonable exercise, for they reveal the potential that the PRC could realize by looking at only the three basic (quantitative) variables. However, Lee (2010) showed that adding a capital account liberalization index to the model could generate different results. By adding policy and institutional variables to the model, we may be able to see how restrictive these variables are for the PRC's reserve-currency ambition. In addition, empirical results, including policy and institutional variables, may also shed light on where the authorities should direct their key reform efforts.

In our study we intend to include a series of potential determining variables for currency shares in global foreign reserves. We start with the basic model, including only the most commonly used variables, mostly quantitative measures. We then estimate several additional models by including new variables, mostly qualitative or institutional variables. The logic of doing this is simple: most studies examine the RMB's potential share in global foreign reserves by looking only at the size of the PRC economy. Although this is useful but it only goes so far: most economies in the world never reach their potential because of institutional deficiencies. For instance, the currency share will not rise alongside economic growth if the currency is not convertible. By estimating the potentials with the policy and institutional variables, we are able to tell what is practically achievable under the current policy and institutional setting. Comparison of different potential estimates can also tell what can be done to increase the RMB's share in global currency reserves.

The currencies identified in the IMF Currency Composition of Official Foreign Exchange Reserves (COFER) database are the U.S. dollar, euro, pound sterling, yen, Swiss franc, and a category of all other currencies. Because some member countries choose not to report the currency compositions of their foreign reserves, the model takes the currency composition of the *allocated reserves* (about 70 percent of total reserves) as the dependent variable representing the reserve currency share.

We use quarterly data for the period 1999 to 2011 because data before January 1999 do not cover the euro. An economy's GDP and trade share in the world are included to represent the impact of the *scale of the economy.* Inflation differential (vis-à-vis OECD average inflation) and exchange rate volatility (three-year monthly average, national currency vis-à-vis the SDR) are added to the model to capture features of the *stability of the currency*. The stock market capitalization as a share of five major financial centers (New York, London, Tokyo, Euronext, and Zurich) combined and the ratio of such a capitalization level to GDP are derived to reflect the *development of financial markets*. Data on stock market capitalization are obtained from the World Federation of Exchanges, while the others are obtained from the IMF International Financial Statistics and CEIC.

We use currency appreciation to proxy market participants' *implicit demand for the currency*.[4] As suggested by Li and Liu (2008), long-term appreciation would also be helpful for achieving the "store of value" function of an international currency. To measure the extent of capital account liberalization, previous researchers have proposed two distinct approaches. The de jure approach is based on legislative restrictions (Chinn and Ito 2008), while the de facto one is often constructed as the ratio of gross cross-border capital stock to GDP (Lane and Milesi-Ferretti 2007). Since the quarterly data are employed, the more refined de facto index is a better fit. The indicator introduced to describe the overall institution is adopted from *Economic Freedom of the World: 2012 Annual Report* by the Fraser Institute. This is a composite index constructed from forty-two variables in five broad areas: size of government, legal system and property rights, sound money, freedom to trade internationally, and regulation.[5]

The following model specification is adopted in empirical estimation:

$$share_{it} = \alpha_1 + \beta_1 GDP_{it} + \beta_2 Trade_{it} + \beta_3 MktCap_{it} + \beta_4 Inf_{it} + \beta_5 FXV_{it}$$
$$+ \gamma_1 FXA_{it} + \gamma_2 KALib_{it} + \gamma_3 MktGDP_{it} + \gamma_4 Institution_{it} + \gamma_5 share_{i,i-1} + \epsilon_{it},$$

where *GDP* is the country's share in global GDP, *Trade* is the country's share in global trade, *MktCap* is total market capitalization, *Inf* is inflation differential vis-à-vis the OECD average, *FXV* is exchange rate volatility, *FXA* is currency appreciation, *KALib* is capital account liberalization index, *MktGDP* is market capitalization relative to GDP, and *Institution* is the economic freedom index. A one-period lag of the dependent variable is also added to control for the inertia of international currency choice, as suggested by Krugman (1984).[6] Table 10-4 shows some statistical characteristics of the data set.

---

4. Currencies used in the first-stage estimation are all from developed economies (eurozone, Japan, Switzerland, UK, and United States). The movement of the exchange rate is generally determined by market forces.

5. Owing to lack of data, the economic freedom index ends at the end of 2010. For variables that do not explicitly cover the eurozone, data are derived from the GDP-weighted average of euro area countries (officially defined as EA-17: Germany, France, Italy, Netherlands, Belgium, Luxembourg, Ireland, Greece, Spain, Portugal, Austria, Finland, Slovenia, Cyprus, Malta, Slovakia and Estonia).

6. Earlier work, such as Chinn and Frankel (2005), recommended the use of a nonlinear logistic transformation model, but the findings from both the linear and nonlinear models are qualitatively symmetric.

In the empirical estimation, we start with the basic model and then add additional variables in the new estimation (table 10-5 shows models discussed here).[7] The F-statistic and Hausmann test validate a fixed-effects panel regression model. The first column of table 10-5 reports estimation results from our first model, Model 1. This basic model replicates previous exercises such as those by Chinn and Frankel (2005) and Chen, Peng, and Shu (2009). It is not surprising that the size of GDP and of the financial market are very important in determining the currency share in global reserve holdings. However, both inflation and exchange rate volatility are not significant, possibly a consequence of the short sample period, as discussed in Chen, Peng, and Shu (2009). The lag-dependent variable, as expected, has very strong explanatory power.

Model 2 considers the development of financial markets by adding the ratio of financial market capitalization to GDP. This variable tells something about the financial development in a country. We should be clear, however, that it only captures the quantity dimension of financial development, nothing about depth, liquidity, and sophistication of financial markets. Model 3 further includes currency appreciation in the model, which reflects implicit demand for the currency. Model 4 adds the capital account liberalization index, which really is a prerequisite for international currency holding. Finally, Model 5 includes the economic freedom indicator to control the impact of a broad range of policies and institutions.

The general findings are that size matters. A country's GDP and share of world trade play very important roles in determining the share of its currency in global currency reserves. Currency appreciation, capital account liberalization, and economic freedom are also quite important in affecting the currency share. However, coefficient estimates of other variables such as inflation volatility and financial market capitalization are not significant in the estimated models. We suspect that these are mainly results of a data quality problem. For instance, market capitalization is probably not an accurate representative of the actual degree of financial market development. In the chapter appendix we report results from various robustness checks to validate our findings.

Having obtained the results, we then predict the likely share of the RMB in global currency reserves. We assume the share to be zero in the first quarter of 1999 and then apply estimated parameters and actual values of the independent variables for the PRC to predict the RMB's share. Since the share of currency in foreign reserve holdings is non-negative, during the recursive process one should always choose the maximum of zero and the predicted value. The predicted RMB shares at the end of 2011 are 10.1 percent under Model 1, 8.9 percent under Model 2, 5.3 percent under Model 3, 6.8 percent under Model 4, and 2.2 percent under Model 5. In general, the more policy and institutional variables are included

7. The second, third, fourth, and fifth columns of table 10-5 are named as Model 2, Model 3, Model 4 and Model 5, respectively. The reason for giving each model a name is to facilitate simulation comparison with figure 10-3.

Table 10-4. *Data Description for the Major Currencies*

	Share	GDP	Trade	Mkt_Cap	Mkt/GDP	Inf	FXV	FXA	KA Lib.	ECOF
Period average, percent (Q1 1999 to Q4 2011)										
CNY		2.57	6.57	7.34	47.50	0.89	1.38	0.39	79.78	5.854
EUR	23.51	7.62	15.01	14.28	32.36	0.42	1.66	0.12	160.94	7.452
JPY	4.05	3.64	5.35	15.50	74.06	0.36	2.52	0.69	88.88	7.693
CHF	0.19	0.30	1.27	3.41	199.50	0.45	1.98	0.63	271.92	8.266
GBP	3.52	1.62	4.14	12.16	130.13	0.45	1.72	-0.24	246.92	8.263
USD	66.52	38.17	12.66	54.64	97.97	0.79	1.39	-0.13	125.62	8.228
End of period, percent (Q4 2011)										
CNY		9.30	10.50	19.10	31.45	0.74	1.69	2.59	116.10	6.180
EUR	24.70	7.85	11.70	14.39	28.08	0.19	2.48	-2.53	205.45	7.450
JPY	3.60	4.42	4.80	14.95	51.77	0.29	2.76	0.29	120.11	7.650
CHF	0.10	0.41	1.20	4.25	160.46	0.47	3.24	-2.55	311.37	8.110
GBP	3.80	1.50	3.10	12.78	130.20	0.28	2.36	0.84	300.99	7.930
USD	62.30	37.41	10.50	53.63	87.76	0.70	1.79	1.72	162.15	7.760

Correlation matrix

GDP	0.98								
Trade	0.72	0.60							
Mkt_Cap	0.95	0.97	0.58						
Mkt/GDP	0.31	0.12	0.62	-0.12					
Inf	-0.30	-0.18	-0.11	-0.19	-0.09				
FXV	-0.42	-0.28	-0.31	-0.21	0.05	-0.07			
FXA	0.05	0.04	0.03	0.04	0.02	-0.01	0.10		
KA Lib.	0.42	0.26	0.42	0.27	0.67	-0.05	0.13	0.00	
ECOF	0.11	0.28	0.05	0.35	0.60	-0.19	0.15	-0.01	0.56

Sources: International Monetary Fund Currency Composition of Official Foreign Exchange Reserve, International Financial Statistics, and Direction of Trade Statistics; World Bank, World Development Indicators; CEIC data.

GDP = the country's share in global gross domestic product; Trade = the country's share in global trade; Mkt_Cap = total market capitalization; Mkt/GDP = market capitalization relative to GDP; Inf = inflation the differential vis-à-vis the Organization for Economic Cooperation and Development average; FXV = exchange rate volatility; FXA = currency appreciation; KA Lib = capital account liberalization index; ECOF = economic freedom index.

Table 10-5. *Panel Regressions of Determination of Currency Shares*

Explanatory variables	Dependent variable: currency share in global reserves				
	(1)	*(2)*	*(3)*	*(4)*	*(5)*
GDP share	0.145**	0.146**	0.0964*	0.0945*	0.103*
	(0.0576)	(0.0576)	(0.0523)	(0.052)	(0.0523)
Trade share	0.146***	0.156***	0.0975***	0.100**	0.092*
	(0.0491)	(0.051)	(0.046)	(0.0464)	(0.052)
Inflation	-0.0664	-0.0612	-0.0364	-0.0513	-0.0133
	(0.086)	(0.086)	(0.0778)	(0.0776)	(0.0871)
Exchange rate volatility	0.0856	0.0991	0.0378	0.0666	0.121
	(0.0726)	(0.075)	(0.0657)	(0.0677)	(0.0811)
Mkt_Cap	0.0349*	0.0327*	0.0193	0.0248	0.0169
	(0.0203)	(0.0195)	(0.0185)	(0.0186)	(0.0194)
Mkt_Cap/GDP		0.00112	0.00137	0.000802	0.000862
		(0.00156)	(0.0014)	(0.00142)	(0.0014)
Appreciation			0.0673***	0.0672***	0.0674***
			(0.00886)	(0.0088)	(0.0093)
Capital account liberalization				0.00631**	0.00849**
				(0.00311)	(0.0036)
Economic freedom					0.0043*
					(0.0025)
Lag of share	0.898***	0.897***	0.925***	0.907***	0.891***
	(0.0198)	(0.0198)	(0.0182)	(0.0202)	(0.0265)
Constant	-0.0151**	-0.0172***	-0.0093***	-0.0141**	-0.048**
	(0.00355)	(0.00370)	(0.00166)	(0.00698)	(0.0226)
Observation	255	255	255	255	235
R-squared	0.948	0.948	0.958	0.959	0.958

Source: Authors' calculation, based on IMF IFS, IMF COFER, CEIC, and World Federation of Exchanges.
* = $p < 10$ percent; ** = $p < 5$ percent; *** = $p < 1$ percent.

in estimation, the lower the estimated share for the RMB in global currency reserves.

Comparison of these predictions also reinforces one of our important arguments: the predicted potentials simply based on quantitative measures are probably too optimistic (figure 10-3). For instance, if we just look at the PRC's GDP and trade shares in the world, the RMB's share should be around 10 percent. This is possible if all policy and institutions in the PRC are similar to those in the United States and other developed countries. Yet we know this is not so. If we take into account several important policy considerations and institutions, such as capital account liberalization and economic freedom, then the RMB's actual potential share comes down to only around 2 percent. However, we think this last number makes sense because it tells us (1) what the PRC can realistically achieve now and (2) what reform actions the PRC needs to undertake in order to realize the 10 percent potential.

Summary

Based on these analyses we propose three sets of factors that are critical for producing an international currency: (1) economic importance in the world—share of global GDP and trade; (2) openness and depth of financial markets; and (3) credibility of economic and legal systems. Comparing the PRC's situation using these criteria may suggest that even though the RMB's international role is likely to expand in the coming years, it would be difficult for it to become a global reserve currency anytime soon.

The first factor, economic weights, should create more chances of using a country's own currency in international transactions; even though they are important, they are perhaps not the most fundamental factors. The Swiss franc is an international currency, although the size of the Swiss economy is relatively small. Conversely, the U.S. dollar was not a global currency before World War I, even though the U.S. economy was already bigger than the economies of the United Kingdom, Germany, and France combined. In spite of these caveats, the PRC's rising importance in global GDP and trade is making a difference and has already generated some demand for the RMB as a settlement currency. It is not too difficult to imagine that such demand will rise rapidly as the PRC becomes the largest economy in the world over the coming decade.

The second factor, openness and depth of financial markets, determines how easily nonresidents can access the currency, make an investment, liquidate their investment, and hedge the risk. The yen provides a good case. For decades, Japan was the world's second-largest economy, and the size of its financial markets was phenomenal. However, the role of the yen as an international currency peaked in the late 1980s. This was partly because the Japanese economy entered a long period of stagnation, but more fundamentally was due to the fact that the Japanese financial markets are not really open to foreign investors. The PRC, too, with

Figure 10-3. *Counterfactual Exercise—Linear Models*[a]

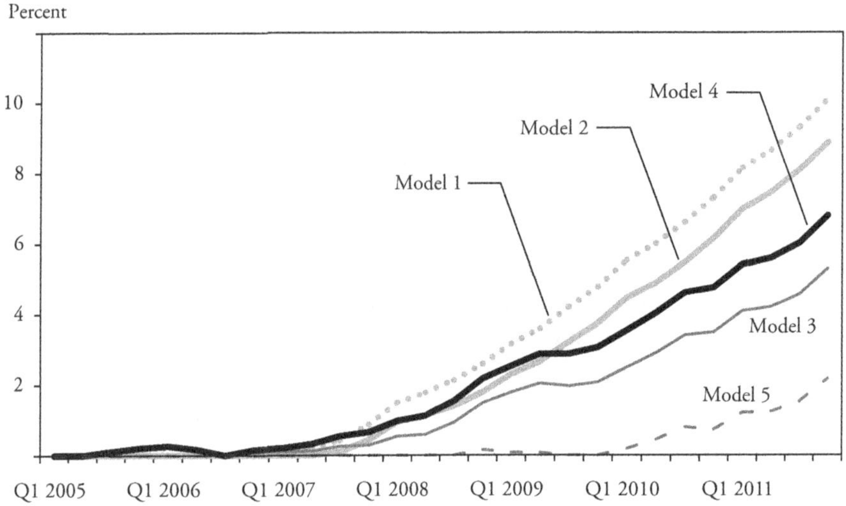

Percent

Source: Authors' calculation.
a. Models 1 to 5 are consistent with the models shown in table 10-2.

its capital account controls and primitive financial markets, lags significantly in this area.

The third factor, credibility of economic and legal systems, increases investor confidence in the currency by supporting currency, financial, economic, and even political stability. It is perhaps no coincidence that all existing global reserve currencies are from developed economies. And the U.S. dollar did not rise to international currency status until after the establishment of the Federal Reserve System. This is probably the most difficult area for the PRC to catch up. The gaps between the PRC and those existing international currency countries in the five categories of the economic freedom index discussed are very wide, especially in the legal system and property rights, sound money, and regulation.

What Needs to Be Done?

The key challenge facing the PBOC and other PRC authorities now is how to raise the RMB's potential share in global reserves from 2 percent identified by Model 5 to 10 percent identified by Model 1 and even higher levels in the future. The main difference between the two model specifications is a set of policy and institutional gaps.

The PBOC has adopted a two-track approach in internationalizing the RMB: one is to promote the international use of the RMB and the other is to liberalize the capital account (People's Bank of China Study Group 2006). We may regard the first track as facilitating nonresidents' use and holding of RMB and the second as creating nonresidents' demand for RMB. The first-track strategies are important because a currency becomes an international currency only if nonresidents use it. The second-track strategies are even more critical: the U.S. dollar has been the global currency mainly because of the strong U.S. economy, its efficient and liquid market, and its sound legal system.

Most of the PRC authorities' recent policy actions are related to the first track. These include use of the RMB in trade and investment settlement, setting up offshore markets, issuance of RMB-denominated securities products overseas, and holding RMB as part of foreign central banks' currency reserves, and so forth. These efforts should continue. The authorities may even take further steps to encourage nonresidents to hold RMB. One such possible step is to add RMB to the IMF's SDR basket and another is to promote intraregional cross-holding of reserve currencies, as proposed by Fan, Wang, and Huang (2013).[8]

The SDR was first established in 1969 as a supplement to the U.S. dollar as a source of international liquidity (Williamson 2009), but it is only an imperfect reserve asset because it does not allow accomplishment of functions such as market intervention and liquidity provision (International Monetary Fund 2011). The SDR basket currently consists of just four major global currencies (table 10-6). Adding the RMB to the basket would not only make it a part of the global reserve assets but also significantly increase its global profile. The IMF was initially reluctant about the idea of including the RMB in the SDR basket but now suggests that "recent reforms that allow nonresidents, including central banks, to hold RMB-denominated deposits . . . could contribute, over time, to resolving some of the technical difficulties in hedging RMB exposure" (International Monetary Fund 2011, 20).

In 2010 Fan, Wang, and Huang (2013) proposed the establishment of an intraregional mechanism for cross-holding of reserve currencies.[9] The key idea is for governments in Asia to reach bilateral agreements to hold each other's currencies as part of their foreign reserves. Weights of such currency holdings may be determined by shares of their bilateral trade in total trade. This arrangement has some similarities to currency swap agreements, which are mainly a crisis response mechanism (although sometimes they are also used as a means to promote trade and investment), whereas cross-reserve holdings are part of regular operations. The new arrangement immediately makes regional currencies available as reserve currencies, opens government bond markets to each other, and also encourages parties involved to monitor others' macroeconomic and policy development.

8. Yiping Huang, "What Likonomics Has to Offer," *China Daily*, July 4, 2013.

9. A version of this chapter was first completed in 2010 as a project report for the PRC Center for International Economic Exchange. It was presented at a joint workshop of the Asian Development Bank Institute and the Center for International Economic Exchange on regional currency cooperation in November 2010.

Table 10-6. *Official Special Drawing Right Weights as Percentage of a Currency Basket*[a]

Currency	1990	1995	1998	2000	2005	2010
U.S. dollar	40	39	39	45	44	41.9
Deutsche mark	21	21				
French franc	11	11				
Euro			32	29	34	37.4
Yen	17	18	8	15	11	9.4
Pound sterling	11	11	11	11	11	11.3
Total	100	100	100	100	100	100.00

Source: International Monetary Fund, Special Drawing Right Statistics.
a. There is no data available for the euro before 1997, and the Deutsche mark and the French franc after 1997.

Our view, however, is that whether or not the RMB can become an international currency will fundamentally be determined by the broadly defined second track of the PBOC. The PRC can encourage nonresidents to hold RMB, but this will be short-lived if the RMB does not possess the essential qualities of an international currency. For instance, the amount of offshore RMB deposits often fluctuates alongside changes in currency expectation. We now discuss some of the important reforms that could improve these three factors.

Economic Importance

So far the hope for the RMB to become an international currency is mainly driven by the rapid rise of the economy. During the first thirty years of economic reform, the PRC maintained an average GDP growth rate of 10 percent. By the end of 2010 it had already surpassed Japan to become the world's second-largest economy. The general expectation is that, if the strong growth momentum continues, the PRC will likely overtake the United States to become the world's largest economy within the next ten years. Growth sustainability should be one of the fundamental factors supporting a rising RMB. The declining international role of the yen in the 1990s as Japan's economy fell into stagnation offers an important lesson for the PRC.

However, the sustainability of the country's growth might be a big question mark. Despite its strong growth performance, economists and officials have long been worried about its growth model. Former Premier Wen Jiabao once pointed out that the PRC growth model is "unstable, unbalanced, uncoordinated and unsustainable."[10] Some of the key structural problems frequently discussed include unusually high investment share of GDP, heavy dependency on resource

10. See *China View* (online newspaper), "Premier: China Confident in Maintaining Economic Growth," March 16, 2007 (http://news.xinhuanet.com/english/2007-03/16/content_5856569.htm).

consumption, large current account surplus, unequal income distribution, and serious pollution. The IMF's latest report on Article IV consultation also confirmed the international community's worry about the PRC's structural problems (International Monetary Fund 2013).

So what lies behind the PRC's growth model, characterized by strong economic growth but serious structural imbalances? One explanation is the so-called "asymmetric liberalization of the market." Product markets have almost been completely liberalized, but distortions in factor markets (for example, labor and capital markets) have remained broad and serious. In general, such policy distortions depressed costs of labor, land, energy, capital, and water; subsidized owners of the endowments (producers, investors, and exporters); and functioned literally at the cost of households. This special mechanism that redistributed income from households to enterprises was the key reason economic growth was unusually strong, but the economic structure became increasingly imbalanced (Huang 2010; Huang and Tao 2010; Huang and Wang 2010).

The good news is that rebalancing of the PRC economy is already under way. There are at least three pieces of evidence supporting this claim (Huang and others 2013): (1) The current account surplus has already narrowed from 10.8 percent of GDP in 2007 to below 3.0 percent in recent years. This is the reason some officials argue that the RMB exchange rate is now close to equilibrium. (2) Recent studies suggest that shares of total and household consumption in GDP started to pick up after 2007 and 2008 (Huang and others 2013). (3) Official estimates of the Gini coefficient point to continued improvement in income distribution among households after 2008.

So far, improvements have been mainly triggered by the rapid rise of wages as a result of the emerging labor shortage problem in the PRC (figure 10-4). Rapidly rising wages squeeze corporate profits and therefore slow production, investment, and export activities. At the same time they also redistribute income back to households from corporations and therefore contribute to faster growth of consumption. However, change of the growth model is only in its nascence and further reforms are necessary to push the PRC's growth model onto a more sustainable path.

Economic policies under the Li Keqiang–led government, the so-called Likonomics, are moving in the right direction. Likonomics is popularly regarded as supported by three pillars: no major stimulus, deleveraging, and structural reforms (Huang 2013). Since late 2012 the government has shown an unusual tolerance for slowing growth, as GDP growth stayed constantly below 8 percent. Although the policymakers are still mindful of downside risks, they take a relatively more relaxed approach toward the growth slowdown as long as it stays close to the new and lower growth potential, evidenced by the robust labor market.

The success or failure of Likonomics will be determined by the outcome of the structural reforms. Policymakers and policy advisers are currently working on proposals for an extended reform agenda that would take in the financial sector, fiscal

Figure 10-4. *Monthly Wages of Migrant Workers in the People's Republic of China, 1978 Prices*[a]

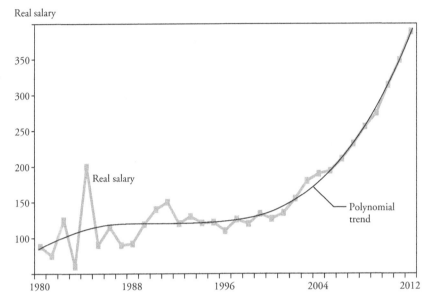

Real salary

Source: Lu Feng (2011).
a. The original data set ended in 2010 and was updated by the authors to include 2012.

policy, land use, factor price, income distribution, administrative controls, and the household registration system. These are all very important, but the following three reforms will dictate the sustainability of the PRC's growth:

1. Change local government behavior from direct involvement in economic activities to public goods provision.

2. Restructure the state-owned enterprises to reduce monopoly power and implicit government support.

3. Liberalize factor, especially capital, markets.

These reforms should support the continuous rise of the country's economy in the global system and further increase the importance of the currency.

In the meantime, it is equally important for the PRC to participate or even lead global liberalization efforts, including the Group of Twenty process and other international initiatives. It is hard to imagine the RMB's functioning as a global currency if the PRC is absent from or even resists such global initiatives.

Openness and Depth of Financial Markets

An international currency must be supported by well-developed financial markets that are freely accessible by nonresidents, sufficiently liquid, reasonably stable, and equipped with effective hedging instruments. To achieve these goals, the bottom

Figure 10-5. *Capital Account Restriction Index*

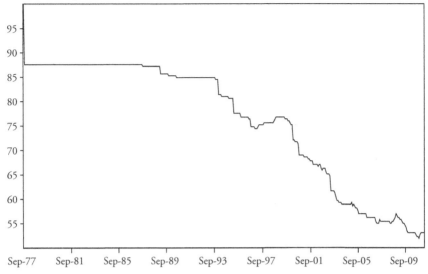

Index = 100 (fully restricted)

Source: Huang and others (2012).

line is that at the very least the PRC must liberalize its capital account to allow the free flow of capital across the border. By itself, though, that is not enough. The lack of capital account restrictions does not necessarily mean that the capital market is open. Here, again, Japan provides another important reference. Japan's capital markets are large, but they are not very liquid and foreign investment remains limited.

The PRC appears to have accelerated its efforts at capital account liberalization after the new government took over in March 2013. One expectation is that the PRC plans to achieve basic convertibility of the RMB under the capital account by 2015 and full convertibility by 2020. Such an expectation is certainly consistent with the monetary authority's plans to introduce market-based interest rates, adopt a deposit insurance system, strengthen market disciplines for financial institutions, and allow residents to access overseas capital markets.

It is important to point out that capital account liberalization did not just start. It has been going on for more than thirty years in the PRC (see quantitative measures of capital account control in figure 10-5). The literature provides two types of measures for the PRC's capital account controls: a de jure indicator, such as the Chinn-Ito index (Chinn and Ito 2008) and Quinn's longitudinal data (Quinn and Toyoda 2008); and a de facto indicator such as the TOTAL Index by Lane and Milesi-Ferretti (2007). The former often has too broad a category coverage and fails to capture important changes over time, and the latter cannot distinguish

Table 10-7. *Capital Account Management in the People's Republic of China*
Number

Instrument/transaction	Nonconvertible	Partially Convertible	Mostly Convertible	Total
Capital and money market instrument	2	10	4	16
Derivatives and other instruments	2	2	0	4
Credit operation	0	1	5	6
Direct investment	0	1	1	2
Liquidation of direct investment	0	0	1	1
Real estate transaction	0	2	1	3
Personal capital transaction	0	6	2	8
Total	4	22	14	40

Sources: People's Bank of China; International Monetary Fund, *Annual Report on Exchange Arrangements and Exchange Restrictions Report (AREAER)*.

impacts of capital account liberalization from those of other macroeconomic changes. The measure shown in figure 10-5 is a de jure index constructed by Huang and others (2012) by going through thousands of policy documents issued by the State Administration of Foreign Exchange over the past three decades.

Huang and his colleagues (2012) assumed complete control of the capital account for 1977, the year before the leaders officially launched the economic reform. They then adopted the classifications used by the Organization for Economic Cooperation and Development and the State Administration of Foreign Exchange: eleven categories of capital account transactions. For each item, a score of 3 denotes full control; 2, strong control; 1, slight control; and 0, liberalized. By updating the classifications in response to legislation passed, an index ranging from January 1978 to December 2010 was constructed to describe the extensiveness of the PRC's capital control. The results clearly show that capital account liberalization has been going on for some time in the PRC. In fact, the authorities adopted a well-established strategy for liberalization: first inflows, then outflows; first long-term, then short-term; and first direct investment, then portfolio investment. Using an index of 100 at the start of the economic reform in 1978, it has already come down to around 50 in recent years.

Yet several areas are still under strict regulation (table 10-7). In opening the securities markets to foreign investors, the government pursued a strategy of segmenting the markets for different investors. Foreign investors can participate in the transaction of foreign currency—denominated shares and debt instruments, such as the B-shares, H-shares, and "red-chip" stocks. However, the RMB-denominated A-shares, bonds, and other money market instruments are not open to nonresident investors unless they have a QFII quota. Restrictions on PRC residents are even stricter. Generally, residents cannot buy, sell, or issue capital or money market instruments in the overseas markets outside the Qualified Domestic Institutional Investor (QDII) scheme.

Currently there is a huge debate in the PRC about planned capital account liberalization, especially its sequencing and timing. Most economists concur that achieving a free capital account is beneficial for the economy by bringing about efficiency improvement, but the critical question is about associated financial risk. Are the financial institutions and markets sound enough to withstand volatile capital flows? As suggested by McKinnon (1991), domestic reforms should be pushed forward along with the opening of the capital account. These reforms consist of reduction of state intervention in the operation of major financial institutions, introduction of market-based interest rates, greater flexibility of the exchange rate, and improvement in the independence of the central bank's monetary policy-making (Dobson and Masson 2009).

Credibility of Economic and Legal Systems

An international currency is one that nonresidents not only use in normal times but also depend on at crisis times. Therefore, just having a strong economy and an open market is not sufficient. The U.S. dollar served as a global currency during much of the twentieth century because of the well-established legal system in the United States and the Federal Reserve System, as well as its efficient market and strong economy. Establishing the credibility of its economic and legal systems is perhaps the highest hurdle that the PRC must clear on its drive to make the RMB an international currency. By definition, developing economies are unstable, volatile (although often with stronger growth), and vulnerable in the face of shocks. If the PRC succeeds at this, it would be a historic achievement because it would be the first time in centuries that a developing country's currency becomes a global currency.

We cannot provide a complete list of the tasks for improving the credibility of the PRC's economic and legal system, but we can start with three.

1. The PRC needs an independent central bank. There are many reasons why the PBOC is not independent—perhaps good reasons—but this lack of independence from the government could seriously affect the achievement of monetary policy objectives in an open economy. Of course, independent monetary policymaking does not mean complete lack of coordination with the government. An independent central bank should possess the following characteristics: First, monetary policies should have clearly defined policy objectives, such as growth or inflation. Supporting state-owned enterprises (SOEs) or local governments, however, should not be a part of the PBOC's obligation. Second, the PBOC should use monetary policy instruments such as interest rates and liquidity measures, abandoning administrative tools such as credit quotas and window guidance. And finally, the PBOC should also improve quality and timeliness of its monetary policies.

2. The PRC needs a fair and transparent legal system to protect property rights and to enforce bankruptcy laws. An economy with many loss-making SOEs and monopoly state-owned financial institutions will never be able to support an international currency. Nonresidents will have confidence in holding RMB assets only if they know that their property rights are effectively protected and they will be fairly treated even if they are involved in economic disputes with PRC SOEs.

3. Political reforms may also be needed to improve the transparency and representativeness of the political system. We do not have a clear vision regarding specific needed political reforms, but we know that to become a global economic leader, the PRC needs to adopt a political system that the rest of the world trusts. Here again, important changes are necessary to systemically crack down on corruption, reduce social tension, and build a harmonious society.

What Are the Likely Implications?

Internationalization of the RMB will likely be an ongoing process, and making it an international reserve currency should also be a long-term goal. Before that, however, the RMB's international role may grow gradually over time. Some PRC scholars speculated that it would take three decades for the RMB to be internationalized: in the neighboring areas during the first decade, within the region during the second decade, and globally during the final decade (Chen 2013). No one can be sure about the exact timing of each of these stages, but the trajectory sounds reasonable—the RMB's role will be extended gradually from the neighboring areas to the global system.

The growing international role of the RMB, even if it is a gradual process, should have significant implications for the PRC, regional economies, and the rest of the world.

First, increasing its use in international trade and investment settlement could remove one important economic risk, exchange rate uncertainty, for PRC households and corporations. Exchange rate uncertainty is one of the main difficulties faced by exporters, especially those of low-margin exports, and importers. Use of the RMB as a settlement currency would means that the exporters no longer would need to worry about potential losses caused by currency appreciation (or by currency depreciation for importers). However, this is true only if exports or imports are priced in RMB. Currently, a large portion of trade and investment settled in RMB is still priced in U.S. dollars, which does not remove the exchange rate risk for PRC exporters and importers. Thus a critical step is for the RMB not only to have the function of means of exchange but also to be used as a unit of account.

Second, in addition to generating seigniorage revenue, turning the RMB into an international reserve currency may help reduce the PRC's balance-of-payments risks. As the PRC is more able to hold both international assets and liabilities in RMB, the risk of a currency crisis—potentially forced upon the PRC by a sudden stop or sudden reversal of cross-border capital flows—is lowered. And if the country suffers from an international payment deficit, the PRC would have the option of printing more currency to meet the shortfall. International investor confidence in a global reserve currency should also be stronger than in other developing-economy currencies, and this should support overall financial stability.

Third, the RMB as a global reserve currency should facilitate regional economic cooperation and integration. East Asia used to be a de facto U.S. dollar bloc. In the 1980s, the yen became an important anchor for some regional currencies such as the won and the NT dollar. This led Mundell (1999) to identify Asia dominated by the yen as one of the three islands of financial stability, the other two being North America, dominated by the U.S. dollar, and Europe dominated by the euro. However, the yen quickly peaked following the stagnation of the Japanese economy. In the aftermath of the Asian financial crisis, there was an important proposal for creating an Asian currency (Kawai 2008), but it lost momentum as its role model, the eurozone, fell into a debt crisis. However, if the RMB becomes an international currency, there is a possibility for it to serve as an anchor of regional currencies in Asia. In fact, our earlier analyses reveal that it already plays some kind of role as a regional currency anchor, alongside the U.S. dollar.

Last, the most important implication of RMB internationalization may be the associated reforms the PRC is about to implement. As discussed earlier, such reforms range from measures to make economic growth more sustainable to those leading to improvement of efficiency and stability of financial markets as well as to economic and political stability. In this sense, we may view RMB internationalization as having similar effects on overall economic reform as accession to the World Trade Organization at the end of 2001, which led to the almost complete revamping of the PRC's economic system. If the government seriously implements those reforms, the economy would certainly become more efficient, more dynamic, and more powerful, regardless of whether the RMB ultimately becomes an international reserve currency. A stronger economy and a more transparent regime can significantly strengthen the PRC's soft power in the world (Helleiner 2003). For this purpose alone RMB internationalization is a worthwhile goal.

Like any other economic strategy, however, internationalization of the RMB could have its own downside risks. One potential risk is premature liberalization of the capital account. Experiences of developing countries with financial liberalization in the 1980s and thereafter were accompanied by frequent financial crises. At the moment, the PRC already suffers from a series of significant risks, including a high M2-to-GDP (M2/GDP) ratio of 200 percent, large local government borrowing, and serious property bubbles. The government's tentative reform program could mean speedy liberalization of interest rates, exchange rates, and the capital account. It is not yet clear how big the shocks will be for financial institutions and manufacturing industries. If the sudden rise of the cost of capital and rapid outflow of capital cause serious dislocations in the economy, growth recession and financial crisis could easily materialize. Even if the RMB becomes an international reserve currency, the PRC will have to maintain a relatively open financial system. It remains to be seen whether the PRC's economy and markets are strong enough to withstand serious economic and financial shocks, including speculative attacks.

Another major challenge is that the RMB could become an international reserve currency in the coming decades while the PRC remains a developing country. Developing countries' currencies are, by definition, less stable. It would be the first time in history that a developing country's currency serves as a global reserve currency, and this circumstance could increase the instability of the international monetary system. More important, if internationalization of the RMB is successful, the currency would likely serve as one of the global reserve currencies, alongside at least the U.S. dollar and the euro. According to some experts, an international monetary system with more than one global reserve currency is actually more unstable than one with a single reserve currency (United Nations 2009). If that is indeed true, the international community should seriously consider proposals for creating a supranational currency (Zhou 2009; United Nations 2009).

Summary of the Main Findings

The PBOC started planning the internationalization of the RMB in 2006 at the latest, but the pace of actual implementation picked up amid the global financial crisis, which raised the possibility of the weakening of the role of the U.S. dollar and a demand for an alternative international currency. This process likely will accelerate further in the coming years, as the new government focuses more on structural reforms. The PRC adopted a two-track strategy for internationalizing the currency, the first track directly promoting the international use of the currency and the second track gradually liberalizing the capital account.

So far, the emphasis has been on increasing the international use of the currency. This includes use of the RMB for trade and investment settlement, mainly with neighboring and regional economies; establishment of offshore markets in Hong Kong, China, evidenced by the rapid growth of RMB deposits held by local residents; issuance of RMB-denominated bonds and other securities in Hong Kong, China and London; a large number of currency swap agreements; and holdings of RMB by some foreign central banks as part of their foreign currency reserves. A significant increase in the international use of the RMB so far is supported by three related factors: encouragement of the government, strong growth of economic activities (the PRC is already the largest trading partner of many regional economies), and expectations of RMB appreciation.

However, the RMB is still far from being an international reserve currency. Many optimists pay a lot of attention to the PRC's already gigantic economy. The logic is simple: the PRC is already a major world economy in the world, so its currency should play an international role. A quick review of experiences of international currencies during the twentieth century suggests that although the size of the economy is an important favorable factor, it is by no means a sufficient condition for the internationalization of the currency. We applied quantitative methods to identify determinants of international currencies' shares in global reserves and then used the results to predict the RMB's potential share. We found that if only GDP and trade weights are used, the RMB's potential share could be as high as 10 percent of the global reserves at the end of 2011. However, if policy and institutional factors such as capital account controls and economic freedom are considered, the RMB's potential share would only reach around 2 percent. These results suggest that the main obstacles for the RMB to become an international reserve currency are policy restrictions and institutional barriers.

So what should the PRC do to effectively internationalize its currency? It can certainly continue to push on the first track: promote the currency's use in international economic transactions, including the establishment of more offshore markets, issuance of more RMB-denominated assets overseas, and use for trade and investment settlement. The PRC may also adopt two additional strategies for this purpose: add the RMB to the IMF's SDR basket, which should significantly raise the international profile of the currency and make internationalization efforts a lot easier, and introduce a new mechanism for intraregional cross-holding of reserve currencies in Asia.

For the purpose of currency internationalization, the broadly defined second track of the two-track strategy is probably more critical, because it creates the foundation of a global reserve currency. We identify three areas for reform on the second track.

1. *Support the sustainable growth of the PRC economy.* To be sure, economic weights are not sufficient conditions for a global reserve currency, but any hopes for the RMB to become an international currency could collapse if the economy suddenly stagnates, similar to what happened to the Japanese economy in the 1990s. An imminent challenge for the PRC economy now is to change the growth model, which may be characterized as a combination of strong growth and serious imbalances. The key is to further economic reforms. The new government's economic policy framework, popularly termed "Likonomics," contains three important pillars: no more major stimulus, deleveraging to control financial risks, and structural reforms. Government officials and policy advisers are working on reform programs for a large number of areas, including the financial system, fiscal policy, land use, administrative controls, factor prices, income inequality, and the household registration system. Successful transformation of the growth model depends critically on liberalizing interest rates, exchange rates, and the capital account; changing the local governments' role from directly engaging in production and investment to providing public goods; and breaking down the monopoly power of the state sector.

2. *Create an open, large, efficient, and liquid financial market.* To serve as an international reserve currency, the RMB needs to be supported by a financial market that is easily accessible by nonresidents. One major step is to liberalize the capital account. This has been an ongoing process, with the capital account control index declining from 100 percent in 1977 to 53 percent in 2011. The government now plans to realize basic convertibility by 2015 and full convertibility by 2020. There is, however, a major debate as to whether this might be too aggressive and could trigger a financial crisis. The answer to this should be to keep a close eye on both the necessary conditions and sequencing of liberalization. Nevertheless, capital account liberalization is also a necessary step for currency internationalization. However, financial markets need to be open, liquid, and efficient, and equipped with well-developed hedging instruments.

3. *Improve the credibility of the PRC's economic and political systems.* The essence of international reserve currency status is that international investors have long-term confidence in it. To support such confidence, the PRC needs to improve its economic, legal, and political systems. The fact that all other existing international reserve currencies are from developed economies that have well-developed economic and political systems highlights the importance of progress in this area. We suggest three starting steps for the PRC: (1) an independent monetary policy-making mechanism, (2) a sound legal system that protects property rights and enforces bankruptcy law, and (3) a political system that is more transparent and representative.

Even if all these efforts are successful, we think the internationalization of the RMB will be a long-term process. We do not think the RMB will become a global reserve currency in the coming decade or anytime soon after that. The RMB's international role, however, may be extended steadily, perhaps first in the neighboring areas, then in the region, and finally globally.

This process could also generate significant implications for the PRC, the region, and the rest of the world. If the RMB is used as a unit of account, it would remove exchange rate uncertainties for PRC households and corporations in international transactions. If the PRC can hold its international assets and liabilities all in RMB, it should generate seigniorage revenue and reduce the country's balance-of-payments risks as well. The most fundamental impact of RMB internationalization could be to push comprehensive reforms in the PRC economy, as occurred in the wake of WTO accession in 2001. For some PRC officials and scholars, this factor alone would make currency internationalization a worthwhile goal.

On the down side, an aggressive reform agenda could increase the risk of financial instability. Even if the RMB successfully becomes an international reserve currency, the PRC will have to withstand more frequent financial shocks or even speculative attacks. It also remains to be seen whether adding a developing country's currency to the global reserve currency basket increases or decreases the instability of the international monetary system.

Appendix

Table 10A-1 shows the results of four types of robustness checks in this analysis. First, as argued earlier, market capitalization is probably not an accurate representative of the actual degree of financial market development. The second column of table 10A-1 redefines financial development as a share of private and public bond market capitalization to gross domestic product (Beck, Demirgüç-Kunt, and Levine 2000). The alternative specification suggests a positive impact from financial development on currency share in global reserves, which is consistent with previous evidence.

Second, instead of classifying institutional development as economic freedom, we choose the variables economic regulation and socioeconomic stability as indicating the development of institutions. The third and fourth columns confirm the results and, not surprisingly, show that there is no significant difference compared with the benchmark model in column 1 of table 10A-1.

Finally, we include log transformation to allow nonlinearity in determining currency share in global reserves, as suggested in Chen, Peng, and Shu (2009). Clearly, as suggested in the fifth column of table 10A-1, there is not much discrepancy in terms of the significance and signs of the estimated coefficients.

Table 10A-1. *Robustness Check of Determination of Currency Shares*

Explanatory variables	Dependent variable: currency share in global reserves				
	Benchmark	Bond Market	Regulation	Socio-Eco.	Log Tran.
GDP share	0.103* (0.0523)	0.102* (0.06)	0.124** (0.06)	0.149** (0.06)	0.738** (0.37)
Trade share	0.092* (0.052)	0.0736 (0.05)	0.0739 (0.06)	0.0517 (0.06)	-0.109 (0.33)
Inflation	-0.0133 (0.0871)	-0.104 (0.11)	-0.047 (0.12)	-0.0905 (0.12)	0.377 (0.72)
Exchange rate volatility	0.121 (0.0811)	0.20 (0.14)	0.08 (0.13)	0.17 (0.13)	0.43 (0.81)
Market capitalization	0.0169 (0.0194)	0.015 (0.02)	0.00997 (0.02)	0.0273 (0.02)	-0.144 (0.12)
Financial development	0.000862 (0.0014)	0.179*** (0.0354)	0.00297 (0.00)	0.00443** (0.00)	0.0405*** (0.01)
Appreciation	0.0674*** (0.0093)	0.048*** (0.0099)	0.0695*** (0.01)	0.0647*** (0.01)	0.289*** (0.06)
Capital account liberalization	0.00849** (0.0036)	0.00726** (0.0042)	0.0162*** (0.01)	0.0206*** (0.01)	0.122*** (0.03)
Institution	0.0043* (0.0025)	0.000278* (0.00)	0.00383** (0.00)	0.00231*** (0.00)	0.0395** (0.02)
Lag of share	0.891*** (0.0265)	0.911*** (0.02)	0.883*** (0.03)	0.865*** (0.03)	0.848*** (0.03)
Constant	-0.048** (0.0226)	-0.0433** (0.02)	-0.0529*** (0.02)	-0.0542*** (0.01)	-0.752** (0.18)
Observation	235	235	235	235	235
R-squared	0.958	0.963	0.958	0.96	0.935

Source: Authors.

$* = p < 10$ percent; $** = p < 5$ percent; $*** = p < 1$ percent.

References

Beck, T., A. Demirgüç-Kunt, and R. Levine. 2000. "A New Database on the Structure and Development of the Financial Sector." *World Bank Economic Review* 14, no. 3: 597–605.

Chen, H., W. Peng, and C. Shu. 2009. "The Potential of the Renminbi as an International Currency." BIS Paper No. 61. Basel: Bank for International Settlements (www.bis.org/repof ficepubl/arpresearch200903.06.pdf).

Chen, Y. 2013. "Toward a Core Country: China's Grand Financial Strategy and Development Path" (in Chinese). *China Think Tank*, vol. 4.

Chinn, M., and J. Frankel. 2005. "Will the Euro Eventually Surpass the Dollar as Leading International Reserve Currency?" NBER Working Paper No. 11510. Cambridge, Mass.: National Bureau for Economic Research.

———. 2008. "Why the Euro Will Rival the Dollar." *International Finance* 11, no. 1: 49–73.

Chinn, M., and H. Ito. 2008. "A New Measure of Financial Openness." *Journal of Comparative Policy Analysis: Research and Practice* 10, no. 3: 309–22.

Cohen, B. 2009. "Toward a Leaderless Currency System." In *The Future of the Dollar*, edited by Eric Helleiner and Jonathan Kirshner, pp. 142–56. Cornell University Press.

Dobson, W., and P. Masson. 2009. "Will the Renminbi Become a World Currency?" *China Economic Review* 20, no. 1: 124–35.

Eichengreen, Barry. 2005. "Sterling's Past, Dollar's Future: Historical Perspectives on Reserve Currency Competition." NBER Working Paper No. 11336. Cambridge, Mass.: National Bureau of Economic Research.

Fan, G., B. Wang, and Y. Huang. 2013. "Intraregional Cross-Holding of Reserve Currencies: A Proposal for Asia to Deal with the Global Reserve Risks." *China & World Economy* 21, no. 4: 14–35.

Fang, Lu. 2011. "Employment Expansion and Wage Growth (2001–2010)." Beijing: Peking University, PRC Macroeconomic Research Center, June 12.

Frankel, J. 2011. "Historical Precedents for Internationalization of the RMB." Paper prepared for the workshop organized by the Council on Foreign Relations and China Development Research Foundation, Beijing, November 1.

Frankel, J., and S. Wei. 1994. "Yen Bloc or Dollar Bloc? Exchange Rate Policies of the East Asian Economies." In *Macroeconomic Linkage: Savings, Exchange Rates, and Capital Flows*, edited by T. Ito and A. Krueger, pp. 295–333. University of Chicago Press.

Fratzscher, M., and A. Mehl. 2011. "China's Dominance Hypothesis and the Emergence of a Tri-Polar Global Currency System." ECB Working Paper No. 1392. Frankfurt: European Central Bank.

Gao, H., and Y. Yu. 2012. "Internationalization of the Renminbi. Currency Internationalization: Lessons from the Global Financial Crisis and Prospects for the Future in Asia and the Pacific." BIS Paper No. 61. Basel: Bank for International Settlements.

Garber, Peter. 2011. "What Drives CNH Market Equilibrium?" CGS/IIGG Working Paper. New York: Council on Foreign Relations Press (www.cfr.org/china/drives-cnh-market-equilibrium/p26292).

Helleiner, Eric. 2003. *The Making of National Money: Territorial Currencies in Historical Perspective*. Cornell University Press.

———. 2008. "Political Determinants of International Currencies: What Future for the US Dollar?" *Review of International Political Economy* 15, no. 3: 354–78.

Huang, Y. 2010. "Dissecting the China Puzzle: Asymmetric Liberalization and Cost Distortion." *Asia Economic Policy Review* 5, no. 2: 281–95.

Huang, Y., C. Fang, P. Xu, and G. Qin. 2013. "New Normal of Chinese Development." In *China: A New Model for Growth and Development*, edited by Ross Garnaut, Cai Fang, and Ligang Song. ANU (Australia National University) Press (link at http://press.anu.edu.au/titles/china-update-series/china-a-new-model-for-growth-and-development).

Huang, Y., and K. Tao. 2010. "Factor Market Distortion and the Current Account Surplus in China." *Asian Economic Papers* 9, no. 3: 1–36.

Huang, Y., and B. Wang. 2010. "Cost Distortions and Structural Imbalances in China." *China and World Economy* 18, no. 4: 1–17.

Huang, Y., X. Wang, Q. Gou, and D. Wang. 2012. "Achieving Capital Account Convertibility in China." *China Economic Journal* 4, no. 1: 25–42.

International Monetary Fund. 2011. "Enhancing International Monetary Stability—A Role for the SDR?" Report prepared for the Strategy, Policy, and Review Department. Washington: January 7 (www.imf.org/external/np/pp/eng/2011/010711.pdf).

———. 2013. "People's Republic of China: Article IV Consultation." IMF Country Report No. 12/195. Washington: July 17.

Ito, T. 2008. "Influence of the Renminbi on Exchange Rate Policies of Other Asian Currencies." In *Debating China's Exchange Rate Policy*, edited by M. Goldstein and N.R. Lardy, pp. 239–58. Washington: Peterson Institute for International Economics.

Kawai, Masahiro. 2002. "Exchange Rate Arrangements in East Asia: Lessons from the 1997–98 Currency Crisis." *Monetary and Economic Studies*, vol. 20, No. S-1. Tokyo: Bank of Japan.

———. 2008. "Toward a Regional Exchange Rate Regime in East Asia." *Pacific Economic Review* 13, no. 1: 83–103.

Kawai, Masahiro, and Victor Pontines. 2014. "Is There Really a Renminbi Bloc in Asia?" ADBI Working Paper Series No. 467. Tokyo: Asian Development Bank Institute.

Kenen, P. 2002. "The Euro versus the Dollar: Will There Be a Struggle for Dominance?" *Journal of Policy Modeling* 24, no. 4: 347–54.

Krugman, Paul. 1984. "The International Role of the Dollar: Theory and Prospect." In *Exchange Rate Theory and Practice*, edited by J. Bilson and R. Marston, pp. 261–78. University of Chicago Press.

Lane, P., and G. Milesi-Ferretti. 2007. "The External Wealth of Nations Mark II: Revised and Extended Estimates of Foreign Assets and Liabilities, 1970–2004." *Journal of International Economics* 73, no. 2: 223–50.

Lee, Jong-Wha. 2010. "Will the Renminbi Emerge as an International Reserve Currency?" Unpublished paper. Korea University, June (http://aric.adb.org/grs/papers/Lee.pdf).

Li, D., and L. Liu. 2008. "RMB Internationalization: An Empirical Analysis." *Journal of Financial Research* 11: 1–16.

Maziad, S., and J. Kang. 2012. "RMB Internationalization: Onshore/Offshore Links." IMF Working Paper No. WP/12/133. Washington: International Monetary Fund.

McKinnon, R. 1991. *The Order of Economic Liberalization*. Johns Hopkins University Press.

McNamara, K. 2008. "A Rivalry in the Making? The Euro and International Monetary Power." *Review of International Political Economy* 15, no. 3: 439–59.

Mundell, Robert A. 1999. "A Reconsideration of the Twentieth Century." Nobel Prize Lecture, Aula Magan, Stockholm University, Stockholm, December 8 (www.columbia.edu/~ram15/nobelLecture.html).

People's Bank of China Study Group. 2006. "The Timing, Path, and Strategies of RMB Internationalization." *China Finance* 5: 12–13.

Quinn, D., and A. Toyoda. 2008. "Does Capital Account Liberalization Lead to Growth?" *Review of Financial Studies* 21, no. 3: 1403–49.

Subacchi, Paola. 2010. "One Currency, Two Systems: China's Renminbi Strategy." IE Briefing Paper 2010/01. London: Chatham House, International Economics, October.

Takagi, Shinji. 2011. "Currency Internationalization: Lessons from the Global Financial Crisis and Prospects for the Future in Asia and the Pacific." BIS Working Paper No. 61. Basel: Bank for International Settlements.

United Nations. 2009. "Report of the Commission of Experts of the President of the United Nations General Assembly on Reforms of the International Monetary and Financial System." Report prepared for the United Nations Conference on the World Financial and Economic Crisis and Its Impact on Development, New York, June 24–26.

Williamson, John. 2009. "Understanding Special Drawing Rights (SDRs)." Policy Brief PB09-11. Washington: Peterson Institute for International Economics, June.

Zhou, Xiaochuan. 2009. "Reform the International Monetary System." Speech of the governor of the People's Bank of China, March 23. *BIS Review* 41 (www.bis.org/review/r090402c.pdf).

11

The Benefits and Costs of Renminbi Internationalization

LIQING ZHANG AND KUNYU TAO

The United States' financial crisis of 2007–08 has created a new wave of discussion about the reform of the international monetary system. Once again, the U.S. dollar–centered reserve system has been strongly criticized for its exorbitant privileges, which not only cause financial instability but also give rise to inequality between rich and poor countries (Stiglitz 2009; Zhou 2009). Although various reform proposals have been repeatedly presented, such as a return to the gold standard, creation of a single world currency, special-drawing-rights-based proposals, and an improved U.S. dollar standard, many economists believe that a multipolar currency system is the most realistic development in the foreseeable future, or even in the coming decades (Eichengreen 2011). Through currency competition, any reserve currency–issuing country could become more disciplined in its monetary and other macroeconomic policies, which could eventually lead to a more stable international monetary system (Zhang 2012).

A consensus has developed that the U.S. dollar, the euro, and an Asian currency should be the main parts of the multipolar reserve system. Until 2009, many economists believed that either the Japanese yen or a sort of synthesized currency, called the Asian dollar, could be popular in Asia and become one of the pillars of the multipolar system. In the event, since 2009 the renminbi (RMB), the currency of the People's Republic of China (PRC), has been used increasingly in trade settlements and other cross-border financial transactions, signaling that the currency structure of the multipolar system may take a different form.

Although some researchers early in this century argued that the PRC should push forward the internationalization of the RMB (Zhao 2001), and more recently some have argued that the internationalization of the RMB should become a new driver of deep economic reform and opening up, the PRC government has never declared such a move or mentioned it in its official documents. Nevertheless, the 2009 removal of restrictions on trade settlements in RMB has spurred a de facto process of RMB internationalization. In the ensuing four years, the scale of RMB use and holdings beyond the borders of the PRC has rapidly increased.

Despite an increasing recognition that the RMB may eventually become a key global currency, several important questions need to be answered. Among them: How should we think about the benefits and costs of the RMB becoming an international currency? What are the key preconditions for it to become a reserve currency, and can this trend continue if the PRC does not fully remove its capital controls? In this chapter we provide some new perspectives on the benefits and costs of RMB internationalization and its related policy issues.

Literature Review

By definition, an international currency is one that is used and held beyond the borders of the issuing country, not merely for transactions with that country's residents but also, and most important, for transactions between nonresidents (Kenen 2011). From a more theoretical perspective, an international currency should function as a unit of account, a means of exchange, and a store of value not only within but also outside the borders of the issuing country. Kenen (1983) provided some early thoughts on the roles that an international currency should play in both governmental and private transactions (see table 5-1 on p. 112 of this volume).

Since the fifteenth century, the currencies of Portugal, Spain, the Netherlands, France, the United Kingdom, and the United States have, in succession, played a role as a leading international currency. In the late twentieth century, in addition to the dominant role played by the U.S. dollar, the Japanese yen, the German deutsche mark, the Republic of Korea's won, the Singapore dollar, and more recently, the euro have played some role as international currencies. The evolution of international currencies suggests that the internationalization of any national currency is basically a market-driven process, mainly reflecting economic fundamentals such as robust economic growth, price stability, a highly developed financial market, foreign confidence in the stability of the convertibility regime, and a healthy situation with regard to the balance of payments (Bergsten 1975).

There has long been academic discussion of the benefits and costs of being an international currency. Indeed, some countries' policymaking has indicated a reluctance to have their currencies internationalized. Cohen (2012) summarized the benefits and risks of being an international currency. He argued that the benefits may include transaction cost reductions, collection of international seigniorage, macroeconomic flexibility, political leverage, and enhancement of a "soft" national power. The costs or risks include a tendency toward currency appreciation, external constraints imposed on domestic monetary autonomy, and a greater global policy responsibility. Genberg (2010) pointed out that there are incremental benefits during the internationalization process; one of the costs is associated with international bond issues, which make domestic interest rates more dependent on external factors.

In a more specific context, Papaioannou and Portes (2008) analyzed the costs and benefits of the euro as an international currency. They argued that the introduction of the euro noticeably reduced transaction costs in both financial markets and financial services and promoted global financial integration. They also found no evidence that currency internationalization made it more difficult to enforce monetary policy. Kim and Suh (2011) compared the gains with the losses during internationalization of the Republic of Korea's won. They argued that one of the main benefits of the won's becoming an international currency was to blunt the adverse effects of external financial shocks, which could be very important for a small, open economy. However, there also was a significant transitional risk. An emerging-market economy hoping to internationalize its currency must liberalize its capital account, which may increase the country's vulnerability to external shocks and even cause financial instability.

The process of RMB internationalization started during the first decade of the twenty-first century and has rapidly gained speed since 2009. The People's Bank of China Study Group (2006) established an index to identify the degree of internationalization of a specific currency. The U.S. dollar was set at 100, the euro was 40, the Japanese yen was 28.2, and the RMB was only 2. Chen and Hu (2013) presented an RMB internationalization index (RII) based on the RMB's role as an invoice, settlement, and reserve currency and found that the RII was still very low, though it had increased dramatically since 2010. Later, the study group announced an annual report on RMB internationalization (Renmin University of China, Institute of International Currency 2012), which extended the RII to 2012. A comparison of these measurements of RMB internationalization is summarized in table 11-1.

Although the internationalization of the RMB is still only beginning, there is a lot of discussion of the pros and cons of the process. Chen, Peng, and Shu (2007) stress the importance of cost-benefit analysis in promoting RMB internationalization for the government of the PRC. Gao and Yu (2010) suggest a road map for RMB internationalization and argue that regardless of whether it was to be an international or a regional currency, the process would be beneficial to the whole economy. Hai and Yao (2010) compare the benefits and challenges of RMB internationalization, arguing that the cross-border circulation of RMB would have a very small impact on the effectiveness of the PRC's monetary policy, based on the

Table 11-1. *Comparison of Measurements of Degree of Renminbi Internationalization*[a]

Year	Renminbi	U.S. dollar	Euro	Yen
2006	2.00	100.00	40.00	28.20
2009	0.02	52.79	26.92	3.60
2010	0.23	53.33	25.58	4.34
2011	0.45	54.18	24.86	4.56
2012	0.87	52.34	23.72	4.78

Sources: For 2006, People's Bank of China Study Group (2006); for 2009–11, Chen and Hu (2013); for 2012, Renmin University of China, Institute of International Currency (2012).

a. The 2006 scores can only be used for cross-currency comparison; the 2009 and 2012 scores can be used both for cross-currency and time series comparison.

VAR (vector autoregression) model. Zhang (2013) points out the arbitrage risks during the process of RMB internationalization. Li and Liu (2008) suggests that, owing to the PRC's high savings rate, the benefit of borrowing internationally may be low, and the benefit of seigniorage income after the PRC's capital account liberalization might be small, when one takes into account financial repression (including interest rate controls, credit constraints, capital controls, and so on). Ba and others (2010) analyze the impact of RMB internationalization on the PRC's finance industry, including the banking sector, the stock market, the bond market, and insurance. They demonstrate that the effects of RMB internationalization on the PRC's financial industry will be long-lasting and profound.

The literature provides a background for further discussion of the benefits and costs of RMB internationalization.

Here we provide a brief review of the development of RMB internationalization since 2009. Then we elaborate on the main benefits and costs of RMB internationalization. Following this we discuss the related policy issues to maximize the benefits and mitigate the costs of internationalization, particularly the costs and risks in the transitional period. Finally we outline our conclusions and suggest a further research agenda.

Main Developments in Renminbi Internationalization since 2009

Since 2009 the RMB has assumed some functions of an international currency, mainly through trade settlements and financial transactions such as bond issuance, foreign direct investment, and bank deposits. It also has become a reserve currency in some emerging-market economies and a denominated currency in bilateral currency-swap agreements. Although its scale is still very limited, over the past few years the RMB has rapidly emerged as an international currency with some functions as a unit of account, a means of exchange, and a store of value.

Trade Settlement in Renminbi

Trade settlement in RMB is probably the most important development in the currency's internationalization. In April 2009 the PRC government announced a pilot scheme of cross-border trade settlement in RMB; as a result, the amount of trade settlements in RMB has increased dramatically. As of the first quarter (Q1) of 2013, the quarterly trade settlement in RMB was CNY1 trillion, or around 11 percent of total trade settlements. About 80 percent of trade settlements in RMB are through Hong Kong, China. As a result, RMB deposits in Hong Kong, China have also risen dramatically since 2010, demonstrating the importance of Hong Kong, China in the internationalization of the RMB.

Cross-Border Direct Investment in Renminbi

Cross-border direct investment in RMB has increased rapidly since 2011, and the scale of RMB settlement for foreign direct investment has been much greater than for overseas direct investment. In 2012 the total amount of cross-border direct investment reached CNY284 billion. Of this, foreign direct investment accounted for about CNY253.6 billion, whereas overseas direct investment was about CNY30.4 billion. More impressively, foreign direct investment in RMB represented 36 percent of total foreign direct investment inflows into the PRC.

Cross-Border Financial Transactions in Renminbi

In 2005, the PRC permitted domestic financial institutions to issue RMB-denominated bonds in Hong Kong, China. More recently, many PRC financial institutions and foreign financial corporate and multinational enterprises have joined in the issuance of RMB-denominated bonds there, and nonfinancial institutions were allowed to issue RMB-denominated bonds in Hong Kong, China, according to a May 2012 provision announced by the National Development and Reform Commission.[1] By August 2012 there had been more than 180 such issues, totaling CNY221.8 billion.

Since 2010, in addition to issuing bonds, the PRC government has launched a series of policies aimed at promoting the financial use of the RMB, and such financial transactions have greatly increased. RMB-denominated qualified foreign institutional investment began at CNY20 billion in 2011 and had increased to CNY270 billion one year later.

Reserve Currency and Currency Swaps with Foreign Central Banks

Over the past few years, the RMB has become a reserve currency for some emerging-market economies and developing countries: Belarus, Cambodia, Malaysia, Nige-

---

1. More information can be found at www.chinabond.com.cn/d2s/cbData.html.

ria, the Philippines, the Republic of Korea, and the Russian Federation. Although the scale is very small, often below 5 percent of the total holdings in these countries, it is somewhat symbolic that the RMB has to some degree emerged as a reserve currency. More impressive, from 2008 to 2009, following the outbreak of the U.S. subprime mortgage crisis in 2008, the PRC signed eight currency-swap agreements with six Asian countries and two others, a move toward RMB internationalization. Since then, the total amount of RMB swapped has increased rapidly, reaching more than CNY2 trillion by March 2013.

Reasons behind the Rapid Development of Renminbi Internationalization

It is fair to say that the internationalization of the RMB has developed so rapidly since 2011 owing to various pilot schemes and related liberalization measures, which have greatly facilitated such development. However, the internationalization of the RMB is basically a market-driven rather than a government-driven process. The following factors have helped push the process forward.

First, increased trade between the PRC and Southeast Asian countries has played an important role. From 2002 to 2011, trade between the PRC and countries in the Association of Southeast Asian Nations (ASEAN) increased from $55 billion to $360 billion. In particular, it rose dramatically after the establishment of the PRC-ASEAN free trade agreement in 2009, which resulted in a 70 percent trade increase from 2009 to 2011. The rapid increase of trade with ASEAN and other Asian countries created a significant opportunity for both sides to use the RMB as a settlement currency.

Second, the continuous appreciation of the RMB since 2005 has encouraged foreign exporters to settle their trades in RMB. It is worth noting that the scale of RMB settlement for imports has been much larger than the scale of RMB settlement for exports over the past years, on average accounting for 80 percent of settlements. The best explanation for the PRC's imbalanced currency structure of trade settlements is probably the expectation of RMB appreciation. Zhang (2013) found that from January 2010 to March 2013, the coefficient of correlation between RMB appreciation and the increment of RMB deposits in Hong Kong, China was 0.54.

Third, given the global financial instability caused by the recent global financial crisis, many emerging economies have suffered from capital outflows and liquidity shortages. To deal with possible liquidity problems, it is natural for central banks from these economies to sign currency-swap agreements with the PRC, which holds the largest foreign exchange reserves in the world (Woo 2010).

Fourth, since its return to the PRC in 1997, Hong Kong, China has been trying to strengthen its role as an international financial center, with support from the central government. To maintain the prosperity of its banking sector, Hong Kong, China has constantly requested that the central government allow banks and other financial institutions in Hong Kong, China to conduct business in RMB.

Benefits of Renminbi Internationalization

The key to most successful international currency use is the trade-off between the benefits and associated losses arising from externalities. Although it is developing very quickly, RMB internationalization is still only beginning, and on the whole it is very limited in scale. Therefore, it might be too early to comprehensively evaluate its economic consequences, from either a national or a global perspective. Nevertheless, it is surely necessary and possible to have some forward-looking discussion about the benefits and costs of the ongoing process.

RMB internationalization, particularly when the RMB eventually becomes a key international currency, may bring significant benefits to the PRC. First, by using the RMB as an invoicing and settlement currency, PRC firms may reduce the exchange risks of international trade and investment, thereby reducing transaction costs. The theoretical description of the benefit of currency internationalization in reducing exchange rate risks and transaction costs is quite similar to the analysis of optimal currency area theories, which was brilliantly made by Mundell (1961). As the second-largest trading country in the world, the PRC accounted for nearly 9 percent of global trade in 2010, and this is expected to reach 12 percent by the end of 2014, according to an estimate by the International Monetary Fund (Maziad and others 2011). In addition, the PRC is probably the largest destination country after the United States for foreign direct investment, and the country is becoming an increasingly important source of overseas direct investment. Obviously, RMB internationalization would create a great deal of monetary efficiency and integrate the PRC more deeply into the world economy.

Similarly, the internationalization of the RMB should be helpful in reducing currency mismatch for financial institutions. It would alleviate the problem of "original sin"—a situation in which a country is not able to borrow from abroad in its domestic currency and one that many emerging economies have to live with.[2] The PRC is a typical emerging market economy, with underdeveloped financial markets. As its economy becomes more deeply involved with the world economy, particularly through a more open financial sector and a more internationalized banking sector, PRC banks may find currency mismatch problems to be a greater challenge. RMB internationalization may help these banks to reduce exchange risks. In addition, the increased weight of RMB-denominated assets in financial institutions would reduce the effects of foreign exchange risk in the Bank for International Settlements' computation of capital adequacy requirements.

Second, RMB internationalization would go hand in hand with a larger, more sophisticated financial sector in the PRC and would benefit the PRC's transformation of its economic growth model. Some writers argue that financial develop-

---

2. Currency "original sin" is a commonly used metaphor in international finance. It was proposed by Barry Eichengreen, Ricardo Hausmann, and Ugo Panizza in a series of papers (two of which are Eichengreen and Hausmann 1999; Eichengreen, Hausmann, and Panizza 2002).

ment should be a precondition of currency internationalization (see, for example, Dobson and Masson 2009; Tavlas 1997). However, the increased use of a domestic currency for international trade and investment would increase the breadth and depth of the financial market by attracting more market participants and strengthening the linkages with the global financial market. Chen, Peng, and Shu (2007) use the currency internationalization experiences of Germany and Japan to illustrate the importance of financial development and the possible gains produced by currency internationalization. Papaioannou and Portes (2008) also argue that currency internationalization would promote the development of financial markets, both domestically and globally. Taking Europe's Economic and Monetary Union following the introduction of the euro as an example, they find that private credit in participating countries increased by roughly 1.15 percent more than in other countries, and that these welfare gains resulted from the internationalization of the euro.

In the case of the PRC, it is recognized that a more developed financial market is the precondition of RMB internationalization. On the other hand, if the RMB internationalization is wide and deep, it would inevitably push forward the development of the financial sector through international trade settlements in RMB and financial services related to RMB-denominated international bond transactions. Indeed, RMB internationalization may become an important driver of the PRC's bond market. In addition, as some researchers have argued, RMB internationalization will largely benefit the rise of Shanghai as an international financial center (Gao and Yu 2010; Ranjan and Prakash 2010). Furthermore, RMB internationalization may actually become a new catalyst for financial reform if PRC authorities believe that a more internationalized currency is in the national interest (Maziad and others 2011; McCauley 2011).

In addition to these arguments, empirical evidence shows the effects of currency internationalization on the development of domestic financial markets. We first look at the global experience and then focus on the PRC's experience.

The Global Experience

Since the 1990s a great deal of literature has described the determinants of financial development, including laws, institutions, political systems, the nature of bureaucracy, culture, social capital, and other elements (Allen and Gale 2001; Chinn and Ito 2006; La Porta and others 1998; Levine 1999). However, little empirical research has focused on the effect of currency internationalization on financial development. We have based our empirical model on Chinn and Ito (2006) and Papaioannou and Portes (2008):

$$(11\text{-}1) \qquad FD_{it} - FD_{it-3} = \alpha_0 + \beta_1 FD_{t-3} + \beta_2 CI_{it-3} + \Gamma X_{it-3} + \epsilon_{it}.$$

The dependent variable is financial development (*FD*), and among the various measurements of financial development (Beck, Demirgüç-Kunt, and Levine

2000), we use the amount of private credit relative to gross domestic product (GDP) and total stock market value relative to GDP to evaluate the degree of financial market development. Our concerned explanatory variable is currency internationalization, denoted as *CI*.

The extent of currency internationalization is determined by complex factors, and there is no uniform measurement of currency internationalization worldwide. The three main functions of a currency (as a store of value, a medium of exchange, and a unit of account) are the general factors to consider when measuring the internationalization of a currency, and among these, the function as a medium of exchange may be the most important in terms of impact on financial development. Therefore, rather than constructing a comprehensive index, we use the currency's share of global trade settlement to estimate a currency's function as a medium of exchange and treat this as a proxy for currency internationalization.

X is a vector of control variables that are in line with the literature. These include the GDP growth rate (growth); log GDP per capita in purchasing power parity terms (income); the inflation rate (*inflation*); trade openness (*openness*), measured as the ratio of the sum of exports and imports to GDP; and financial openness (*KAopen*), which measures the degree of capital account openness. Subscript i refers to the country, subscript t refers to the year, and ε_{it} is the error term.

The sample covers Japan, the United Kingdom, and the United States from 1980 to 2005 and the eurozone from 2000 to 2005. Financial development and most of the control variables come from the International Monetary Fund's *International Financial Statistics* and the World Bank's *World Development Indicators*. The share of currency settlements for the U.S. dollar and the euro are from Kamps (2006), and the share for the pound sterling and yen are collected from national central banks and statistical offices. The index for financial openness comes from Chinn and Ito (2006).

To avoid problems of endogeneity, we specify our model as a growth rate on levels regression, similar to a panel error-correction model with non-overlapping data. We only sample data every three years between 1980 and 2005, and we use the three-year average growth in the level of financial development as the dependent variable and the "initial conditions" for time-variant explanatory variables, including the initial level of financial development indicator for each three-year panel.

The regression results for equation 11-1 are shown in table 11-2. We can see that when we control for economic indicators, currency internationalization in terms of trade settlement has a significant and positive effect on the development of a financial market; a one-unit rise in currency internationalization will increase the development of the financial market by 0.2 percentage point in terms of private credit and 0.7 percentage point in terms of stock market total value. For the control variables, higher income levels and greater trade openness will assist the

Table 11-2. *Impact of Currency Internationalization on Financial Development*[a]

Variable	Private credit (I)	Total stock market value (I)	Private credit (II)	Total stock market value (II)
CI	0.0022** (0.0009)	0.0071* (0.004)	0.0024** (0.0011)	0.0088** (0.0041)
Growth	. . .	. . .	0.0022 (0.0015)	0.0024* (0.0013)
Income	. . .	. . .	0.0031** (0.0014)	0.0037** (0.0015)
Inflation	. . .	. . .	−0.0212** (0.0121)	−0.0302** (0.0133)
Openness	. . .	. . .	0.0122** 0.0055	0.0117** 0.0051
KAopen	. . .	. . .	0.0027** (0.0014)	0.0088 (0.0071)
Observations	32	32	32	32
Adjusted *R*-squared	0.18	0.16	0.24	0.22

Sources: Authors' calculations, based on International Monetary Fund, *International Financial Statistics*; World Bank, *World Development Indicators*; Kamps (2006); Chinn and Ito (2006).

a. In the first two columns, we only use the key explanation variable (financial development: private credit, stock market value), so all the other control variables (growth, income, etc.) are not in the regression model, so there are no records.

* = $p < 10\%$; ** = $p < 5\%$; *** = $p < 1\%$.

development of financial markets, and inflation has a negative impact on the dependent variable.

The Case of the People's Republic of China

Based on the global experience, we try to analyze the case of the PRC. In general, RMB internationalization may affect the PRC's financial development in the banking industry, the stock market, the bond market, and the insurance market. To examine the general effect, we have constructed the following regression model, based on Chinn and Ito (2006) and Papaioannou and Portes (2008):

$$(11\text{-}2) \qquad FD_t = \alpha + \beta_1 rmb_t + \beta_2 Control_t + \epsilon_t.$$

The dependent variable is financial development; we use only the share of private credit relative to GDP to evaluate the extent of the PRC's financial market development. The main explanatory variable is RMB internationalization, for which we use two indicators. The first is the RMB internationalization index (RII) published by Chen and Hu (2013). Chen and Hu based this quarterly index on the three major functions of an international currency and found that the index increased dramatically from 2010 to 2013. The other indicator is the

Table 11-3. *Basic Estimation of the Impact of Renminbi Internationalization on the Financial Development of the People's Republic of China*[a]

Variable	1 *RII*	2 *RII*	3 *Settlement*	4 *Settlement*
RII	0.006* (0.0033)	0.0078** (0.0032)	. . .	. . .
Settlement	. . .	. . .	0.012** (0.004)	0.018*** (0.005)
Growth	. . .	0.052*** (0.0189)	. . .	0.048** (0.0147)
Income	. . .	0.024** (0.0102)	. . .	0.021* (0.0101)
Observations	16	16	16	16
R-squared	0.68	0.76	0.74	0.82

Source: Authors' calculations, based on Chinn and Ito (2006); Papaioannou and Portes (2008); Chen and Hu (2013); National Bureau of Statistics data, December 209 to June 2013.

a. Numbers in parentheses are associated standard errors.

* = $p < 10\%$; ** = $p < 5\%$; *** = $p < 1\%$.

RMB cross-border trade settlement ratio (settlement), because one of the most important functions of an international currency is its use as a medium of international payment, and the rise of payment demand will promote its use in the international reserve. The control variables, which are in line with the literature, include the GDP growth rate (growth) and GDP per capita (income). The final item is an error term.

All of the variables are quarterly data and most are compiled from official National Bureau of Statistics data from December 2009 to June 2013. Due to the limited sample period we cannot use the same regression method as for the global experience, and instead use a simple ordinary least squares regression with robustness check.

The results are presented in table 11-3. Columns 1 and 2 are estimated with *RII* and columns 3 and 4 are based on settlement. First, we find a significant and positive relationship between RMB internationalization and the PRC's financial development, which indicates that RMB internationalization will promote the PRC's financial market development as a whole. Second, a 1-percentage-point rise in *RII* will boost the PRC's financial market development by 0.6 percentage point. Third, among the three major currency functions, international payment can be regarded as the leading index. Given that the effect of cross-border RMB trade settlements on financial development is greater, a 1-percentage-point increase in the settlement ratio can increase the share of private credit relative to GDP by 1.8 percentage points.

This regression may include an endogeneity problem because financial development may also promote RMB internationalization. Because the sample period

Table 11-4. *Robustness Check of the Impact of Renminbi Internationalization on the Financial Development of the People's Republic of China*[a]

In FD	1 RII	2 RII	3 Settlement	4 Settlement
Lagged RII	0.0055* (0.0026)	0.0062** (0.0028)	...	...
Lagged settlement	...	...	0.010* (0.004)	0.016*** (0.005)
Lagged growth	0.044** (0.0142)	0.048*** (0.0149)	0.032** (0.0124)	0.038** (0.0117)
Lagged income	0.020* (0.01)	0.021* (0.010)	0.015 (0.009)	0.019* (0.009)
Observations	16	16	16	16
R-squared	0.62	0.67	0.72	0.76

Source: Authors' calculations, based on Wooldridge (2002); Ba and others (2010); Papaioannou and Portes (2008).

a. Numbers in parentheses are associated standard errors.

* = $p < 10\%$; ** = $p < 5\%$; *** = $p < 1\%$.

is short, we refer to Wooldridge (2002) and use the lagged value of the explanatory variable as the instrumental variable to deal with the endogeneity issue and the simultaneity problem, because the lagged RMB internationalization index will affect financial development but current financial development will not influence previous currency internationalization.

The results listed in table 11-4 indicate that even when the reverse causality and endogeneity issues are considered, RMB internationalization will still have a positive effect on the PRC's financial development. What is more, even though we cannot testify to the nonlinear effect in the previous regression, due to the sample size, many studies have revealed a non-monotonic effect, arguing that the long-run effect will be greater than the short-term effect (Ba and others 2010; Papaioannou and Portes 2008).

Third, RMB internationalization would allow PRC firms and financial institutions to borrow in RMB, which may reduce costs in two ways. First, PRC firms and financial institutions may borrow in domestic financial markets at a lower cost, due to increased foreign demand for RMB-denominated securities. Second, PRC firms and financial institutions may get loans or issue bonds at lower cost in offshore RMB markets if the restriction on borrowing abroad is loosened.

Similarly, RMB internationalization would allow the government of the PRC to borrow at lower cost and thus to maintain higher fiscal deficits than it can at present. This benefit is akin to so-called monetary privilege or macroeconomic flexibility (Cohen 2011). By selling RMB-denominated government bonds and treasury bills to foreign investors, the PRC may get low-cost funding from the rest of the world. Looking forward, as a consequence of the aging of the population, the PRC may face more fiscal deficit pressure than it faces today. RMB internationalization may provide the PRC with a new channel for dealing with these challenges. Of course, such a benefit will largely depend on how sophisticated the PRC's financial market (particularly the bond market) is in the future. And it would certainly be a big mistake for the PRC to abuse such a benefit and lose control of its fiscal deficits.

Fourth, RMB internationalization would benefit the overseas expansion of PRC firms and financial institutions and would increase the ability of PRC firms to invest abroad. Generally, investors prefer to operate in their domestic currency, where it is allowed, because it is more convenient and less expensive for them to hold. In the future, the renminbi not only will increasingly be used in foreign and direct investment but will also increasingly function as an international currency in contracts and claims documents. Accordingly, the PRC's capital and financial accounts may show big deficits, something both the United States and Japan have experienced in the past. For instance, from 1953 to 1971 (except for 1968 and 1969), U.S. capital and financial account deficits increased dramatically; the deficit in 1971 was 51.39 times the deficit in 1953. Likewise, since 1981, when Japan began to promote the international use of the yen, Japan's capital and financial accounts have been in deficit, with the deficits from foreign investment increasing from ¥4.71 trillion in 1981 to ¥21.35 trillion in 1998 (International Monetary Fund 2012).

As the RMB becomes an increasingly important currency in global financial markets, financial institutions will conduct more and more RMB business, and in comparison with foreign banks, the PRC's banks could be more competitive in this area. Therefore, it is reasonable to speculate that RMB internationalization would push forward the overseas expansion of PRC financial institutions; in the early stages, this would be particularly true of the commercial banks.

Fifth, RMB internationalization would allow PRC monetary authorities to collect seigniorage from the rest of the world, although this should not be considered a primary benefit. Seigniorage is defined as the profit resulting from the difference between the nominal value of a currency and its cost of production. The government that issues a specific currency can gain seigniorage by exchanging its paper money for goods and services. Cohen (2011) pointed out there are two components in seigniorage: the first results from foreign accumulations of actual cash bank notes and coins; the second derives from foreign accumulations of financial claims denominated in the local currency. The latter actually means an increase of effective demand for assets, which drives the cost of borrowing below what it might be otherwise.

The first component—holding of notes and coins abroad—represents the equivalent of an interest-free loan to the issuing country. We can define this part of seigniorage based on Hai and Yao (2010) as

Table 11-5. *Seigniorage Revenue of Renminbi, March 2010 to June 2013*
CNY billions

Month	Renminbi settlements in cross-border transactions	Share of import transactions	Share of net import transactions	Seigniorage revenue
Mar 2010	18.35	0.60	0.2	0.1101
Jun 2010	48.66	0.60	0.2	0.29196
Sep 2010	126.48	0.60	0.2	0.75888
Dec 2010	312.85	0.60	0.2	1.8771
Mar 2011	360.32	0.65	0.3	3.24288
Jun 2011	597.25	0.65	0.3	5.37525
Sep 2011	583.41	0.65	0.3	5.25069
Dec 2011	539.02	0.65	0.3	4.85118
Mar 2012	580.40	0.70	0.4	6.9648
Jun 2012	671.55	0.70	0.4	8.0586
Sep 2012	798.96	0.70	0.4	9.58752
Dec 2012	889.09	0.70	0.4	10.66908
Mar 2013	1,003.92	0.80	0.5	15.0588
Jun 2013	1,046.08	0.80	0.5	15.6912

Source: Authors' calculations, based on data from the Chinese Academy of Social Science.

$$(11\text{-}3) \qquad\qquad S = r^* \Delta Mr,$$

where S is the international seigniorage; r is the zero-risk interest rate of RMB in the offshore market; and ΔMr is the increment of money supply held by other countries.[3] The overseas outflow of RMB is mainly the result of cross-border trade, cash payments made during cross-border travel, and underground foreign exchange. Because it is difficult to get accurate data on cash payments and underground exchanges, we use the net import settlements in RMB to represent ΔMr.[4]

Estimated RMB seigniorage is presented in table 11-5. The rough estimate of the share of import transactions comes from the Chinese Academy of Social Science. Assuming that the zero-risk interest rate for offshore RMB remains at 3 percent during the sample period gives us estimated results. For example, in 2012, current account transaction settlements in RMB were valued at roughly CNY3 trillion. Due to the appreciation expectation, more than 70 percent of

3. With the development of RMB internationalization, r could be different. In the case of the U.S. dollar, r is measured as the difference between the rate of return on long-term assets (such as what U.S. investors earn on foreign direct investment and portfolio investment) and the rate of return on short-term U.S. dollar liquidity.

4. Because RMB deposits in Hong Kong, China and other offshore RMB markets are basically sourced from the overseas outflows of RMB in trade settlement, we ignore them to avoid a double calculation.

these transactions related to the import of goods or services, so the net import transaction share was 40 percent, equating to around CNY1.2 trillion in net outflows. Supposing that these funds remained outside the PRC for one year in the form of bank deposits or various financial assets, and that the zero-risk interest rate of RMB in the offshore market was 3 percent, the seigniorage on these RMB could be CNY36 billion. If the RMB plays a more important role in trade settlements and becomes a more attractive store of value, its seigniorage would be more significant.

Sixth, RMB internationalization may help the PRC reduce its reliance on the U.S. dollar. The PRC is an emerging-market economy with a very large and sometimes volatile export sector, and financial reform and liberalization of its capital accounts are listed on the country's policy agenda. To avoid external shocks and to maintain financial stability, it is reasonable for the PRC to accumulate sufficient foreign exchange reserves for insurance purposes, though it should also seek to avoid excessive holdings. However, because the U.S. dollar is currently the main reserve currency, the PRC may have no choice but to hold U.S. dollars in large amounts, and it is clear that overreliance on U.S. dollar–denominated assets not only offers low returns but also is risky.

Developing countries that have not carried out currency internationalization must hold a large amount of foreign exchange reserves as a safety net against external shocks. Central banks in developing countries cannot be the lenders of last resort for foreign currency, because they have no power to print it. They can play a limited role as quasi lenders of last resort in foreign currency, if they have large foreign reserve holdings. However, even if they do hold massive foreign reserves, they can use only a limited amount of those reserves in the event of a crisis, due to their fear of losing those international reserves (Aizenman, Chinn, and Ito 2008). Therefore, RMB internationalization and the emergence of the RMB as a main reserve currency may help the PRC reduce its demand for foreign exchange reserves and thereafter reduce its reliance on U.S. dollar holdings.

What is more, RMB internationalization can help the PRC prevent large losses in its foreign reserve management. Zhang, Wang, and Hua (2010) constructed three measures of the returns on the PRC's foreign exchange reserves, looking at goods and services, a basket of currencies, and the U.S. dollar. They found that returns on the PRC's foreign exchange reserves held in a basket of currencies or in goods and services were much lower and more volatile than the returns on reserves held in U.S. dollars. The average value of real returns on the PRC's foreign reserves in goods and services was 3.2 percent, whereas the dollar-denominated return was 5.72 percent, and both of these were lower than the PRC's benchmark loan rate. The unsatisfactory return on the PRC's current foreign reserves represents a huge welfare loss resulting from overreliance on the U.S. dollar. With the acceleration of RMB internationalization, the PRC can not only reduce its reliance on the U.S. dollar but also improve the efficiency of its foreign reserve management.

Seventh, RMB internationalization would improve the PRC's political position in the world and strengthen its influence. As a reserve currency–issuing country, the PRC could play a more important role in global macroeconomic policy dialogue and coordination, particularly when the RMB becomes a key currency. For instance, if the RMB were an important global financial asset, the PRC might contribute to world peace by monitoring and freezing the assets of terrorist organizations, if needed.

Costs of Renminbi Internationalization

The costs of RMB internationalization may be discussed from two perspectives. The first is in terms of the general costs that may accrue to any international currency, whether it is the pound sterling, the yen, the U.S. dollar, or another currency. As long as a national currency plays a role as an international currency, such general costs may always exist. The other perspective relates to transitional costs or challenges, which may exist only during the period in which a national currency is becoming an international currency, particularly if the internationalization happens in an emerging-market economy. Such costs or challenges are usually temporary and may disappear after a certain period of time.

General Costs of Renminbi Internationalization

First, RMB internationalization may complicate the PRC's monetary policy and reduce its effectiveness and independence. This cost, which may be the main challenge for an international currency, is similar to the problem that Mundell (1961) described as the "impossible trinity" of an open economy, meaning that no country can simultaneously reach the policy goals of free capital movement, exchange rate stability, and independent monetary policy. Normally, a highly internationalized currency must be combined with a convertible capital account. In such a circumstance, the country must forgo its domestically oriented monetary policy if it wants to keep its exchange rate stable.

Some economists argue that the effectiveness and independence of the PRC's monetary policy may not be a big problem at the current stage, because the country still maintains relatively strict capital control. As the RMB becomes a leading international currency, however, the PRC's monetary policy may become less effective at keeping its exchange rate stable. For instance, Aizenman, Chinn, and Ito (2008) argue that with a reduction in the effectiveness and independence of the PRC's monetary policy as the RMB is becoming an international currency, the PRC's position in the impossible trinity will move from its current status to a more extreme point. Similarly, Hai and Yao (2010) indicated that although RMB internationalization would not have a significant influence on the effectiveness of PRC monetary policy in the short to medium term, in the long term, the growing scale of RMB cross-border circulation and enhancement in other currency functions that follow from RMB internationalization might affect the independence of the PRC's monetary policy through endogenous monetary transmission mechanisms.

It is noted that RMB internationalization does not necessarily involve the removal of all restrictions on capital movement. The government of the PRC may continue to impose restrictions on residents' financial transactions in foreign currency instruments. Nevertheless, RMB internationalization will broaden the scope for residents and nonresidents to buy and sell domestic currency instruments, which will limit the ability of the People's Bank of China to influence domestic interest rates and the money supply through open market operations.

Specifically, the rapid development of Hong Kong, China, the offshore RMB market, and its increasingly close links with financial markets in the mainland PRC (Maziad and Kang 2012) could make it harder for the People's Bank of China to control monetary aggregates and maintain its autonomy in setting domestic interest rates. To some extent, the Hong Kong, China offshore RMB market is a pool of hot money. At any point it could present a shock to the mainland PRC's monetary policy.

Second, RMB internationalization could similarly reduce the autonomy of exchange rate policy. As the RMB becomes an international reserve currency, it could become an anchor currency for other countries, and the exchange rate of the RMB against that currency would lose its flexibility. Without this exchange rate flexibility, the PRC could lose its macroeconomic flexibility and trade competitiveness. Since the Bretton Woods agreement (1944), the United States has often suffered from such exchange rate inflexibility, particularly from its inability to devalue the dollar (Bergston 1975).

Third, should the RMB become a key international currency, the PRC would bear more responsibility in the rest of the world. It is widely recognized that the macroeconomic policies of a reserve currency–issuing country often have significant spillover effects to the rest of the world. In addition, a key reserve currency–issuing country is responsible for keeping the international financial and monetary system in order. Among others, it should play the role of being a lender of last resort, meaning that it will have some responsibility to provide liquidity support during periods of global financial stress, even though such support may have an adverse effect on its domestic economy.

Therefore, any reserve currency–issuing country must be very careful about its policies. Although we should not forget the notion made famous by one U.S. policymaker that "the dollar is our currency, but your problem," it is more important to remember that any persistent misuse of macroeconomic policies will lead to a significant depreciation of a currency, and sooner or later a country will lose its currency privilege. Under the multipolar reserve currency system, such a risk could be much greater than in other situations.

Transitional Risks of Renminbi Internationalization

First, RMB internationalization may increase the probability of asset bubbles and financial instability. This challenge could be regarded as a transitional cost. Since 2009, the volume of RMBs circulating beyond the borders of the PRC has increased very rapidly. Except for the RMBs that remain in Hong Kong, China as offshore currency, most of these circulating RMBs return to the PRC through the export of goods and services from the PRC or through foreign direct investment and other security investment in the PRC, such as RMB-denominated qualified foreign institutional investment. At present, because of capital controls, the purchase of RMB-denominated financial assets is not fully liberalized and is only possible through managed channels. However, should capital accounts become more convertible, the PRC might face increased demand for RMB-denominated assets, especially if the RMB is under pressure from exchange rate appreciation and tight monetary conditions. Given the constrained scale of the PRC market, increased asset demand could cause an asset bubble, and if RMB-denominated assets are widely held domestically and abroad and the holders come to believe that the PRC's asset prices are likely to fall sharply, the PRC could suffer an asset bubble collapse. Such a collapse would likely be accompanied by a great depreciation of RMB or a currency crisis.

The PRC is an emerging-market economy, and even if the RMB were not internationalized, the country could experience "boom and bust" cycles if it makes mistakes in its macroeconomic policies and opens its capital accounts in the wrong way. However, RMB internationalization would surely increase the probability of suffering from an asset bubble cycle. Even the United States, a developed reserve currency–issuing country with the largest bond market in the world, was unable to avoid such problems, as its subprime mortgage crisis of 2007–2008 demonstrated. This crisis illustrates one of the risks of being an international currency. Due to increased demand for dollars as a reserve currency by many emerging market economies at the end of the 1990s and the early 2000s, the long-term interest rate was continuously kept at a historically low level, and the asset bubble, which to a large degree caused the subprime debt crisis, became a big problem during those years.

Second, RMB internationalization may induce exchange rate appreciation as a result of nonresidents' demand for RMB-denominated assets, and may depress the PRC's trade competitiveness. The more popular a currency becomes, the more likely it is that a certain degree of appreciation will occur. For domestic consumers, currency appreciation represents a benefit, but for producers and exporters, the effect of RMB appreciation will be negative, because the competitiveness of exports and import-competing industries will be damaged. Reserve-issuing entities such as the European Union, Japan, and the United States all had similar experiences, at least in the early stages of their internationalization (Maziad and others 2011).

However, there is no evidence that such exchange rate appreciation would exist indefinitely. It is more likely that the exchange rate would stop appreciating and would begin to depreciate after a certain point, partly as a result of the earlier appreciation. Another interpretation of the depreciation could be the well-known Triffin Dilemma, which states that a reserve currency–issuing country will find it difficult to keep its exchange rate stable or avoid currency depreciation while still satisfying the constantly increasing demand for sufficient liquidity unless it maintains current account deficits. Because the RMB is just in its beginning stage of internationalization, there is certainly no immediate worry about its depreciation. However, it could be problematic if the currency appreciates too much in a short period because exports are still so important to the PRC's economic growth.

Third, there are some risks related to the offshore RMB market. Due to the capital controls in the PRC, the offshore RMB market in Hong Kong, China has been developing rapidly and actually has played a key role in the ongoing internationalization of the RMB. However, because the RMB exchange rate is under severe management in the mainland PRC whereas it appears fully market-determined in the Hong Kong, China offshore market, the exchange rate difference often becomes a source of arbitrage and speculation. Arbitrage in parallel markets is not always a bad thing, because it can encourage equilibrium. According to Zhang and He (2012), however, because the RMB is under appreciation expectation, the arbitrage on RMB exchange rates between onshore and offshore markets will cause an unbalanced trade settlement structure——RMB settlement would be used more for imports but less for exports (Maziad and others 2011). Eventually, this would result in a greater accumulation of foreign exchange reserves in the PRC.

Moreover, the offshore RMB market could become a conduit for speculative attack, as Thailand's hard experience during the Asian financial crisis in 1997 demonstrated. In that case, the Thai baht's offshore center played a significant role in the speculative attack, because foreign speculators were easily able to obtain Thai baht, which they then sold short within a very short period. Massive short selling of the baht eventually triggered the financial crisis on July 2, 1997.

Policy Choices for a Sustainable Process of Renminbi Internationalization

Although RMB internationalization has made rapid progress since 2009, it is still in an early stage. A research team from Renmin University created an index to identify the extent of currency internationalization. According their calculations, by the end of 2011, the RMB's internationalization index was only 0.45, whereas the index of the U.S. dollar was 54.18, the euro was 24.86, the yen was 4.56, and the pound sterling was 3.87 (Renmin University of China, Institute of International Currency 2012). Similarly, the International Monetary Fund indicated that the international currency status of the RMB remains very low—in some respects

Table 11-6. *Benefits and Costs of the Renminbi as an International Currency*

Benefits	Reduces exchange risk
	Promotes financial development, thus benefiting the PRC's economic transformation growth model
	Allows PRC firms and financial institutions to borrow in renminbi, which may have lower cost
	Assists the overseas expansion of PRC firms and financial institutions
	Earns international seigniorage
	Helps the PRC reduce its reliance on U.S. dollars
	Improves the PRC's political position in the world
Costs	
General costs	Complicates the PRC's monetary policy and reduces its effectiveness and independence
	Reduces the autonomy of the PRC's exchange rate policy
	Increases responsibility to the rest of the world in terms of policy spillover
Transitional risks	Increases the probability of asset bubbles and financial instability
	Induces exchange rate appreciation and reduces the PRC's trade competitiveness
	More risks linked to the offshore renminbi market, which may transfer back to the mainland

Source: Authors.

even lower than the currencies of some other emerging-market economies (Maziad and others 2011).

The internationalization of the RMB and its emergence as a leading international currency will take time—perhaps a decade or even longer. The time required will largely be determined by the PRC's future economic, trade, and financial situation. Scale, stability, and liquidity will be the other main determinants (Eichengreen 2013). Although RMB internationalization is a market-driven process, successfully building up the required preconditions would certainly help shorten the time required.

An analysis of the benefits and costs of RMB internationalization is summarized in table 11-6. The question is how we should judge the overall economic consequences of RMB internationalization. For a few reasons, it is fair to speculate that the benefits of RMB internationalization should surpass its costs, particularly in the long run. First, most of the benefits elaborated here, such as reduced exchange rate risks, development of the financial sector, and increased economic openness to the rest of the world, are related to the real economy and would gain in significance if the RMB were to become a leading international currency. Second, although the costs should not be ignored, most of these costs could be alleviated by some appropriate policy mix. For instance, a more flexible exchange rate regime or optimal capital account management may increase the independence of monetary policies. Third, transitional costs will be reduced with the improvement of RMB internationalization. The current limited variation in the RMB's exchange rate against the U.S. dollar and the early stage of development of the financial market are probably the main factors that explain the concern about the potential destabilizing effect of the external demand for the RMB. However, increased exchange rate flexibility and progress in financial sector reform and development should help increase the domestic economy's resilience to external shocks over time and reduce the transitional cost of RMB internationalization. Finally, the history of the U.S. dollar and other leading international currencies has shown that it is not a bad decision or a wrong choice to allow a currency to be internationalized. Therefore, the related policy suggestions should focus on how to deal with the transitional costs and sustain the lasting gains.

First, for a smooth and sustainable RMB internationalization, it is important that the PRC maintain strong and sustainable growth in the coming decades. Economic size is probably the most important precondition for the RMB's becoming a leading international currency. Although the PRC has become the second-largest economy in the world, it is still a developing country, with a per capita annual income of around $5,000. After maintaining nearly thirty years of high growth, the present increase in labor costs, income disparity, environmental deterioration, and other social problems as well as a declining comparative trade advantage increasingly raise concerns about whether the PRC will soon step into the "middle-income trap" (Asian Development Bank and Peking University 2012).[5] If it should do so, the PRC may fail to maintain its steady economic growth in the coming years.

To avoid this middle-income trap, the PRC should accelerate technology innovation and industrial upgrading, deepen its market-oriented economic reform to improve economic efficiency after the development strategy gradually switches to the domestic market, build up and improve the social security network to deal with the income disparity problem, and implement political reform to create a more transparent and democratic society.

Second, although the PRC is moving toward a more domestic-oriented economic structure, maintaining a competitive trade sector and a leading role in global trade is still extremely important. In order to reach this goal, the PRC should improve its capacity for technology innovation, build up new trade advantages, broaden its trade network, and further enlarge its share of global trade. It is important to have more export settlement in RMB, so as to alleviate the imbalanced trade structure.

Keeping the RMB exchange rate stable is very important for RMB internationalization. Significant appreciation in a short period may encourage more import settlement in RMB and rapid accumulation of RMB deposits in Hong

---

5. "Middle-income trap" refers to a theorized economic development situation that occurs when a country's income per capita reaches a certain level and gets stuck at that level owing to lack of economic growth momentum.

Kong, China, as reflected in the rapid development of RMB internationalization since 2009. However, if such appreciation goes on continuously, the PRC's current account could be negatively affected—the RMB's position might weaken, and the trend toward RMB internationalization might go into reverse. Of course, keeping the RMB exchange rate stable does not mean that the PRC should stop its reform of the exchange rate regime. Instead, the PRC should maintain a balanced external economic position, avoiding both a significant balance-of-payment surplus and deficits.

Third, if the RMB is to be a reliable and convenient store of value, it is extremely important for the PRC to accelerate its domestic financial reform, especially building up a highly liquid bond market, and gradually push forward the liberalization of capital accounts.

Economic size does matter for RMB internationalization, but it is not a sufficient precondition, as the precedent of the U.S. dollar indicates. Although the United States surpassed the United Kingdom in economic size in the mid-1870s and was twice its size by 1914, the U.S. dollar only surpassed the pound sterling in the mid-1920s. The critical incident that enabled the dollar to surpass the pound was the creation of the Federal Reserve Bank, which preceded the rapid development of trade acceptance markets (Eichengreen 2009).

Although the PRC created its central bank in the early 1980s and has been trying to build up a modern financial sector, its financial market is still under development, with limited scale and openness. According to statistics from the Bank for International Settlements and the People's Bank of China, the PRC's share of the global financial market is very small, although its stock market represents roughly 10 percent of the world market. For instance, the foreign exchange turnover in RMB was only about 0.9 percent of total world turnover in 2010, and cross-border bonds and notes denominated in RMB represented only about 0.16 percent of world cross-border bonds and notes in 2011.

The PRC has sped up its financial reform since last year. The People's Bank of China made significant progress on the liberalization of interest rates in 2012, increasing the restrictive deposit rate ceiling by 10 percent and fully removing controls on the interest rates on loans. Meanwhile, various measures have promoted the development of capital markets, particularly the bond markets, to change the indirect finance-dominant and bank loan–dominant structure.

The PRC also is going to liberalize its capital account, although at a more cautious pace. After nearly ten years of effort, the PRC has already removed many restrictions on its capital account. According to the International Monetary Fund (2012), the PRC has fully or partly liberalized thirty-four of forty items related to capital account restrictions, or 85 percent of the total. Specifically, since 2010 the PRC has launched several liberalization measures directly linked to RMB internationalization, including introducing RMB-denominated qualified foreign institutional investment; allowing foreign central banks and other qualified institutions to invest in its domestic bond markets; and allowing Hong Kong, China offshore banks to lend RMB to the firms in the Qianhai special pilot areas. The restricted six items, or 15 percent of the total, mainly relate to the issuance of money market instruments, collective investment instruments, and financial derivatives.

There is some evidence that the PRC will continue to liberalize its capital account. However, it is not necessarily the case that there will be no progress on RMB internationalization until the PRC has fully liberalized its capital account. The rapid development of the Hong Kong, China offshore RMB market over the past years has shown that RMB internationalization could make much progress even if the PRC partially retains capital control. In fact, the eurodollar market in the 1950s and 1960s provides a very interesting historical precedent. In that case, the U.S. domestic financial market retained many restrictions, including controls on cross-border capital movement, and it was through the offshore market that the U.S. dollar became much more influential as an invoice and settlement currency.

There has been a consensus that external financial liberalization should be the last step of economic liberalization in a typical emerging-market economy (McKinnon 1991), yet this is not always true in practical experience. Because the PRC's domestic financial reform is still under way, financial supervision is not very adequate, and the exchange rate regime still lacks flexibility. Any big push for capital account liberalization could present significant risks to the PRC's economic and financial system and economic growth. If a crisis developed, the process of RMB internationalization could be stopped or even reversed.

Fourth, the PRC needs to reform its exchange rate as soon as possible in order to better address the speculation between onshore and offshore markets. Given that full liberalization of the capital account may take time, the offshore RMB markets in London, Singapore, and Hong Kong, China and perhaps other international financial centers will likely continue to play an important role in the coming years. If the RMB exchange rate continues to be strictly managed with very limited flexibility, the difference between onshore and offshore markets may well remain in a constant state of arbitrage. When the RMB is under pressure of appreciation, arbitrageurs may try to use permitted capital account or disguised trade channels to make RMB accumulate in offshore markets. Likewise, when the RMB is under pressure of depreciation, arbitrageurs may try to make RMB accumulate in the offshore market. These kinds of speculation may cause an abnormal fluctuation in demand for RMB and therefore affect the effectiveness of the PRC's monetary policies. In extreme situations, as with Thailand's experience in 1997, it may become a source of speculative attack or even trigger a financial crisis. Increasing the flexibility of the RMB exchange rate regime could be the best way to abolish speculation between onshore and offshore markets. In addition, it is very important to the further liberalization of the capital account and therefore crucial for RMB internationalization.

Finally, strengthening global and regional financial cooperation may help create a good environment for RMB internationalization. RMB internationalization is a market-driven process and is basically a by-product of the PRC's steady economic growth and continuous opening up to the rest of the world. However, this does not mean that the government plays no role in the process.

The U.S. dollar's early experiences show that a government can significantly promote its currency as a key international currency. In addition to the crucial influence of the creation of the Federal Reserve Bank in 1914 (Eichengreen 2009), the Bretton Woods system, which was undoubtedly driven by the U.S. government, represented another important milestone in the dollar's becoming the dominant international currency. According to the International Monetary Fund agreement, each country was requested to peg its currency to the U.S. dollar. Through this institutional arrangement, the U.S. dollar received an advantageous chance to become an official reserve currency.

The PRC should strive to play a greater role in the G-20 and other international macroeconomic coordination processes. In particular, the PRC should continue to actively push forward the reform of the international monetary system and work for a more representative and democratic international financial architecture. It would be meaningful to the PRC to have the RMB become a special-drawing-right-basket currency in 2014. Such an arrangement would increase the RMB's chance to become an important reserve currency.

The PRC also should actively promote Asian monetary and financial integration. Given that Asian countries, particularly ASEAN countries, have increasingly close economic and financial relations with the PRC, it would be beneficial for both sides to push forward monetary integration. In fact, the RMB could become a nominal anchor for most of the Asian economies. As more and more currency-swap agreements, intraregional trade, and investments are denominated in RMB, it would be helpful for Asian countries to keep their currencies pegged or partially pegged to the RMB, and eventually to make the RMB one of their main reserve currencies.

Conclusion

Although it is developing very quickly, RMB internationalization is at an early stage, and its scale is very limited, so it might be too early for a comprehensive evaluation of its economic consequences, either nationally or globally. Despite increasing recognition that the RMB may eventually become a key global currency, several important questions remain to be answered:. What are the benefits and costs of the RMB becoming an international currency? What are the key preconditions for it to become a reserve currency? And can the ongoing trend continue if the PRC does not immediately remove all of its capital controls?

In this chapter we have tried to offer a comprehensive analysis of the pros and cons of RMB internationalization. We have discussed seven primary benefits:

1. By using the RMB as an invoicing and settlement currency, PRC firms may well reduce the exchange risks of international trade and investment, thereby reducing transaction costs.

2. RMB internationalization would be accompanied by a larger and more sophisticated financial sector in the PRC and would benefit the PRC's transformative economic growth model. Our empirical evidence suggests that, controlling for other economic factors, currency internationalization will help the development of the domestic financial market; this is applicable not only globally but also in the PRC.

3. RMB internationalization would allow PRC firms and financial institutions to borrow in RMB, which may cost less.

4. Internationalization would benefit the overseas expansion of PRC firms and financial institutions.

5. RMB internationalization would enable PRC monetary authorities to collect seigniorage from the rest of the world. As the RMB plays a more important role in trade settlements and becomes a more attractive store of value, its seigniorage will be more significant.

6. RMB internationalization may help the PRC reduce its reliance on the U.S. dollar and reduce the welfare loss caused by the low returns on foreign reserves.

7. Internationalization would improve the PRC's political position in the world and increase its influence.

However, RMB internationalization also brings with it general costs, which are permanent, and transitional risks, which are usually temporary and may disappear after a certain period of time. The general cost is that RMB internationalization may reduce the effectiveness and independence of the PRC's monetary policy and the autonomy of its exchange rate policy. There also are some transitional risks during the process of RMB internationalization. For instance, internationalization may increase the probability of asset bubbles and financial instability, and it could induce exchange rate appreciation and depress the PRC's trade competitiveness. However, these transitional risks would be eliminated if proper policy responses were undertaken.

In general, comparison of the benefits and costs of RMB internationalization indicates that the pros overweigh the cons. In order to accomplish RMB internationalization smoothly and sustainably, it is important that the PRC maintain strong and sustainable growth and a competitive trade sector in the coming decades. Second, it is vital to accelerate domestic financial reforms, though this should be done in a cautious manner, especially in the case of capital account liberalization. Third, the PRC should reform its RMB exchange rate and reduce speculation between onshore and offshore RMB markets. Finally, strengthening global and regional financial cooperation may foster a good environment for RMB internationalization.

RMB internationalization began in 2009 and is still at a preliminary stage, so it is difficult to conduct solid empirical studies. However, with the development and acceleration of RMB internationalization, there will be more and more interesting aspects to study. Our next research priorities will be to focus on a specific benefit or cost of RMB internationalization and develop more reliable evidence; to find the key preconditions for the RMB to become an international currency; and to explore the obstacles to RMB internationalization and ways to deal with the transitional risks during the process.

References

Aizenman, J., M. D. Chinn, and H. Ito. 2008. "Assessing the Emerging Global Financial Architecture: Measuring the Trilemma's Configurations over Time." NBER Working Paper No. 14533. Cambridge, Mass.: National Bureau of Economic Research.

Allen, F., and D. Gale. 2001. *Comparative Financial Systems: A Survey.* University of Pennsylvania, Wharton School Center for Financial Institutions.

Ba, S., B. Wu, P. Yuan, M. Wang, and Z. Yin. 2010. "Effects of RMB Internationalization on China's Finance Industry." In *Currency Internationalization: Global Experiences and Implications for the Renminbi,* edited by P. Wensheng and C. Shu. New York: Palgrave Macmillan.

Beck, T., A. Demirgüç-Kunt, and R. Levine. 2000. "A New Database on Financial Development and Structure." *World Bank Economic Review* 14: 597–605.

Bergsten, C. F. 1975. *The Dilemma of the Dollar: The Economics and Politics of United States International Monetary Policy.* New York University Press.

Chen, H., W. Peng, and C. Shu. 2007. "The Potential of the Renminbi as an International Currency." *China Economic Issues* 7, no. 7.

Chen, Y., and B. Hu. 2013. "Internationalization of the RMB: An Evaluation Framework." *Economic and Political Studies* 1, no. 1: 5–20.

Chinn, M., and J. Frankel. 2005. "Will the Euro Eventually Surpass the Dollar as the Leading International Reserve Currency?" NBER Working Papers No. 11510. Cambridge, Mass.: National Bureau of Economic Research.

Chinn, M. D., and H. Ito. 2006. "What Matters for Financial Development? Capital Controls, Institutions, and Interactions." *Journal of Development Economics* 81, no. 1: 163–92.

Cohen, B. J. 2012. "The Benefits and Costs of an International Currency: Getting the Calculus Right." *Open Economies Review* 23, no. 1: 13–31.

Dobson, W., and P. R. Masson. 2009. "Will the Renminbi Become a World Currency?" *China Economic Review* 20, no. 1: 124–35.

Eichengreen, Barry. 2009. "The Irresistible Rise of the Renminbi." *Project Syndicate* (online journal), November 23 (www.project-syndicate.org/commentary/the-irresistible-rise-of-the-renminbi).

———. 2011. *Exorbitant Privilege: The Rise and Fall of the Dollar and the Future of the International Monetary System.* Oxford University Press.

———. 2013. "ADB Distinguished Lecture. Renminbi Internationalization: Tempest in a Teapot?" *Asian Development Review* 30, no. 1: 148–64.

Eichengreen, Barry, and Ricardo Hausmann. 1999. "Exchange Rates and Financial Fragility." Working Paper 7418. Cambridge, Mass.: National Bureau of Economic Research.

Eichengreen, Barry, Ricardo Hausmann, and Ugo Panizza. 2002. "Original Sin: The Pain, the Mystery, and the Road to Redemption." Paper presented at a conference on Currency and

Maturity Matchmaking: Redeeming Debt from Original Sin, Inter-American Development Bank.

Gao, H., and Y. Yu. 2010. "Internationalization of the Renminbi: Implications and Preconditions" (in Chinese). *Review of International Economics* (January): 1–21.

Genberg, H. 2010. "The Calculus of International Currency Use." *Central Banking* 20, no. 3: 63–68.

Hai, W., and H. Yao. 2010. "Pros and Cons of Internationalization: Use of the RMB for China." In *Currency Internationalization: Global Experiences and Implications for the Renminbi*, edited by P. Wensheng and C. Shu. New York: Palgrave Macmillan.

International Monetary Fund. 2012. *Annual Report on Exchange Arrangements and Exchange Restrictions.* Washington: International Monetary Fund.

Kamps, A. 2006. "The Euro as Invoicing Currency in International Trade." ECB Working Paper Series No. 665. Frankfurt: European Central Bank.

Kenen, Peter. 1983. "The Role of the Dollar as an International Currency." Group of Thirty Occasional Papers No. 13. Washington: Group of Thirty.

———. 2011. "Currency Internationalization: An Overview." *BIS Papers 61,* pp. 9–18. Basel: Bank for International Settlements, December (www.bis.org/publ/bppdf/bispap61.pdf).

Kim, Kyungsoo, and Young Kyung Suh. 2011. "Dealing with the Benefits and Costs of Internationalization of the Korean Won." *BIS Papers 61,* pp. 151–71. Basel: Bank for International Settlements, December (www.bis.org/publ/bppdf/bispap61.pdf).

La Porta, R., F. Lopez-de-Silanes, A. Shleifer, and R. W. Vishny. 1998. "Law and Finance." *Journal of Political Economy* 106, no. 6: 1113–15.

Levine, R. 1999. "Law, Finance, and Economic Growth." *Journal of Financial Intermediation* 8, no. 1: 8–35.

Li, D., and L. Liu. 2008. "RMB Internationalization: An Empirical and Policy Analysis." *Journal of Financial Research* 11, no. 4: 1–16.

Maziad, S, P. Farahmand, S. Wang, S. Segal, and F. Ahmed. 2011. "Internationalization of Emerging Market Currencies: A Balance between Risks and Rewards." IMF Staff Discussion Note. Washington: International Monetary Fund, October 19.

Maziad, S., and J. S. Kang. 2012. "RMB Internationalization: Onshore/Offshore Links." IMF Working Paper WP/12/133. Washington: International Monetary Fund.

McCauley, Robert. 2011. "Renminbi Internationalization and China's Financial Development Model." CGS-IIGG Working Paper. New York: Council on Foreign Relations Press, November.

McKinnon, R. 1991. *The Order of Economic Liberalization: Financial Control in the Transition to a Market Economy.* Johns Hopkins University Press.

Mundell, R. 1961. "A Theory of Optimum Currency Areas." *American Economic Review* 51, no. 4: 657–65.

Papaioannou, E., and R. Portes. 2008. "Costs and Benefits of Running an International Currency." *Economic Papers* 348, November.

People's Bank of China Study Group. 2006. "The Timing, Path, and Strategies of RMB Internationalization." *China Finance* 5: 12–13.

Ranjan, R., and A. Prakash. 2010. "Internationalisation of Currency: The Case of the Indian Rupee and Renminbi." *Reserve Bank of India Reports,* May.

Renmin University of China, Institute of International Currency. 2012. *Annual Report on the Internationalization of the Renminbi.* Renmin University of China Press.

Stiglitz, Joseph. 2009. "The Global Crisis, Social Protection and Jobs." *International Labour Review* 148, nos. 1–2: 1–13.

Tavlas, G. S. 1997. "Internationalization of Currencies: The Case of the US Dollar and Its Challenger Euro." *International Executive* 39, no. 5: 581–97.

Woo, Wing Thye. 2010. "A Realistic Vision of Asian Economic Integration" (www.econ.uc davis.edu/faculty/woo/0.0.transfer/Econpercent20Growthpercent20Notes/Raw/Realistic AsianIntegration.pdf).

Wooldrige, J. M. 2002. *Econometric Analysis of Cross Section and Panel Data.* MIT Press.

Zhang, B., X. Wang, and X. Hua. 2010. "The Nominal and Real Returns of China's Foreign Reserves." *Economic Research* (January).

Zhang, L. 2012. "Reforming the International Monetary System and Internationalization of RMB: A Chinese Perspective." Paper presented at the international conference International Monetary System, Energy and Sustainable Development. Korea Development Institute, Seoul, September 21.

Zhang, M. 2013. "Internationalization of Renminbi: Policies, Progress, Issues and Prospect" (in Chinese). IIS Working Paper 201303. Beijing: Institute of World Economics and Politics/ Chinese Academy of Social Sciences, July 2.

Zhang, M., and F. He. 2012. "Arbitrage between Onshore and Offshore Markets in the Internationalization of Renminbi" (in Chinese). *Studies of International Finance* 10.

Zhao, H. 2001. "Promoting the Renminbi to Be One of the World Currencies" (in Chinese). *Finance and Trade Economics* 5.

Zhou, Xiaochuan. 2009. "The Reform of the International Monetary System." Speech of the governor of the People's Bank of China, March 23. *BIS Review* 41 (www.bis.org/review/ r090402c.pdf).

Contributors

Yin-Wong Cheung
City University of Hong Kong

Menzie Chinn
University of Wisconsin

Benjamin J. Cohen
University of California, Santa Barbara

Prince Christian Cruz
Asian Development Bank

Barry Eichengreen
University of California, Berkeley

Fan Gang
National Economic Research Institute

Yuning Gao
Tsinghua University

Yiping Huang
Peking University

Hiro Ito
Portland State University

Masahiro Kawai
University of Tokyo

Victor Pontines
Asian Development Bank Institute

Eswar Prasad
Cornell University and Brookings Institution

Changyong Rhee
Asian Development Bank, formerly

Lei Lei Song
Asian Development Bank

Lea Sumulong
Asian Development Bank

Kunyu Tao
*Central University of Finance
and Economics*

Daili Wang
Peking University

Yu Yongding
Chinese Academy of Social Sciences

Naoyuki Yoshino
Asian Development Bank Institute

Liqing Zhang
*Central University of Finance
and Economics*

Index

ASIAN DEVELOPMENT BANK INSTITUTE

The Asian Development Bank Institute (ADBI), located in Tokyo, is the think tank of the Asian Development Bank (ADB). ADBI's mission is to identify effective development strategies and improve development management in ADB's developing member countries. ADBI has an extensive network of partners in the Asia and Pacific region and globally. ADBI's activities are aligned with ADB's strategic focus, which includes poverty reduction and inclusive economic growth, the environment, regional cooperation and integration, infrastructure development, middle-income countries, and private sector development and operations.

BROOKINGS INSTITUTION

The Brookings Institution is a private nonprofit organization devoted to research, education, and publication on important issues of domestic and foreign policy. Its principal purpose is to bring the highest quality independent research and analysis to bear on current and emerging policy problems. The Institution was founded on December 8, 1927, to merge the activities of the Institute for Government Research, founded in 1916, the Institute of Economics, founded in 1922, and the Robert Brookings Graduate School of Economics and Government, founded in 1924. Interpretations or conclusions in Brookings publications should be understood to be solely those of the authors.